CULTURE AND SOCIETY IN
CLASSICAL WEIMAR

Wie es die Welt jetzt treibt, muß man sich immer und immer dar sagen und wiederholen: daß es tüchtige Menschen gegeben hat und geben wird, und solchen muß man ein schriftlich gutes Wort gönnen, aussprechen und auf dem Papier hinterlassen. Das ist die Gemeinschaft der Heiligen, zu der wir uns bekennen.

GOETHE TO ZELTER, 18 JUNE 1831

1 (a)   VIEW OF WEIMAR FROM THE SOUTH

In the foreground, centre, the house of Frau von Stein (from 1777), behind it the
Fürstenhaus, where the Duke and Duchess lived until 1803, and to the right of
this the Ducal Library, surmounted by the surviving tower of the burnt-out
Wilhelmsburg.

1 (b)   GOETHE'S GARTENHAUS IN THE WEIMAR PARK

The drawing shows the house and part of the Weimar Park in 1806, after the
improvements made by Goethe and the Duke from 1778 onwards.

CULTURE AND SOCIETY IN CLASSICAL WEIMAR
1775-1806

BY

W. H. BRUFORD

*Fellow of St. John's College and Emeritus Professor of German in the
University of Cambridge*

CAMBRIDGE
AT THE UNIVERSITY PRESS
1962

PUBLISHED BY

THE SYNDICS OF THE CAMBRIDGE UNIVERSITY PRESS

Bentley House, 200 Euston Road, London, N.W.1

American Branch: 32 East 57th Street, New York 22, N.Y.

West African Office: P.O. Box 33, Ibadan, Nigeria

©

Cambridge University Press

1962

Printed in Great Britain by Spottiswoode, Ballantyne & Co. Ltd,
London and Colchester

CONTENTS

LIST OF ILLUSTRATIONS

LIST OF ILLUSTRATIONS

ACKNOWLEDGEMENTS

MY work on this subject would have been impossible without the resources of the Cambridge University Library and the Beit German Library, for which my teacher, Professor Karl Breul, had patiently collected much material, now almost unobtainable, about life in Weimar. Visits to the *Nationale Forschungs– und Gedenkstätten in Weimar*, the Marbach *Schiller National–Museum*, the Düsseldorf *Goethe–Museum* and the Frankfurt *Freies deutsches Hochstift* filled in many gaps. I am greatly indebted to the staffs of all these institutions for help and advice, and to the Directors of the German ones for permission to reproduce pictures and drawings from their collections.

To the Syndics of the Cambridge University Press I am most grateful for so readily accepting a bulky manuscript, and to their team of experts for transforming it into a handsome book.

What I owe to my own teachers, finally, and to my colleagues and pupils in three universities, is beyond expression. I have tried to put into these pages what I have come to understand through them about the part played in our lives by what Herder calls the 'chain of culture'. It was some such idea, I think, that was aroused in me vaguely on my admission to this College some fifty years ago, and ten happy years as professorial fellow have deepened that awareness in all sorts of ways.

W. H. B.

ST JOHN'S COLLEGE, CAMBRIDGE
15 OCTOBER 1961

INTRODUCTION

'A CULTURE, while it is being lived, is always in part unknown, in part unrealised', writes Mr Raymond Williams in his *Culture and Society, 1780-1950*,[1] the stimulating book to which I owe my title, and helpful ideas related to a subject that has occupied me for many years, the 'advance in consciousness' achieved in classical Weimar. The aim of the present work is first to describe Goethe's Weimar as we see it now, from documents of the time and from the research, mainly of German scholars, into the most brilliant period of their literary and philosophical history, and secondly to interpret the connections that may be found, after so many eventful years, between German culture and German society, both in the age of Goethe and later.

Wieland and Herder, Goethe and Schiller, it is well known, have come to have a representative quality which makes them the supreme classics of German literature, and their close association with Weimar has made the name of this previously obscure provincial capital into a symbol for 'Geist', as the Germans call it, for all that is best in German thought and aspiration. There is a unity of content in these Weimar writers resulting, it is generally agreed, from a view of man and the world shared in essentials by them all in what is called the age of 'Humanität', a philosophy of life resting on the belief in the perfectibility of man.

How greatly this humanistic philosophy enriched the subsequent literature and thought of the surrounding world is clear, for instance, from a work like Fritz Strich's *Goethe and World Literature*,[2] and no one acquainted with German classicism can read Mr Williams without being constantly reminded of problems common to Germany and England. John Stuart Mill used to think of the 'Germano-Coleridgian school', as Mr Williams tells us, as 'the first . . . who inquired with any comprehensiveness or depth into the inductive laws of the existence and growth of human society', who 'looked upon the culture of the inward man as the problem of problems' and were aware that 'the culture of the human being had been carried to no ordinary height, and human nature had exhibited many of its noblest manifestations, not in Christian countries only, but in the ancient world, in Athens, Sparta, Rome; nay, even barbarians . . . all had their own education, their own culture'. These ideas are pure Herder, and Mill describes them as 'the characteristic feature of the Goethian period of German literature' and as 'richly diffused through the historical and critical writings of the new French school, as well as of Coleridge and his followers'.[3] Coleridge saw 'a continuing and progressive civilisation' as the supreme goal, but as one unattainable 'where this civilisation is not grounded in cultivation, in the harmonious development of those qualities and faculties that characterise our humanity'.[4] Whatever may be thought about Coleridge's claim to originality, it is indisputable that what he says here had been said repeatedly, in much the same language (for 'cultivation' is surely 'Bildung'), by Herder, Goethe, Fichte and others, and Carlyle and Arnold openly acknowledged their debt to Germany. In relating ideas about culture to ideas about society, the German and the English writers did not lay the emphasis in the same places, of course, for the problem of industrialism, for instance, central in Victorian England, had in Goethe's age not yet emerged in Germany, but both schools of thought have common roots in the post-Renaissance belief in reason and the rejection of supernaturalism, the idea that it is man's duty, as an individual and as a member of society, to make himself. The story of Weimar is therefore relevant to a good deal more than an understanding of German civilisation alone.

There were, as we shall see, special reasons why the Germans should develop, earlier than their neighbours in Europe, a strong theoretical interest in the connection between the ideas of culture and of society. As a first indication of these reasons we may point to the interpretation of German classicism on which leading historians of thought such as Dilthey,[5] Troeltsch[6] and Korff[7] are in all essentials in agreement. According to this view, poetry

2

and philosophy from Lessing to Hegel, roughly speaking in the last third of the eighteenth century, represent a single sustained effort of the German mind to make sense of its own peculiar world. Unlike their fellow-countrymen earlier in the eighteenth century and in the nineteenth, and unlike their French contemporaries, they were little concerned with improving the material conditions of life. Their ideal, as Troeltsch puts it, was rather 'a full and free development of the mind and heart for its own sake', and many members of the intellectual élite began to see in the realisation and propagation of this ideal the specific mission of the Germans. Culture had become a supreme good, an ideal to live for.

But we must now ask ourselves what we mean by culture. In this context it is clearly personal, as opposed to national, culture that is meant, and we shall find important differences between individual authors in their valuation of the various possible types of personal culture, but for all of them an ethical and social factor was involved in personal culture that rarely entered into the English conception of it before Matthew Arnold's time, though Coleridge and even Burke had insisted, as Mr Williams points out, 'on man's need for institutions which should confirm and constitute his personal efforts. Cultivation, in fact, though an inward was never a merely individual process. What in the eighteenth century had been an ideal of personality—a personal qualification for participation in polite society—had now, in the face of radical change, to be redefined, as a condition on which society as a whole depended.'[8]

'Culture' is in English, as Mr T. S. Eliot reminded us a few years ago,[9] a highly ambiguous word, and one that for various reasons we tend to avoid. Yet the concept or rather the concepts for which it stands have become indispensable tools of our thought, though it is necessary to distinguish the various possible meanings of the English word, for which German, for example, often uses separate terms. Apart from its scientific use in a phrase like 'bacterial culture', with which we are not concerned, the word seems to have now in English three principal meanings, all connected with the notion of tending and improving by education or training. The first is the process of the cultivation of an individual mind. This seems to be the basic meaning from which the others were later derived, and is clearly a metaphorical extension of the literal sense of 'culture' that still survives in 'agriculture', 'horticulture' and so forth. From Cicero's 'cultura animi' down to 'la culture de l'esprit' the object of the cultivation was still explicitly stated, but from the middle of the seventeenth century (see Appendix II) examples can be found of the use of 'cultura' alone, or of its equivalent in a modern language, particularly in the second or third sense that we shall distinguish, though this absolute use of the word only became common in the second half of the following century.

In its second sense, 'culture' means the result, in the individual, of the process of cultivation, as in 'a man of the widest culture'. In Goethe's day it became usual to use 'Bildung' in both of these first two senses, though 'Kultur' was still a possible synonym, along with some other expressions. Goethe himself, in his maturity, always associates this particular kind of 'Bildung' with the formation and transformation which he sees going on in all living nature, the object of his morphological studies. 'If we consider structures (Gestalten) in general,' he writes in 1806, 'particularly organic ones, we never come across anything stable or completed, but always things trembling in constant movement.' Accordingly our language, appropriately enough, is wont to use the word 'Bildung' both of the product of formation and of the process.[10]

The third common meaning of 'culture' is what in German is usually called 'Kultur', in English 'civilisation', and is applied not to individuals but to groups, usually whole nations. The personal culture that results from the cultivation of an individual's mind and feeling is stored in his memory and affects his behaviour every moment, but it dies with him. Civilisation or group culture outlives individuals, though it could only come into existence through them, and has to be given a new lease of life by each succeeding generation. It is the result for society of 'cultivation'

4

and 'personal culture', stored in the form of habits and traditions, which are handed on partly from individual to individual, by example and by word of mouth, and partly impersonally, through institutions and organisations of a thousand kinds, kept alive by successive individuals. In both kinds of transmission material objects, fashioned by a particular generation, play an all-important part in the resurrection, in each successive generation, of 'culture' in individuals and 'civilisation' in groups. These accumulated material objects may be subdivided into the useful and the significant. We may include under the former heading the humanised landscape, buildings and technical installations of every kind, everything in fact that is a product of man as toolmaker. The 'significant', on the other hand, includes all things to which man has given a symbolic meaning, first language in its most fleeting and insubstantial form, the puffs of breath that convey so much from one human being to others, then the language of gesture, dancing, miming, vocal and instrumental music and all their possible combinations. No civilisation has developed very far without the invention of some way of recording these fleeting expressions of meaning through a secondary symbolisation, marks on paper and so on which last, and enable anyone, at any distance in space and time, who has in his individual life been able to acquire the traditional skills required, has been 'cultivated', that is, to recover the original meaning of the signs before him. The plastic arts, working from the beginning with material substances, hand on their meaning from generation to generation much as writing does, but only if they too can be resurrected by a duly 'cultivated' individual mind. It is not necessary to carry this elementary analysis further, or to attempt a catalogue of the types of object which accumulate as any civilisation grows, to remind the reader that in any civilisation we are concerned with what Nicolai Hartmann calls 'objectified mind',[11] the imprint on a material substance of the activity of human minds, capable of evoking in other minds, given suitable conditions, which always include 'cultivation', an activity of a more or less similar kind. These are the material heritage from the past that Faust has in mind when, looking round his cramped Gothic room, he cries:

> Was du ererbt von deinen Vätern hast,
> Erwirb es, um es zu besitzen!*

In German, the word 'Kultur' is now commonly reserved for the higher manifestations of what we call civilisation, those expressed mainly in symbolic forms—religion, philosophy, literature, art and music, but also law and the forms of political and social life. The history of 'Kultur' deals exclusively with this kind of thing. That side of civilisation which ministers to man's material welfare—transport, housing, sanitation, cooking and everything technological, for instance—is called 'Zivilisation'. The Russians, on the other hand, seem to use the word corresponding to 'cultural' more freely than either we or the Germans do, speaking of such an activity as nursing, for example, as eminently cultural, because it is regarded as unselfishly devoted to the purposes of the community. We are often reminded, when we read of Russian cultural activities, of the contrast drawn by Mr Koestler between the 'Commissar', who looks to planned institutions for the improvement of life, and the 'Yogi', who relies on change from within, and in discussing Weimar we shall be much concerned with an 'inward' point of view very close to that of the 'Yogi'.

A fourth meaning of 'culture' must also be noted, now very common because of the widespread interest in prehistoric archaeology. The archaeologist and anthropologist speak of 'cultures' in the plural, distinguishing them from each other by some descriptive name. Here it is the whole way of life of a human society that they have in mind, as far as it may be revealed, for prehistory, by the spade from material remains, or as it is scientifically observed among primitive peoples by the visiting anthropologist. The word was apparently first used in this sense in English by Tylor, in the title of his work on 'Primitive Culture', in 1871,

---

* That which your fathers have bequeathed to you,
  Win it afresh, to make it really yours!

and this is a direct imitation of the German. Herder, we shall find, already used 'Kultur' with this meaning, as well as all the others. Sociologists now study culture, understood in this comprehensive sense, in every kind of society, ancient or modern, primitive or advanced. Mr E. A. Hoebel defines culture as 'the integrated sum total of learned behaviour traits which are manifest and shared by the members of a society', and Mr T. S. Eliot too says: 'By "culture", then, I mean first of all what the anthropologists mean: the way of life of a particular people living together in one place. That culture is made visible in their arts, in their social system, in their habits and customs, in their religion.' But all are parts of a living whole, 'in trembling movement'. 'These things all act upon each other, and fully to understand one you have to understand all.'[12]

To possess culture is clearly a human prerogative. Lower creatures can evolve a kind of social life based on instinct, such as we find at its most complex in an ant-hill, but only men, with their highly developed nervous system, have that capacity to learn during their individual lives, and to remember sufficiently well, which makes culture possible. Further, only men living together in a society can have culture, for which it is necessary that each generation shall be influenced not only by its own experience, but by the accumulated results of its ancestors' experience, handed down to it not only by direct contact, but indirectly by means of its civilisation, with all its material embodiment of the thought and feeling of the past. A Kaspar Hauser could not have even the rudiments of culture in any sense, any more than the 'wolf children' who have occasionally been discovered in India. 'At the time of his capture', we read of one of them, then eight years old, 'the boy was drinking on all fours at the side of a forest pool in the company of a she-wolf, which afterwards followed the party for a considerable distance. He is undersized for his age and after six months in human care still prefers raw meat to other foods, and has a tendency to bite. He has not yet learned to speak.'[13] Hobbes perhaps imagined creatures something like this boy when he described the life of man in primitive society, before the emergence of the state, as 'solitary, poor, nasty, brutish and short', and Pufendorf, countering the arguments of the *Leviathan*, anticipated the modern sociological view of the rôle of culture in raising man above 'the state of nature', employing the Latin word 'cultura' perhaps for the first time absolutely, in 1686.[14] (See Appendix II.)

The comparative poverty of our English vocabulary in these matters seems to indicate that an interest in the theory of culture developed later here than in Germany. German writers were apparently also the first to take up philosophically the subject of general aesthetics. 'Culture', like 'art' in its modern sense, which embraces all the particular arts, is a late conception everywhere, the result of a process of classifying concepts by similarity gradually carried further and further, with results which may easily mislead the unwary, but cannot be ignored. When we boggle at the word culture, it is generally because we disagree with some view about what is best in culture that is implied in the context. There must inevitably be such disagreements, because cultures and ideals of culture are so various. The summary attempted above does not tell half the story. As Mr Eliot clearly showed us, in any one national civilisation at present there are different co-existent levels of culture, as well as big regional differences, and this is desirable, though some degree of integration is desirable too. Progress in civilisation, he says, brings into being more specialised culture-groups, to the advantage of the whole society, but also at a certain risk to it.

The emergence of such a culture-group, with the risks and advantages thereby entailed, is the theme of the following pages, a group of particular interest to the student of culture because it was so fully conscious of its own cultural effort, to the extent of sometimes defeating its own end, for culture is as shy a bird as happiness and often eludes a too direct approach. This group has the advantage for the student of being, for modern conditions, relatively closed, and its history is very fully recorded. We can therefore trace clearly the main stages in the development of Weimar, one quite unforeseen at the outset of our period, and we can understand something of the complex interplay of social and intellectual factors, of environment and individual genius. Broadly humanitarian aims were honestly pursued by the leading figures, but inevitably, an element of 'contingence', as the theologians say, entered into all the ideas and ideals of the time, and it is particularly interesting to try to see how it modified them, and thus perhaps to explain in part some of the moral and aesthetic contradictions in later German history. It is a 'civilisation grounded in cultivation' that I see and wish to present in my picture of Weimar, concentrating attention on those typical features in the life of its intellectual leaders and their patrons which seem important for my purpose. The story is carried only as far as the end of the old Reich, a year after Schiller's death, but in a final chapter the later history of the ideas of cultivation and civilisation (Bildung and Kultur) is outlined, to indicate how a diffused and diluted Weimar humanism was sometimes perverted to strange purposes in the struggle for national unity and power, sometimes transformed into an inner refuge, divorced from influence on everyday life.

> Weimar, thou wert assigned a special fate,
> Like Bethlehem in Judah, small and great.

So Goethe poses the problem which faces us in the first chapter: why Weimar? The first step towards Weimar's cultural leadership, it is generally agreed, was taken by Duchess Anna Amalia when, all unknowing, she asked Wieland to be the tutor of her elder son, and we can find reasons for her choice of a novelist and poet, and this particular one, in her character and earlier history, and in his. Wieland already made Weimar into something of a literary centre with his *Deutscher Merkur*, but he would hardly, on his own initiative, have sought out such a brilliant rival as the young Goethe. To understand Goethe's advent, we must know what a boy-duke could see in him, and bring in Knebel as intermediary.

The second chapter describes first the obscure German court, in a modest town whose society was quite normal for the times, into which Goethe burst like a 'Voltairian Huron' when, being at a loose end, he accepted a casual invitation to go there. Why he stayed on, how he became the Duke's trusted friend and adviser, and what exactly he did in the official posts that he filled for the next ten years are the questions to which the second half of the chapter attempts an answer.

The third chapter deals with the arts, especially the amateur theatre, as they developed in these years under Goethe's leadership, then with the new interest in natural history and science evoked in the poet by the demands of practical life and followed up for its own sake, an interest shared by Knebel, Herder and others, and finally with Goethe's inward growth, his conscious efforts at self-mastery and his relation with Charlotte von Stein, until his escape to Italy, to be himself again, in 1786.

The fourth chapter leads up to the discussion of classical Weimar's cultural institutions by analysing the theories of culture put forward by those principally responsible for the final shaping of those institutions, Herder, with his pioneering history of civilisation and humane ideas, Goethe, with his notion of individual self-improvement, closely connected with his scientific and aesthetic ideas and most fully expressed at this stage in *Wilhelm Meister's Apprenticeship*, the first 'Bildungsroman', and Schiller, with his *Letters on Aesthetic Education*.

In the fifth chapter the connection is established between the cultivation and creative effort of the leading figures in Weimar and Jena (the university of the state) and various important institutions that made their work fruitful for society in Weimar and further afield, and gave it permanence in a material embodiment, through which it became a lasting feature of German civilisation. Wieland's influence was exerted chiefly through his *Deutscher Merkur*. His assistant in the early days, Bertuch, spread Weimar ideas far and wide through a whole series of periodical publications, one, the *Allgemeine Literatur-Zeitung*, of the greatest importance, and he greatly benefited local arts and crafts through his *Modejournal* and his Centre for Local Industries. Herder left his mark on history mainly through his books, but as 'Generalsuperintendent' he was the head of the Protestant clergy and responsible for all the schools in the state, and he effected some reforms. The enormous influence of Goethe and Schiller during the decade of their friendship is considered, after a brief study of their earlier relationship, mainly in connection with certain periodicals: *Die Horen*, the *Musenalmanach* with its satirical 'Xenien', and the *Propyläen*. Their notion of classicism is further illustrated from the history of the Weimar Art Competitions, and finally of the Weimar Court Theatre. Goethe's work for the University of Jena, especially its scientific institutes, is brought into relation with the general history of the University in crucial years following the French Revolution, and the story of his 'Friday Society' in Weimar is followed by an account of his various series of organised readings and lectures to the ladies of the court.

The last chapter discusses briefly the later history of Weimar and the influence of Weimar ideals on later German civilisation as a whole, sketching first the new ideas of the Romantic School, a group of younger men associated during our period with Jena, but best considered as a new departure. The effects on German conceptions of culture and civilisation of the emergence of 'state' nationalism, of the economic and technical transformation of Germany and of the struggle for world power are briefly outlined, as some of the topics that would form the high-lights of any continuation of the present volume.

CHAPTER I

DUCHESS ANNA AMALIA AND WIELAND,
1756–1775

I. DUCHESS ANNA AMALIA AS PATRON

OUR object being to study the emergence and development of a new élite or culture-group in Weimar, the first step is to determine when, how, and if possible why this process started there. The analogy which is implied in the very word culture makes it natural for us to look for someone corresponding to a gardener, who introduces new plants and improves the existing soil to receive them. In the general conditions of the time, political, economic and social, which I have described in an earlier work, it was indeed a prerequisite for any considerable cultural movement in eighteenth-century Germany that some individual, possessing ample means and high authority, should take the lead, and in that pre-industrial age it had to be a member of the landed aristocracy, or best of all, one of the many petty princes, most of whom we should think of as having more in common with an English peer than with the King of England. Private patronage retained its importance far later in Germany than in countries with a more highly developed trade and industry. It did indeed gradually become possible, in the second half of the century, for a literary man to live as a free-lance writer, as Lessing was one of the first to prove, but he was put to all sorts of shifts to do so, for he could not yet exchange private for public patronage and count on a well-defined body of readers. Copyright could not yet be enforced in Germany, and the reading public, though it was growing rapidly, was scattered, amorphous, undecided in its views and tastes, and disposed, like the rest of the population, to follow the lead of the courts. What was possible without patronage may be seen from the history of the group of writers in Berlin, including

Nicolai, Mendelssohn, Garve, Engel and many others, with some of whom Lessing was for years closely associated, men not lacking in talent or energy. Through their periodicals in particular they reached an extensive public in northern Germany, and started a tradition of rationalism which persisted into the nineteenth century, affecting thinking men of all classes throughout Berlin, though not without the help of wealthy emancipated Jewish hostesses, whose continuing influence in the diffusion of thought and taste and the encouragement of the free intellectual life will concern us later. But the Philosopher on the Throne, though he granted them a certain licence, while it suited his purposes, never changed his own French tastes in art and literature, and the absence of his patronage long delayed a reform of the theatre and discouraged native German talent in almost every branch of the arts.

It was no novelty for high aristocrats, in Germany as elsewhere, to exercise patronage; it was in fact naturally expected of them that they should, and in a small way quite a number of courts did something now and then for the encouragement of German writers, scholars, actors and so on, but their favours were more often reserved for the more spectacular arts, and as they or their advisers were guided by the international aristocratic norms of the time, they employed the best talent they could afford, native or foreign, though they often took steps to build up a supply of local skill for their needs. A letter written by Goethe, on his way to Switzerland in 1797, illustrates what happened in scores of places and incidentally shows us how well he understood the importance of patronage for the fostering of the higher forms of culture in his day. As a sort of Minister for Cultural Affairs in Weimar, he is reporting to his Duke on the state of the arts in Stuttgart, and indirectly hinting at the Duke's own responsibilities at home. Duke Karl Eugen of Württemberg (Schiller's 'tyrant' who reigned from 1744 to 1793), though he had not been particularly enlightened, and had aimed in the main at external show, had yet through his need for artists unintentionally greatly benefited the arts, Goethe says. Operas, festivities, masquerades had all required trained talent, and had led to the foundation of an academy, later extended to cover music, acting and the ballet. For a time Stuttgart had had perhaps the best opera in Europe, and to build and adorn his palaces the Duke had had architects, painters and sculptors trained in Paris and Rome. The love of the arts was still widespread in Stuttgart, Goethe found, though unfortunately people had not a good word to say for German music and singing. What a pity it was, Goethe added, that they so seldom realised what a precious possession they had in this artistic skill, a capital slowly built up in the past. Together with science and scholarship, fine craftsmanship and well-managed industry, it was of the greatest importance for the whole life of the country.[1] With all its insight, the letter was apparently rather wasted on Karl August, who wrote to Knebel that Goethe was sending him letters like official reports, and that it was too funny to see how solemn the man was getting.

His mother had more understanding for such things, and it was to her in the first place that the Weimar 'Court of the Muses', as it came to be called, owed its origin. As Princess Anna Amalia of Brunswick she had been married in 1756, 'as princesses are married', as she herself put it, while still hardly more than a child, to Ernst August Konstantin of Weimar, who at eighteen had just attained his majority. His little duchy could then boast of nothing remarkable in its present position or its past history. The original partition of the Wettin lands in 1485 between the Ernestine and Albertine branches had been followed by innumerable further subdivisions, the principle of primogeniture having been established in Weimar, for instance, only in the reign of Ernst August Konstantin's father. Various independent lines belonging, like the Weimar house, to the Ernestine branch, ruled one or more scraps of territory in the patchwork that was marked Thuringia on the maps, with the lands of other fragmented small states filling up the gaps in between, so that in mid-century the area was divided among nearly thirty princes, nearly all closely related by generations of intermarriage. Most of these small states were made up of smaller portions that had been combined and recombined in the course of the centuries, as the result of successive wills and marriage contracts, like the scattered mansions and estates of any big landowner in England at that time. Weimar consisted now of the combined duchies of Weimar and Eisenach, together with the former duchy of Jena and the bailiwick (Amt) Ilmenau, inherited from a Count of Henneberg in Franconia. Weimar and Eisenach had been united since 1741, through the extinction of the Eisenach line, and Jena, which for fifty years they had shared, had been reunited through the same circumstance and was now administered from Weimar. All four portions had their separate taxation systems still, and Eisenach, which made up nearly half the area of the whole, had an almost entirely separate administration, supervised by a common Privy Council in Weimar. The larger neighbouring state of Sachsen-Gotha was still divided among four lines (earlier it had been seven): Sachsen-Gotha-Altenburg, Sachsen-Coburg-Saalfeld (Prince Albert's ancestors), Sachsen-Meiningen and Sachsen-Hildburghausen.

It is readily understandable that the separate portions of such conglomerate states held firmly to their own traditions, and that it was almost impossible even for an energetic and able ruler either to imitate Brandenburg-Prussia in its centralisation of power and bureaucratic efficiency, or with its scanty resources to build up a fund of musical and artistic talent such as Goethe found in Württemberg, which had six times the population of Weimar. Weimar had had no personality among its dukes and duchesses to compare with the great Ernst der Fromme (1640–75) or with Duchess Luise Dorothea (1732–67), the correspondent of Voltaire, in the neighbouring state of Gotha. The best of them had been patriarchally benevolent, but as Hartung says, 'Weimar had experienced the drawbacks rather than the blessings of particularism in the eighteenth century. Ernst August (Konstantin's father) had shown less regard than most German princelets for the financial position of his tiny duchy, in indulging his expensive taste for a toy army, his love of the chase and above all his passion for building. . . . The patriarchal benevolence even of Ernst

August Konstantin and Anna Amalia was soon exhausted when their own privy purse was affected; they too looked upon Treasury funds simply as their private banking account as rulers, and found it more than superfluous to spend their money on enterprises for the future good of their country. This attitude easily led to heavy demands on the country for the upkeep of the court, resulting in serious debts and a heavy burden of taxation.'[2]

Patronage of the arts began then in Weimar, gradually and on a modest scale, with Anna Amalia. It is true that the organist of the Schlosskirche between 1708 and 1718 had been Johann Sebastian Bach, and that he had composed there some of his best early cantatas and much organ music, but music was fostered from religious motives in many German states, following the Lutheran tradition, and the gloomy Duke Wilhelm Ernst in Bach's time had no doubt simply engaged him as a local man, from Eisenach, of known talent, without realising in the least what a genius he had in his service. Anna Amalia, however, knew what she was doing, because of the tradition which she had herself inherited at Brunswick. When she married Ernst August Konstantin in 1756 she was not yet seventeen, and her husband under nineteen years of age. Before he died, two years later, she had borne him a son, Karl August, and a second son, Konstantin, was born soon after his father's death. Anna Amalia became Regent during her son's minority, and in the nineteen years between her accession and that of her son (in 1775, when he was eighteen) she had changed the tone of the Weimar court and made the later developments there possible.

One can understand this new turn of events as the result partly of her individual endowment, partly of her upbringing. Before her marriage she had been shy, awkward and rather plain, the fifth child of a large family, put into the shade especially by her beautiful older sister Caroline. 'I withdrew myself wholly into myself', she wrote later (1772), when she looked back on what seemed to her a rather unhappy childhood which, if it made her something of an introvert, left her spirit unbroken. Her father,

Duke Karl I of Brunswick and Lüneburg (born 1713, reigned 1735–80), found the state on his accession deeply in debt, and he seems to have done his best, following the example of his neighbour, Frederick William I of Prussia, to increase the prosperity of his much smaller country. But he was not made in the Hohenzollern mould. He tried to imitate Frederick William in strengthening the central government at the expense of the Estates and in economic experiments, but he was a man of pleasure, not a dour fanatic, affable and generous, but extravagant and lacking in foresight. His canal-building and silkworm-breeding only led to further debts, which were reduced for a time through the sale of his soldiers to England and other powers, but finally brought the state to bankruptcy. He did leave his mark, however, largely owing to the good influence of F. W. Jerusalem, the tutor of his sons, later one of the leading enlightened Protestant churchmen of his day, on cultural developments. He went further than Prussia in his improvement of primary education, setting up some of the first teachers' training colleges in Germany, and he founded what became one of the best schools in Germany for boys of good family, the Carolinum in Brunswick. This aimed at taking the boys further than the ordinary 'Ritterakademien', boarding-schools, where they were given a more modern and practical education than in a 'Gymnasium', with its concentration on the classics. The classics were taught, so that for the day-boys it could serve as a Gymnasium or grammar school, but the emphasis was on subjects useful for the future diplomat or civil servant, and an exceptionally good staff, including several well-known writers (even Klopstock had been approached), paid special attention to the writing of good German. The school was considered good enough for the Hereditary Prince of Brunswick.

F. W. Jerusalem and his friends at the Carolinum cannot have been without influence on Anna Amalia. In his capacity as tutor Jerusalem certainly wrote reports on her, all very favourable and stressing her sensitive nature. He was to attempt in his last years to overcome Frederick the Great's prejudice against German literature (1781) and must certainly have encouraged his pupils to take an interest in it. But it was naturally French literature and art and the French stage that made the deepest impression on Anna Amalia in her youth. Her mother, a younger sister of Frederick the Great, bore philosophically the unfaithfulness of her husband and consoled herself with reading and the arts. The Duke was quite willing to spend money on performances of Italian opera and French plays, and the Duchess, though her whole education had been French, like her brother's, was open-minded enough to take pleasure in occasional visits of north German touring companies. Lessing, of course, only went to Wolfenbüttel as the Duke's librarian over twenty years after Anna Amalia's marriage. A royal library and a picture gallery were amongst the things that any court of standing tried to keep up in rivalry with its neighbours. Anna Amalia was used to such luxuries, and through her mother was accustomed to looking upon art and literature, music and the theatre as indispensable elements in the life of anyone of cultivation. In Weimar later we find her writing, acting, composing, painting and even taking lessons when in her thirties in Latin and Greek. She had no great talent perhaps, but a genuine liking for literature and the arts, combined no doubt, as it was in her much more gifted uncle, with the desire to prove that she did not owe everything to her position, but had some right to consideration for her native intelligence and taste. Schiller, it is true, on first meeting her, though she treated him extremely well, found 'her mind very limited. Nothing interests her but what is connected with the senses. This explains her taste, real or assumed, for music and painting and so on.'[3] In interpreting this outspoken opinion, we have to remember Schiller's state of mind during this first, rather embarrassing visit to Weimar, his extreme idealism and instinctive rejection of the 'attachment to nature and resignation to one's five senses' with which he found Goethe had infected his whole circle. But he probably felt rightly that Anna Amalia belonged to the rococo world, and that the supersensuous left her cold.

During their all too short married life Anna Amalia and Ernst

August Konstantin, who was fond of drawing and picture-collecting, and played the fiddle, at least had time to do something for the theatre in Weimar. They brought Döbbelin's touring company to the town and after a few months set up a court theatre for German plays, the first of its kind. The troupe consisted of six married couples and gave performances before the court and invited guests in a small theatre in the ducal palace, the Wilhelmsburg. The auditorium, only about as big as the stage, held a hundred. The Duke's death of consumption in 1758, before he was quite twenty-one, soon put an end to this venture, and the times were far too serious and difficult for his widow to think of any further patronage of the arts until the Seven Years War was over. The troops of both Frederick and his opponents were constantly marching through Weimar territory and requisitioning what they needed, so that even although the government sent as few troops as possible to fight for the Reich, it proved impossible, in spite of the strictest economy, to reduce the burden of debt inherited from Ernst August's time and further debts had to be incurred. Though anxious to improve the music at court, Anna Amalia had to be content for fifteen years with the very modest orchestra, a wind octette dating from Ernst August's time —he had himself performed on the trumpet, and liked particularly the sound of trumpet and drum. Later some strings were added, but in 1783 there were still only about a dozen players. E. W. Wolf, who with his wife became the centre of Weimar musical life in the 'seventies, went there first in 1761, to give private lessons, began to take part in court concerts and presently became organist. His wife, the daughter of the Master of the King's Music in Berlin, Franz Benda, had gone to Weimar on a private visit and been engaged as court singer before marrying him. Other singers seem to have been either simply engaged for particular performances, or to have been amateurs.

It was not until several years after the end of the war that Anna Amalia could think of bringing a troupe of actors to Weimar again. In the winter of 1767-8 the Starcke company performed in the Riding School, and from 1768 for three years the Duchess subsidised the well-known troupe of G. H. Koch, a veteran trained by Karoline Neuber. Goethe, as a student in Leipzig, had been present at the opening in 1766 of Leipzig's first permanent theatre, built for Koch, and Koch had been so successful there with comic opera that the town council, at the request of the university, had cut down the number of performances to two a week. Koch was therefore very glad to move to Weimar, returning to Leipzig only at fair time. In Weimar, the enterprising musician Wolf soon felt impelled to try his own hand at composing comic operas similar to those put on by Koch. These 'Singspiele' had begun with German adaptations of Coffey's *The Devil to Pay*, a ballad opera like the earlier *Beggar's Opera*. Many were adapted from French operettas, in which social criticism, already to be found in Gay, was made a prominent feature. They were all the rage in Germany at this time, and they led straight to Mozart's German operas. It is interesting to note who were Wolf's local collaborators. For his *Rosenfest*, first performed on 4 September 1770, it was one of the two 'instructors' of Karl August, Councillor of Legation G. E. Hermann, who adapted the French libretto, and for the second, *Das Gärtnermädchen*, in the following September, it was J. K. Musäus, tutor to the pages and a part-time teacher at the Gymnasium. He made his name later of course with his *Volksmärchen*. It is hard to think of anyone else Wolf could have turned to in Weimar at that time, except the small staff of the Gymnasium, the ministers at the two churches (who were unlikely to be interested), or the court librarian.

In the next few years, however, the number of the 'literati' steadily increased, and long before the end of the century there was an unparalleled concentration of talent in Weimar. The first decisive step, for which Anna Amalia was personally responsible, was the appointment in 1772 of one of Germany's leading authors, Wieland, as tutor to Karl August, now fifteen, during the final stage of his education.

Her elder son's education had been a matter of much concern to his mother from the beginning. From his fifth year, it had been entrusted to Graf Görtz, one of the young noblemen turned

2 WIELAND

out by the Carolinum at Brunswick, recommended no doubt by Jerusalem. He was assisted by two instructors, Hermann, already mentioned, and a mathematician, Albrecht, as well as special masters for dancing, riding, and so on. The University of Jena later on provided professors to lecture to him on law, and Anna Amalia's chief minister, Jakob Friedrich von Fritsch, advised that other professors should be called in from there to give the Prince a finishing course in philosophy. But the Duchess decided that it was even more necessary to bring in a tutor who could teach him some of the things that he himself would have preferred to learn by making the Grand Tour, for which his mother considered him, at fifteen, still too young. Moreover she no longer had complete confidence in Graf Görtz, who was something of an intriguer and seemed to her to have more influence over the young prince now than she had herself. Karl August was certainly very much attached to him and felt, perhaps encouraged by Görtz, that his mother treated him too much like a child. He would have liked to begin already to live in the style of the duke he felt himself to be, even though he was still a minor. Anna Amalia would have let him go abroad in the company of her own former tutor Jerusalem, but the old clergyman, who was soon to receive a great shock through the suicide of his son Karl at Wetzlar, the event that precipitated Goethe's *Werther*, was too busy and not in the best of health. Instead of sending her son on his travels with Görtz, Anna Amalia called in Wieland to give him at home some of the worldly wisdom and polish that were supposed to result from a visit to Paris and Italy. Wieland had not to be brought very far, being now a professor at the University of Erfurt, he was recommended by Karl Theodor von Dalberg, the Statthalter of Erfurt, a detached portion of the Catholic Electorate of Mainz with which Weimar had many dealings, and it is not difficult to understand why this particular writer appealed to Anna Amalia, and why he was attracted by the Weimar offer, after some bargaining, of a salary of 1,000 gulden a year while he was acting as tutor, and thereafter a pension of 600 gulden a year for as long as he remained in Weimar.

2. WIELAND AND HIS PHILOSOPHY

By appointing Wieland, Anna Amalia brought a literary man of middle-class origin into the closest association with her family and the court, and thus unwittingly started a process which was to result in that partial fusion of two culture-groups, an aristocratic and a middle-class one, that finds its literary expression in Weimar classicism. To appreciate the significance of this step, we must remember how slight the part played by aristocratic writers in the revival of German literature since mid-century had been, and how strong a hold French literature and culture possessed over the German courts. In Paris, a bourgeois writer of talent had long been able to win for himself a perhaps slightly precarious place in good society, as he could, with more security, in London, but in Germany social distinctions were much more rigid, and aristocratic circles were all the more prejudiced against native literary ambitions because of the high prestige so long enjoyed by French literature, and the ridicule with which French wits greeted any suggestion that a German might rival them. Even in the 1770's, it was only at one of the smaller German courts, which had to be content with the second-best, that a German poet or a German troupe of actors had much chance of finding a patron. Lessing had been persistently cold-shouldered in Berlin, and even Klopstock, who did indeed enjoy extensive patronage, more as a religious teacher than a poet, found his chief benefactor in Denmark. Yet for a number of reasons, it was possible for Wieland to gain a foothold, not in Vienna, certainly, as he had hoped, but at least in Weimar.

It was already one of Wieland's admitted distinctions that, more than any of his contemporaries, he had attracted the approving attention of aristocratic readers, previously uninterested in German work. Though simple and unpretentious in his normal way of life, he had for some years, while occupying the position of Senator in his native town, Biberach, been accepted on equal terms in the entourage, comparable with a court, of Count Stadion, formerly Chancellor of Mainz, and now living in retirement near Biberach. With experience of the world Wieland combined, as professor of philosophy at Erfurt, some standing as a scholar, and most important of all perhaps, as a recommendation for the Weimar post, he had just written a work, *Der goldene Spiegel*, which, in the palatable form of a novel, presented a political philosophy.

The story of the kings of Scheschian, told in instalments by the wise Danischmend to the Sultan Gebal as a sort of night-cap, was intended by his prime minister to convey to him indirectly some wholesome truths about the art of government. With a certain effort one can still enjoy the liveliness of the narrative and of the frequently ironical exchanges it evokes from the hard-headed monarch and his courtiers, but it is hard to believe that the reflections here offered to the reader, on the successes and failures of these imaginary rulers in their efforts, while maintaining their power, to harmonise the interests of the various classes among their subjects, can ever have been of the slightest practical value to Anna Amalia or anyone else. Wieland had written the book in the hope of finding favour in the Vienna of Joseph II, so his ideal king, Tifan, is an enlightened despot ruling a great empire, but the charming picture that is drawn at another point of the idyllic life led in a small, obscure state that happens to be well governed— and very lucky—seems equally well designed to procure the patronage of some such minor sovereign as Karl August. The book was in the tradition of *Rasselas* and the *Lettres Persanes*, with its criticism of current affairs in Europe in a fanciful oriental disguise. One of Wieland's contemporaries, Mercier, a favourite of the Sturm und Drang for his unsparingly realistic pictures of Paris, was already using the device in a revolutionary spirit. Wieland's tone was anything but revolutionary, and that was essential if the book was to be a success in Germany. It emphasised the importance of a prince's education and suggested, for example, that 'the man who teaches a young prince history should combine the sincerest rectitude with wide and penetrating vision, the most refined moral feeling with the keenest discrimination'.[4] 'Man', says Tifan's tutor to his pupil, 'issues from the hands of Nature imperfect, but with innate powers fitting him to attain admirable perfections. The same plasticity makes him equally capable of assuming, under pressure, either the shape of a God—or the repellent features of a monster. Everything depends on the circumstances into which he is born and the impressions that his waxen brain registers in early youth.'[5] And later Tifan himself, in a long paean to education, announces that 'education is the first, the most important, the most essential concern of the state'[6] —good 'Enlightened' doctrine which, along with the spirit of humanity breathed by the work, could not fail to make a deep impression on a Regent in that age, anxious to do her best for her son.

Although there was really no solid political wisdom to be gained from such a hotchpotch of conflicting views, the speakers who voice them are plausible enough, and Anna Amalia was delighted to find a German writer who could discuss such themes without boring her. If she had been more critical, she would never have taken Wieland seriously enough as a philosopher to ask him, as she did at first, to obtain leave from Erfurt in order to give her sons a six-month course in philosophy. He had been appointed to the chair in Erfurt because a rapidly declining university badly needed men with a name, to attract students. Philosophy was not yet the technical subject that it was to become when Kant had made the theory of knowledge its central concern, and Wieland had as good a claim to the title of philosopher in this non-professional sense (that of the French rather than the German word) as, let us say, the 'Philosopher on the Throne'. He had put forward persuasively his views on the general conduct of life, in the novel *Geschichte des Agathon* (I and II, 1766–7), and it was on the strength of this achievement that he was chosen.

Agathon is the story of how a young man learns through personal experience that the excessively spiritual 'enthusiasm' of his youth was folly. A wise man does not imagine, he comes to think, that only those experiences are valuable where the instinctive life is repressed and a man tries to be pure mind.

'I am sorry for you, Kallias' (the new name given to Agathon when he has been sold as a slave), says the Sophist Hippias, his master.

You have a figure and gifts that justify you in aiming at all the happiness possible to man; it is only your thinking that will make you unhappy. Accustomed as you are to seeing yourself entirely surrounded by ideal beings, you will never learn to profit from the society of men. In a world that will know as little of you as you do of it, you will stray like a man from the moon, never at home save in a desert or in Diogenes' tub. . . . Yet if you will but learn, you may easily rid yourself of this strange kind of madness, that you regard as wisdom.[7]

Agathon does indeed prove teachable, when he meets the charming hetaira Danae, like many an innocent in French novels of that age, or like the hero of Fielding's *Tom Jones*, who acquires a wholesome knowledge of the world as it is, and not as Richardson drew it. The story has many other episodes, and in a third part added nearly thirty years later Wieland provided it with a much more respectable philosophy, but its rococo sensualism is the heart of the book. *Musarion*, the short philosophical idyll in verse written alongside the first version of *Agathon*, a poem Goethe soon had by heart and never ceased to admire, and that Wieland held to be the best expression he had ever given to his own view of life, shows us a similar young dreamer cured in exactly the same way. The philosophy of both is:

Die reizende Philosophie
Die, was Natur und Schicksal uns gewährt
Vergnügt genießt und gern den Rest entbehrt . . .
Nicht stets von Tugend spricht, noch, von ihr sprechend, glüht,
Doch, ohne Sold und aus Geschmack, sie übet.*

We have not yet reached here the mystical conception of the

---

* The charming philosophy that enjoys gladly what nature and fate allow us, and willingly gives up the rest . . . is not for ever talking, with hectic enthusiasm, about virtue, but practises it from taste, and without thought of reward.

'eternally feminine'. Feminine influence does not so much draw men on to higher planes of existence as release them from inhibitions imposed by outdated creeds. An attractive young woman cures some man of an obsession with high-falutin' ideas by reminding him that he is human-all-too-human. Wieland's ladies often do this by calculated indiscretions that remind us of rococo paintings and book-illustrations, as when Musarion produces a slight disorder in her dress (ll. 839 ff.) to put Theophron off his stride, in his description of the pure spirituality that results from chastity and a diet of beans. But Wieland did not see his Greeks only through the eyes of the French; he was indebted also to Winckelmann, with his spiritualisation of antiquity, and above all to the third Earl of Shaftesbury (1671–1713), whose influence on serious minds in Germany throughout the eighteenth century was so profound.

It was exercised both directly, through his *Characteristics of Men, Manners, Opinions and Times* (1711), much of which had been translated into German by this time,[8] and through British (particularly North-British) authors who followed him in his optimistic view of human nature, like James Thomson, in his *Seasons*, and the Scottish school of philosophers, notably Ferguson, Hutcheson and Adam Smith. Combining some ideas of the Cambridge Platonists with others from the English Deistic tradition, Shaftesbury rejected the notions of a special revelation and of original sin, and found in the Greeks the best guides he knew to the good life for a cultivated man. A gentleman does not need to be constantly reminded of the gallows to behave decently, any more than of possible rewards or punishments in a future life. Virtue, properly understood, is its own reward, and everyone with a good nursery and a humanistic education behind him will have developed a 'moral sense' that is a sufficient guide to right conduct, just as he has acquired good taste and good manners. We hear in Shaftesbury, whose education had been directed by Locke, the message of the Enlightenment, delivered in the persuasive tones of a Wykhamist, well versed in the classics, in an age when, as Professor Basil Willey has said, the wealthy and educated of Europe must have enjoyed almost the nearest approach to earthly felicity ever known to man. Centuries of superstition, error and strife lay behind; most of the medieval ghosts had been laid; a revolutionary era had been successfully weathered; liberty and philosophy and the arts were raising their heads once more. . . . The universe had been explained.[9]

In Germany, Shaftesbury's ideas fitted in well with the prevalent desire of moderate men of the Enlightenment, following Leibniz and Wolff, to be completely 'modern' in their views without abandoning what they considered the core of their inherited religion, the belief in God, freedom and immortality, and thus leaving ethics without a foundation. They were reinforced by the humanism of the lawyers, with their notion of natural law. Pufendorf, its great German exponent, had held that there was an inborn social sense (socialitas) in man, that tended to restrain individual selfishness. It was for him the psychological basis of civilisation, and he held it to be part of a man's duty towards himself to foster it, by consciously cultivating his own mind and heart, a process of self-improvement that he calls 'cultura' (this being, as we have mentioned, the first known use of the Latin word in an absolute sense). Here it has the meaning of 'Bildung'. (See Appendix II.) The notion of natural religion was encouraged by, or at least flourished in the same atmosphere as, this of natural law, and it was widely believed in Wieland's youth that the religion that underlies all historical religions could be taught to the young from what Bacon called God's second bible, the book of nature, and from the writings of the great poets and philosophers. In this way formerly religious ideas and attitudes were being increasingly secularised.

The loss of faith common to all the leading European writers of the Enlightenment seems to have caused far more heart-searching in Germany than in France or England, where it is an age of confident belief in the power of the human reason to solve the problems of existence. The kind of conflict of conscience which we associate with the Victorian Age occurred in Germany from mid-eighteenth century. Most serious writers have already something about them that reminds us of the young man in Heine's poem 'Fragen', who stands by the shore at midnight and asks the wild waves

> Was bedeutet der Mensch?
> Woher ist er kommen? Wo geht er hin?
> Wer wohnt dort oben auf goldenen Sternen?*

or of Chekhov's engineer in the story 'Lights', who gives himself up to the sensation of terrible loneliness, imagining that in the whole universe, dark and formless, nothing exists but himself, and pondering over the aimlessness of life, and the darkness beyond the grave. Though treated with irony by these late writers, the metaphysical thrill was a genuine and frequent experience of unbelievers in Germany long before the Romantics. As to the philosophers, Heine was not far wrong when he wrote in *Die romantische Schule* that German philosophy, though it now claimed a place by the side of the Protestant Church, or even above it, was nevertheless only its daughter, and literary men too, sometimes unconsciously, were concerned to answer just those questions about life which their childhood religion had made all-important for them, but which today, for many English philosophers at least, seem to be literally without meaning, so much do our intellectual interests depend on the intellectual climate we live in. The clear-headed Lessing never lost his passion for apologetics and was almost entirely occupied in his last years with thoughts of religion. Herder, Goethe and Schiller, in their different ways, not to speak of dozens of lesser writers, display in their work and expect of their readers a bias towards metaphysics and ethics so pronounced that H. A. Korff can rightly claim, as a justification for his method of writing the history of classical and romantic German literature, that it is more truly a 'literature of ideas' than any comparable body of world literature. Wieland, though so often accused of frivolity, is not, if we consider his work as a whole, an exception to this rule.

As a student of eighteen he composed for his cousin Sophie

---

* What is the meaning of man? Where has he come from? Where is he going to? Who dwells up there on the golden stars?

Gutermann a long didactic poem in alexandrines, *Die Natur der Dinge*, where we see, as Sengle writes, 'how a parson's son secularises the Gospel of Love and a Christian sermon into a love-myth', which begins with a proof of the existence of God on lines familiar from Paley's *Evidences*:

> Ja, spricht er, ja, ein Gott bewegt die Wunderuhr
> Der Welt, die er erfand, beseelet die Natur.*

Though this precocious boy had had a pietistic upbringing, he had read at fifteen Bayle's *Dictionnaire historique et critique*, where he found all the reasons for and against believing so persuasively set out that it seemed most reasonable not to accept any belief as final, but to be tolerant of all. The best commentary on the religious phase of Wieland's writing, when he had first his family and Sophie, then the pious Bodmer circle and similar Swiss groups in mind as his audience, is still Lessing's (in the 11th of the *Literaturbriefe*): 'The Christian religion comes into almost every sentence Herr Wieland writes.—People often boast of something they do not possess, in order at least to seem to possess it.' All along he had inwardly doubted, and when he returned to Biberach and came into close touch with the completely rococo and scep-tical entourage of Count Stadion, he quickly shed his etherial tone and began to write the graceful, frivolous verse tales which captured the ear of aristocratic readers, and in which 'metaphysics is for him a joke'.[10] In prose writings he had however already expounded the common-sense compromise which represents his own convictions, so far as he had any, and here his chief guide is Shaftesbury.

From Shaftesbury Wieland learned that a man of the world can still maintain what can be called a spiritual view of life, in that he lives in the main for knowledge, art and reflection, the enlarge-ment of his mind, yet shirks no duty and accepts cheerfully what-ever fate decrees. At first he was attracted chiefly by Shaftesbury's often rather wordy Platonism, but he soon saw that there was

---

* Yes, he says, a God keeps the miraculous clock of the world, which he invented, in motion, and gives a soul to nature.

nothing repressive or ascetic in his philosophy, no one-sided soulfulness, but rather a plea for the full development, so far as it was possible without conflict, of all sides of a man's personality. The easy assurance, common-sense tolerance and infectious optimism of a cultivated nobleman made a deep impression on a bookish provincial, very unsure of himself, as Wieland was at that time. It may be useful here, because of the importance of so many of Shaftesbury's ideas for the movement of thought we are describing, to re-state in a more systematic form the chief arguments of the *Characteristics*.

1. Shaftesbury rejects both atheism and Christian orthodoxy and puts forward a rational deism, taking that term in the then current sense of theism, 'belief in the existence of one God as creator and supreme ruler of the universe' (*Oxford Dictionary*), but with denial of revelation. In their emotional effect, some of his purple passages in *The Moralists* come near to pantheism and remind us, at a certain remove, of Goethe's (or J. C. Tobler's) *Naturfragment* of 1781–2. There are even sentences in the later essay that sound like a more pregnant expression of Shaftesbury's thought. Compare, for instance, this in the *Naturfragment*: 'Her spectacle is always new, because she is always creating new spectators. Life is her finest invention, and death is her device for ensuring that there shall be much life', with Shaftesbury's: 'All lives: and by Succession still revives. The Temporary Beings quit their borrowed Forms, and yield their Elementary Substance to Newcomers. Called, in their several turns, to Life, they view the Light, and viewing pass; that others too may be Spectators of the goodly Scene, and greater numbers still enjoy the Privilege of Nature.'[11]

We should however remember, in reading the much-quoted and frequently imitated rhapsody in *The Moralists* to 'Glorious Nature! Supremely Fair and Sovereignly Good', and to the 'Impowering Deity' approached through her,[12] that, according to the author's own comment,[13] there is an element of parody, not surprising in an author so fond of 'raillery', to be discounted in some of the rhetoric of Theocles, who is a character in a dialogue. For Shaftesbury, his own reason, stimulated and tested in free discussion, is his guide to truth, and for him 'a freedom of Raillery, a Liberty in decent Language to question everything, and an Allowance of unravelling or refuting an Argument, without offence to the Arguer, are the only Terms which can render such speculative Conversations any way agreeable'.[14] He detests any kind of sectarian fanaticism or 'enthusiasm' (what Lessing and Wieland called 'Schwärmerei'), but his attitude is far from negative. He rejects the Hobbesian view that there is 'no such thing as natural Faith and Justice', or that 'only Force and Power constitute Right'.[15] Like Pufendorf, he holds that social feeling is 'natural', that 'Faith, Justice, Honesty and Virtue must have been as early as the State of Nature, or they would never have been at all'.[16] Even now, 'they who live under a Tyranny, and have learnt to admire its Power as Sacred and Divine, are debauched as much in their Religion, as in their Morals'.[17]

2. Though a strong individualist in his insistence on free thought, Shaftesbury remains a neo-classicist, an Augustan, in his view of literature and art. A painter, he says, 'knows he is even then unnatural, when he follows Nature too close, and strictly copies Life'. For 'all Beauty is Truth', and the true artist and poet 'hates Minuteness and is afraid of Singularity',[18] even though the poet is to be regarded in some respects as 'a second Maker, a just Prometheus, under Jove'.[19] It is not unfettered creative genius that Shaftesbury has in mind here, as the Sturm und Drang would have it, but a talent for harmonious composition, for producing a single, unified impression. 'Like that Sovereign Artist or universal Plastic Nature, he forms a Whole, coherent and proportioned in itself.' In his ethical writings, similarly, Shaftesbury is seeking a norm for those who reject authority, and he holds that a man of good breeding can find sufficient guidance in the 'moral sense' that has gradually matured in him, as the nucleus of social feeling with which he was born has acquired a definite character, under the influence of those around him and of his own self-criticism. He is well aware that moral sense, like good taste, with which it is exactly analogous, is the result of cultivation and owes

almost everything to the accumulated culture or civilisation of his society. No one can get very far without learning to 'know himself' (the Socratic formula), which he does through discussion with friends and through 'Soliloquy', an inward discussion with his better self.[20] Great stress is laid on this exercise in *Advice to an Author*. Ready-made metaphysical systems, on the other hand, seem to him quite useless. 'The most ingenious way of becoming foolish, is by a System.'[21]

3. The good, the true and the beautiful have an irresistible appeal for a sensitive, well-bred man. They are sought for their own sake, and are in the last resort identical. The refinement of inborn tendencies, under guidance and by self-criticism, is the process governing advance in all three realms. 'If the Love of doing Good, be not, of itself, a good and right Inclination; I know not how there can possibly be such a thing as Goodness or Virtue.'[22] 'The Taste of Beauty, and the Relish of what is decent, just and amiable, perfects the Character of the Gentleman and the Philosopher. And the study of such Taste and Relish will, as we suppose, be ever the great Employment and Concern of him, who covets as well to be wise and good, as agreeable and polite.'[23] Platonic and neo-Platonic notions of harmony, and of the fundamental identity of the supreme values as reflections of an eternal world of ideas, are reconciled here, it seems, with habits of thought that one expects to find in an Augustan gentleman. There is, for instance, the aristocratic insistence on being oneself, on doing nothing under compulsion and following one's native inclination, the 'Eigenwüchsigkeit' that Goethe was later to admire so much in Byron, and in English visitors to Weimar. They were completely themselves, complete fools sometimes, but that was better, he thought, than the conformity that comes from having had the beadle after you from your earliest years if you made a noise in the street, like the children outside his door.[24] A gentleman admires things that are done easily and gracefully, as from long habit, like a stylish stroke at cricket, not following some theory or principle, or acting from fear. Only 'the mere Vulgar of Mankind stand in need of such a rectifying Object as

the Gallows'.[25] 'A man of thorough Good-Breeding, whatever else he be, is incapable of doing a rude or brutal Action. . . . He acts from his Nature. . . . 'Tis the same with the Honest Man.'[26] Out of self-respect, a gentleman dislikes 'being nasty' even when there is no one to see him, and he cannot see himself.[27]

In all this we have the point of view of one of the privileged, who takes his privileges, but also his obligations, completely for granted, at a moment in history that, as is pointed out by Basil Willey, was peculiarly favourable. Paul Valéry has emphasised the same point in discussing Montesquieu and the origins of liberalism: 'L'ordre bien assis, — c'est à dire la réalité assez déguisée et la bête assez affaiblie, — la liberté de l'esprit devient possible. L'oubli des conditions et des prémisses de l'ordre social est accompli; et cet effacement est presque toujours le plus rapide dans ceux mêmes que cet ordre a le plus servis ou favorisés.'[28] But we should note that there is nothing mysterious or mystical in Shaftesbury's conception of the 'virtuoso', the 'real fine Gentlemen, the Lovers of Art and Ingenuity; such as have seen the World, and informed themselves of the Manners and Customs of the several Nations of Europe, searched into their Antiquities, and Records' and into their whole culture.[29] Shaftesbury has a clear understanding of how culture develops, both in the individual and in a nation. 'What difficulty to be in any degree knowing! How long e'er a true Taste is gained! How many things shocking, how many offensive at first, which afterwards are known and acknowledged the highest Beauties! For 'tis now instantly we acquire the Sense by which these Beauties are discoverable. Labour and Pains are required, and Time to cultivate a natural genius, ever so apt or forward.'[30] The taste of the tiro on his first foreign tour has to be corrected, and it has always been the same, even in Greece, where the arts and sciences were first formed, in 'that sole polite, most civilised and accomplished nation', where or through which alone real perfection has ever been attained.[31] Here too taste was only gradually perfected—Shaftesbury sketches its history—and each budding 'kalos kai agathos' had to start at the beginning, like any modern gentleman and wit.[32] *The*

Moralists ends with a recapitulation which is an exhortation to the pursuit of perfection by the individual:

And thus, O Philocles! may we improve and become Artists in the kind; learning to know Ourselves, and what That is, which by improving, we may be sure to advance our Worth, and real Self-Interest. ('Tis the height of Wisdom to be rightly selfish', as we read elsewhere —I, p. 121.) ... He only is the Wise and Able Man, who ... applies himself to cultivate another Soil, builds in a different Matter from that of Stone or Marble; and having righter Models in his Eye, becomes in truth The Architect of his own Life and Fortune: by laying within himself the lasting and sure Foundations of Order, Peace and Concord.[33]

This is not the place to trace in detail the ideas of Shaftesbury that proved fruitful for his many German admirers, or even for Wieland. H. Grudzinski has examined Wieland very thoroughly and described Shaftesbury's general influence in Germany down to 1760.[34] In later chapters we shall be constantly reminded of Shaftesbury whenever we discuss 'Bildung', and in particular with regard to the idea of the 'beautiful soul', the early history of civilisation and aesthetic education. Shaftesbury is an enduring presence for German writers in the age of Goethe. In their repeated attempts to find a substitute for the Protestant metaphysical and ethical system, Shaftesbury's 'aesthetic optimism, his aesthetic theodicy', as Grudzinski calls it, was an indispensable link with Plato and Plotinus. Even when Kant's rigorism seemed to be carrying everything before it, the leading poets were unshaken in their 'aesthetic optimism', and Schiller, in so many respects a disciple of Kant, made a sustained effort to get back to something very like Shaftesbury's views.

Goethe himself gives an important place to Shaftesbury in his address to the Weimar Freemasons in 1813 in honour of Wieland, who had just died, and the way in which he speaks of him is clear evidence of the English writer's high standing in Germany.[35] It is only necessary to mention this name, Goethe says, to recall to every cultivated man an excellent thinker. But he has evidently not re-read him recently, for though he contrasts the English nobleman's background with Wieland's in well-chosen phrases, his brief indication of Shaftesbury's way of thinking is quite misleading. He remembers only the 'Frohsinn' and 'Heiterkeit' with which he faced the serious problems of his time. There is far more in Shaftesbury, as we have seen, than the dubious idea that 'Anyone who can look into his own heart with unperturbed good humour must be a good man. Everything depends on that, and all other good things follow.' To call Wieland a 'twin brother in spirit' to a man so little understood is therefore not so revealing as has usually been thought. Although Wieland was not really so 'exactly similar' to Shaftesbury, it is true that by temperament and education he was predisposed to welcome the gospel of sweet reasonableness that he read in him. He was tolerant, good-humoured, somewhat sceptical but with a good conceit of himself, he knew his Plato and Xenophon, and above all, he revelled in Horace. The seeds of religious doubt had long lain in his mind and he had discovered that he had no talent for asceticism. Through Shaftesbury's ideal of the virtuoso, which combined 'Platonic enthusiasm for beauty with Horatian urbanity' (Grudzinski), and was persuasively présented to him by an esteemed fellow-author of the highest social prestige, he found, with a sense of relief, a way of adjusting his philosophy to the kind of life he really desired.

Exactly when and how Wieland became acquainted with Shaftesbury's writing is a matter of dispute and is not important for our purpose. He mentions the name frequently from 1775, but may possibly have known some of the works a year or two earlier. In the *Plan for a New Kind of Private Tutoring* that he drew up in February 1754, when he was himself a tutor in Zürich, there is much that seems to have come directly or in-directly from Shaftesbury, particularly the idea of an aesthetic basis for education. He quotes Plato to show 'that correct taste in manners and the arts, and true beauty of soul' are both to be attained through a knowledge of the nature of beauty, and that young people can be taught to distinguish good from evil correctly by the help of taste alone.[36] His dependence is quite explicit however in the *Plan for an Academy for the Training of the Mind and Heart of Young People*, published in 1758 but completed two years earlier. The Greeks, he says here, believed in exercising the powers of both mind and body. 'They thought that man comes into the world as a sort of embryo, that has still to be developed (*ausgebildet*) into a man.'[37] He describes their ideals and methods, how they appealed to the imagination of the young, brought them into the company of wise elders, taught them a philosophy of right action and the art of expressing themselves. 'They expected a noble and well-bred young man to be kalos kai agathos, a Virtuoso, as the most brilliant and subtle of modern writers, Shaftesbury, puts it.' A paraphrase of the passage quoted above (p. 33) is added, together with some names of Greek and Roman model 'virtuosi', Xenophon, Plato, Pericles, etc. There was an 'air de grandeur' about such men, as we see from their statues, but it was combined with a noble simplicity and an easy elegance. What a contrast to the usual results of German education! 'Education cultivates (*bildet*) man', but our normal methods produce nothing but pedants.

Nearly thirty pages of detailed provisions follow, for a small, well-staffed boarding school for gentlemen's sons, each of whom is to bring his silver spoon with him and to leave it behind as part of the college plate when he goes. Several features suggest that Wieland had read a description of English schools or colleges. At any rate, his aim is not to produce scholars, but to train the pupils for the life ahead of them, above all to develop in them 'moral sense' and taste and the requisite skills, rather than abstract knowledge. Everything will depend, he sees, on the quality of the masters, and they must be constantly in touch with their pupils, sleeping in the same room with them and sharing their meals. Wieland's ideas had no practical effect in Basel, where the town-clerk Iselin, the historian, had invited them, but they were discussed by Lessing in the *Literaturbriefe* (nos. 9–14) and, more sympathetically, by Herder, in the chapter 'On Greek literature in Germany' in the *Fragmente*. Both took up the point of the identification of the Virtuoso with the 'kalos kai agathos' and between them they at least contributed towards making

Shaftesbury's notion very widely known and determining the connotation of the word 'Bildung', which Mendelssohn, as late as 1784 (in his essay, *Über die Frage: was heißt aufklären?*) classed along with 'Kultur' and 'Aufklärung' as a literary, not a popular word. It was acquiring the ethical colouring, that was super-imposed on the word culture in Shaftesbury's own country only in Arnold's time, as we have mentioned, under his influence and indirectly that of Germany. At the same time and for the same reasons it was coming to be opposed to vocational as well as to formal education (Erziehung), being felt to be rather what a man learns for himself, through his experience of the world, his private reading and hobbies, than what he is expressly taught. The locus classicus is in Goethe's *Tasso*, where the Duke is made to say:

> Ein edler Mensch kann einem engen Kreise
> Nicht seine Bildung danken. Vaterland
> Und Welt muß auf ihn wirken,*

and the Princess to respond with:

> Es bildet ein Talent sich in der Stille,
> Sich ein Charakter in dem Strom der Welt†.

The Duke stresses the widening of Tasso's horizon (*An*bildung) and the Princess the unfolding of his native gift (*Aus*bildung). One or the other of these two aspects was often given a pre-ference in later writers,[38] but they are not yet distinguished by Shaftesbury or Wieland, who have both alike in mind.

This notion of 'Bildung', of man making himself, comes up often in Wieland, in central works like *Agathon*, in some respects the first 'Bildungsroman', and *Musarion*, as we have seen, and also in essays and stories long since forgotten, like the tale of *Koxkox und Kikequetzel*, in the anti-Rousseauistic miscellany *Beiträge zur geheimen Geschichte der Menschheit*, 1770. This is a variant on the theme of *Paul et Virginie*, and describes the coming together, in the woods of Mexico, of a boy and a girl miraculously

---

* A man of noble mind cannot owe his cultivation merely to a narrow circle. He must come under the influence of his nation and of the world.

† A talent forms itself in retirement, a character in the stream of the world.

spared from the disastrous effects of a very odd comet, with a watery tail. The treatment is purely rococo, the reader being kept wondering the whole time how far the author will go in his description of the love-making of two children of nature, but Wieland adds a perfunctory conclusion, supposed to illustrate the natural history of morals, and interpolates, after the description of 'pure nature' in the first part of the story, a philosophical passage on nature and culture. 'Man,' we read here, 'as he emerges from Nature's moulding hand, is little more than a potentiality. He has to develop, to shape himself (*sich ausbilden*), to give himself the last touch of the file that will bathe him in glory and grace—in short, man must, in a manner of speaking, be his own second creator.'

There are innumerable further specific references to Shaftesbury in Wieland's work, and he never ceased to revere him as a sage. As late as 1808 he says in a letter that on warm summer evenings at Belvedere he enjoys the companionship of Cicero, Horace, Lucian or Shaftesbury. We have seen already how deeply Shaftesbury influenced his most characteristic writings, the poem *Musarion*, with its praise of good things done for their own sake and from taste, and *Agathon*, though Wieland did not get much further than the conversion of the hero to more sensible principles in the early editions, and only added the positive philosophy, put into the mouth of the wise Archytas, in the edition of 1794. This is almost pure Shaftesbury, about the necessity of harmonising the animal and the spiritual in man, instead of trying to suppress the former. Shaftesbury probably altered Wieland's whole attitude to writing, as Grudzinski suggests, through what he said in his *Advice to an Author* about 'self-study and inward converse', after wide reading, as well as by his praise in various essays of the efficacy of wit and humour against every kind of 'enthusiasm'. Wieland was more ready now to accept an uninteresting post, if it gave him time to think, and he was well prepared to make the best of his contacts with the *beau monde* round Count Stadion, whose factotum Laroche, the husband finally chosen by Sophie, Wieland's cousin, was called by Wieland a perfect virtuoso. His role as mediator between the middle class and the aristocracy was a natural development from this experience, and his move to Weimar was another step in the same direction.

3. WIELAND IN WEIMAR

What Wieland had principally in view, no doubt, in accepting the Weimar post, was to provide himself and his rapidly growing family with some degree of security, in pleasant surroundings, with the prospect of devoting himself before long entirely to his writing. He had also not quite given up the hope of using Weimar as a stepping-stone to Vienna. He arrived at the end of September 1772, and immediately began to make plans for starting a new literary monthly, *Der deutsche Merkur*. The first number came out in 1773. Meanwhile Wieland had been teaching Karl August, a rather sulky boy, to judge by his portraits, much more interested in riding and shooting than in his books, a formidable array of subjects. They included psychology, cosmology and philosophical theology, all said to be based on Adam Ferguson, whose Edinburgh lecture summaries, the *Institutes of Moral Philosophy*, had just been translated and commented on by Garve. Wieland instructed Karl August also in natural law, political economy and the principles of what was called 'Polizei', the control exercised by absolute governments over the whole economic and social life of their subjects. For these lectures he probably brought out again his own old notes from Zürich, where he had already given his private pupils an 'Introduction to the knowledge of the present states in Europe' (50 pages as printed from his pupils' notes in the Prussian Academy edition of Wieland's works, volume 4) and 'Foundations of the Christian religion' (150 pages), not to speak of a 'Theory and history of rhetoric and poetry' (120 pages), in which he gives Shakespeare only five marks out of twenty for composition, and James Thomson full marks in everything. The Prince was allowed an hour of something like this occasionally in the afternoons, as a relaxation. He seems to have liked Wieland as a teacher, and certainly as a person. One can imagine that he would be more entertaining than Professor Mayer of Jena, who lectured for four hours a week on German history, followed by public law, or Privy Councillor A. L. Schmidt, a former professor, on civil law and Saxon constitutional law. For a boy of fifteen or sixteen all this was heavy going, and Wieland could at least talk easily and wittily, and illustrate theory with anecdote, in the manner of *Der goldene Spiegel*. Anna Amalia herself, however, was disappointed to find her son as headstrong as ever, and by no means drawn away from Count Görtz by Wieland, as she had hoped. Wieland had written, while the plans for the last stage of the Prince's education were still under discussion, that it was not 'a teacher of philosophy he needed, but a philosopher', clearly meaning himself. Anna Amalia now found that he had promised too much, and described him to Fritsch, after a year, as a 'weak enthusiast, full of vanity and self-love'. He meant well, but he could not stand up to his young charges, and anyone (meaning Count Görtz) could get round him by flattery.[39]

Perhaps Wieland had not really been such a failure as Anna Amalia in her personal disappointment declared. She evidently did not look forward to the day, now not far off, when she would, as Dowager Duchess, retire into the background and see her young son and his favourites undoing her work. 'They are all looking towards the rising sun', she wrote to Fritsch. It was naturally impossible for her to realise the importance of the cultural advance that she had unconsciously set in motion through her employment of Wieland. Yet the first signs of it were already clear when she wrote. Wieland had made a good beginning with his periodical, *Der deutsche Merkur*, which was to flourish for nearly forty years and provide southern Germany, as Goethe put it, with its literary culture. It was a sounding-board for the Weimar writers, diffusing a knowledge of their work and of everything that went on in Weimar, and thereby contributing much towards making the little town into the cultural capital of Germany. As Goethe himself says, Weimar entered German literature with the first volume of the *Merkur*.[40] Wieland had also, with his *Alceste*, produced the first of the many dramatic symbols through which the Weimar poets, responding to the needs of the court, yet drawn towards a timeless Greek ideal, were to give their modest capital the reputation of being a second Athens.

With his new periodical, modelled on the well-known *Mercure de France*, Wieland hoped to earn an honest penny and at the same time to do something he considered necessary at this stage for Germany's literary and artistic development. His programme is explained in the preface to the first number, published in January 1773. It is unsigned, and his name did not appear on the title-page until 1790, but everyone knew who the editor was. He draws attention in this preface to his countrymen's uncertainty in matters of taste, contrasting Germany with England, where the reputation of a Milton and a Shakespeare is quite secure, whereas Germany has no established 'classics', as we should say, though Wieland does not use the word. The translator of Shakespeare (for Wieland had been the pioneer in the translation of Shakespeare, producing twenty-two prose versions in Biberach in five years) and the admirer of Shaftesbury are speaking, a writer who hopes now, by example and impartial criticism, to lay sure foundations for the future German literature. In a comment that he prints after some rococo verses by J. G. Jacobi, the first item in his review, he suggests that what Germany now needs is a more serious kind of verse than these trifles, thoughtful, even philosophical poetry, though it should still aim at giving pleasure. Without false modesty he points to his *Musarion* as a model— this was one advantage of remaining anonymous as editor—and half the number is taken up with letters to a friend about the German 'Singspiel' *Alceste*, again his own work, explaining his intentions in departing in his plot from the play of Euripides. He claims that the new version is more touching and more humane. The second number gives less space to self-advertisement, though the letters on *Alceste* are continued. Some points in Herder's *Origins of Language* are discussed, and the current Göttingen *Almanach of the Muses* is reviewed in a rather ironical, patronising

41

tone. It is not surprising that a few months later Wieland's portrait was solemnly burnt by the Göttingen poets, and the pages of his *Idris* used to light their pipes, when they formed themselves into a brotherhood which they called 'The Grove', a Teutonic counterpart to the 'Hill' of Parnassus. The choice of this name was an act of homage to Klopstock, whose ode, *Der Hügel und der Hain* (The Hill and the Grove), had been a plea for a truly German poetry like that of the bards of old, as he imagined them.

Wieland was feeling his way towards a new ideal of poetry for Germany, and was not so sure of himself as Klopstock, but it is clear from the article about Joshua Reynolds's Royal Academy *Discourse* of 1771, which followed in the March number of the *Merkur*, that he had reserves about the classicistic tendencies of Winckelmann and had some sympathy with the realistic aims of the young writers of his day, who were later to be called the 'Sturm und Drang' school. The principle followed by Reynolds that the painter must improve on nature, we are told, leaves no room for an art that can truly be said to be modelled on life. 'Through too much attachment to the calm of the Ancients modern truth is sacrificed.'

The *Merkur* had not so far published any new writing of much merit and its critical line, we see, was not very novel, but it had maintained a quality at least comparable with that of Nicolai's periodicals in Berlin, it made some appeal to the rapidly expanding public of ordinary tradesmen and their wives, as well as to the highly educated, and it had the field almost to itself in southern Germany. Wieland had aimed from the first at combining literary and artistic topics with features of more general interest, and the surprisingly high circulation proved that he had at least aroused a great deal of curiosity. Over 2,500 copies of the *Merkur* were printed and sold in the first year, though, as we shall see, this figure could not be maintained, for all the editor's ingenuity, for he was constantly experimenting with new features. For our present purpose, a particularly interesting venture was a section in the issue of March 1773, headed 'Theatrical news. Weimar.'

The *Mercure de France*, of course, made a wide appeal through its accounts of the Paris theatre, but there was nothing at all comparable to report in Germany at this time, and it was decidedly bold to try to interest a wider public in Seyler's productions in Weimar.

From the beginning, what Wieland emphasises is the cultural importance of the theatre. Drama and the stage, it is claimed, which were a political institution for the Greeks, have now become, in the enlightened parts of Europe, a moral institution, capable of exercising a wholesome influence on the thought and the manners of a whole people. In the hands of a wise government, they are one of the most effective means of cultivating (bilden) the intelligence and the heart of its subjects. In England, men of the highest rank and even clergymen write or edit plays for the stage, and great actors are buried in Westminster Abbey. To appreciate the force of Wieland's remarks, we must remember when he is writing, between the failure of the Hamburg National Theatre in 1769 and the establishment of the Court Theatre at Gotha in 1775.[41] Even in Hamburg the greatest actor-manager of the time, F. L. Schröder, was only being moderately successful in trying to interest the public in German plays of literary merit and had still to contend with the hostility of the clergy to the stage. But Wieland was writing from Weimar, where, he says, it is less necessary than anywhere else to defend the theatre against unjust accusations.

Being convinced that the proper kind of theatre can do much to improve and refine the ideas and sentiments, the taste and manners of a people, our admirable Duchess-Regent was not content to provide her court, through the theatre, with the seemliest of entertainments, her officials with relaxation in the worthiest form, and the more leisured classes with the most innocent amusement. She did not wish the lower classes to be excluded from a form of public entertainment which is at the same time a school of good manners and of virtuous sentiments for them. So Weimar enjoys the privilege, which it has reason to recognise with gratitude and which no other town in Germany can boast, of having a German theatre that anyone may visit three times a week free of charge.

High praise follows of the manager of the troupe which had succeeded Koch's in Weimar in 1772, a remnant of the Hamburg

National Theatre company under Abel Seyler, which remained there until fire destroyed the Wilhelmsburg and its small theatre in 1774, and which, after a year on the road, finally became the nucleus of the Gotha Court Theatre.

After the theatre article, another novelty makes its appearance, 'Political news', an essay which must certainly also have been used for the instruction of his pupils, and which shows again his conciliatory attitude, his hope for reform from above. Under this rubric he will mention only important items of general human interest, 'examples of magnanimity, generosity, philanthropy on the part of the Great of this earth and their advisers, but also of any virtuous citizens of the world'. He hopes that each year will see some improvement, and closes with the appeal: 'You Ruling Princes of the earth, procure for yourselves, procure for the world this most god-like of delights!' Political articles were to come to the fore only after the French Revolution, on which Wieland commented on the whole with good sense. At the moment he has no quarrels with the existing political condition of Germany. Although, in the April number, he has already to complain of literary piracy of his work, the bane of German writers who lived by their pen, and an evil that only a stronger central government could have eliminated, he states with approval in the next number that 'the German nation is not really a nation, but an aggregate of many nations, like ancient Greece'. He criticises current attempts to give German literature a national character which it cannot have in the same degree as that of France or England because of these political facts. There is a special strength and fire in primitive poetry, he admits, but modern German writing has its own flavour too, and he deplores the attempts of some of his contemporaries (like Klopstock) to put themselves back in Ossianic times, just as in the preceding article objections had been raised to the revival of old words like 'Minne'. It is not national differences but international similarities that need to be stressed in the search for a common perfection. Nature has provided for differences enough.

These opinions were not in line with the ideas of the early

Sturm und Drang writers who were now emerging, the Göttingen poets, sworn enemies of his frivolities, the young Goethe and those associated with him in Strassburg and Frankfurt, and his mentor, Herder, whose two essays on 'Shakespeare' and 'Ossian und die Lieder alter Völker' were published in this same year 1773, along with Goethe's 'Von deutscher Baukunst', all anonymously, in the collection *Von deutscher Art und Kunst*, a sort of manifesto of the new movement. In June 1773 Goethe's *Götz von Berlichingen*, the first major work on the new lines, made its appearance. All these were duly reviewed in *Der deutsche Merkur*, and with surprising understanding, *Götz* in September and the essays in December. *Götz* was hailed as 'the most beautiful and interesting of monstrosities, worth a hundred of our sentimental comedies'. Wieland, who thought so little of Shakespeare's powers of composition, could hardly be expected to approve of a 'raree-show' of this kind, yet he greatly admired the imaginative power it revealed and toned down the mild criticisms of his reviewer, C. H. Schmid of Giessen, in a postscript. Next month he returned to the subject, still pointing to Lessing as a better model in some ways, but showing that he could well conceive how others might fall in love with Shakespeare's eccentricities, as with the scars on the face of one dear to them.

Goethe displayed no such tolerance as yet for the older man's weaknesses, though it seems to have been due to Lenz that Goethe's *Götter, Helden und Wieland* appeared in print (in March 1774). This amusing short skit was evoked by Wieland's *Alceste* and his letters about it in the *Merkur*. The libretto of *Alceste*, in about 1,200 lines of verse, is not a great work, but it is extraordinarily characteristic of the Weimar atmosphere. Sengle says of it and of Goethe's *Iphigenie*: 'The spirit of Anna Amalia, of Weimar in general, is at the bottom of the two similar treatments of a Greek theme by dissimilar poets; what dilettantes from the Duchess down to the obscurest of her ladies-in-waiting express in endless verses with much feeling the poets take up and handle with a master's skill.' The only question is whether the amateur verses did not come later than Wieland's, and how much they all owed to the widely diffused sentimental classicism of the time, expressed not only in poetry but in painting, sculpture and even in ornaments for the drawing-room and the garden.

Wieland's essay of 1775, *Versuch über das deutsche Singspiel*, shows that in replacing the popular 'Singspiel', a speciality of the Seyler troupe, with something more to Anna Amalia's taste, he had wider aims in view. The earlier 'Singspiel', going back through French light opera to English ballad opera, was a light-weight affair, meant to please and amuse but not to edify, though it might contain a hint of social criticism. Gluck in Vienna, with his librettist Calzabigi, had already made several attempts to move away from the pomp of grand opera, back to the simplicity of the earliest Italian opera, which had been intended as a revival of Greek drama. But his *Orfeo* (1762), *Alceste* (1767) and *Iphigénie en Aulide* (1774) had still been works in the grand style, destined for Vienna or Paris, with their large orchestra, chorus and corps de ballet. The text was in French. Wieland's essay hints at the difficulty he had in following Gluck's lead, with the modest resources of Weimar and the Seyler troupe, and speaks of other obstacles in the way of the reformer which may surprise us, familiar as we are with the later history of German opera. Dr Burney on his recent travels, he says, had been surprised to find no 'lyrical theatre' in Germany, in spite of the abundance of musical talent there. There are far too few trained singers, Wieland admits, though given enlightened patronage they would soon be forthcoming. A footnote reminds us that behind his proposals is his belief in the humanising influence of the arts in general; music, poetry, the drama and the fine arts are not there simply for our amusement, as the *beau monde* tends to think. Many of the German aristocracy, he says, cling to their German estates and privileges, but in matters of culture disclaim all German ties. German is no language to sing in, they say, but Dr Burney at least does not agree. It is true that Charles V may have thought German only fit for his horse, but modern German poets have clearly shown its musical qualities. There is a deeply rooted prejudice, further, that opera seria must present to us a fairyland, a magnificent spectacle that charms the senses with a combination of all the arts. In all Europe, only a few princes are rich enough to maintain an opera of this ambitious kind. But the 'Singspiel', using poetry, music and action alone, can move and satisfy us at a far lower cost. It should have a serious subject, but not every subject suitable for tragedy will do, because music, he thinks, must give pleasure. It should add beauty to the presentation of characters, passions and situations, and calls for a straightforward plot, free from violent scenes, which might lose truth through musical embellishment. It must be free from distracting episodes and involve only a small number of characters, who express their feelings directly in song rather than in action.

In *Alceste* Wieland uses the classical idiom, it will be seen, in a way that reminds us of Goethe's *Iphigenie* indeed, though his motives were by no means the same. Its smooth and graceful verse, mainly blank verse in the dialogue, is much closer to Goethe's than that of the more famous *Nathan der Weise* (1781), and is so freely varied in length and rhythm that metrists now classify it as 'madrigal verse' and look on it as a possible model for large parts of *Faust*. *Alceste* has still another feature that it shares with *Iphigenie*, the uniformly noble humanity of its characters, but they are so little developed, so flat, that they only come to life in a few lyrical passages. Pretentious monotony is one of the weaknesses of *Alceste* seized on by Goethe, in *Götter, Helden und Wieland*, where Euripides is made to say: 'Your people belong one and all to the great family that you have decked out with 'human dignity', a thing abstracted from God knows where— you poets building on our ruins. They look as like each other as so many peas, and you have stirred them all up into a meaningless porridge. There is a wife who wants to die for her husband, a husband who wants to die for his wife, a hero who wants to die for both of them.' 'Ganz verteufelt human', too humane for words, Goethe might well have called the play, as he did his own *Iphigenie* (to Schiller, 19 January 1802), when he had outgrown the stage at which he had written his 'would-be Greek play' for Charlotte von Stein and those who shared her tastes. What particularly annoyed him in 1773 was the way in which Wieland spoke in his *Letters on Alceste* about the 'uncouth' Hercules in Euripides' play. The only other lyrical drama of this kind that Wieland wrote for Weimar, again composed by Schweizer, the musician employed by the Seyler troupe, brought Hercules in again in a role that must have pleased Goethe even less. It was the frankly moralising *Die Wahl des Hercules*, performed on Karl August's sixteenth birthday in September 1773, where Hercules, whose language often reminds us of Sturm und Drang heroes, with their superabundant virility, is given the choice between the alluring Kakia, who promises him unalloyed pleasure, and the stern Arete, who bids him remember his fatherland and mankind. 'Two souls are at war in his breast', but of course he chooses the path of virtue.

Goethe's criticism naturally stung Wieland, but with remarkable restraint and generosity he carried out his already expressed intention of doing justice to *Götz* in a continuation of his earlier footnote to Schmid's inadequate review, prefacing his remarks with some comments on Goethe's satire, to the effect that young geniuses are like unbroken foals, bursting with spirit. Let them bite and kick for a while, and these wild youths will become great men. When Johanna Fahlmer showed Goethe in Frankfurt the new *Merkur* (of June 1774) with the second *Götz* review, he was ashamed of 'the rubbish that he had written when he was drunk' and quite overwhelmed when he came, further on, to the actual review of his skit by Wieland, which said that if *Götz* had shown that he had the makings of a Shakespeare in him, this 'heroic-comic-farcical pasquinade' proved that if he liked he could be an Aristophanes too.

4. CHANGES AT THE COURT OF WEIMAR

Meanwhile there had been developments in Weimar which were to bring Goethe himself to this sedate little capital, and for a time a whole host of 'geniuses' in his train. Again, as when Wieland was appointed, those responsible had no intention of providing further literary patronage, and it was not Wieland himself who wanted other writers to join him in Weimar, least of all a Goethe. It was in fact to counter Wieland's influence that Fritsch suggested, late in 1773, that Wieland and Görtz should at any rate have nothing to do with the education of the younger prince, Konstantin, who seemed best suited for a military career. Fritsch wanted for him a tutor with military experience as well as humanistic interests, and a young man happened to visit the famous Wieland in the autumn of 1773 who seemed very suitable. This was Karl Ludwig von Knebel, whose father, a Prussian official, had been ennobled by the Emperor for his meritorious services, at the request of Frederick the Great. To please his parents Knebel had entered, without enthusiasm, the Regiment of Guards at Potsdam, after a brief period at the university, and now, at thirty, he had asked to be released, being unable to bear any longer the boring and intellectually unsatisfying life of a guards officer in peacetime. He had done a little writing and had long been in touch with literary circles in Berlin and elsewhere. He was glad to accept the post as tutor to Prince Konstantin that was finally offered to him, some months after he had gone on to his father's home at Ansbach. Some difficult negotiations had been necessary first, because Count Görtz clearly saw what was in the wind, the gradual undermining of his own influence. Fritsch, however, had his way, and Knebel was appointed in October 1774, on the same terms as Wieland previously. At the same time, in accordance with the advice tendered by Fritsch to the Regent after her despairing letter, Karl August's programme of tuition was much reduced, so that he might gain some practical experience of the work of his Privy Council. As the nucleus of a court of his own he was given a companion in the person of the Equerry to the Regent, Josias von Stein, the husband of Goethe's Charlotte, an accomplished horseman, 'a perfect cavalier in every sense of the word, but without claims to intellectual distinction', as Karl von Lyncker puts it.

Karl August's father had married at eighteen, and his son wanted to follow his example. His mother agreed, with the idea of assuring the succession, and began to look round among the eligible princesses. Her choice fell on Luise of Hesse-Darmstadt, who had lost her mother a year before this and was living at Karlsruhe with her sister, Amalie, recently married to the Hereditary Prince of Baden-Durlach. Karl August had met her once, two years earlier, when she had passed through Erfurt on her way to Russia, with her mother and two unmarried sisters. It had been arranged that the Princesses should make this long journey at Russia's expense, so that the Grand Duke Paul, or rather his strong-willed mother, Catherine the Great, might choose one to be his bride. It was Princess Wilhelmine who was chosen. Another sister, Friederike, was already married to the Prussian Crown Prince, Frederick William, so Anna Amalia and her advisers had good political reasons for looking with favour on Luise. It only remained to see whether the two young people could bear each other before uniting them, 'as princesses are married'. Accordingly, Karl August was at last allowed to begin his grand tour, which provided an excuse for visiting Karlsruhe on the way to Paris. The Prince, now just over seventeen, was accompanied by his brother, with Görtz, Stein, Knebel and a medical man in attendance.

Making for Mainz, the party spent a few hours in Frankfurt, and there Knebel, interested as he was in all young writers, paid a surprise visit on 11 December 1774 to the young lawyer Johann Wolfgang Goethe, a literary celebrity in Germany since the preceding year with his *Götz*, and now, at twenty-five, in Europe generally, with *Die Leiden des jungen Werthers*. Goethe and Knebel took to each other at once, and the young princes were delighted with Goethe when Knebel took him round to see them and their party at the inn, the Rotes Haus. Goethe saw the *Patriotische Phantasien* of his friend Möser lying uncut on the table, and was able to talk to them in the liveliest fashion about Möser's high opinion of what could be done for culture in Germany's numerous small states. As they had to hurry on to Mainz, it was arranged that Goethe should follow. He did so, much against the advice of his father, who, as a good republican—

for a Free Town like Frankfurt was a kind of republic—had no trust in princes, and reminded his son how Voltaire had fared at the hands of Frederick the Great. In further conversations with the Weimar party, Goethe had a chance of explaining in how light-hearted a fashion he had written *Götter, Helden und Wieland*, all at one sitting, over a bottle of burgundy, for his father was sure they wanted to lure him to Weimar to punish him for his insolence.[42] Karl August and his companions then went on to Karlsruhe, where everything went as planned, and after a few weeks' interval, spent in Strassburg, Karl August went back and was officially betrothed to Luise.

The journey to Paris was resumed. Twelve weeks were spent there, much as they were usually spent by young aristocrats under close supervision, seeing the sights, visiting artists in their studios, and the salons of the literary ladies, going to the theatre and opera, and above all, playing cards.* They were of course presented at Versailles and were invited out by the nobility and the ambassadors and ministers of foreign powers in Paris. Their principal guide was Friedrich Melchior Grimm, the author of the *Correspondance littéraire*. The whole tour cost nearly 12,000 taler, ten times the annual salary paid to Goethe later as minister. It had naturally given Karl August new standards for his own court, though he felt himself more German on his return than ever. He spent a fortnight in Karlsruhe on the way back, and there, as it happened, he came across Goethe again, who was on his way to Switzerland with three young aristocratic admirers, all in Werther costume, Baron Kurt von Haugwitz and the two Stolberg brothers. The good relations between Goethe and the Weimar princes had nearly been wrecked two months before this by H. L. Wagner's publication, anonymously, of his satire in doggerel verse, *Prometheus, Deukalion und seine Rezensenten*, which everyone took for a work of Goethe's, until he disclaimed it. It deals

* That Karl August also contrived, or was permitted, to sow some wild oats is suggested by the following footnote in W. Bode's *Karl August von Weimar, Jugendjahre* (Berlin, 1913), p. 230: 'As to alleged relations between Karl August and French girls of the poorer classes we only know that for a generation he had 500 francs a year paid to a certain Jeanette Brossard of Epernay.'

with Nicolai's parody and the various criticisms of *Werther*, but it also ridicules Wieland and refers ironically to Goethe's contacts with the princes in Mainz. Now good feeling was completely restored and Goethe was invited to visit Weimar.

On 3 September of this same year Karl August came of age, and his succession to the title was celebrated with due pomp. His first thought was of course to emancipate himself from his tutors and his mother. Wieland had been a free man since the beginning of the Duke's grand tour, and Görtz had been handsomely pensioned soon after their return, but the manœuvring for position when the Duke should come of age had continued in a series of unpleasant intrigues, with Görtz and Fritsch on opposite sides. The Duke pushed forward the preparations for his marriage, which took place on 3 October, and the Duke and Duchess were given a great reception in Weimar on 17 October. Weeks of festivities followed, in the midst of which Goethe was expected any moment, so Wieland wrote. The continued opposition of Goethe's father, who, like most of the middle class, thoroughly distrusted all courtiers, the delay because of a misunderstanding about the carriage that was to be sent for Goethe, its arrival finally when he was at Heidelberg, on his way to Italy, and the words he used to allay the fears of his hostess, an old friend of the family, a passage taken from the new play, *Egmont*, which he was writing, about the necessity of taking risks and trusting one's fate —all this is familiar to every reader of *Dichtung und Wahreit*, which unfortunately ends at this dramatic moment. The drama is perhaps partly 'Dichtung', but if so, it is natural that Goethe should have seen, looking back in old age, a turning-point in his life in the journey that brought him to Weimar for the rest of his life on 7 November 1775.

3(a)   DUKE KARL AUGUST

3(b)   DUCHESS LUISE

3(c)   DUCHESS ANNA AMALIA

3(d)   CHARLOTTE VON STEIN

CHAPTER II

SOCIAL CONDITIONS IN WEIMAR AND GOETHE'S REACTIONS

I. WEIMAR IN 1775

THE analysis of Goethe's motives for going to Weimar is a matter for his biographers. To his admirers in France or England, where in the last two or three centuries Paris or London, the political and therefore the cultural centre of the country, has exercised an almost irresistible pull on most great writers, it is naturally surprising to find a man like Goethe, no recluse by temperament, content to remain so long in what must seem to them the petty conditions of a minor German court, with only one long interruption, the years in Italy. The truth is, of course, that Germany had no real metropolis, a fact deeply deplored by Goethe in later life, though he still, like Möser, saw compensating advantages in Germany's possession of many small centres of culture, and consequent diversity of tastes. In the first instance what he chiefly wanted, perhaps, after the breaking off of his engagement to Lili Schönemann, was to get away from Frankfurt, a 'nest' that he had never intended to make his home for good. In the conditions of that day, to go to court was for him something of an adventure, in his father's view, as we have seen, a risky step. He had only vague ideas of what awaited him and no definite plans for his future, but according to his autobiography, he had for some time been looking out for a lucrative way of employing his uncreative periods. His poetry, he says, came to him without his needing to take much thought about it, but at unpredictable intervals. He had not yet reconciled himself to the idea of accepting payment for these gifts of nature, and in any case, no author could depend for a livelihood on his writings, because piratical publishers immediately pounced on any successful work.

Friends had suggested that he might become the political agent or consul of some foreign power in Frankfurt, but that kind of occupation was too dull for him. He was attracted however by the prospect of a period in quite new surroundings.

The move to Weimar meant for Goethe, as Karl Viëtor has well said,

a complete change of cultural climate. From the middle-class medio-crity and ceaseless but unhurried bustle of a town of capitalists and traders where, as the pampered son of a family of independent means, he has been able to live according to his own pleasure, he found himself transported to a stricter sphere of life in a small aristocratic society gathered round a clever and highly cultivated duchess. Whereas he had hitherto been able to treat the world as an arena for the free indulgence of his genius, he now entered a circle where demands were made upon him, demands which at first he could not meet.[1]

How he responded to his new surroundings is clear from his letters. Out of many that could be quoted, here is one passage in which he is reassuring his mother, after six years in Weimar, about the turn that his life has taken:

The disparity between the narrow and slow-moving middle-class circle I lived in and the many-sided and quick responsiveness of my nature would have driven me crazy. With my lively imagination and antici-pation of human affairs, I should have remained ignorant of the world, a child who had never grown up, unbearable to myself and others, as such unfortunates usually are, through conceit and the defects that go along with it. How much more fortunate it was for me to find myself placed in conditions for which I was not in any way prepared, which gave me ample opportunities of getting to know myself and others through the mistakes I made in my ignorance and over-hastiness, going through trials that hundreds of men may not require, but that I urgently needed for my full development ('Ausbildung').[2]

Much can be learned from the letters, but we miss greatly the continuation of *Dichtung und Wahrheit* which Goethe planned, and for which at least some notes have come down to us.[3] They begin by referring to the

efforts of the Germans to attain to culture of the mind (innere Kultur), especially in opposition to that of the French, [and continue] Literary culture, especially of the middle class, spreading through the nobility to the ruling princes. The Catholics gave some stimulus too. The Electoral State of Mainz, Minister Stadion and his relations with Wieland. Laroche his protégé. Later Emmerich Joseph [von Breidbach-Bürresheim] (Elector of Mainz, 1763–1774). Karl von Dalberg, the star of hope at that time of the Catholic world, Governor of Erfurt. The Natural History Society, the University. Diffusion of these influences—the Count at Bückeburg, attracting first Thomas Abbt and then Herder. Amalia Duchess of Weimar.

This first section is evidently a skeleton description of the steps leading up to Anna Amalia's summoning of Wieland to Weimar, followed by her son's invitation to Goethe, such as we have attempted in the first chapter, and Goethe sees all this as part of a wide movement on the part of the small princes, following the aristocracy, to catch up with the middle class. Karl (Theodor Anton Maria) von Dalberg, descended from a very old noble family, appointed Governor of Erfurt at twenty-seven in 1771, was a man of such outstanding gifts and cultivation that many thought of him already as a future Archbishop and Elector of Mainz.* We must remember the position of Erfurt, only about as far to the west of Weimar as Jena is to the east, some ten miles as the crow flies. Dalberg's presence there spurred on his neighbours to new efforts, Goethe suggests. He had brought Wieland to Erfurt, and it was through him, as we have seen, that Anna Amalia first thought of Wieland for Weimar. Dalberg was a frequent visitor at Weimar down to the 'nineties, intimately acquainted with Goethe, Herder, and almost everyone of note in the arts. But Goethe seems hard put to it to find a forerunner for Anna Amalia among the princes if he can only think of the eccentric Count of Schaumburg-Lippe, whom Herder soon found more of a hindrance than a help when he went to be his Court

* Karl von Dalberg's younger brother Wolfgang Heribert (1750–1806) was the Director of the Mannheim National Theatre who played an important part in Schiller's career. A granddaughter of this brother married into the Acton family of Aldenham Hall, and through her the Cambridge historian, Lord Acton, was the great-grandson of Wolfgang Heribert. (See Karl Freiherr von Beaulieu-Marconnay, *Karl von Dalberg und seine Zeit* (Weimar, 1879), I.)

Preacher in 1771. Goethe meant to go on, it is clear from a second section of notes, to speak of the established tradition of hospitality to distinguished visitors at Weimar, a natural characteristic of small states, evident even in Ernst August's time, and then of the condition of Weimar during the Regency, both among the nobility and the middle class. He ends the section with this phase: 'Cheerful mediocrity (gutmütige Beschränktheit), with aspirations towards knowledge and culture.'

The notes do not include any topographical descriptions, but before we discuss Goethe's remarks on his own activity in these early years, it may be useful to sketch the place and its inhabitants, to provide what follows with a concrete setting. The external appearance of Weimar was that of a duodecimo capital. As the stranger approached it by one of the wretched roads of Thuringia, he saw, standing out above the town's six or seven hundred houses and their enclosing wall, the towers of a couple of churches and of the ducal Schloss. Entering at one of the four gates, he would be asked his name by the gate-clerk for inscription in his book. All wheeled traffic was strictly controlled because of the excise levied on goods passing through, and even pedestrians, unless they were of the nobility, had to pay the porter a small due. 'If you don't want your name taken down at the gate,' Goethe wrote to Frau von Stein one morning in 1782 when they were to go for a country drive together, 'it will be best for you to get in and out of your carriage at the Stern bridge (outside the walls). Order the carriage to pick you up there and I will call for you (on foot). There is no other way, unless you tell the gate-clerk not to enter you, and that would look odd.'[4] From the gates, cobbled streets led past low thatched or shingle-roofed houses with no pretensions to beauty to the Renaissance market-place, with its sixteenth-century townhall and assembly-rooms (the Stadthaus) and a few other high-gabled buildings, such as the two good inns, the Erbprinz and the Elefant, and the house where Lukas Cranach died. Cranach had painted the altarpiece in the town church, and introduced his own portrait and Luther's into it, for Luther had preached there. All the town to the east of the market-place, quite one-third of the area within the walls, was taken up by the complex of buildings round the Schloss. Mme de Staël felt Weimar to be in fact 'not a small town, but a large château'. Within walking distance of the town were three country residences of varying size, Ettersburg to the north, Belvedere to the south, and the modest but charming Tiefurt to the east, and further away a few hunting-lodges, like Goethe's beloved Dornburg. There were promenades for the *beau monde*, the 'Stern' across the Ilm to the east, and the 'Esplanade' just inside the old walls. The extensive park that became one of Weimar's chief attractions was only laid out by Goethe and the Duke in the 'eighties, in imitation of the English Park at Dessau.

Most of these external features Weimar had in common with the usual small capital. The larger ones, Dresden, Munich, Stuttgart and so on, were much more impressive, but the generic resemblance between them all was close, for all were in origin extensions of the palace of some absolute prince, great or small. Late foundations like Karlsruhe, Mannheim or Ludwigsburg had, as can still be seen, a town-plan of geometrical regularity, in which great gardens, a chapel, a picture-gallery, a theatre, a riding-school and so forth were disposed in a pleasing and convenient relationship to the central Schloss. Broad streets afforded charming vistas and led to palaces a few miles out in the country, the counterpart of Versailles and Saint-Germain. In old Free Towns like Frankfurt, Nürnberg or Rothenburg, on the other hand, there was little evidence of planning. They had their functional features, market, churches, townhall, fortresses and walls, but their private houses and twisting streets were the outcome of individual caprice, their public buildings spoke of communal wealth and civic pride. Beyond the vicinity of the palace, Weimar's streets too were narrow and winding, its houses for the most part mean and small, so that some travellers speak of it as more of a village than a town. Yet it bore the unmistakable stamp of a small capital and court, though in 1775 its main palace, the Wilhelmsburg, was a pitiful sight, a fire having gutted it completely in the previous year, leaving only the outer walls and the tower standing. Rebuilding was long delayed for lack of funds and not completed till 1803. Till then, the Duke and the Dowager Duchess were both in temporary quarters, houses designed one for the offices of the Estates, and hastily adapted as the 'Fürstenhaus', the other for Herr von Fritsch, the Prime Minister. The destruction of their small theatre in the palace had forced Seyler and his company to leave Weimar.

Weimar in 1775, then, was not impressive to look at. It lacked the attractions of the greater courts as well as those of old centres of commerce. Its trade and its home industries were alike almost negligible. Karl von Lyncker mentions only three shops, two in the market-place, court-agent Paulsen's for fine dress materials, gold and silver braid, trinkets and similar luxuries and Monsieur Gambu's for perfumery and cosmetics, and a third in the square in front of the town church, a cloth merchant's. There were of course butchers and bakers, grocers and chemists (the court chemist's in the market-place was owned by one of the medical men, Dr Buchholz) and the tradesmen required for making the furniture, clothing, footwear and all the ordinary necessities of life; they would not have shops in the modern sense, where goods are displayed in a large window, but ordinary small houses, where customers were received in the front room, as happened in small villages right down to the present century. The baker's window, and perhaps some others, might be fitted with shutters that could be let down to form a counter such as we see in Ludwig Richter's illustrations. A nail-smith plied his trade under the inner Erfurt gate, making the horses shy as the sparks flew out, the butchers' stalls stood side by side under one of the arcades below the Stadthaus, and the inner Jakobstor was generally called the 'Trödeltor', because second-hand clothing was hung up for sale under its long archway. The inner Frauentor was also made use of, the tower surmounting it serving as a prison. These inner gates were no longer needed because a new wall had been built to take in a larger area, with gates of its own.[5] As in most small towns then, there were a number of people in Weimar who cultivated land outside the walls and even kept a few cows, which were collected and driven out to pasture in the morning by the town herdsman, and back again at night. The streets would therefore in places have a farmyard look—and smell, as drainage was still of the most primitive nature. By 1786, a guide-book tells us,[6] the town could be lit by five hundred lanterns, but they were expensive to maintain and the order to light them all was seldom given. Carriages were preceded at night, therefore, by a footman carrying a torch. Every hour throughout the night a half-blind watchman, whose voice could be heard all over the town even when he was seventy years old, says Herr von Lyncker, bawled out the time.

The town of Weimar, with its five or six thousand inhabitants ('6163 and 102 paupers' in 1786, according to Leonhardi), was a market for the surrounding country, and the seat of government for the combined duchies of Weimar and Eisenach, which at the first census in 1785 had 106,398 inhabitants on some seven hundred square miles of territory.[7] Apart from this it was a place of residence and centre of consumption for the ducal family, the members of the court and a number of gentry who, for one reason or another, had taken a fancy to this quiet corner of Thuringia, some miles from the main road running east and west, from Frankfurt-am-Main to Leipzig, which passed to the north, through Buttelstedt, so that letters had to be brought to Weimar by the postman there. Herr von Lyncker's memoirs have rescued from oblivion many features of everyday life before the French Revolution, when everyone knew and accepted his place in society, and from week to week and from year to year little ever occurred to break the long-established routine of the different social classes. A few details will be quoted to suggest the atmosphere in Weimar, before we turn to the statistical analysis of conditions there.

Karl von Lyncker, born near Weimar in 1767, was the son of parents who were, as Bode says, 'of the nobility, bore high titles and seemed well-to-do, but were always in need of the bounty of their prince. They were therefore no exception among the

Weimar nobility.' Their son also gratefully mentions considerable gifts which he himself received, 'with deep emotion', from the Duke. After being taught at home by a tutor, as all young aristocrats in Weimar were, because the Gymnasium served also as a primary school for the ordinary burghers' sons, he became, between the age of thirteen and seventeen, one of the six pages at court, receiving his board, free education from the special pages' tutors and 'card money' from visitors at court. In effect, the court was for him a kind of free finishing school, as it had been for many of his like since the Middle Ages. At seventeen he went to the University of Jena for three years and at twenty entered the Prussian army, leaving it after five years to become a sort of factotum at another Thuringian court, at Rudolstadt, and finally to return to Karl August's service as 'Landrat' at Jena. His notes were written in his old age for the then Grand Duke of Weimar, not for publication. They are of course mostly concerned with personalities and events at court. He is practically our sole informant about many of the amateur performances of plays in the early years of Karl August's reign, having often taken a part in them himself. But interesting sidelights are thrown on the relations between the different classes and on the life of the middle class.

We hear for instance that in his boyhood the highest officials were seldom seen in public. In the streets they were always followed by a man-servant and greeted deferentially by those standing by. They wore well-powdered bag-wigs with many side curls. The clergy too lived a retired life, and if they went out appeared fully robed and in powdered wigs. Like the lawyers and doctors, they walked with dignity, very slowly. Boys were taught by their tutors not to run 'like tailors'. The four doctors visited the families who had entrusted themselves to them (mainly of the better classes, no doubt) once a week, inspecting the whole household. Every quarter all patients were systematically purged. All gives the same impression of a static and relatively contented society, seeing few strangers and hearing little of the outside world. In such conditions it was normal for a man to remain in the class, or rather the estate, into which he was born. There had been much legislation in the past aiming at the 'freezing' of traditional ways of life for the various grades or estates of society, the nobility, the burgher, the peasant or workman, notably so-called sumptuary laws. A new one was decreed in Weimar by Karl August in September 1778, designed to check the use of garments made of cotton from the new mill at Eisenach. These cheap materials, it was feared, would make it hard to tell mistress from maid, so cotton dresses were to be stamped by the police before use. It is hard to imagine that the law can have been strictly enforced. In the same way the common people were restricted in what they spent on weddings or funerals, in the credit they could accept from shopkeepers, with a limit of 10 talers, in their 'Dorflaufen' or village pub-crawling on Sundays. The men fore-gathered happily however in the many small beerhouses, and the women and old people liked to sit on summer evenings before their cottage doors like old Kaspar. There were occasional dances, and until the shooting-range, with its big garden, was made into part of the new park, early in Karl August's reign, there were the usual contests of marksmen, with their traditional ritual, that are found all over Germany. They called it here 'das Vogelschiessen' (presumably clay pigeons were used) and made it a festival for all, attended even by the Duchess and the young princes during the Regency, and by Karl August when the range was rebuilt, after thirty years. Throughout the year the working man managed to get his little bit of excitement by imitating his betters in one form or another of gambling.[8]

Some figures will be given later which prove that even fifty years after the time of which we are speaking, over one-third of the adult population of Weimar were in domestic service or were casual labourers, nearly two-fifths were shopkeepers or craftsmen, the larger half of these self-employed masters, and over a quarter were government or town officials or professional men. The so-called officials, however, though the better-paid made up much the larger part of the higher-income groups, were to be found in all groups, from the highest to the lowest, and five-sixths of them were in the bottom third of the income scale, in which were all the craftsmen, whether masters or apprentices, and over three-quarters of the shopkeepers. This means that the handful of court nobility, the more successful professional men and the higher officials stood out from the general mass of the population far more noticeably than in recent times, with little or no real middle class in between. There is no reason to think that conditions had changed in this respect to any great extent since 1775; the middle layer will have been, if anything, rather thinner then. For the 'Bürger' generally, the ducal family and their immediate entourage were superior beings whom they admired from a distance, when they appeared on the Esplanade on Sundays and holidays, or drove through the streets, preceded by a running footman. They were most picturesque in winter, when ladies wrapped in furs rode behind gaily betasselled horses in sleighs shaped like shells, or swans, or mermaids, each driven by a cavalier standing behind, as in Goeckingk's charming poem, 'Als der erste Schnee fiel', which ends with this picture:

> Aus allen Fenstern und aus allen Türen
> Sieht mir der bleiche Neid aus hohlen Augen nach;
> Selbst die Matrone wird ein leises Ach
> Und einen Wunsch um mich verlieren.

> Denn der, um den wir Mädchen oft uns stritten,
> Wird hinter mir, so schlank wie eine Tanne, stehn,
> Und sonst auf nichts mit seinen Augen sehn,
> Als auf das Mädchen in dem Schlitten.*

But there was often room for a small audience of the under-privileged in a gallery at a court concert or a play.

As in the rest of Germany, a rigid distinction was normally made between those admissible at court (Hoffähige) and others, the necessary qualification being a title of rank. It was for this

---

* From all windows and all doors pale hollow-eyed envy stares at me as I pass; even the matron will breathe a gentle sigh and a wish at the sight.

For the youth who has made us girls so often rivals of each other will stand behind me, slim as a young fir, and have eyes for nothing but the girl in his sledge.

reason that Goethe reluctantly consented to the Duke's proposal
that he should be raised to the nobility in 1782, and the same
happened with Schiller and Herder twenty years later, when
Schiller had been two years in Weimar without being asked to
court, though his wife was of aristocratic family and her sister
was the wife of the chief court official. 'Lolo is quite in her
element', he wrote to Humboldt a little later, 'now that she can
waggle her train about at court'. The Dowager Duchess, certainly, was no stickler for etiquette. At her Wednesday dinner-
parties, Lyncker says, there were only one or two people of rank
present, and 'several so-called *beaux esprits*'. He was often there,
as a fourteen-year-old page, enjoying their lively, rather noisy
conversation, when good wine had loosened their tongues, and
they discussed plays and masquerades in which he had sometimes
had a part. The waiters at table for the reigning Duke and
Duchess were always pages, sometimes with disastrous results,
and the Dowager Duchess had them too for special occasions.
Trained waiters would have done the job better, but it was
beneath the dignity of high personages to have menials in such
intimate attendance on them. All six pages stood behind the
chair of the Duchess, even in the absence of the Duke, when she
sat down to dine every day with a minimum of nine to keep her
company, her regular household of three ladies and three gentlemen-in-waiting, the captain 'du jour' and two permanent guests,
old Privy Councillor Schardt, 'the greatest gourmand of his
time', and Chief Equerry von Stein—the former the father of
Frau von Stein, and the latter her husband. Unlike her mother-
in-law, the young Duchess took etiquette seriously. It is characteristic that the well-known drawing by Kraus of a group of
people round a table, listening to Goethe reading, some busy
with embroidery, others sketching or looking at prints, represents an informal evening with the Dowager Duchess. Those
present with her are two ladies and one gentleman-in-waiting,
two writers, an artist (as well as Kraus himself), and three English
residents in Weimar.

The regular formal occasions in the season were a reception

open to all the nobility on Sunday afternoon, followed by a concert and cards in the evening, the Dowager Duchess's Wednesday concert, and card-parties twice a week for the ladies and gentlemen of the household, visiting guests, and one or two invited for the evening. Then there were masked balls ('Redouten') every week or fortnight, preceded by supper at court for a number of guests. At these and the Sunday receptions there were always card-tables laid out by the pages, and it was not uncommon to play for high stakes. Gambling and extravagant habits reduced many of the young gentlemen of the court to borrowing from the two Jewish bankers, Uhlmann and Elkan, who had been allowed to settle in Weimar by Anna Amalia and soon made their fortunes. The court uniform was almost exactly the same as that of the foresters, so velvet and satin suits embroidered in gold and silver were favoured instead, and it became more and more common in the 'eighties for young noblemen, from the Duke downwards, to race about in light phaetons, and for their elders to drive four-in-hand, whereas before 1775 nearly all had been content with sedan chairs. Cards were the chief attraction for the men at the 'assemblies' given regularly by three or four aristocratic hostesses in the town, while the ladies gossiped, in German larded with French phrases, worked at their 'réseau', or teased out gold braid. The untitled higher officials and literary and professional men started clubs which were closed to the nobility, by way of retaliation, but they often divided the middle class more than they united it, because their committees wanted to make them exclusive also. When Schiller saw Wieland at one of these clubs, in 1787, he was always playing cards, he says. It was one which had just been founded, called the 'Mittwochsgesellschaft' or Wednesday Club, for men and women, where 'we played cards, talked, sometimes danced a little and then had supper together'. Wieland was also a leading light in the Weimar Freemasons' Lodge, the 'Loge Amalia', founded in 1764, with Fritsch as its Grand Master. One of the attractions of freemasonry was of course that, theoretically at least, it recognised no distinctions of rank, unlike most other associations and clubs of the time, though it was so expensive to hold office that those high up in the masonic hierarchy tended to be men of rank. Later the lodge was joined first by Goethe, in 1780, and then by the Duke himself, though they both lost interest fairly soon. Social barriers were broken down too in the main group of amateur actors in Goethe's first few years in Weimar, but there were also separate aristocratic and middle-class groups, as we shall see, the former presenting only French plays.

What we badly need, in addition to contemporary descriptions, in order to form a clear idea of social conditions in the past, are reliable statistics about the size of various groups and their relative importance as measured, for example, by their purchasing power. For Weimar in 1775 such figures are unobtainable, but we have some for later dates from which, in that slow-moving society, much of value may be deduced. For 1786 there are precise population figures for the first time, which have been quoted. In that year the number of births in Weimar was 1,861, 79 illegitimate, and the number of deaths 1,615, so that there was apparently a healthy natural rate of increase, but bad hygiene, it must be remembered, led to the death of a large proportion of the children in infancy. We learn nothing however about the social classes, except that in Weimar itself there were 102 paupers living on alms.[9] Fortunately a document has recently been discovered and analysed which, though relating to the year 1820, allows us to make a fair approximation to many of the figures we are seeking for the preceding half-century, for it contains no indication that rapid changes had been taking place in the social structure, through industrialisation or movements of population.[10]

This document is an 'assessment roll for the town Weimar in 1820', apparently prepared for the committee which, between 1819 and 1821, was going into the question of a reform of the system of taxation, one long overdue, as we shall see, and finally carried through fairly successfully in 1821. Hartung[11] tells us that, for all its defects, the new system put Weimar ahead of all the other German states in the direct taxation of income, at a time when even England had given up the elaborate income-tax system worked out in the war-years. In interpreting the document we must however remember that the new system was still a compromise, in that it retained, in a modified form, the traditional tax on land, formerly much the most important of all the taxes. The landed nobility resident in Weimar, and other landowners, are not therefore included in the roll unless they had also an income from some office or employment there. Moreover the government, and much more the preparatory committee, shrank from harsh methods of obtaining information about a man's income, as searching inquiries into the citizen's private affairs were still greatly resented. They relied in the main on statements made by the tax-payer 'in good faith', and it was generally admitted, for instance, that most landowners' estimates of the value, or even the area, of their land were very much on the safe side. Too much reliance should not therefore be placed on the information given in our document about the estimated income of some of those in the higher income groups. One of the objections made against income-tax had always been that it was hard on civil servants and others with easily ascertainable incomes.

As will be seen from the summary of the assessment roll given in Appendix I, the income of those on whom it is proposed to levy the new tax range from the 3,100 talers received annually by Privy Councillor von Goethe—his income had only recently, in 1816, been raised from 1,800 talers—to a sum of under 100 talers a year earned by messengers, maids, private tutors, petty tradesmen, journeymen, coachmen and so forth. There are only ten other persons along with Goethe who earn more than 2,000 talers a year, but there are 1,475 with under 100 talers. Eventually three categories of income were distinguished, high, middle and low, and the rates of tax were made uniform for members of the same category, not graduated according to the amount of the individual income. If we make a similar tripartite division in order to convey a general impression of the social structure revealed by the table, we may assign to the lowest class those in receipt of less than 200 talers, who numbered 2,171. We may call this the journeyman class, as no journeyman is recorded as receiving more than 200 talers. The middle class might be taken as ranging from 200 to 600 talers. It comprises 430 individuals and may be described as the master-craftsman class, for no self-employed craftsman, except a certain Herr Burgmüller, rise above 600 talers, though a great many, 324 out of a total of 440, fall below 200 talers. There remains the upper class, with incomes over 600 talers, and this includes all the more successful professional men, officials, bankers, industrialists, innkeepers and shopkeepers. There are only 114 in all. The three classes stand therefore in roughly the following numerical proportions to each other: upper class (excluding landed proprietors), 1; master-craftsman class, 4; journeyman class, 20. As the total population of Weimar in 1820 was 8,673, 5,968 persons are unaccounted for in the list. This number must include most of the wives and nearly all the children of the 2,715 persons who were earning a taxable income, as well as the nobility not holding any office and the military, who were exempt from taxation unless they were above the rank of lieutenant. The proportions are surprising, and would seem to indicate either that many wives were in paid employment, or that there were very few young children.

Many features in the social structure indicated by the tax-assessment roll strike us as typical of the old, pre-industrial order. It will be seen that 590 people in all are accounted for in the first two columns of the table. Together with the 241 pensioners, they bring the total of those dependent on court or government up to 30 per cent of the whole number on the list. The only industry in Weimar of any note is still Bertuch's 'Landesindustriecomptoir', of which more will be heard. Bertuch was a struggling young writer, not long down from the university, when Wieland went to Weimar. He helped Wieland with the *Merkur*, looked after the young Duke's privy purse, and gradually, we shall find, made himself indispensable in Weimar, as a practical man who created a market for the product of other men's brains, and steadily built up a considerable fortune. He made capital out of Weimar culture, and at the same time played a big part in its diffusion. Along with him in the first group we find the two bankers already mentioned, who profited by the extravagance of the courtiers, with the proprietors of the two leading inns, and ten shopkeepers, all in the lower half of the group. Numerically, the civil service and local administration are best represented, with fifty-four people, then come the chief office-holders at court and a dozen of the staff of the opera and theatre, making twenty-four in all. Sixteen professional men, clergymen and grammar-school staff complete the group, headed by the Duke's private doctor, who made twice the income of the headmaster of the grammar school and four or five times that of an assistant master.

In the second group, along with the more successful butchers and bakers and master-craftsmen, there are the middle ranks of the officials, probably without university training, and at court a variety of actors and musicians, the higher kitchen staff and personal servants. Of these three categories the numbers are roughly equal, rather more than a hundred of each, but there are only about a quarter of this number of advocates, teachers, barber-surgeons and assistants to the clergy, and about the same number of middling shopkeepers and innkeepers. There seem to have been large numbers of tailors and shoemakers, all in a small way of business and so mostly in the lowest group, with a host of unskilled and semi-skilled workers of all sorts. The members of the opera chorus might be part-time staff, but we note that the instrumentalists are in the lower half of the middle group, and we are reminded of the evidently low social standing of the professional musician in Schiller's *Kabale und Liebe*, Herr Müller. Advocates too seem to have an unexpectedly low status, at the head of the second group.

One is encouraged in thinking that the social structure revealed by the tax assessment of 1820 was very similar in essentials to that of thirty or forty years earlier by the fact that it tallies so well with the general descriptions by travellers of their impressions of Weimar. Here is a particularly acute analysis by the anonymous author of the *Travels in Thuringia* published in Dresden and Leipzig in 1796, so about half-way through the period between 1775 and 1820 during which, we suggest, the rate of social change was extremely slow, in spite of the Revolution.[12] This writer begins, certainly, with a gross over-estimate of the population of Weimar, which was then about 7,000, but apart from that his picture has a convincing ring about it.

Of the 11,000 inhabitants of the town, much the greater number belong to a type of small-town provincials who show no signs either of the refinement of a court-town or of any particular prosperity. They are all kept going by the luxury requirements of a small court whose prince is not in residence, and whose lesser nobility are partly too poor, partly made up of scholars and writers who think too philosophically to follow the expensive tastes of the court. Weimar has neither factories, nor trade, nor tourist traffic. Herr Bertuch's 'Industriecomptoir' has indeed for some time acquainted the people of Weimar with the word industry, but that is the only industry that exists here.

About the nobility resident in Weimar, we are well informed by Herr von Lyncker for the early years, and by the constant mention of their names in the correspondence of Goethe and the other writers throughout the period. After the accession of Karl August, the Dowager Duchess had as her Oberhofmeister Graf Putbus, and as gentleman-in-waiting the former page, Friedrich von Einsiedel, a versatile and agreeable young man of twenty-five, who played the cello and acted well, wrote skits and operettas, adapted foreign operas and later translated Latin and Italian plays. The lady-in-waiting was Thusnelda von Göchhausen, now twenty-three, whose lively mind enabled her to bear with cheerfulness the burden of her misshapen body. Knebel stayed on for some years as gentleman-in-waiting to his former pupil, Prince Konstantin.

At the court proper, the household officers of the Duke and Duchess included one or two intellectuals, but the majority were of a more conventional type. Count Görtz, the Duke's former tutor, became Oberhofmeister, but resigned his post after about a year and took service in Prussia. The Oberhofmarschall was Herr von Witzleben, old and sick, whose duties were mainly taken over by the Reisemarschall, Herr von Klinkowström. Herr von Stein remained Chief Equerry. The Duke's gentlemen-in-waiting were the young Herr von Wedel, a former page, even-tempered and dependable, Karl August's favourite companion when he went shooting and riding, August von Kalb, son of the Weimar Kammerpräsident or head of the Treasury, and Siegmund von Seckendorff, a gifted young nobleman of thirty-one, composer, translator, and author of sketches and plays. The Duchess had brought two colourless ladies-in-waiting with her, Frl. von Wöllwarth and Frl. von Waldner, and the formidable Countess Gianini was called in from Brunswick to be Oberhofmeisterin. She was intelligent and experienced, but what the page Lyncker remembered about her was 'an enormous nose, protruding, rolling eyes edged with red, black hair round her mouth and a fondness for snuff that gave her a mannish appearance in spite of all her rouge'.

The main departments of the government were presided over by noblemen, Herr von Kalb at the Treasury, Herr von Lyncker at the 'Konsistorium' or Ministry for Church Affairs, Herr von Fritsch as Prime Minister and Herr von Oppel as Treasurer of the Estates. In memoirs and correspondence of the time we hear much of other aristocratic families settled in or near Weimar, in addition to those mentioned, especially of their ladies. There were two elderly Counts von Werthern, brothers, one of whom (Graf von Werthern-Beichlingen) had been Master of Ceremonies at the Prussian court and the other (Graf von Werthern-Neunheilingen) Saxon Minister in Spain. His charming wife was a sister of the later Prussian Minister Freiherr vom Stein. Then there was a Freiherr von Werthern-Frohndorf, who lived for horses and the pleasures of the table, and became Second Equerry to the Duke. He had married in 1774 a young lady of seventeen who became a great favourite in Weimar society. Amalie (or Emilie) von Werthern, pretty, coquettish, intelligent, and childless, was naturally active in the amateur theatre when it started. A great friend of hers was Sophie von Schardt, who married in 1777 an equally boring husband, Frau von Stein's brother Geheimer Regierungsrat von Schardt. Both of them later ran away from their husbands. Knebel was the confidant of the one, and Herder, surprisingly, for she was an empty-headed little creature, of the other. Sophie von Schardt was a cousin of the Danish statesman Count Bernstorff, who became her guardian during her minority, and after the Count's death his widow followed her to Weimar and settled there in 1779. Countess Bernstorff became one of the great ladies of Weimar, and in her train Christoph Bode, the translator, who looked after her affairs, came to Weimar too. Finally we must mention, among the more prominent young ladies of Weimar who are constantly coming into Goethe's letters, the younger sister of Frau von Stein, Luise, married, again to an unattractive older man, Freiherr von Imhoff, as his second wife. He is said to have literally sold his first wife to Warren Hastings. Luise came to Weimar in 1776 to have her first baby, the later poetess Amalie von Imhoff. Three or four other families are mentioned by Lyncker, as well as a number of young men who came as unpaid Hofjunker, and young ladies who were all friends of his family and all soon found husbands. For one motive that brought families with marriageable daughters to Weimar, as to other courts, was that they had good opportunities there of meeting eligible young men. These débutantes are the 'Misels' (Mslles) of whom we hear so much in Goethe's early years in Weimar. Many of these families who made up court society had estates, usually in Thuringia, that provided them with a sufficient income. Others, as we have seen, derived their income, or most of it, from salaried offices in the court or government service, and others again, often birds of passage, came, like Freiherr von Imhoff or Count Brühl later, in the hope of mending their fortunes or at least enjoying the Duke's hospitality for a while.

The atmosphere of an eighteenth-century German court is something so difficult for us in the twentieth century to imagine that it may be helpful at this point to interpolate a few impressions written down only thirty years ago by Mrs Desmond MacCarthy, who, at the age of eighteen, in the year of King Edward's coronation, had spent six months at a German court where it was still possible to recapture the spirit of the age with which we are deal-ing, in a Schloss where 'an old Grand Duke and Duchess, their son and his wife, the hereditary Prince and Princess, and their daughter, the young Princess' lived in the summer, 'surrounded by any number of retainers, Gentlemen-in-waiting, foreign visi-tors from Sweden, Denmark and France, a Chamberlain, a Vice-Chamberlain, a Master of the Horse, a Chief Jaeger and an Under-Jaeger ... chefs and scullions ... an enormous French butler like a Velasquez painting and innumerable lackeys', all this, be it remembered, at the beginning of the present century.

It would be quite easy [Mrs MacCarthy wrote] to give a carping and critical account of the daily life led in the Schloss; of the standing about and bowing and curtseying; of the elaborate and enormous meals; the changing of clothes; all the arranging of expeditions; and tucking up into carriages, and heavy mounting of fat cobs and horses for drives and rides. But the life, as a matter of fact, had many graces. There was a mellow dignity about the quiet, traditional way of doing things that had been done for generations and generations at the country Schloss that had its charm. From the moment I woke the next morning I felt I had gone back a hundred years.

Dinner parties were a great affair at the Schloss—these were often given to the surrounding neighbourhood. The hour of the banquet would be three o'clock although the sun was shining outside; all the shutters would be closed and hundreds of wax candles lit. Grafs and Gräfins, having driven long distances from all directions, would emerge from landaus, the ladies' silks and old gentlemen's coat-tails somewhat crumpled from long hours in the carriage. They were cheery, straight-forward, plain people. They all seemed to have shrill voices, and they shouted; but they had a rather pleasing provincial intonation. In England gentlefolk ceased to speak with the accent of their county after the eighteenth century. But certainly in the late nineteenth century many North German county families were still proud of keeping the accent of their country provinces. One of the Gentlemen-in-waiting by whom I was seated at dinner told me that it was supposed that the country guests dining round us had such cracked high voices from shouting against the whistling winds that blew over their cold northern estates all the winter. We laughed over this; we could not be heard, there was such a noise at the table.

The Court met once more in the evening, having changed out of its smart clothes again—this time only for a short informal meal, it must be said—after which everyone strolled and smoked out of doors for the rest of the evening. There was no 'sitting out'; everyone walked about. That was the invariable custom. The younger members of the household got together, always feeling the relief from formality and always managing to have a good deal of fun. . . .

The stables of the Schloss were filled with a hundred horses, all, to a steed, milk-white as in a fairy story. Behind a pair, and sometimes behind four of these, we would drive out on long drives, visiting the farms about the country. . . .

I confess I did not at all like the exchange to the modern town. The palace in which we now took up our abode was shaped like a small barrack. Flower beds, urns and statues outside—inside, parquet floors, chandeliers, cabinets and central heating. There were two other palaces just like it in the town, lived in by other princes. The members of the Duke's family all met in the evenings at the theatre in a huge box, like a room, opposite the stage. Those of princely rank sat on chairs in a long row in the front of the box, and the Ladies-in-waiting and Adjutants in uniform, with their swords at their side, sat behind. The operas were excellent. The Grand Duke was a great supporter of the arts, and the best opera singers came to perform in the Little Theatre.

The dwellers in all three palaces lived much the same lives; occupied by charitable works, the opera, social life, a little sport, and riding and driving about the surrounding country. . . .

Dinner parties were much more formal and grand here than they had been in the country; also the guests were more sophisticated. The dinner parties took place in the evening now, and, of course, here in full evening dress—officers in full dress uniform. The custom was for the guests in uniform to approach up the room and make their bow and kiss hands, fully accoutred.[13]

In its picture of both the formal and the informal aspects of German court life before the First World War, Mrs MacCarthy's account of her experiences fills some gaps in the descriptions we have found in Herr von Lyncker and others of that other, smaller court before the French Revolution. Above all, through reminding us of the continuity of development between the past and the present, it stimulates our effort to imagine the figures of a distant age not as actors in a pageant, but living people like ourselves.

2. GOETHE'S RECEPTION AND HIS REACTIONS

This then was the court which Goethe came to visit late in 1775, a young poet, novelist and dramatist of twenty-six, much discussed in the literary reviews, especially for his most recent work, *Werther*, the most eloquent apology for passion in German, a book that gripped and disturbed even the older readers who did not like this apotheosis of 'the heart', and swept the young and sensitive, like K. P. Moritz, quite off their feet in their enthusiasm, so that they felt, as he did, that 'they could not talk to a friend as they could converse with this book'. It brought home to them their separateness, as conscious beings capable of feeling, in an unfriendly world. When Anton Reiser, in whom Moritz drew himself, read *Werther*, or Shakespeare, he felt 'superior to the circumstances around him; the increased awareness of his isolated existence, in that he thought of himself as a being, in whom heaven and earth are reflected as in a looking-glass, made him proud of being a man, instead of being ashamed of his insignificance in the eyes of others'. That a creative writer who could speak to millions, who had fragments like the *Urfaust* in his papers, not only went to Weimar for a month or two, as anyone might out of curiosity, but stayed there and got himself so much involved in the domestic affairs of a rural community of 100,000 that for twelve years he published nothing but an occasional lyrical poem—it is not surprising, as we have said, that many foreign biographers of Goethe find something here that baffles them and fills them with regret.

What we have to ask ourselves in our present inquiry is what the coming of Goethe did to Weimar, and what Weimar did to him, in the particular field we are considering, the interaction of personal cultivation (Bildung) and group civilisation or culture (Kultur). In other words: how did the way of life he encountered and shared in Weimar enrich Goethe as man and poet, and how did his inner wealth affect the society in which he lived? In this chapter we are concerned with his attempts to bring a little more order into this small world in which he unexpectedly acquired

4   GOETHE IN 1779

considerable authority. In the next, we shall try to follow his own inner development down to his Italian journey. But all through we are trying to explain to ourselves, through a fresh examination of the facts, how the, broadly speaking, romantic tendencies of German literature in the 'seventies, the tendencies that seemed to Coleridge and others, later, immoral and revolutionary in their extreme subjectivity, were halted and to some extent reversed in German Classicism. 'Their peculiar moral "revolutionary" significance', Professor Pascal says of the Sturm und Drang, 'lies not in an attack on particular social evils, but in the depiction of the unease of man in modern society, of the contradiction between inner values and social forms.'[14] Social forms were at their most rigid in a petty German state, and inner values at their most uncompromising, it might seem, in the young Goethe, the poet of heart-felt experience, yet the contradiction was so far resolved in Weimar that when the French Revolution for freedom, equality, fraternity seemed in danger of spreading to Germany, Goethe and Schiller besought their fellow-countrymen, in the interest of a better future, not to abandon over-hastily their traditional social forms.

In the already mentioned notes for the continuation of *Dichtung und Wahrheit*, Goethe speaks of his nature, as it revealed itself in the new environment, as like that of Voltaire's Huron—the Huron, that is, who in Voltaire's short story, *L'ingénu*, arrived like a bolt from the blue on the shores of Brittany and surprised and delighted a certain prior, his sister and their neighbours with his naïveté and natural charm. 'On m'a toujours appelé l'Ingénu', he tells them, 'parceque je dis toujours naïvement ce que je pense, comme je fais tout ce que je veux.' Voltaire satirises, through the words and actions of his noble savage in a French and Christian environment, the inconsistency and irrationality he finds in contemporary religion and social behaviour. Goethe's comparison is apt, because he too, as he says, surprised and delighted, he too pleased particularly the ladies and the younger men, both in person and through his writings, whereas older people, however transparent they might find his character, felt uneasy and uncomfortable in his presence. The Huron was a handsome fellow in

75

Voltaire's tale, quick and spontaneous, but affectionate and tactful in his own way. Spontaneity and rude 'genius' were not enough in Weimar either, as the reception accorded to Goethe's Sturm und Drang friends was soon to show, but his own meteoric rise to power there would be inexplicable, the next note in our draft seems to say, but for the possibility that existed in this kind of society of becoming a prince's favourite, and the self-confidence with which he seized his chance. It reads simply: 'Favoritism. Self-confidence. Conceit.' Another note hints at the intrigues occasioned by his advance to favour: 'Contributory influence of people who had their own advancement in view. To their advantage to get me promoted. They flatter me and encourage my weaknesses.'

The remaining notes, not yet logically arranged, deal with three themes: first the folly and the inevitable failure of his own efforts to take a share in government, because of faults in his nature that made him unsuited for a man of action, secondly the ideals pursued by enlightened rulers, and thirdly the history of some sides of his work. On the first point he reminds us in self-defence of the small scale of everything in Weimar, which made things visible at a glance, but in old age he regards the hopes he had had of translating ideals into practice, even in this miniature state, as 'a pretty dream, naïve madness'. Not realising, in his ignorance and over-confidence, the difficulty of his task, he had laboured like a Sisyphus, though he can see now that his approach was always too theoretical, too little concerned with everyday technical details. He had no gift for temporary expedients, preferring work that allowed of long-term planning, yet he was over-hasty in his decisions and his answers to inquiries. As to political ideals, Goethe says that it had come to be expected of rulers great and small that they should take heed of the recent spread of humane ideas, put forward originally by Beccaria and other liberal thinkers of cosmopolitan outlook. Princes aimed now therefore at contentment among their subjects, by improving the organisation of justice, economic life and 'police' measures, measures designed, that is, not only to provide for the order and safety, but also for the prosperity and general welfare of the community. It is not so much the greater German states, it would seem, that Goethe has in view, as the patriarchal smaller ones, where welfare legislation was not subordinated, as in Prussia, to the pursuit of power. Karl August's free-and-easy ways seem to the older Goethe, enjoying the advantage of hindsight, to have been in line with 'Sansculottist' tendencies that he discerns even in the Duke's greater contemporaries: 'Frederick the Great isolates himself from his court. A bed of state stands in his bedroom, but he sleeps beside it on a camp bed. Lampoons are treated with contempt and posted up again. Joseph pays no attention to external forms. Instead of sleeping in state beds on his travels, he uses a mattress laid on the floor. Disguised as a courier, riding an old nag, he orders the horses for the Emperor. The maxim is proclaimed that the ruler is only the highest civil servant. The Queen of France renounces etiquette. This self-depreciation goes so far that finally the King of France considers himself an anachronism.' All these things are for Goethe symptoms of a bad conscience in the monarchs of the day produced by the general movement of ideas, just as we find 'conscience-stricken gentry' later in Russia, ashamed of the privileges of their class.

Goethe's efforts to see his own life in the light of eternity are invaluable to us who attempt now to imagine how things really were in Weimar. There is clearly much that is legendary in what has been written about Goethe's life there, much that is inspired by local patriotism and dynastic loyalties or by a vague idealising 'Schwärmerei', seen perhaps at its worst in some reconstructions by painters like Kaulbach, in his 'Goethe Gallery' in Munich. When we study the documentary evidence about Goethe's conquest of Weimar that has been assembled by generations of 'Goethe-Philologists', from Düntzer to Wilhelm Bode, it seems less of a romantic fairy-tale. Our present aim is not to attempt another general description of Goethe's life and writings in Weimar, but to inquire how it was possible for a young poet to gain so quickly, or to have thrust upon him, a position of political authority, and to describe the results, both for Weimar and for his own growth, of his attempt to perform conscientiously the duties of a high official and at the same time to develop to the utmost his innate gifts.

The first few months in Weimar, it is clear, were a time of tensions and uncertainties that no one would suspect from some of the accounts we have of the 'Court of the Muses'. Never was life such a provisional affair, so much a mere apprenticeship for Goethe, as Gundolf rightly says, as in these early years.[15] The desire for 'a firm mind and a stout heart' (*Menschengefühl*) is one of the chief themes of the few lyrical poems he wrote then. In confident moments he assures himself that he has this strength (*Seefahrt*), in weaker mood he longs for peace (*Wandrers Nachtlied* and poems to Charlotte von Stein). Perhaps the most evocative of these poems is one first entitled *Dem Schicksal* (later revised under the title *Einschränkung*):

> Was weiß ich, was mir hier gefällt,
> In dieser engen kleinen Welt
> Mit leisem Zauberband mich hält!
> Mein Karl und ich vergessen hier,
> Wie seltsam uns ein tiefes Schicksal leitet,
> Und ach, ich fühl's, im stillen werden wir
> Zu neuen Szenen vorbereitet.
> Du hast uns lieb, du gabst uns das Gefühl,
> Daß ohne dich wir uns vergebens sinnen,
> Durch Ungeduld und glaubenleer Gewühl
> Voreilig dir niemals was abgewinnen.
> Du hast für uns das rechte Maß getroffen,
> In reine Dumpfheit uns gehüllt,
> Daß wir, von Lebenskraft erfüllt,
> In holder Gegenwart der lieben Zukunft hoffen.*

* *To Fate.* How can I say what it is that pleases me here, in this narrow little world, and binds me as by a gentle magic spell? My Carl and I forget here how strangely we are being led by an inscrutable fate and, I feel, quietly being prepared for new scenes. You love us, you gave us the feeling that without your help we rack our brains in vain, and will never win anything from you prematurely by impatience and frenzied activity without trust. You have decreed the right measure for us and wrapped us in pure passivity, so that, conscious of strength within, we enjoy the present and have dear hopes of the future.

Trust in life, in spite of all the riddles and trials of the present, confidence that he can safely leave his future to the guiding hand of Providence, that is the feeling expressed in this poem, which was enclosed on 3 August 1776 in a letter to Lavater, with whom Goethe so often discussed questions of religion. The Christian trust in God has been given an undogmatic, generalised expression, very similar in essentials to what we find, a few years later, in Iphigenie's great monologue:

> So steigst du denn, Erfüllung, schönste Tochter
> Des größten Vaters, endlich zu mir nieder! (ll. 1094 ff.)*

While the poet might seem to be wasting his time in trivialities, the slow ripening of his wisdom is perceptible as early as this.

For several months, of course, Goethe regarded himself and was regarded by others simply as a visitor, invited by the young Duke because he had taken a personal liking to him and thought he would be excellent company. If Goethe had been a nobleman, like the young Stolbergs, in whose company the Duke had seen him in May at Karlsruhe, he would certainly have been asked to become a gentleman-in-waiting, a 'Kammerherr', as Fritz Stolberg was when the two brothers also came to Weimar, on their way back from Switzerland, three weeks after Goethe. The Duke was not going to be content, like his predecessors, with having mere Kammer*junker* about him like the ordinary minor ruler. He wanted Kammer*herren* like the Electors, a great extravagance, his neighbours thought, and a celebrity like the author of *Werther* would obviously add the distinction to his court which was the boy-duke's first aim. The idea of literary patronage was probably far beyond him at this time. He wished, in the first place, to use his new-found freedom and to enjoy himself, and in the round of revels that followed his return home, Goethe was not uppermost in his mind, or there would have been no hitch in sending a

---

* Do you now come down to me at last, Fulfilment, fairest daughter of the greatest Father?

carriage for him. But when Goethe was once there, and living in the house of the head of the Treasury, Herr von Kalb, whose son had fetched him, he proved so much a man after the Duke's own heart that he could not part with him. What surprises us most is Goethe's adaptability. The difference in age between him and the Duke was after all greater than that between himself and Herder, who had claimed and obtained so much deference in Strassburg, when Goethe was twenty-one. Now Goethe was twenty-six, and the foremost among the Natural Geniuses, as the Sturm und Drang poets were called, yet he was soon as much at home with Karl August as Wedel, a boy of eighteen like the Duke himself, whom he had known for years and who shared his passion for the chase. 'This young enthusiastic Herr Doctor—for that is what he was called at that time—brought about a remarkable revolution in this place, which till then had been rather philistine and was suddenly invaded by a "natural genius",' says the sober Dr Hufeland, about whom more will be heard in chapter 5. 'It was no wonder. One cannot imagine a handsomer young man . . . the rarest combination of intelligence and physical perfection. . . . He was the first in all physical accomplishments, riding, fencing, vaulting, dancing.'[16]

This shows at any rate the reputation Goethe enjoyed, for Hufeland was a boy of thirteen when he arrived, and his imagination perhaps idealised things a little in his old age. Goethe was probably not really a great horseman, though everyone in his position in life could ride of course in those days; he had no taste at all for shooting or cards, and in society he held himself stiffly, the courtiers said, and bowed awkwardly, for he had naturally something to learn in ease of deportment, and that is perhaps why his Wilhelm Meister attaches what may seem to us undue importance to 'vornehmer Anstand', the bearing of a gentleman, in his letter to his boyhood friend Werner (Book V, Chap. 3) about a German middle-class man's difficulty in making himself into a 'personality'. Like Wilhelm before the Prince, Goethe constantly gave himself away by unseemly enthusiasm. All that is what Frau von Stein later corrected in him. To begin with, it constituted part of his Huronic charm, 'a source of surprise and amusement', but tolerable, for a time, in a literary lion.

It is certain, at any rate, that in spite of his different upbringing and infinitely superior gifts, Goethe threw himself for a time into the activities that Karl August considered fun, with that power of chameleonic mimicry that he was so often to display and that led his old friend Fritz Jacobi, as late as 1793, to warn Princess Gallitzin against that 'Proteus', Goethe, who seemed this time, by what he had heard, to have been adapting himself only too well to her Catholic entourage. With Wedel then and the Duke, and sometimes Einsiedel or Kalb, and the Stolbergs during their ten days in Weimar soon after his own arrival, he went riding and shooting, and danced sometimes with village girls at a 'Vogelschießen', sometimes with the 'Misels' in Weimar. He often dined with the Duke and one or two others in the Duke's private apartments, and he accompanied him every few weeks to consultations with Dalberg in Erfurt, who was often also in Weimar.

Christian Stolberg's first impressions of the informality of life at this court, recorded at the time in a letter home, bring back something of the atmosphere. He was asked to supper with Prince Konstantin at Tiefurt, probably before Goethe and the Duke were back from a visit to Erfurt.

All at once [he writes] the door opened, and in came the old Duchess, with the wife of the Chief Equerry, a Frau von Stein, a splendid person, both good and nice to look at; both had old swords in their hands from the Arsenal, a foot or two longer than I am tall, and they dubbed us knights. We stayed in our places at table and the ladies went round pouring out champagne for us. After supper we played Blind Man's Buff, and we kissed the Equerry's wife, who was standing next to the Duchess.—At what other court can you do things like that?

Earlier he had said: 'The whole family of the Duke is quite unlike any princely family. You behave with them all just as if they were people like ourselves.'

All the same, certain basic conventions had to be observed, or the older courtiers would have been even more scandalised than they were. So we find that Goethe had only dined once at the 'fürstliche Tafel', the official high table of the Duke and Duchess, by the end of the year, and that was at the country palace, Belvedere. He had had dinner, however, a dozen times at the 'Marshal's table', to which high officials were invited, for example, after the meetings of the Conseil. His exclusion from the 'fürstliche Tafel' continued for six months longer, until he had been made a 'Geheimer Legationsrat' and a member of the Conseil.[17] Böttiger tells a long story, which he had heard from Kalb, about how the Duchess was led into according Goethe the honour of joining her at cards, after a precedent had been created at Meiningen, where manners were easier. Herr von Stein, who was at her table, was called out, by arrangement, and Goethe asked in to play his hand.[18] This may well be gossip, because Goethe never played cards if he could avoid it, but the story shows how the shy and rather starchy young Duchess, whom Goethe nevertheless describes in letters as 'an angel', had to be humoured before she would accept her husband's unconventional friend. We know from the letters of Countess Gianini, Countess Görtz and others that Goethe was blamed by the writers and the conservative spirits at court for all the silly things that Karl August insisted on doing, like cracking his long whip in the market-place.[19] 'You would not believe how many good fellows and intelligent people there are here', Goethe writes to Johanna Fahlmer and his mother (14 February 1776). 'We keep together, agree wonderfully and play into each other's hands, and hold the court at arm's length.' One of his own party, Einsiedel, gentleman-in-waiting, as we have seen, to the Dowager Duchess, conveys the feelings of their opponents well in some verses he wrote at New Year, 1776, about the Duke and several of his intimates, including Wedel, Goethe and himself:

> Nun denk' man sich 'n Fürstensohn,
> Der so vergißt Geburt und Thron
> Und lebt mit solchen lockern Gesellen,
> Die dem lieben Gott die Zeit abprellen.
> Die tun, als wär'n sie Seinesgleichen

Ihm nicht einmal den Fuchsschwanz streichen,
Die des Bruders Respekt so ganz verkennen,
Tout court ihn 'Bruderherz' zu nennen.
Glauben: es wohne da Menschenverstand,
Wo man all' Etikette verbannt,
Sprechen immer aus vollem Herz',
Treiben mit der heil'gen Staatskunst Scherz.[20]*

The people with literary leanings, like Einsiedel, were soon all imitating Goethe in writing satirical doggerel like this about each other. They read it aloud at special parties the Duke began to hold on Saturday mornings, so that compositions of this kind came to be called 'matinées' and formed a genre peculiar to Weimar and no doubt of some importance in maintaining the cohesion of the group. Goethe had also begun to give readings from his unfinished *Faust* (the *Urfaust*, as we call it now), first when the Stolbergs were there and then later. Anna Amalia and her lady-in-waiting liked it so much that Frl. von Göchhausen borrowed the manuscript and copied it out in full—it is only through this copy, discovered in Dresden in 1887, that we know the *Urfaust* at all. We may be sure that it made a deep impression too on Frau von Stein, who soon became Goethe's most intimate confidante and knew depths of his nature hidden from all others. The Duke took him to call on her a few days after his arrival, but their acquaintance does not seem to have ripened until after New Year, 1776. The first of nearly 1,800 surviving letters and notes addressed to her by Goethe dates from the beginning of January.

It was only in the new year, too, that Goethe began to be active in amateur theatricals. The first play in which he acted was Cumberland's *The West Indian*, possibly put on at his suggestion. He tells us in his autobiography that in Frankfort they had called

---

* Now imagine a young prince who forgets his birth and throne and lives with queer fellows such as I have described, who have nothing to do but to waste time. They behave as if they were his equals and don't even flatter him. They forget respect for his brother so far as to address him simply as 'brother soul'. They think that common sense prevails where all etiquette is banished, always speak from the heart and make fun of the sacred art of politics.

him, as the child of nature that he was, sometimes a 'Voltairian Huron' and sometimes a 'Cumberlandian West Indian', and this may easily have led him to propose the play. But it was in any case very well known by now, having been translated by Bode for Schröder in Hamburg, and performed by Seyler's company in Weimar three years before this. It is an effective sentimental comedy with well-marked character roles but a very artificial plot, a great favourite in Germany for a generation or more. Goethe was the dashing and unconventional young West Indian planter, on his first visit to London. He has succeeded to the estate of the wealthy Belcour and bears his name, though he is really the son of the virtuous London merchant, Stockwell (Knebel). He gives away money and jewels right and left, and in particular helps Charlotte Rusport (Charlotte von Stein) to escape from her dreadful old aunt (Frl. von Göchhausen) and marry Charles Dudley (Prince Constantin). Belcour follows a pretty girl, with whom he has fallen in love at first sight in the street, into the house where Charles Dudley and his sister are lodging, is repulsed by Luise Dudley (Frau von Werthern) and leaves some jewels with the wicked landlady (played by Seckendorff), at her suggestion, in the hope of gaining his lady's favour. This he eventually does, when various complications have been dealt with by a stage Irishman (the Duke) and others, though when Luise is asked whether he has made any professions to her, she can only reply: 'He has, but always in a style so whimsical and capricious, that the best which can be said of them is that they seemed more the result of good spirits than good manners.' It is interesting to see how the personalities of the players are reflected in the roles chosen for them, mainly no doubt by Goethe, who certainly organised the rehearsals. The first performance was on 29 February 1776, and on this evening, at any rate, Goethe supped at the 'fürstliche Tafel'. He was the only untitled person in the cast.[21]

It was not Goethe, however, who started the amateur acting in Weimar. It was not until nearly a year after his arrival that the Duke asked him to take charge of it (from 1 October 1776). It had begun a few weeks before Goethe came, with a performance in French, to welcome the Duke and his bride, of Voltaire's *Nanine*, by a group of ladies and gentlemen of the court, led by Count Putbus. This was not followed up until the new year, when probably much the same people did *Adelaide* in the second week of January, while the other, middle-class group led by Bertuch put on Ayrenhoff's comedy *Der Post zug* on 25 January, followed by Anseaume's operette *Les deux Chasseurs et la Laitière*, in German. In February, before *Der Westindier* on the 29th, there were six performances, *Minna von Barnhelm* by Bertuch's group, *Le Glorieux* (Destouches) by that of Count Putbus, and a comic opera, *Les deux Avares*, apparently also by them, together with three repeat performances. Goethe was only concerned with *The West Indian*, but he took the part of the Devil of Pride in a piece of dumb show at the masquerade on 23 February, which he may have devised. The only new play in March was Voltaire's *Mahomet*, by the Putbus group, and in April they did Legrand's operette *Le Maître en Droit*. It was not until 24 May that one of Goethe's own works was produced, the short operetta *Erwin und Elmire* which he had written and published a year before this. Anna Amalia composed the music for this performance. It proved extremely popular and was repeated four times in this same year. It was also performed in at least six German theatres outside Weimar, usually to music by André. The only other novelty in May was a performance for children of Engel's *Der Edelknabe*. Then there was nothing new until August, when Audinot's *Le Tonnelier*, one of the most popular French operettas, was given in German, by much the same people, probably, who had performed in the very similar *Les deux Chasseurs et la Laitière*. Finally, before Goethe took over, there was a performance by the middle-class group (without Bertuch this time) of another English comedy like *The West Indian*, Colman and Garrick's *The Clandestine Marriage*, translated by Schröder. In their choice of plays, it will be seen, neither group showed any originality, always attempting tried favourites which were dramatically effective.[22]

In all this we have been anticipating, in order to show that Goethe became involved in duties connected with the theatre only by easy stages, his time being very much taken up with other matters in this first year in Weimar. He had been kept continually on the move by the young Duke, and months went by before he definitely made up his mind to stay, on receiving at last from the Duke the offer of an important office. Early in December 1775, consulted by the Duke about filling the vacant post of 'General-superintendent', or head of the clergy in the state, he had suggested Herder and written to him about it on 12 December. He felt then that he must stay at least until this matter was settled, but he was running short of money, and an appeal to his father through Johanna Fahlmer, on 5 January 1776, producing no result, he was obliged to borrow from friends like Merck and Fritz Jacobi. Acknowledging receipt of some money on 22 January, Goethe told Merck that he was now involved in all court and political affairs and would hardly be able to get away. 'My situation is advantageous enough,' he wrote to Merck, himself a man of affairs, 'and the duchies of Weimar and Eisenach at least give a man sufficient scope for him to see how a role in the world would suit him. I am not hurrying matters, and the chief conditions of the new arrangement will be freedom and a sufficiency.' A week later he told Frau von Stein that he was still undecided and rather worried, but on 26 January Wieland wrote to Merck: 'Goethe will not be able to leave this place. Karl August can neither swim nor wade without him now. But nothing is decided yet.' By 14 February Goethe was writing to Johanna Fahlmer:

Herder has accepted the post of 'Generalsuperintendent'. I shall probably stay here too and play my part as well as I can and for as long as seems good to me and to fate. Even if it were only for a few years, it is still better than the ineffectual life at home, where I cannot do anything, however much I want to. Here I have at least a couple of duchies in front of me. Now I am busy getting to know the country— that in itself is great fun. And the Duke is acquiring a taste for work in this way too, and because I know him I am not at all worried about a lot of things [you will have heard of].

On 19 February he prepares his parents for a visit from Herr von Stein, the Chief Equerry, who will be passing through Frankfurt. They are not to seem too delighted about his present position, and he warns them that Stein, like nearly all the court, is not quite happy about the Duke, because he does not dance to their tune, and they consider Goethe responsible.

On 6 March he is still trying to persuade his father to give him money, to furnish the rooms he has now rented and to fit him out with clothes. His mother should try not to be so timid with his father about this, he writes, 'seeing that I am brother and everything of a prince. The Duke has again made me a present of 100 ducats. I am everything I can be for him, and he for me. ... I owe money to all sorts of people, but that doesn't matter.'

By this time the Duke had informed his chief minister, Fritsch, who had felt uncomfortable for many months and had asked in the preceding December that he might be transferred to the vacant post of 'Regierungspräsident', the head of the Court of Appeal, of the changes he proposed to make. He wanted Fritsch to remain in his present position, but to accept as colleagues on the Conseil, the central organ of government, to set the experienced Privy Councillor Schmidt free for the Court of Appeal, a senior official from outside, recommended by Dalberg, and along with him another new member, Goethe. He also proposed that young Herr von Kalb should succeed his father as head of the Treasury. At the interview in the middle of February when these proposals were made, Fritsch had raised serious objections and had begged the Duke to think the matter over carefully. It was quite natural that from all he had seen and heard of Goethe and the frivolities in which he and the Duke seemed to be spending their time, Fritsch should be aghast at the thought of a Council dominated by such a favourite. In March it seemed as if the Duke's health was breaking down under the strain of his wild life. Against Goethe's advice, in reality, he had insisted on riding to Erfurt and back when he was not feeling well, bringing on an attack of rheumatism that kept him in for weeks. All kinds of stories reached the outer world and even Hufeland speaks of a 'mortal illness' brought on by the Duke's cold baths, taken on Goethe's advice. Hearing the rumours, Klopstock wrote a moralising letter to Goethe, in which he said he could not advise his friend Fritz Stolberg to go to such a court as Kammerherr. At the end of the month 'Goethe's shadow', the poet Lenz, turned up unexpectedly, penniless and expecting favours from Goethe's patron. Goethe was away in Leipzig for a few days, with various commissions from the Duke, trying, amongst other things, to persuade the singer Corona Schröter to come to Weimar as Hofsängerin. While he was away, the Duke, through Bertuch, bought for Goethe the now famous Gartenhaus, then a long-neglected cottage in the fields just beyond the Ilm.

On 23 April the Duke repeated his proposals in a letter to Fritsch, dropping only the one about Dalberg's protégé, who had declined his offer. The draft of this letter, in the Duke's hand-writing, uses stronger language about Schmidt than the version sent, speaking of 'distrust'. The tactful emendation, we know from the draft, was suggested by Goethe, being written in at the side in his hand. Fritsch sent a long and dignified reply the very next day, to the effect that to appoint Kalb to the Treasury over so many better men would be rank favouritism, and that he would rather resign than serve on the Conseil with Goethe. He had to wait about a fortnight for the Duke's answer, which took back nothing, but defended Goethe against the implications in Fritsch's letter with the greatest firmness and warmth. It is a really remarkable letter for a young man of eighteen, and shows every sign of being his own work, with its blots and corrections. If Goethe had been a man of ambiguous character, the Duke says, everyone would approve of the minister's decision. 'But Goethe is a man of integrity, with an extraordinarily good and sensitive heart; not only I [think so,] but men of insight congratulate me on having this man. His intelligence and genius are well known. You will see yourself that a man like this would not be able to bear the tedious and mechanical tasks necessary for him to work his way up in a Department.' It would be a waste of talent not to make use of him at the top, where he (the Duke) must have men he can trust, and if the world disapproves of his taking a man without the usual training, that makes no difference. 'The world judges according to its prejudices, but I, like everyone who wants to do his duty, do not work to gain fame, but to be able to justify myself before God and my own conscience.' He is surprised that Fritsch feels he must leave his service at a time when he needs him so badly, instead of finding pleasure in giving so able a young man as Goethe the benefit of his long experience.[23]

It is evident from this letter that the young Duke had the courage to follow his own judgment, whatever others might say, and that he had the highest possible opinion of Goethe. In this respect events proved him to be right, but Fritsch naturally considered him to be merely pig-headed, especially as he went on to express a confidence in Herr von Kalb which soon proved to be misplaced, and to voice opinions about the competence of the officials in Weimar, and about desirable changes in procedure, which Fritsch rightly thought to have little foundation. It is not surprising that the Minister immediately replied that he was still of the same opinion, and asked for time and a short leave of absence to think things over. In this impasse the Duke evidently realised that the resignation of Fritsch would create an awkward problem, because Schnauss, who, if both Schmidt and Fritsch left the Conseil, would be the only one left with experience of its work, had not enough initiative and strength of character to be made Prime Minister. He therefore turned to his mother for help, knowing Fritsch's high admiration for her, and a gracious and tactful letter from Anna Amalia to Fritsch, in which she too spoke of Goethe in the highest terms, ascribing to him not only talent amounting to genius, but the religious views 'of a true and good Christian, which teach him to love his neighbour and to try to make him happy', finally induced the Minister's assent. Fritsch would know, she said, that she always put people to the test before making up her mind about them, and that she was not without experience of men. She urged him to get to know Goethe better, and judge for himself. He had made his protest, and it was the Duke who must bear the responsibility. She closed with an appeal to the conscience and the devotion of her old and trusted adviser.

On 16 May, the day after Fritsch had briefly acknowledged his defeat, the Duke got Kalb to write to Goethe's parents, asking for their consent to the appointment of their son in his ministry, with the title of Geheimer Legationsrat, a salary of 1,200 taler and a seat in the Conseil. It was 11 June before the Conseil passed the proposals, and with his letter of appointment Goethe received half a year's salary. Meanwhile, on 22 May, Goethe had politely but firmly told Klopstock to mind his own business, and it was in the same week, between 17 and 24 May, that he had written the long and delightfully fresh diary-letter to Auguste zu Stolberg about his life in the newly acquired Gartenhaus, which was only just ready for occupation. The letter introduces in turn all the ducal family, Frau von Stein, 'an angel of a woman', Wieland, Kraus and several more of their circle, in snapshots from the apparently idyllic life that he is leading, in the garden, where they all visit him informally, and at Belvedere, Tiefurt and so forth, where he is their guest. The letter ends with a contrasting picture of a village fire at a place a dozen miles or more away from Weimar, to which he had ridden with the Duke, as he did to three others in May and June, using the technique which he had first tried out (according to *Dichtung und Wahrheit*, Book 16) in the ghetto in Frankfurt. A chain of helpers passing the water along, he found, was twice as effective as the same number each running with his pail.

Repeatedly in the letter to Auguste there come remarks like this: 'What will come of it all? I have still a lot to go through, that is what I felt in all difficult moments of my youth, but I am hardened too, and will stick it out to the end.' It is the letter of a man who has come through a crisis, and it produces a misleading impression if one does not know that. It was also meant no doubt to counteract Klopstock's alarming picture of what was in store for Auguste's brother Fritz if he went to Weimar, as the Duke still hoped he would. He did not go, however, but Lenz was still there, a continual embarrassment to Goethe, and just as they had decided to invite him to go to Berka, in the country, for a few weeks, Klinger too arrived, on 24 June, and both of them spent the summer in or near Weimar. In the autumn (21 September) Klinger brought Christof Kaufmann, the extraordinary creature who had taken in Lavater and was recommended by him to all his friends as a kind of primitive apostle. In his shaggy green tweeds, with long beard, hair floating in the wind and chest bare, he was considered by sentimentalists like Karoline Herder a martyr for truth and the good of mankind, until he was revealed as the hypocrite he was. Fortunately he continued on his way to Basedow's model school at Dessau on 9 October—the Herders had arrived on the 1st—and Klinger left at the same time, soon to become an actor. Lenz, after some unknown final foolish escapade, was given his travelling expenses and sent away at the end of November, and Goethe settled down to his new duties, somewhat disenchanted already with Sturm und Drang.

The events of Goethe's first year in Weimar have been recounted at some length, trivial as some of them are, because a more summary treatment would not have revealed the true nature of his reception there. A middle-class poet of his quality, transplanted to a court, could only take root there as he did after a lengthy process of adaptation. Popular biographies too often give the impression that the brilliant young man had only to show his face in Weimar to win all hearts, and that from the beginning he was doing half-a-dozen things at once, sharing the Duke's sports and amusements, running the amateur theatre, undertaking many official duties and passionately making love to Charlotte von Stein.[24] In reality the majority of the courtiers were indignant at the favour shown to him, and it was only after months of discussion and conflict, culminating in the Duke's over-ruling of his principal minister, whose views were shared by all the high officials and most of the court, that Goethe was given an official standing and title. At one stage the most distinguished German author of the day, Klopstock, had felt it his duty to intervene, and even to make his views known to other courts.

Goethe owed his position in Weimar entirely to the fact that a young Duke, just beginning his reign as an absolute monarch, conceived a liking for him, more as a person than as a poet. It was a position that Goethe might easily have abused, and he had evidently pondered over this question when he said in his old age to Kanzler Müller: 'A parvenu like myself could only maintain his position by making it quite clear that he did not wish to feather his own nest. I was urged to do so from many sides, but I have contributed to my expenses here with my literary earnings and with two-thirds of what my father left to me, serving first for 1,200 and later for 1,800 talers.'[25] In the notes for the continuation of his autobiography too he reflects on the fact that parvenus are honest and not self-seeking, partly by nature and partly on principle, a fact which gives them a dignity of their own.

There is much evidence that Goethe was soon uncomfortably aware of the responsibility that rested on him, and that almost from the beginning of his friendship with the Duke he tried tactfully to remind him that in his desire for a full and natural life as a man he ought not to neglect the inescapable duties imposed upon him by his station. The first open and public reminder was the poem with which, dressed as a peasant, Goethe greeted the Duke, probably in January 1776, when they were on a shooting expedition outside Weimar territory, perhaps near Erfurt.[26] 'Turn a gracious eye on me too', the peasant is made to say:

> Gebt auch mir einen gnädgen Blick,
> Das ist schon Untertanen-Glück;
> Denn Haus und Hof und Freud und Leid
> Hab ich schon seit geraumer Zeit.
> Haben Euch sofern auch lieb und gern,
> Wie man eben liebhat seinen Herrn,
> Den man wie unsern Herr-Gott nennt
> Und auch meistens nicht besser kennt ...
> Sind doch immer Euer bestes Gut,
> Und könnt Euch mehr an uns erfreun
> Als am Park und an Stuterein.*

* Turn a gracious eye on me too; that in itself is happiness for your subjects, for I have had for a considerable time my own house and farm and joy and sorrow. You are as dear to us as our own lord, whom we refer to with the same word as

Earlier letters and verses often express too the Sturm und Drang love of the natural as opposed to the conventional. At the end of 1775, for instance, when the Duke and Duchess were spending Christmas at the court of Gotha, Goethe, with Einsiedel, Kalb and Bertuch, had ridden through the woods beyond Jena to Waldeck, to stay with the Duke's head keeper, whose daughter Bertuch was soon to marry, and this is part of Goethe's verse epistle to Gotha:

> Gehab' dich wohl bei den hundert Lichtern,
> Die dich umglänzen,
> Und all den Gesichtern,
> Die dich umschwänzen
> Und umkredenzen.
> Findst doch nur wahre Freud und Ruh
> Bei Seelen grad und treu wie du.*

To this the Duke replied: 'How much I should like to be watching the dear sun rise and set in the hills round Jena, my heart and breast free and you (du) at my side! I see it every day, but the palace is so high and set in such an unattractive plain, it is full of so many attendant spirits, that have veiled their light and airy being in satin and silk, that I get quite dizzy and sick, and feel every evening ready to give myself up to the devil. People here are so comme il faut.'

This rejection of the conventions of court life was represented in a different light, of course, by those who were interested in their maintenance, like Karl August's new gentleman-in-waiting, Siegmund von Seckendorff. Before he came under the influence of Goethe, the Duke had, as we have seen, naïvely thought of adding distinction to his court by multiplying offices and giving them grander titles. Seckendorff had expected to be the senior of half a dozen 'Kammerherren', but when he arrived, he found the Duke

to the Lord our God, and usually do not know any better. . . . We are after all still your best possession, and you can rejoice in us more than in your park and your studs.

* Fare you well under the hundred candles that shine around you, and all the faces that mince around you and attend on you with meat and drink. You will still only find real joy and repose with souls as frank and true as your own.

never had time for such matters and seemed fully won over to what Goethe later himself called the 'Sansculottist' view.

The prevailing dislike of any kind of court has led the Duke and his following to look upon holders of court offices as useless encumbrances, whom it would be better to throw out than to add to. . . . You will understand that my little equipment of court manners and courtly ideas are contraband today. I would do better to exchange them for a hunting whip, high boots, a great sabre and a hat with heron's feathers in the Polish style. . . . According to the system of the Duke's advisers there is no such thing as decorum. The conventions now observed had their origin in the whims of some man or men, and the head of the state can abolish them.[27]

For the first few years the two tendencies, the return to nature and humanitarian reform, are both to be found in the Duke's activities and way of life, sometimes alternating, sometimes in combination or in conflict with each other, and Goethe threw his weight more and more on the side of the second. He wrote a masterly analysis of the process in his poem *Ilmenau* in 1783, and explained the background of the poem in detail to Eckermann forty-five years later (23 October 1828), after the Duke's death. He spoke first of the extraordinary range of Karl August's interest in science and natural history, and recalls how it all started. 'He used to sit whole evenings with me deep in conversation about art and nature and other serious topics. We often sat up late into the night and sometimes fell asleep on my sofa side by side.' The distractions of court life made it difficult for him to get to know about anything thoroughly—a young ruler is expected to take notice of everything, but of nothing for long. But he was a man of character, and a good judge of it in others. He inspired instinctive liking and respect in his people, and desired with his whole heart to do good. He liked to see things for himself and form his own opinion. His love of travel and his shooting expeditions into all the corners of his lands opened his eyes to possible improvements in agriculture, forestry, cattle-breeding and industry. Eckermann interjected that his own memory of him was of someone in an old overcoat and military cap, smoking a cigar, driving to a shoot in his almost springless open carriage with two horses. He had always despised appearances, Goethe continued, as well as comfort and any kind of softness, and had a taste for things coarse and plain. He was very young and they certainly did some mad things together.

He was like a good wine that was still in violent fermentation. He did not know how to work off his excess of vigour, and we often came near to breaking our necks. Riding to hounds over hedges and ditches and through streams, tiring himself out uphill and downdale for days on end, and then camping out under the stars, perhaps beside a fire in the woods—that was what he enjoyed. It was nothing to have inherited a dukedom, but it would have been something after his own heart if he could have ridden and fought for one and taken it by storm.

Finally he quoted the lines about the young Duke in the poem, which we shall have to look at again in the next chapter for the light it throws on Goethe himself:

Der Vorwitz lockt ihn in die Weite,
Kein Fels ist ihm zu schroff, kein Steg zu schmal;
Der Unfall lauert an der Seite
Und stürzt ihn in den Arm der Qual.
Dann treibt die schmerzlich überspannte Regung
Gewaltsam ihn bald da bald dort hinaus,
Und von unmutiger Bewegung
Ruht er unmutig wieder aus.
Und düster wild an heitern Tagen,
Unbändig ohne froh zu sein,
Schläft er, an Seel' und Leib verwundet und zerschlagen,
Auf einem harten Lager ein.*

The picture is humanly credible, and it tallies with the facts we know. This young ruler would of course seem to most

* Recklessness entices him into strange places, no cliff is too steep for him, no path too narrow; mischance lurks beside his ways and thrusts him into the arms of agony. Then excitement painfully intense drives him helplessly this way and that, and from unsatisfying exertions he seeks unsatisfying rest. And gloomy and boisterous on his good days, intractable and yet not happy, bruised and sore in mind and body, he falls asleep on a hard couch.

95

onlookers to be wasting his time, but he had a fund of common sense and human kindness that made his rural rides fruitful in practical suggestions for improvement, encouraged as these were by the friend beside him, whose own urge to enter imaginatively into all kinds of experience was, quite simply, Faustian, and whose supple intelligence saw analogies and connections everywhere that led him on to search for principles and laws. The Duke's life was no doubt too restless, his economic and technical knowledge too limited and his good intentions often too fleeting to allow of the translation into practice of many of the good ideas that occurred to him sporadically, but he could listen to complaints on the spot, make suggestions to his civil servants and offer constructive criticisms of their measures. The real importance to Goethe of the experience he gained of the daily life of all classes was to nourish his poetic imagination and to arouse his interest in several branches of science.

3. GOETHE'S OFFICIAL ACTIVITIES

An elaborate bureaucratic system of government had been built up in Weimar, as in all German states, since the sixteenth century, with whole-time officials, partly noblemen, partly university-trained lawyers of middle-class origin in the higher positions. It was from Germany that Russia borrowed the idea of its sixteen grades of 'chin' or official rank, and most of the names attached to them. In little Weimar there was quite a hierarchy. At the top were 'Wirkliche Geheime Räte', with the predicate Excellency —for these the guard presented arms. Then came the 'Geheime Räte' attached to departments, 'Geheime Regierungs- and Justiz-räte', 'Kammerräte', 'Konsistorialräte', then the ordinary 'Regie-rungsräte' and so forth. The lowest of these received the same pay as a captain, in the tax assessment roll already referred to, the highest the same as a colonel. Below all these came 'Assessoren', 'Revisoren', 'Registratoren', 'Kalkulatoren' and 'Kanzlisten' or clerks, the lowest of whom were paid the same as a (probably very junior) lieutenant. Finally, along with messengers and porters were the 'Kopisten', in what we have called the apprentice class.

Routine business and minor decisions were left to various 'Kollegien' on boards, but all major issues came to the Duke's Privy Council or 'Conseil', consisting, after June 1776, of the Duke and three advisers, Fritsch, Schnauss and Goethe. Decrees were put out in the name of the Duke, beginning with the formula: 'Von Gottes Gnaden Karl August, Herzog zu Sachsen, Jülich, Kleve und Berg, auch Engern und Westphalen pp.' There were three boards subordinate to the Conseil, the 'Landesregierung', a court of appeal and senior administrative body; the 'Kammer' or Treasury, with a branch in Eisenach, responsible for the Duke's demesne estates and the collection of the standing 'ordinary' tax and the indirect tax on liquor; and finally the 'Oberkonsistorium' or Consistory Court, responsible for church affairs and education. In theory, all new taxes were granted for a limited period by the 'Landschaft' or Diet, representing the University of Jena (instead of the Prelates, who had gone at the Reformation), the 'Ritterschaft' or landed gentry, and the towns. In practice, it was only a committee of the Diet that was called together, about every six years, and it was content to grumble, always complying in the end with the Duke's wishes and never initiating any action. The office, nominally under the control of the Diet, through which these special taxes were collected, the 'Landschaftskasse', really considered itself as a government department. It looked after the so-called 'extraordinary taxes' and the 'excise', levied on goods entering the towns.

Goethe was introduced by the Duke as a member of the Conseil on 25 June 1776, and took the oath of allegiance. From then onwards he went regularly, wearing the laced coat that was customary, to the meetings of the Conseil, which took place usually once or twice a week, and took his due part in the deliberations, though he was not at first responsible for any particular department. His attendance, we know from the records, was exemplary until February 1785, after which time (so already eighteen months before his Italian Journey) he asked to be excused from the petty detail of these meetings. He evidently behaved tactfully and soon convinced Fritsch of his seriousness and good sense. In surviving letters to Fritsch, even from Switzerland in November 1779, he seems to have adopted the official style so completely that his own individuality is nowhere in evidence and he signs as His Excellency's most obedient servant.[28]

The heaviest part of Goethe's official duties until 1785 was the share he took in the general business of government as a member of the Conseil. For Fritsch and Schnauss it was a whole-time occupation, and though they evidently did much more work than Goethe, it must have been impossible for any one member of so small a body, if he was regularly present at meetings, to avoid reading a mass of papers in order to take part in the discussion that followed the presentation of each item by one of the members, until the council was ready to vote. Questions of policy came up for final decision from the Treasury, the Court of Appeal, the Consistory Court and from various standing committees—for military matters, for questions concerned with 'police', fire-assurance and so forth—as well as the more important personnel questions, petitions from individuals, monetary matters concerning the ducal family and their court, and a host of others. The items were distributed beforehand, more or less haphazard, for preparation and presentation by a member. They were so varied that no one could confine himself to one particular type of question. In difficult cases a decision had often to be deferred, or handed over to a suitable committee, perhaps one specially set up for the purpose, but when it was reached, the decision was a collective one, although the Duke's opinion naturally carried great weight and he had a final veto. A short minute was prepared by the secretary who was present, without voting powers, the 'Geheimer Referendar', and this was elaborated by the Chancery into a 'Reskript' or 'Dekret' or 'Fürstenschreiben' or 'Extractus Protocolli' or 'Ordre', in due form and traditional language, according to the nature of the matter and the authority or person to whom it was addressed. There was a long history behind the 'chancery style' employed. Its involved periods often annoyed the Duke, but when, in 1785, he wanted all documents to be written in plain German, to avoid delay and misunderstanding, Goethe defended traditional practice, with its suggestions of mature deliberation and its air of decorum, well befitting the solemn pronouncements of a prince. A first draft of the final document was circulated among the councillors in their homes, in inverse order of seniority, for approval or correction, before a fair copy was made for the Duke to sign.[29]

The very nature of the procedure, it will be seen, involved every councillor in much home-work; it also makes it very difficult for us now to assess the personal share of any one of them, except in unusual circumstances. Among the two hundred documents assembled by Professor Flach in the first volume of *Goethes amtliche Schriften*, all concerned with Goethe's activity in the Conseil between 1776 and 1786, there is little, merely a few official letters and memoranda, wholly attributable to Goethe himself, though there is something that is demonstrably his in each of the two hundred. These are, however, only a very small part of the twenty-three thousand cases considered in all in that period. In 99 per cent of this total, that is, Goethe's participation cannot now be proved, except that he is known to have been present at over five hundred meetings, or about five-sixths of all that were held down to February 1785. Even among these two hundred items the range of the business dealt with is astonishing wide. There is foreign policy—the question of Prussian recruiting in Weimar in 1779, the encroachments of Saxon troops in 1781, the request of the Netherlands for mercenary troops in 1784, the Duke's attitude to the League of Princes in 1785. There is financial and economic policy—consideration of Treasury budgets, court and stables budgets, new emergency taxation, questions of rent and repairs on ducal estates; of the sale of government corn in Bremen and of oak for shipbuilding, a debate on the banning of coffee imports, the settlement of gild disputes, and above all, measures for restoring Ilmenau's prosperity, Goethe's special concern. There are disputed legal decisions, about the penalty for infanticide or a breach of promise case.

There is university business, appointments to chairs in Jena, the acquisition of the Büttner library, the punishment of a drunken student. Appointments of higher civil servants come up for approval, and an allowance is made to Prince Konstantin. Building projects are considered, for a theatre in Weimar (Hofjäger Hauptmann's reception rooms, with removable stage) or for a bridge at Tannroda, or new butchers' stalls in Weimar. Finally there are momentous trifles like the provision of new leather breeches for the Hussars, or the renewal of the law about the delivery by each village of a specified number of sparrows' heads.

Speaking to Eckermann (on 10 February 1829) about his first ten years in Weimar, Goethe said that his poetic talent was in conflict with the realities of life, with which he was forced to acquaint himself through his relationship to the court and his work in various branches of the civil service. This was in the end to his advantage, although in those years he wrote nothing of importance. Goethe was not a 'chiel with a notebook', but he was, or he came to be, 'in love with the real', and our increased knowledge about his work on the Conseil shows what opportunities it gave him of seeing every aspect of life, in a tiny agrarian state, certainly, but one far removed from primitive simplicity. Social, economic and legal relationships in this community were made plain to him on the Conseil in repeated instances, and this paper knowledge was continually gaining concreteness from his expeditions with the Duke to courts, towns and villages of all kinds in Thuringia. The effect on his writing is already quite clear in the *Briefe aus der Schweiz*, composed from actual letters after his three months' journey to Switzerland with the Duke in 1779. The feeling expressed here from the beginning, anticipating the *Italienische Reise* and the *Kampagne in Frankreich*, is his conscious delight in seeing things as they are, the feeling that nature has far higher powers of invention than his own.

My eye and my mind could grasp these objects, and as I was at peace with myself ('rein'), and this feeling (for the mountains) awakened no false echoes, it achieved its full effect. It is only if such a feeling is compared with the one we have when we laboriously occupy ourselves with small things, use all our skill to lend them significance and touch them up, giving pleasure and food to our mind through its own creations, that we see what a wretched makeshift this is.

And on the next page there is evidence of that equally characteristic pleasure in the recognition of the order of nature that marks all Goethe's mature writing: 'We are filled with the feeling that here we have nothing arbitrary, here is the slow working out in everything of eternal law, and what is of human making is only the convenient path on which we make our way through these wondrous regions.'[30]

The feeling for natural law ripened in Goethe, as is well known, through the new passion for the scientific study of nature, first aroused in him by the demands of council business for which he was made personally responsible. There were a number of small-scale but important activities in the state of Weimar which required continuous governmental supervision, like many which in larger states like Prussia gave rise in time to new government departments. They were looked after in Weimar by standing committees (Kommissionen). Those with which Goethe came to be associated were, first, the Mining Commission, in February 1777, eight months after he had joined the Council, and secondly the Military Commission, closely connected with the Roads Directorate, both of which he took over after two years more, in January 1779. His last and most exacting task was to fill the gap temporarily when the head of the Treasury, Kalb, had to be summarily dismissed in 1781. Goethe was never himself Kammerpräsident, but he took over many of the duties of the office.

Goethe seems to have entered light-heartedly and by slow degrees into the first of these commitments, for Ilmenau, where the mine was, was associated for him from the beginning with the memory of holidays from court, among the wooded hills of the Thuringian Forest. The idea of re-starting the copper and silver mines there, once very productive but abandoned in 1739, was not his.[31] It had been brought up by the Duke at the Council before Goethe joined it, and an inspection by a mining expert from

Claustal, Herr von Trebra, had been arranged. Goethe first saw Ilmenau, which was in the smallest of the three portions of Weimar territory, the Henneberg inheritance, up the Ilm, about twenty-five miles south-west of Weimar, when he rode over with a hussar on 3 May 1776, while his fate in Weimar was still in the balance. The Duke had heard that morning of an outbreak of fire there, and Goethe, who had helped to fight several village fires, was sent to see what could be done, but the fire was out by the time he arrived. The Duke himself was not yet fit, after his illness in the spring, for a six-hour ride. Goethe had heard about the mining project and naturally visited the old mines when he was looking round the little town next morning. It had been in a bad way since an earlier disastrous fire in 1752, traces of which were still to be seen. Its poverty was evident, and there had been a highway robbery near it in the previous week. Goethe spent a week exploring the neighbouring country, which he found delightful, and riding back the long way round through Arnstadt and Erfurt. Later that summer he was one of a party from Weimar which spent a month in and near Ilmenau with the Duke (18 July to 14 August), primarily in order to be shown round the old workings by Trebra, who had reported favourably, and partly also to shoot, ride, walk, dance and enjoy themselves. This the young men of the party did sometimes like students on the spree, at the popular shooting-match arranged in their honour in Ilmenau, and particularly on visits to smaller places like the glass-making village of Stützerbach, near the source of the Ilm and some seven miles from Ilmenau. For once we have a detailed description of some of these goings-on, instead of vague rumours. It was written by Trebra himself in his old age, and he claims to have seen that Goethe only joined in the Duke's frolics in order to humour him, and so to have a chance of steadying him down later on. Trebra was a sensible, kindly official of nearly forty and was at first rather taken aback at the tone in the Duke's circle, where everyone was expected to forget his inhibitions and be boisterously cheerful.[32]

Goethe himself, to judge by a letter he wrote to Frau von Stein from Ilmenau five years later, when his attiude to Sturm und Drang had completely changed, seems to have had rather a bad conscience about the old times, the spirits of which, he says, still haunt him and give him no peace. One of Trebra's anecdotes shows us perhaps the kind of thing he had in mind. One day at Stützerbach, where the director of the ducal glass-works put them up, they had dinner in the house of his brother-in-law, a well-to-do and rather self-important shopkeeper called Glaser, whom they found very funny. They were evidently not his guests, at least he was not present, and after the bottle had circulated freely, some bright spirit suggested ragging him in his storeroom down below. They trooped down and made havoc among his stocks, carrying full and empty casks and cases into the street and rolling some barrels down the hill. Goethe had stayed behind, but with equally irresponsible notions in his head, for he cut out the head of a portrait of Glaser, displayed in all his finery, that hung in the dining-room, and, just before his companions came back for coffee, he sat down, covered his legs with a cloth, rested the gold frame on his knees and poked his head through the hole. Some biographers make great play with the contrast between poor stupid Glaser's new face, with the flashing dark eyes, and the old, but perhaps it was not really such a good joke. Glaser anyhow became a favourite butt, and on two later visits of Goethe with the Duke, we read in his diary 'Glaser mercilessly ragged' ('Glaser geschunden'). One of these entries reads: 'After dinner dancing with the peasant girls. Uproariously merry till one in the morning. Slept well.' Another speaks of 'free and easy girls'.

But all this was only one side of Goethe's life in the Ilmenau neighbourhood. From the beginning we hear in his letters the poet and nature-lover, the author of *Werther*, as well as the boon companion of Karl August. While the Duke went shooting, Goethe often made pencil drawings of the landscape for Frau von Stein, and he wrote to her during this first visit about his walks and his favourite views, praising especially the cave under the Hermannstein. This is where he carved an S in the rock, after she had visited Ilmenau for a day and gone with him to his cave where, holding his hand, she had bent down and playfully made this sign in the dust. In his diary Goethe used the sun symbol for the name Stein, and this initial is perhaps a variant. Two poems[23] refer to these incidents, but there are many other reflections in Goethe's work of experiences on this and other visits. The episode in *Werther*, added in 1782 to the second edition (published 1787), of Lotte and her tantalising canary (12 September) was suggested by what happened when Goethe called on Frau von Stein at her inn.[37] The scene between miner and peasant in *Wilhelm Meisters Lehrjahre* (Book II, Chapter 4) is based on a traditional miners' play he saw in Ilmenau, and the little town with the two inns, where Wilhelm first meets Philine, seems to have many features of Ilmenau too. Lines written to Herder (9 August 1776) remind us immediately of the scene 'Forest and cavern' in *Faust*: 'I lead my life in ravines, caves, woods, in pools beneath waterfalls, among the subterranean spirits, and God's world is my green pasture.' No wonder that with so many currents of feeling and uncertainties about his future to contend with he wrote in Stützerbach on 3 August 1776 the poem *To Fate* quoted above.

But above all, Ilmenau brought him in the end months and years of tedious work and endless worry, for which he could only console himself with the thought that it had been good for his soul and had developed in him a lasting interest in geology and mineralogy. It was six months after his first visit to Ilmenau that the Mining Commission was set up (in February 1777), consisting at first of Goethe, Kalb and a lawyer, J. L. Eckardt, from the Regierung. There were serious legal and financial problems to be tackled before any beginning could be made in Ilmenau itself, and it took years to solve them even provisionally. It is true that promises to take up shares in the new company came in quickly enough from the people present at the Duke's first visit to the mine, and their friends in Weimar, but two other states, Saxony and Gotha, were joint owners of the mine with Weimar, and some shareholders in the old company had earlier advanced large sums that had never been paid back. All these soon proved willing to leave the further exploitation of the mine to Weimar and a new company, but only on conditions which were painfully negotiated, mainly by Eckardt, in the next few years. Goethe too had a share in them. He took thirty folio pages of notes written by himself for his opening statement at a conference with representatives of Saxony and Gotha in 1781, for instance. One set of negotiations dragged on till the end of 1783, the other till 1784. Meanwhile Goethe had made the journey to the Harz in winter about which he wrote his poem with that title (5 to 12 December 1777) to see the flourishing mines in that district, visited Blankenburg, to see an old miner who had worked in Ilmenau, and taken a share in many discussions on the technical problems involved in the reopening. A prospectus was published and a sufficient number of shares subscribed to provide capital for the first stage, and at last, on 24 February 1784, the first turf was dug, or rather the first pick buried, by Goethe, for the new shaft that had to be sunk to get at the previously worked ore-bearing seam, after a confident speech by Goethe, a church-service, music and a procession to the mine. Then a quite small number of miners worked their way with pick and shovel, day by day and month by month, down the deepening shaft towards the seam.

It was while this preparatory work was still going on that Goethe wrote his poem *Ilmenau*, on the Duke's twenty-seventh birthday, 3 September 1784, while hopes were high but before any ore at all had been brought up. The 'new Eden' (l. 10) was a hope, not yet a fact, but his cares, and the poverty of the district, were realities:

> Laßt mich vergessen, daß auch hier die Welt
> So manch Geschöpf in Erdefesseln hält,
> Der Landmann leichtem Sand den Samen anvertraut
> Und seinen Kohl dem frechen Wilde baut,
> Der Knappe karges Brot in Klüften sucht,
> Der Köhler zittert, wenn der Jäger flucht.*

* Let me forget that here too the world holds so many creatures fast in fetters of earth, the peasant entrusts his seed to light sand, and grows his cabbages for insolent game to eat, the miner seeks a meagre livelihood in clefts in the rock and the charcoal-burner trembles at the sportsman's oaths.

What is said in the central portion of the poem about the inner development of Goethe and the Duke is matter for our next chapter, but we may note that in describing the new prosperity of Ilmenau at the close, Goethe does not make extravagant claims about the mine:

> Und Seil und Kübel wird in längrer Ruh
> Nicht am verbrochnen Schachte stocken.*

The stagnation of the last forty-five years has ended, that is all. Unfortunately, the reopening proved a complete fiasco in the end, but buoyed up by what proved to be misleading advice by experts, the Commission would not accept defeat. Legal difficulties, then disagreements on the staff, a serious accident, and above all, technical difficulties of ever-increasing magnitude, which led to further calls on the shareholders and finally a loan backed by the Duke, all had to be faced in turn. The seam had not been reached by the time Goethe went to Italy, but increasingly complicated pumping arrangements had proved necessary to keep the workings dry, with idle months in between, while they were waiting for new machinery. Prospects were still so doubtful three years after Goethe's return from Italy that a meeting of representatives of the chief shareholders had to be called to decide whether to go on. Goethe had the unenviable task of explaining the situation, and he weathered this storm too. Then at last, on the Duke's birthday, 3 September 1792, as it happened, the seam was reached, after eight and a half years of work, when the water had at last all been pumped out. There were great rejoicings; a procession, music, a church-service and a big ball were organised a few days later, and ore was at last brought to the surface. But now came the greatest disappointment of all. Repeated tests failed to reveal any significant quantity of metal in it. Still they went on, hoping to strike a better part of the seam by further operations. Goethe comforted a meeting of shareholders in December 1793 with a reflection that has a familiar ring to many of us, namely, that great as their difficulties were, they were nothing like those being faced by the

* And rope and tub will no longer be kept still in the broken shaft.

armies opposing the French invader. Then at last, in October 1796, the final catastrophe occurred: a gallery in one of the old workings, used to carry away the water pumped away from the face, collapsed and the miners below narrowly escaped drowning. The water rose and rose, and though maintenance work was continued in one shaft till 1812, in the hope that with better times work could be resumed, it was at the expense of the Weimar Treasury, for the shareholders were not to be persuaded to put any more money into an obviously very doubtful enterprise. Practically no ore of any value had been obtained, and all that could be said was that a certain amount of employment had been created in Ilmenau, though all the shareholders had lost their money, and the Weimar Treasury still more. The total amount expended seems to have been about 40,000 or 50,000 talers.

The Mining Commission probably did not take up very much of Goethe's time in the early years, while Eckhardt was struggling with legal problems, but 1777 and 1778 were the most active years of the amateur theatre, as we shall see in the next chapter, Goethe himself busily writing, acting and producing for it, while continuing his work on the Council. In 1779, however, no performance is recorded in the first three months, and then on 6 April came the most notable of all, Goethe's prose *Iphigenie*. It was in these early months of 1779 that he was learning his business on the Roads Directorate and Military Commission. In these too, as in the Mining Commission, though he was the responsible head and had to keep an eye on all correspondence and reports, he did not have to keep office hours, and he had a permanent assistant who did most of the day-to-day work. In the Roads Directorate it was Engineer J. A. J. de Castrop, who in 1768 had been given the title of captain in the so-called Artillery in Weimar. He was a self-made man of forty-eight, born and bred in Germany, in spite of his name, and had come into the service of Weimar permanently in 1766, after previous experience in Kassel and Eisenach. His status is indicated by his low salary then of 100 talers. For years he had engaged and directed the labourers who, under two foremen, did the actual road-making and repairing, mainly the latter so far. Periodically he surveyed sections of road to see where repairs were necessary, and he provided all the material for the report annually written until now by his nominal chief, the President of the Treasury. Under Goethe all this went on as before, though de Castrop, who had been restive because his pay was low and in arrears, was delighted to have a new chief who took an interest in him and what he was doing. He was a thoroughly reliable, practical man with a sense of humour, the kind of man with whom Goethe got on splendidly. Within a year Goethe had secured for him a rise in pay of 150 talers.

De Castrop had evidently kept abreast of modern techniques in road-building, for he himself wrote several pamphlets on the subject and a book *Projet sur la construction des chaussées*, from which we can learn how he went to work. It was on the lines followed in France earlier in the century, on which Pierre Trésaguet, the best road engineer of the day, had by now improved, in his book of 1764. The French had been the pioneers in training engineers and directing road-building systematically, and only three or four German states had built good metalled roads before 1779.[35] De Castrop's method was to lay a foundation of flat, carefully fitted stones, and to cover them with progressively smaller stones to a depth of fifteen inches in the middle and several inches less at the sides, producing a marked camber. To build roads like this was an expensive operation and one peculiarly difficult to carry through in Germany, where it was often only possible to use statutory labour and where the authority responsible might be a different one every few miles on a stretch of road that passed through several states. The long-term policy followed by Goethe was to build good *chaussées* between Weimar and Erfurt, to the west, and from Weimar in the direction of Naumburg, to the east, in order to offer an inducement to traffic moving east and west to pass through Weimar, instead of well north of it through Buttelstedt, the post-route, as we have seen, in 1775 and for many years to follow. So far, with the same aim in view, the Buttelstedt road had been purposely left in bad repair. A good road to Jena seemed an obvious necessity, and this was the first *chaussée* to be completed. It was built between 1782 and 1787, at a cost of over 11,000 talers. The road to Erfurt was greatly improved, but not very much progress was made with the continuation eastwards from Weimar to Auerstädt, on the way to Naumburg, for lack of funds. In general, it was difficult enough to carry through the most urgent repairs. It is clear from Weimar's later experience, in the early nineteenth century, that good roads would not alone have greatly improved the economic condition of the state, without the co-operation of more-powerful neighbours in reducing other hindrances to trade. These neighbours used their age-old rights to exact a payment from carriers for the use of certain roads, a due formerly justified by their policing of the roads, and under another set of treaties they could prevent the use of alternative by-roads. Weimar could not one-sidedly alter the complicated past agreements governing the use of the Frankfurt-Leipzig highway, and it exacted its own dues by virtue of the Duke's possession of the Thuringian 'Geleit' or safe-conduct, a right that his Treasury, like the others, was most unwilling to renounce. The Roads Directorate had therefore a whole mass of legal negotiations on its hands as well as financial and technical problems.[36] Goethe's long final report before going to Italy, in 1786, shows that his hopeless task had left him with a sense of frustration.

Stones are carted to a road, with a view to making it into a *chaussée*, but so many of them have to be used for temporary repairs to keep the road open at all that the *chaussée* is never built. Chronic lack of funds makes it impossible to plan ahead and to accomplish with economy the task undertaken. Compelled as he is to leave so many defects unremedied, the person in charge of these activities loses all interest, a thing that would never happen if he could work on a proper basis and feel that his efforts were producing some result.[37]

Equally pettifogging business claimed his attention with regard to water regulation, for the prevention of flooding, etc., which came under the same Commission, and in which he continued to take some share even after 1790, when he was put on to a special Commission for that purpose, remaining a member until it was reabsorbed by the Roads Directorate in 1803. Here again there was the same trouble, multiplicity of authorities, which could seldom be persuaded to co-operate. One good thing that Goethe felt he was getting out of his work on these Commissions was a sort of discipline, in that the matters he was concerned with had very little interest for him. This was particularly so with the Military Commission, where he was again battling with trifles. He told Kanzler Müller that he only joined this committee as the most obvious way of effecting economies. His aim from the beginning was to reduce to a minimum an 'army' which had no useful function. Karl August's grandfather had been much given to playing at soldiers, a traditional weakness of the petty princes of Germany, but the number of troops had been greatly reduced during the Regency. In 1775 there were only twenty-two Hussars and fifty Gardes du Corps, whereas Ernst August had had a bodyguard of one thousand. There were still seven hundred infantry, but for most of the year the men were working in their villages, only being called up for manœuvres. The young Karl August found an outlet for his energy in taking command himself. He pensioned off the senior officers and brought in a Prussian officer to train his Hussars, who were given a new riding-school and new stables. They were a picturesque sight in their red uniforms, with blue dolman and brown fur cap, as Rittmeister von Lichtenberg, notorious for his severe punishments, led his men on parade every day, thirty-six of them now, while a trumpeter played the cavalry march. They were useful for patrol duties, as a sort of gendarmerie, a few of them escorted the Duke on his journeys, they took a hand in fire-fighting, they made a brave show on state occasions, at court balls, shoots, and so on, and they carried messages for the Duke, or even notes from Goethe to Frau von Stein.

Some economies had been accepted by the Duke before Goethe was called in. The last twenty-four of the Garde du Corps were dismissed in 1779, the 'artillery' were virtually pensioners, a corporal and half a dozen cannoniers in green and red, who looked after the obsolete cannon at the Wartburg and in Weimar and

5 (*a*) SELECTING RECRUITS FOR THE INFANTRY

5 (*b*) THE ROMAN HOUSE IN THE WEIMAR PARK
The house was built 1792–6 (see p. 390) and frequently used as a
summer retreat by Karl August until his death.

fired them for ceremonial purposes. Their captain was of course the Roads Engineer. But there were still eight companies of infantry, four in Weimar and two each in Eisenach and Jena, under Colonel von Lassberg and a dozen or more subordinate officers. They wore blue coats with red facings like the Prussian infantry, and for a time after the Duke's visit to Berlin in 1778, he had a passion for drilling them before breakfast. It was for this branch of the service that a levy was made every three years among the peasantry and apprentices. To conduct it was one of Goethe's first duties, first in Weimar, at the end of February 1779, soon after he had begun the prose *Iphigenie*, then in Jena ('Menschenklauberei', man-grabbing, he calls it to Frau von Stein), then in quiet Dornburg, noisy Apolda, and so on, always with the thought of his drama in his head, so that, though in this activity too he was extending his first-hand knowledge of life, and rejoiced to find so many things 'different from what we can imagine', his 'inner life continued unshakably on its own course'. In Apolda, however, he admitted, it was difficult to make 'the King of Tauris speak as if no stocking-weaver there were hungry'. Here too 'the cripples all wanted to be called up, and the stalwarts to get an exemption certificate'. In March 1782, three years later, he was doing the rounds again, but not in between these two periods.

By this time he was the temporary head of the Treasury, and instead of merely cheeseparing, always hampered by an unco-operative colleague, nearly twenty years older than himself, Herr von Volkstedt, whom he could not get rid of for a year or two, he was able, in view of the desperate state of the finances, to make whole-sale reductions. He persuaded the Council in 1783 to reduce the court and stables budget to 30,000 talers, which was possible by halving the size of the infantry force, now 248 instead of 532 men. The Hussars were kept, as policemen and glorified lackeys. A few years later, while Goethe was in Italy, Karl August was given the command of a Prussian regiment, which he drilled to his heart's content as Aschersleben.[38]

A particularly difficult and responsible task was imposed upon

Goethe when he was asked, in June 1782, to take charge of the Treasury, a few days after the dismissal of its President, Kalb. The Duke had made him a Geheimer Ratin 1779, and he had just learned that at Karl August's request the Emperor had now raised him to the nobility. At Easter he had rented the house on the Frauenplan that we know as the Goethehaus, after using in turn four different unpretentious *pieds à terre* in town, the 'Gartenhaus' given to him in April 1776 being unsuitable for regular winter use, and rather inaccessible when he was kept late in town. 'His Excellency' had now therefore all the outward signs of his high position. As a member of the Council with much experience of financial problems on his various Commissions, he was to try to deal with the financial emergency that had arisen through Kalb's inefficiency, with a view to becoming Kammerpräsident himself, but he never actually held this office, and was not concerned with the routine administration of the department. Surviving documents amply prove how difficult were the negotiations conducted by Goethe with the three separate bodies representing the Estates of Weimar, Eisenach and Jena respectively, which controlled new taxation.[39] Without their help, the Duke had only the income from the ducal demesnes and the small sums yielded by the old-established 'ordinary tax' and beer-duty, not only to maintain his court but to pay a number of officials whose services were essential to the whole duchy, and not merely to the dynasty. As in other small states, the older 'patrimonial' conception of the state still exerted a considerable influence, and the distinction was not yet quite clear between the ruler's public and private liabilities.

In the summer of 1776, soon after Kalb had become Treasurer and Goethe a member of the Council, this body had gone carefully into the already rather disturbing financial condition of the country. While urging the Duke to observe the strictest economy, it had increased his allowance for court and stables about 23 per cent. This meant that Kalb had to find an additional sum of 10,000 talers a year, and his first proposal had been a strict excise levied on imported goods, similar to that exacted in Prussia and in the Electorate of Saxony, in accordance with the prevailing mercantilist theory. The difficulties were, however, too great in Weimar, with its scattered territories, and a poll-tax was introduced instead, with the consent of the Committee of the Estates, which met in 1777. The levy ranged from 16 talers on a Privy Councillor (with a salary of 1,800) to 4 groschen (one-sixth of a taler, about a day's wages) on day-labourers. This was unpopular, because the poorer people were already so heavily taxed that they found it hard to pay anything more in ready money. With the help of the Estates Treasury Kalb was able to keep things going for a year or two, but in August 1779, not long before the Duke and Goethe went on their Swiss journey, the Treasury had had to borrow 50,000 talers from Berne, and during the journey Goethe had noticed, and pointed out to the Duke, how well the Swiss towns and cantons managed their finances. The crisis in 1782 arose through Kalb's inability to pay the interest on this Swiss loan. He had continued, however, to produce bright ideas, the latest being to sell in Bremen the surplus stocks of corn accumulated by the government from tenants' payments in kind. Unfortunately it was discovered, soon after he had gone, that the transport costs were much higher and the price realised lower than had been anticipated, so that 8,000 talers had been lost on the transaction.

Goethe was not able to do anything sensational, but by insisting on the strictest economy, particularly, as we have seen, in military matters, he had been able to win the confidence of the representatives of the Estates, and their committee, called together in 1784 again, as in 1777, because of the financial crisis—it had not met at all in between—agreed to take over the Treasury's debts, though not that to Berne, and to pay military pensions. In return, the Duke had to agree, as we have seen, to a reduction of his court and stables allowance from 59,000 talers to 30,000. It was possible now to abolish the poll-tax, much to Goethe's relief, though the peasants' lot, as he clearly saw, was in general still a hard one in Weimar. It is about this time (20 June 1784) that he writes in a letter that it is the poor who must always 'carry the sack, and it makes no difference whether it is too heavy for a man on his right shoulder or on his left'. A series of remarks in his letters between 1782 and 1784 show how well he understands the socially unjust world in which he lives, though he can think of no fundamental remedies, and fears disorder more than injustice. 'The class we call the lower', he says, is 'in God's eyes the higher.' 'One is ashamed at being favoured above so many thousands. We are always hearing how poor a province is, and how it is getting poorer; sometimes we tell ourselves that it isn't true, at others we put it out of our minds. But what when we see things for ourselves with open eyes, and see how incurable it all is, and how many botched efforts are made!' (2 April 1782). In one bitter letter to Knebel (17 April 1782) he compares the peasantry, wresting a bare living from the ground, with the aphis on the rose-bushes; as soon as they have fed themselves full and green, ants come along and suck them dry. 'We have got so far now,' he goes on, 'that more is consumed in a day at the top than can be produced in a day at the bottom.' These remarks are made in the period when Goethe was most occupied with the general economy of the state he knew so well.

Before finally giving up the struggle with so many insoluble practical problems, Goethe was called upon to serve on a new Commission, set up in July 1784 to investigate and reorganise the tax system in the isolated district of Ilmenau where, in difficult conditions partly due to the great fire, followed by the Seven Years War, the accounts of the tax-collecting office had been in a muddle for a generation. The little oligarchy of prominent citizens that ran the town's affairs had long been hopelessly corrupt. A new 'Amtmann' appointed in 1779, probably helped, as Goethe was himself, by information supplied by Goethe's protégé known under the alias of 'Krafft', whom he had settled there earlier in that year at his own expense, reported his suspicions about the tax-collector, and after due investigation this official was dismissed and put in prison in December 1782. This is what is referred to in the poem *Ilmenau* in the line:

Es wird der Trug entdeckt, die Ordnung kehrt zurück,

though the next line expresses only a hope for the future:

Es folgt Gedeihn und festes irdsches Glück,*

for the town was still almost as poor as ever, but the taxes were now at least properly collected. The main tax was a land-tax, for which the land-register was in a chaotic state and (as in most places) hopelessly out-of-date. It was to have it put right that the new Commission, consisting simply of Goethe and a lawyer from the Regierung (e.g. Voigt from 1786), was set up. It could not make its recommendations, which were accepted, until 1796, after a complete new survey and valuation of the district, and Goethe continued to have a little to do with it until 1805.[40]

In addition to the specific duties that have been mentioned, many others devolved upon Goethe in the course of the first ten years in Weimar. It was through him, as we have seen, that Herder was won for Weimar, and it was he who conducted most of the negotiations both before and after Herder's arrival. We shall return to his later relations with Herder and his support of Herder's efforts. Whenever difficult negotiations were necessary with the neighbouring courts, Goethe was the first person to be thought of as envoy. His ennoblement made missions of this kind less troublesome. Here is a glimpse of one such visit, to Meiningen. 'As envoy, I have had a formal audience of the two Dukes', he writes to Frau von Stein (12 May 1782). 'In the great hall attendants in livery, the court officials in the anteroom, two pages at the double doors and their Highnesses in the Audience Chamber.' What he considered his most important duty was to guide the young Duke into ways of wisdom, and *Ilmenau* shows us how difficult this was:

> Doch rede sacht! denn unter diesem Dach
> Ruht all mein Wohl und all mein Ungemach:
> Ein edles Herz, vom Wege der Natur
> Durch enges Schicksal abgeleitet,
> Das, ahnungsvoll, nun auf der rechten Spur

* The fraud is discovered, order returns, prosperity and well-founded happiness ensue.

Bald mit sich selbst und bald mit Zauberschatten streitet
Und, was ihm das Geschick durch die Geburt geschenkt,
Mit Müh und Schweiß erst zu erringen denkt.*

As time went on, Goethe could venture to speak more plainly, and the Duke continually gave him cause, with his extravagance, his amours, his unmethodical and inconsistent direction of affairs. In spite of his 'passion for going wrong', he had 'a deep desire for truth', a genuineness that gave Goethe confidence and earned his sincere devotion. The difficult lesson he had to learn was what Goethe too was learning from his contact with hard facts: 'Entbehren sollst du', or, as *Ilmenau* puts it:

Der kann sich manchen Wunsch gewähren,
Der kalt sich selbst und seinem Willen lebt;
Allein wer andre wohl zu leiten strebt,
Muss fähig sein, viel zu entbehren.†

When we read the history of Goethe's official activity, we realise that a day was bound to come when he would no longer be able to console himself for the comparative ineffectiveness of most of his work by the thought that it was a wholesome discipline. From 1782 there are repeated indications in his letters. Speaking of a storm in which he had been caught, he writes to Frau von Stein (2 April 1782): 'I am glad that I am quite indifferent to discomfort if it is unavoidable, and if I am making for something. It is aimless activity that makes me furious, and I have vowed never to be reconciled to it.' It was his growing conviction that much of his work could never lead to the desired ends that gradually made him lose interest. By the beginning of 1785 this feeling is reflected in his almost ceasing to attend the

---

* Yet speak softly! for under this roof lies all my happiness and all my pain: a noble heart, prevented by a narrow fate from following the way of nature. Prompted by feeling, he is now on the right track, but still has to contend, sometimes with himself and sometimes with phantoms, and what fate presented to him through his birth, he is trying to make his own by toil and sweat.

† The man who, cold and selfish, lives for his own will, can grant himself wishes in plenty; but he who would be a good leader to others must be able to refuse himself many things.

Council, though up till now he had hardly missed a meeting. A new junior member, J. C. Schmidt, formerly secretary to the Council, had been admitted to full membership six months earlier and could now relieve him of much work. We gather from the *Dichtung und Wahrheit* notes already referred to that Goethe now regarded the work of the Council as being mainly concerned with devising temporary expedients, and in a characterisation of himself written in 1797 he says: 'In affairs he is useful, if consistent application is necessary, leading to some lasting achievement, or showing tangible results. . . . What necessity or art or craftsmanship produce, he can always tolerate, but he must look away, when men act according to instinct and claim to be acting with a purpose.' Though not sorry to have been through this experience, he feels more and more, he writes in 1782 (17 September), that he was 'born to be a private individual'. 'He must content himself with watering his garden if he cannot bring the country rain', he writes another time (9 June 1784), and this is his consolation, that he has at least grown in will-power and insight through attempting his 'Sisyphean task'. It is to this inward growth that we must now turn.

CHAPTER III

GOETHE'S CULTURAL LEADERSHIP AND PERSONAL LIFE, 1775-1786

I. GOETHE AS LEADER

W E have now seen something of the social condition of Weimar at the beginning of Karl August's reign and of Goethe's activities as one of his ministers. We have noted the humanitarian spirit that informed his work, without examining in detail the development of his thought on culture and society. What the outside world learned of all this did little at first to distinguish Weimar from the general run of small courts. A series of rumours was current, especially in court and literary circles, about a young Duke who was kicking over the traces, encouraged by the rather irresponsible author of *Werther*. Surprise and apprehension were aroused by the news of the favourite's appointment to a high official position. Wieland's numerous references to Goethe, on the other hand, in his extensive correspondence, were consistently favourable, pitched, in fact, in so high a key that to modern ears they sound extravagant. 'He is in all respects and from all sides the greatest, best, most wonderful human being God ever made', he writes, for instance, on 8 January 1776, to the fashionable doctor Zimmermann, who had visited Goethe in Frankfort. The scandal-mongers were the disappointed Seckendorff, Görtz and their friends. Frau von Stein, by now a close friend of the neglected Duchess and herself a strong upholder of the conventions, wrote (on 6 March 1776), also to Zimmermann, who had been corresponding with her, largely about Goethe, since November 1774, a year before she met Goethe: 'Goethe was wild at your letter.' (Zimmermann had apparently, in spite of what he heard from Wieland, sounded a warning note in a recent letter to Goethe, or to Charlotte herself.)

I defended you, confessed to him that I myself wished he would drop some of his wild ways, that make people here misjudge him, though at bottom they amount to nothing more than that he goes shooting, careering about on horseback, and cracking a long whip, all in the company of the Duke. These are certainly not his own tastes; but he must carry on like this for a time, to win over the Duke and be able to exert a good influence. That is how I think about it—he did not defend himself in that way, but with all sorts of strange excuses that did not convince me.[1]

Her interpretation entirely fits in with Trebra's (see above, p. 102), or, for that matter, with that of Goethe's manservant at this time, Sutor, with whom Eckermann chatted one day, many years later, about Goethe at the age of twenty-seven. In cheerful company he had been in high spirits too, the old man said, but never beyond measure. When things began to go too far he generally turned serious.

Knowing as we do now, as the result of documentary research, how extraordinarily conscientious Goethe's service to the Duke must have been, we are more than ever convinced that Frau von Stein was right. In the absence of her half of the long correspondence with Goethe, this letter is, incidentally, very valuable also for the light it throws on the writer. Goethe's picture of himself in the poem *Ilmenau* is proved to be entirely fair, and this impression is strengthened by a consideration of his other writings at this time, to which we now turn. They are, with few exceptions, and these consist mainly of works that remained fragments, plays and poems written for particular occasions, seldom published at the time, so that their influence was confined to Weimar, some neighbouring courts, and a few literary men who were in close touch with Weimar. When Goethe returned to literature and Göschen began to publish his collected works, during the Italian journey, he was with the general public a half-forgotten author. Wieland and Herder had, however, in the meantime, writing also in Weimar, made important contributions, Schiller had moved to this neighbourhood before Goethe returned, and in the next fifteen years or so the fruits of a long period of cultivation were abundant.

(i) *The Theatre*

Goethe's particular commitment at first, as unofficial 'maître des plaisirs', was of course to the amateur theatre, and though the immediate results were not particularly striking, for he did not give much time to it and had many other things to do, recent work has shown how much the later manager of the Weimar Court Theatre owed to his experience in these years, as playwright, producer and actor, with a group of keen amateurs whose performances relied much on improvisations, so that often in an emergency, 'the poet himself had to snuff the candles'. These words are a quotation from the fine poem *Auf Miedings Tod*, in which Goethe looks back early in 1782 on the past six years and recalls highlights in the little theatre's history, as well as some of its anxious moments. Everything speaks of a typically amateur theatre, 'where everyone goes his own way and a factotum is indispensable', and it is this factotum's self-forgetful service that is the theme of the poem. An unassuming stage-carpenter has in this way gained an immortality denied to all but a few idols of the theatre, and with him are mentioned Schuhmann, the scene-painter, and the two tailors responsible for costumes, Hauenschild, for the men's, and Thiele, for the women's, and even 'Jew Elkan' (p. 64, above) 'running up with many an unconsidered trifle', no doubt for properties. All these names figure in the still existing accounts paid by the Duke's Keeper of the Purse, Bertuch, and carefully filed, on the basis of which Dr Gisela Sichard has been able to fill in many gaps in our knowledge. We know, for instance, that Corona Schröter, the only professional in the group of actors and actresses, when she played Iphigenia, to Goethe's Orestes, needed, for the 'Greek' costume in which we see her in the well-known painting by Kraus, no less than eighteen yards of white linen, eight yards of white taffeta and thirty yards of white butter-muslin (the flowing veil). It came from Paulsen's shop (p. 58, above) and cost over 36 talers.[2] For amateur performances, these were evidently very well dressed. In modern plays the actors wore their own clothes, but when fantastic or oriental costumes were called for, as in *Lila, Der Triumph der Empfind-samkeit,* or Gozzi's *Die glücklichen Bettler,* they were specially made at court expense. For scenery, Mieding worked wonders with lath and cardboard and ingenious effects:

> Des Rasens Grün, des Donners lauter Knall,
> Der Laube Schatten und des Mondes Licht—
> Ja selbst ein Ungeheu'r erschreckt' ihn nicht,*

though he was apt to leave things till the last minute, and was often busy with poles and ropes and nails when the court party had already entered and the overture had begun.

It is not possible even now to say exactly what share Goethe had in the sixty or more entertainments listed by Dr Sichardt down to 1783, when a professional company was again engaged. As we have seen, apart from acting in *The West Indian,* he did practically nothing in the first year, and by then he had the regular business of the Conseil to occupy him, was called in for advice about building projects, for improvements to the park and gardens and many other matters, and after a further two years had special responsibilities that took up more and more of his time, besides which he was constantly on the move with the Duke. He did not write more than two or three plays or playlets a year, and nothing that took him very long except the prose *Iphigenie* in 1779. He acted in his own new plays and perhaps took a small part in one or two other performances, usually either round about Christmas-time or during the court's residence at Ettersburg in the summer, when there were none but members of the court, and perhaps a few guests, present, whereas at the ordinary performances in Weimar, all given in Hauptmann's Rooms (the 'Redoutenhaus' built by Hofjäger Hauptmann in 1775, with some help from the Duke), a certain number of people from the town could be admitted. There were four benches for them in the gallery, taking eight or ten each, and apparently fifteen in the parterre, the rest of the space being reserved for the chairs occupied by the court.[3]

* Green sward, the loud report of thunder, shady arbours and moonlight—yes, even a monster does not frighten him.

Until November 1776, the only play by Goethe himself that was performed was the very popular *Erwin und Elmire*, as has been mentioned, not a new work. It was a domestic comedy of young love, only remarkable for its songs, which include gems like 'Ein Veilchen auf der Wiese stand'. Goethe was so dissatisfied with the plot, based on a romance in *The Vicar of Wakefield*, and with the prose dialogue, that he rewrote it completely in Italy and made of it the verse 'Singspiel' that now appears in his works. The cast of four had to be singers, some of those who regularly performed in court concerts and in operettas, being partly professionals like Mme Wolf, partly amateurs like Consistorial Secretary Heinrich Seidler. Goethe was no doubt called in for advice. The music for the songs, we have seen, was specially composed by Anna Amalia, who was helped as usual in the orchestration by Seckendorff. For his own first production on 21 November 1776 Goethe wrote a new prose one-act play, *Die Geschwister*, perhaps the best of his early prose plays, admirably natural in its dialogue. This was conceived, Goethe's diary tells us, on 26 October and written between 28 and 30 October. There are only three characters. Goethe played Wilhelm, devotedly loved by Marianne, who thinks she is his sister, until Wilhelm is forced to reveal the truth on her receiving a proposal of marriage from his business friend, Fabrice. It is the opposite of the theme common in novels of that time, of the lovers who find themselves to be brother and sister. Wilhelm has brought up as his sister the child entrusted to him by a widow with whom he had been in love, whom he would have married but for her early death. He now loves her again in her daughter. It is a situation into which Goethe could completely enter in imagination, closely attached as he was to Cornelie, his own sister, now unhappily married and exchanging the friendliest letters with Charlotte von Stein, his 'sister or wife' in an earlier existence. His alter ego in the play has ambivalent feelings similar to his own, but a happier lot, for he is united finally with the woman he loves.

In 1777 Goethe began by producing and acting in his early verse comedy, *Die Mitschuldigen*, on 9 January. Preparations had begun for this production months before, but it had been delayed, and now Corona Schröter was able to make her first appearance on this stage, as Sophie. Goethe played Alcest, Bertuch Söller, and Musäus the inn-keeper. For Duchess Luise's birthday on 30 January, which was always marked from now on, and even in the days of the Weimar Court Theatre later, by a special performance, Goethe provided a new 'Singspiel', *Lila*, a rapid improvisation, as is soon evident, with a plot probably borrowed from Rotrou. Thanks to the skill of Dr Verazio (Goethe), Lila is reunited in happy love with her husband, Baron Steinthal, as the poet would have liked to see the Duke and Duchess. The husband, in this, the original form of the play, on hearing what proves to be a false report of his wife's death, almost loses his reason at the shock, does not recognize his wife when he sees her, and cuts himself off from all society. A fairy play, devised by Verazio, and acted by friends and relations, restores him to mental health. In the play as published, in 1790, we have a slightly revised version, apparently never acted at court, as the only recorded repeat performance took place a month after the first, and the revision was not begun, according to Goethe's diary, until a year later, on 15 February 1778. Here the roles of husband and wife are reversed. If the wife had been the unhappy victim of the estrangement in the acted play, the allusion to the Duchess would have been too transparent. Seckendorff provided music, and Mieding and his helpers the most elaborate scenery attempted so far, painted by Hofmaler Schuhmann from a sketch by Oeser in Leipzig, whose help Goethe had enlisted. Because of the regular fancy-dress balls for which they were mainly designed, Hauptmann's Rooms could not have a permanent stage, but only one constructed by Mieding in portable sections, specially erected for each play and immediately taken down again. Though it was not so small as used to be imagined—the proscenium opening was about seven yards wide, and the stage as broad as the hall, nine or ten yards—the system of staging had to be simple, as it was in the theatres for which, for instance, Lessing's plays had been written. Wings and backcloth, and a middle curtain if required, had to do all, with simple devices for changing the scenery quickly, at first 'folding wings', simply nailed to the stage, then after the *Lila* performance, for which the stage was slightly enlarged, a simple arrangement for wheeling the wings in and out, but without the under-stage machinery such as we find at Schwetzingen, which was by now common on permanent stages.[4] In the summer, the same scenery could be used in the hall in the west wing of the palace at Ettersburg, where a stage was put up in the autumn of 1777. We have no records of performances in the open-air theatre there.

The rest of the year 1777 seems to have been uneventful in the theatre as far as Goethe was concerned. He acted in the repeat performance of *Lila* early in March and of *Die Mitschuldigen* at the end of December, *Erwin und Elmire* was given again in March, no doubt with Corona Schröter in it this time, but the other plays and operettas were of the usual popular type, some of them repeat performances. With Seckendorff, Einsiedel and Bertuch all ready to help in producing, and the dancing-master Aulhorn to prepare an occasional ballet, Goethe probably had little or nothing to do with these entertainments. They more or less ran themselves, and for the young people appearing in them, even the rehearsals were pleasant social events at which refreshments were provided, sometimes at the Wittumspalais or Frau von Stein's, but more often at the house of Musäus or Seckendorff or Goethe, if the play was one of his own, or in the theatre, for dress rehearsals. Musäus and Hauptmann duly sent in bills to the Duke for the wine or punch or coffee provided. Reading rehearsals seem to have been quite usual—Goethe attached much importance to them later, of course—and for the more difficult plays up to six or eight rehearsals might be held in all, as well as many hours of ballet practice with Aulhorn, who sometimes charged the Duke for fifty or more hours for one show.

In 1778, Goethe's birthday piece for the Duchess in January was a better one than *Lila*. It was *Der Triumph der Empfindsamkeit*, originally described as a 'festival play with songs and dances'. It contained in its fourth act the fine 'monodrama' *Proserpina*.

Rousseau's *Pygmalion*, the first of these showpieces for a favourite actress, had been much imitated in Germany, by Bertuch among others with his *Polyxena*, published in the *Deutscher Merkur* in 1776, and by both Brandes, the actor-playwright, and Gotter in the neighbouring Gotha, for Mme Brandes, though these were called 'duodramas', because a man was introduced too, in a secondary role. They were popular in Hamburg, Berlin and elsewhere, and it was natural that Goethe should write one for Corona Schröter. They were all lyrical monologues, or near-monologues, with a few lines given to other figures, as in *Proserpina* to the Fates, and like Gluck's operas, or Wieland's *Alceste*, they dealt with themes from Greek mythology, carefully selected themes of a Winckelmannish simplicity and dignity. The text was introduced and occasionally supported in its emotional appeal by music, and part of it might even be sung. Something of the effect of grand opera was in fact obtained by the simplest possible means. For an audience accustomed to works like these, Goethe's *Iphigenie* would not be so surprising an innovation as it seems to us, for it too was intended at first as another festival-play, starring the same actress as *Proserpina*. The themes treated in *Proserpina* are in fact very close to those of *Iphigenie*. We see a noble woman, banished for ever from her loved ones and the happy scenes of her youth, full of humane pity for the tortured Tantalus and his fellow victims, unwilling to be a queen to an unloved husband, and innocently suffering at the hands of the Fates. One could almost call the monologue a 'Parzenlied' dramatised. The 'nächtliche Höhle' where this 'Verbannte' sings is Avernus itself, turned into an Inferno, where Tantalus, Ixion and the Danaids are tortured for ever. All hope is here abandoned, so the dominant note is accusation of the gods, as in the *Prometheus* fragments of 1773 and the 'Hymne' distilled out of them, and published by Jacobi in 1785. Goethe had been turning Greek themes over in his mind since before he wrote *Götz*, and they were familiar to him and to his age in opera, and particularly in paintings in the Poussin and Claude Lorrain tradition beloved of Oeser, who had been asked by Goethe for a design of the same type, or alternatively for 'an engraving from Poussin', for the park scene in *Lila*.

The rest of the play was quite separately conceived, as a satire against sentimentalism, full of local allusions, particularly to what everyone had heard about poor little Lenz (not yet known to be a mental case) and the hopeless passion he affected for a newly-married Weimar lady, the attachment written up by him in his unfinished *Werther* imitation, *Der Waldbruder*, which he had left behind with Goethe. One of Wieland's mock-heroes (in his *Idris*, 1767) had been in love with a statue, as Prince Oronaro is here with a life-size doll, a portrait of Queen Mandandane (also played by Corona Schröter), whom her husband Andrason (played by Goethe) finally cures of her sentimental weakness for the Prince by the revelation of the fact that the Prince is not in love with her, but with this image of her that he can take about with him wherever he goes, together with his 'Reisenatur', packing-cases filled with stage-properties, bubbling springs, singing birds, bottled moonlight and so on, only requiring a suitable tapestry back-cloth to convert any room into a fitting natural setting, free from midges and other inconveniences, and entirely at his disposal, as the doll is. These scenes are not only excellent comedy. They unmask the egocentric 'pathetic fallacy' that Goethe already sees in much Pre-Romantic love of nature. The literary satire reaches its climax when the doll is found to be stuffed with a sackful of sentimental stories and plays, including *La nouvelle Héloïse*, of course, and *Werther*, the source of all the trouble, as well as later manifestations like Miller's *Siegwart*, Jacobi's *Allwill*, and Goethe's *Stella*. Goethe does not spare himself here, it will be seen, any more than in the introduction to the fourth act, where Mandandane's lackey describes the English park he has laid out, as 'court-gardener in hell', as a fit setting for the monodrama which his mistress is about to perform. Goethe had evidently talked a good deal about his ideas for a park at Weimar, not seriously taken in hand until later, and he satirises the craze for the picturesque, with many local allusions. That the Queen makes a hobby of acting monodramas provides a tenuous link in the plot between the *Proserpina* and the rest of the play. If there is any deeper meaning in the combination of two so diverse creations in the same work, it is perhaps that *Proserpina* provides a standard of genuine and natural feeling, discovered in Greek art, by which to judge the aberrations of the present, but it is more likely that in this improvisation for a special occasion, Goethe was less concerned about unity of impression than about variety of entertainment, and the provision of a good part for the best actress.

The sentimental Prince is accompanied, in a manner by now traditional in comedy, by a down-to-earth Sancho Panza of a gentleman-in-waiting, Merkulo, and we are reminded of the contrasted pairs found so often in Goethe's works, in particular in *Faust*, pairs that reflect the Faustian and the Mephistophelian in himself. The verses he wrote as a prologue when he first thought of the play, but later dropped, with lines like these:

> Was hilft uns alle Herrlichkeit
> Ohne Seelen-Behaglichkeit
> Und ohne des Leibes Liebesleben?*

even make one wonder whether, behind it all, the Mephistopheles in himself is not mocking at the lover who allows himself to be fobbed off by Charlotte von Stein with 'thoughts' that, like the prince, he 'embraces with the arms of his soul'. The verses the Prince speaks in Act II are a slightly caricatured form of Goethe's own serious love-poems. But Goethe did not suggest this interpretation by acting the Prince himself, and it is probable that no one thought of it. Though so much depended on local allusions that a contemporary audience in Weimar could alone fully appreciate, Goethe was annoyed, his diary tells us (10 February 1778) by stupid misinterpretations, such as taking Proserpina, perhaps, like Lila, for a picture of the Duchess. What everyone could admire was the lavish production, which cost the really quite large sum of 400 talers. Mieding must have had his hands

---

* What is the use of all these glories without a comfortable frame of mind and a love life in the flesh?

full, especially with the transformation scene, when a room in the palace becomes a sylvan paradise before the eyes of the audience, as the Prince produces his 'Reisenatur'. For lack of stage machinery Mieding needed five assistants at the crucial moment, to change boxes into bushes, and so on, by manual manipulation.

Earlier in January Goethe had acted again, after three rehearsals, in the *West Indian*, with the famous Ekhof, from the Gotha Court Theatre, as guest actor, in the part of Stockwell. Ekhof's life-story, heard from his own lips, helped him with *Wilhelm Meister*, begun a year before this. Then on 27 March he played a comic character in another expensively dressed production, Gozzi's 'tragi-comic fairy-tale' *The Happy Beggars*, in an oriental setting, and after a long break he acted a small part at Ettersburg, as the nurse's husband, Lucas, in Einsiedel's translation of *Le médecin malgré lui* of Molière. But the great event of this Ettersburg season was another dramatic satire, *Das Jahrmarktsfest ʒu Plundersweilern*, presented after the Molière on 20 October and again on 6 November. These lively scenes, in Hans Sachsian doggerel like that of the *Urfaust*, introduce us to a world in small, in the varied types to be seen at a south German fair. There is really no plot. By way of prologue, a quack talks, as to a colleague, to the doctor who has obtained permission for him to perform a play, as mountebanks frequently did then, to get a crowd round. Goethe played the quack, and also a character in each of the two scenes of his play. It is part of a biblical play about Esther, 250 lines in all, a caricature of the crude tragedies in alexandrines that were the stock-in-trade of travelling players. Before and after it, the fair-ground characters pass before our eyes in turn, vendors of all kinds with their traditional street-cries, a ballad-singer, some visitors. Finally a shadow-play man shows the story of the world down to the flood, with naïve comments in his broken German. It is interesting to note how exclusively biblical the imaginative world of the ordinary man still is, and the popular tone of the piece must have added to its attractions for an audience at court, where in their 'Wirtschaften' and so on ladies and gentlemen delighted in masquerading as common people. The *Jahrmarkts-fest* had been written in 1773. It recalls the fragments of *Der ewige Jude* and parts of the early *Faust*. For the performance, Goethe adapted and expanded it considerably and entirely rewrote the inset play, which consisted originally of eighty lines of doggerel. Anna Amalia provided tunes for the street-cries, other music was adapted for overtures and so on, much care was taken with costumes and properties, and the whole was an enormous success. After this the actors seem to have rested on their laurels until *Iphigenie* was ready to be acted in the following spring. It had been Goethe's busiest year with the theatre, while he was still not too much taken up with official duties to spare time for it. It was at the beginning of the next year that he became responsible for the Roads Directorate and the Military Commission.

There is apparently no evidence of any performances during the winter of 1778–9 after the *Jahrmarktsfest*, except possibly of a short Hans Sachs play, *Das Narrenschneiden*, on 11 December. Goethe may have played in it; he acted the doctor at any rate when it was repeated at Ettersburg in July. The first performance recorded in 1779 is of the prose *Iphigenie* on 6 April, in Haupt-mann's Rooms, with a repeat performance there a week later, and another, mainly for the benefit of Merck, who was in Weimar on a visit, at Ettersburg in July, when Karl August played Pylades, instead of Prince Konstantin. In all performances, Goethe was Orest, Corona Schröter Iphigenie, Knebel Thoas and Seidler Arkas. The early *Iphigenie* is of course the outstanding work among all that Goethe wrote and produced for the amateur theatre, and it is very nearly the last. It will concern us often, but let us now look at the handful of plays with which he was concerned before a professional company was engaged again in 1783. On 20 May 1779 at Ettersburg, Goethe acted Eridon in the charming little pastoral play in alexandrines, *Die Laune des Verliebten*, his first surviving play, written in the Gellert tradition eleven or twelve years before this and never printed or acted. It is as if he had wanted to remind himself of the distance he had covered between writing this rococo trifle and *Iphigenie*. A few songs composed by Seckendorff, probably from poems by Goethe, were introduced, to make the playlet into a kind of 'Singspiel'. Goethe did not think enough of it to publish it in the first collected edition of his works. The theatre was becoming a more and more intimate one, confined to the small Ettersburg circle, and the plays were all short, because interest was flagging. Apart from one or two repeat performances, Goethe's only other appearance that year was in a small part in Einsiedel's parody (from the English) of *Orpheus und Euridice* in September, just before setting out with the Duke on a three-month tour of Switzerland.

The year 1780 was comparatively uneventful, except for Goethe's *Jery und Bätely*, a product of his Swiss journey, and *Die Vögel*, a modernisation of Aristophanes. Goethe described *Jery und Bätely* to Dalberg as 'a little operetta, in which the actors will wear Swiss costume and talk about cheese and milk. It is very short and merely designed for musical and theatrical effect.' Goethe had wanted his Frankfurt friend, Christoph Kayser, now in Zürich, to compose the music, but as he could not do it in time, Seckendorff again undertook the task, for the performance on 12 July, which was twice repeated. If *Jery und Bätely* relied on music and a little local colour for its effect, in *Die Vögel* it was the costumes and scenery that attracted most attention. So it is with all these later productions—the chief source of appeal is non-literary. The back-cloth for *Die Vögel* was painted by Oeser, who was there on a visit, and Mieding took great trouble with the bird-costumes and the rocky valley. Herr von Lyncker's description makes clear at any rate what fun the performers had.

The birds appeared in papier-mâché coats of feathers, very naturally painted; the people dressed as birds, of whom I was one, could turn their heads freely and move their tails to and fro by means of a string; the horned owl and owl could even make their eyes roll; the voices were clearly to be heard. These scenes had to be frequently rehearsed, of course, and the whole troupe was generally driven to Ettersburg once or twice a week in the afternoon. We were given refreshments there, followed later by a lavish supper at which, if the Duchess had already retired, we became very merry over wine and punch (champagne was very seldom served in the old days), and sang songs together. I remember that Franz von Seckendorff organised a regular students' drinking-party, attended by Goethe and even by the Duke himself, that the 'Landesvater' was sung and that we only reached Weimar, singing and shouting, at three in the morning.'

The text is a rather weak adaptation of the beginning of Aristophanes' comedy, with vague literary instead of sharp political satire and some private references to the Swiss journey, including one to Goethe's botanising and geologising. To get from Athens to Ettersburg was only possible, as the epilogue explains, by a *salto mortale*.

A fortnight later another entertainment was offered to the court by Einsiedel which also depended on external effect, the 'forest drama' *Adolar und Hilaria* or *The Gypsies*, the main attraction of which was that it was presented in the open air, in the so-called Klosterholz at Ettersburg, on a specially constructed stage, probably with lighting effects through the trees that suggested Goethe's *Fischerin* two years later.[6] Goethe and Corona Schröter took the leading parts, as in *Iphigenie* and, in this same year, in Seckendorff's tragedy *Robert und Kalliste*, with music by the author. This performance, on 26 May, was probably the first in the new assembly-rooms and theatre, erected by Hauptmann with a grant from the Duke. This was the building opposite the Wittumspalais that was to be used throughout the time of the Weimar Court Theatre, until it was burnt down in 1825. It had for the first time a fixed stage, with a proscenium opening about a yard wider than before, and provision for five pairs of wings instead of four.

There was a marked decline of interest in the theatre in 1781, when Goethe seems to have had little to do with it except at the beginning, in a revival of *Iphigenie* for the Duchess's birthday. Seckendorff again provided the novelties, two shadow-plays, 'ombres chinoises', a form of entertainment introduced to Weimar by the Prince of Meiningen. The first, to celebrate Goethe's birthday, was called *Minerva's Birth, Life and Exploits* and was given in the little 'Mooshütte' in the Tiefurt Park. The following description reminds us how naturally, in this intimate circle, classical mythology was resorted to, following a well-established tradition, for the expression of feeling on special social occasions.

Jupiter (painter Kraus with a colossal cardboard head) swallowed Metis, and had a dreadful headache. Ganymede, borne on the eagle, handed him in vain a bowl of nectar and went to fetch Aesculapius who, also in vain, got a Cyclops to give him a blood-letting, in the nose. But after Vulcan (the Duke) had split his skull open, Minerva (Corona Schröter) emerged, appearing first small and then full size. She was praised and adorned and given presents by her father and the other gods. In the third act the goddess found the day of the performance marked as one of the most auspicious in the book of fate, since one of the best and wisest of men had been given to the world thirty-two years previously. A genius wrote Goethe's name in the clouds, Minerva wound a wreath round it and dedicated to him the gifts received by her from the gods, Apollo's lyre, the garlands of the Muses, etc. She had laid aside the whip of Momus, on the lash of which 'aves' was to be read, while the titles *Iphigenie* and *Faust* appeared in fiery letters. But at the close Momus returned and hung this attribute too with the other offerings.[7]

The pantomime, in shadows thrown on a stretched sheet, was accompanied by music and by explanatory rhymes, both by Seckendorff. In the second of the shadow-plays, presented to a larger audience in the new theatre on 20 November under the title *The Judgement of Midas*, Goethe was one of the players.

Shows of this kind clearly called for far less preparation by the performers than a regular play, and the same is true of Goethe's sole new contribution for the year, the satire *Das Neueste von Plundersweilern*, not a play but a poem in doggerel, declaimed at court on Christmas Eve by Goethe, dressed as the Quack from the *Jahrmarkt*, and helped only by Aulhorn, as Hanswurst. Kraus had painted a large water-colour illustration to the poem (reproduced in many editions of Goethe) to which Goethe pointed, in the manner of the itinerant ballad-singer, as he spoke. Asked repeatedly for the latest news of this imaginary little German village, now supposed to have grown into a town, he gives us here a lively satire on the growth of the reading public, piratical publishers, Ramler and other critics, the imitations of *Werther*

6(a)   AN EVENING WITH ANNA AMALIA

The figures, from left to right, are: H. Meyer, Frau von Fritsch, Goethe, Einsiedel,
Anna Amalia, Elizabeth, Charles and Emily Gore, Frl. von Göchhausen, Herder.

6(b)   A SCENE FROM 'DIE FISCHERIN'

Performed on the wooded banks of the Ilm at Tiefurt. Corona Schröter,
as Dortchen, is in the foreground.

and *Göt̨*, the work of the Göttingen poets and of Klopstock himself, and above all, on the Sturm und Drang dramatists. It is as clear a renunciation of Sturm und Drang as he was to make in *Ilmenau* two years later, and at the same time Goethe praises Wieland's new poem, *Oberon*, as immortal, though not without a sly dig at the solemnity of the *Merkur*. Anyone who thinks that Goethe had no sense of humour should read these verses, where it is seen at its freshest and most spontaneous. No poet could have been more directly in touch with his audience, who appreciated every allusion and insisted on two repeat performances early in the new year. This and the shadow-plays just described seem to indicate that a high degree of unity in intellectual interests and culture had already been attained in Weimar, chiefly owing to Goethe's presence and leadership. Individuals naturally differed widely in their tastes, but a small group of people who were always in each other's company, who read the same books and contributed actively in plays, concerts and a private magazine, the *Tiefurt Journal*, to pleasures that were eminently social and shared by the whole group, though decisively influenced by Goethe and one or two others, could not fail to have much in common in their general interests and in their attitude to life.

In the last full year of the Weimar amateur theatre, 1782, the only notable performance was that of Goethe's 'forest and water drama' *Die Fischerin* on 22 July, though half a dozen other plays were acted, in one of which, a parody of *Zaïre* done at Ettersburg in the summer, not only Goethe but the Duke, Einsiedel, Kraus, Frl. von Göchhausen and some other ladies of the court and pages took part. Performances like this must have been very like charades at a house-party. The author's own note in the text of *Die Fischerin* tells us that this short 'Singspiel', acted at night beside the Ilm at Tiefurt, was designed to lead up to a particular visual effect. When Dortchen's father and sweetheart think she is drowned and call on their neighbours to light fir-tapers and torches to look for her, moving lights appear, first near by and then in the distance, colouring the trees and glittering in the winding Ilm, a long stretch of which could be seen by the audience.

The play itself is a quickly improvised 'ballad opera', in a rather unusual sense. It begins with the magical ballad *Erlkönig*, which Dortchen, the fisherman's daughter, is singing to pass the time. This was Goethe's re-handling of a Danish ballad translated by Herder, and four of the principal songs of *Die Fischerin* are directly borrowed from the same collection of Herder's translations from the folk-songs of many nations. The situation Goethe invents for their display is taken from the life of simple people and is very like that in *Jery und Bätely*, turning on the unwillingness of a girl in love to be rushed into marriage, but the artless dialogue, almost all in short phrases, is surprisingly expressive.

Kraus has left us an illustration to this play, as also to *Iphigenie* and several others, including the one play, *Zobeis*, that is known to have been acted in 1783, on 21 March, another adaptation by Einsiedel from their favourite Gozzi, again in an oriental setting, and with a musical accompaniment.[8] But the best memorial to the theatre of Goethe's early years in Weimar is the already mentioned poem *Auf Miedings Tod*, written in the spring of 1782, following Mieding's death in January. Here, as Emil Staiger has said, 'Weimar' perhaps for the first time becomes a definite concept. The little capital is revealed certainly as conscious of itself and its reputation:

> O Weimar! dir fiel ein besonder Los!
> Wie Bethlehem in Juda, klein und groß.
> Bald wegen Geist und Witz beruft dich weit
> Europens Mund, bald wegen Albernheit.*

The feeling that inspires the poem is no doubt the same that is summed up in the marvellous lines of Goethe's second theatrical elegy, *Euphrosyne*:

> Jenes süße Gedränge der leichtesten irdischen Tage,
> Ach, wer schätzt ihn genug, diesen vereilenden Wert!†

* O Weimar, a special fate was dealt out to you, to be, like Bethlehem, small and great! You are the talk of all Europe, for your genius and wit, or for your follies.

† Those sweet crowded hours of light-footed earthly days, ah! who treasures enough this swift-vanishing blessing!

and there is something very satisfying in the fact that in both elegies it is an obscure professional servant of the theatre who is celebrated, one whom life, for Goethe's feeling, had not rewarded as it might have done:

> Bedauert ihn, der, schaffend bis ans Grab
> Was künstlich war, und nicht was Vorteil gab,
> In Hoffnung täglich weniger erwarb,
> Vertröstet lebte und vertröstet starb.*

After a little moralising in the familiar Augustan way on death the leveller, there come lines that remind us of Goethe himself:

> Du, Staatsmann, tritt herbei! Hier liegt der Mann,
> Der, so wie du, ein schwer Geschäft begann;
> Mit Lust zum Werke mehr als zum Gewinn ...†

and after celebrating Mieding as 'Direktor der Natur', the poet takes us in imagination to the simple funeral of this poor craftsman, and reminds the muses of the theatre of his achievements:

> In engen Hütten und im reichen Saal,
> Auf Höhen Ettersburgs, in Tiefurts Tal,
> Im leichten Zelt, auf Teppichen der Pracht,
> Und unter dem Gewölb der hohen Nacht.‡

Then he describes the variety of entertainments that have been offered:

> An weiße Wand bringt dort der Zauberstab
> Ein Schattenvolk aus mythologschem Grab.
> Im Possenspiel regt sich die alte Zeit, [Hans Sachs]
> Gutherzig, doch mit Ungezogenheit.
> Was Gallier und Brite sich erdacht,
> Ward, wohlverdeutscht, hier Deutschen vorgebracht;
> Und oftmals liehen Wärme, Leben, Glanz

---

* Pity him who, busy till the end with the things of art and not with what brought him gain, though ever hopeful earned less every day and lived on promises until his death.

† You, statesman, come this way! Here lies the man who, like you, attempted a heavy task, delighting in his labours rather than in gain.

‡ In cramped huts and in the luxurious hall, on the heights of Ettersburg and in Tiefurt's vale, in a flimsy tent or on rich carpets, or under the vault of high night.

Dem armen Dialog—Gesang und Tanz. [Singspiele]
Des Karnevals zerstreuter Flitterwelt
Ward sinnreich Spiel und Handlung zugesellt.
Dramatisch selbst erschienen hergesandt
Drei Könige aus fernem Morgenland;
Und sittsam bracht auf reinlichem Altar
Dianens Priesterin ihr Opfer dar.*

Finally, Corona Schröter, sole star of this theatre, is described as she comes to express Weimar's thanks at Mieding's grave:

Wir sind erhört, die Musen senden sie.
Ihr kennt sie wohl; sie ist's, die stets gefällt:
Als eine Blume zeigt sie sich der Welt,
Zum Muster wuchs das schöne Bild empor,
Vollendet nun, sie ists und stellt es vor.
Es gönnten ihr die Musen jede Gunst,
Und die Natur erschuf in ihr die Kunst.
So häuft sie willig jeden Reiz auf sich,
Und selbst dein Name ziert, *Corona*, dich.†

(ii) *Contributions to the 'Tiefurt Journal'*

The poem *Auf Miedings Tod* takes up the whole of the twenty-third number of the *Tiefurt Journal*, a private court magazine, of which about eleven copies were made by hand. It was started by Anna Amalia and Einsiedel in August 1781 and kept up, with increasing difficulty, till June 1784, forty-seven numbers in all.[9] Soon after she had begun to reside in the summer at Tiefurt,

* There a magic wand brings on to a white screen a shadow tribe from their mythological grave. Old times come to life in the farce, with kind hearts but manners rough. The creations of Gaul and Britain, in good translations, was presented to Germans, and often faulty dialogue was given warmth, life and lustre by song and dance. The disjointed tinsel world of carnival was enriched by plot and action full of meaning. Even the Three Wise Men were summoned from the far East to appear in dramatic shape, and Diana's priestess in all propriety offered sacrifice on an unsullied altar.

† Our prayer is heard, the Muses send her to us. You know her well; it is she who always gives pleasure, she shows herself to the world like a flower. Her fair form grew to be a paragon; perfected now, she represents the ideal in herself and in her acting. The Muses granted all their favours to her, and Nature in her created Art. So does she eagerly add to herself every grace, and even your name, Corona, is an adornment.

originally a farmhouse, then the home of Prince Konstantin, whose companion and tutor, Knebel, had greatly improved its gardens, the Dowager Duchess had had the idea of producing in the court circle, simply for their own amusement, as they did their plays, an imitation of the *Journal de Paris*, a little paper for the *beau monde* about literature and the arts which had been appearing daily since 1777, and had been a great success, attracting subscribers even in Germany, for it was a kind of *Correspondance Littéraire* for a much larger public than the handful of courts that could afford Baron Grimm's literary newsletter. Weimar could not, but often received titbits from Gotha, where it had started. The new venture, whether intentionally or not, might have shown Frederick the Great that German could become the language of a court far sooner than he had considered possible in his *De la littérature allemande*, published six months before the *Tiefurt Journal* began. The author of the 'dégoûtantes platitudes' which were all that Frederick was able to see in *Götz von Berlichingen* wrote for the new magazine four superb poems, the prose *Fragment* on Nature, a few translations of folk-songs and a version of one taken down near Weimar; he sent in also poems from Lenz's papers and got visitors and friends, like Prince August of Gotha and Merck, to contribute. In No. 24 Frl. von Göchhausen, in her story about Ritter Eckbert von Tiefurt, makes a twelfth-century knight see in a magic mirror the Tiefurt of her own time, admire Knebel's handiwork and above all Anna Amalia's way of life in this rural retreat. One passage refers to the leading contributors to the *Journal*:

He saw now too how Amalia erected a small temple to the Muses in an unseen quiet place. How she herself sets up Psyche and Amor (a serial re-telling the Greek myth), how Goethe set up in it the statue of Imagination and Wieland those of the Graces. How Herder moulds those of Wisdom and Virtue, for Love, Wisdom and the Graces are sisters to each other.... Then he saw how the little temple was adorned by Herder's charming wife, by Prince August, Seckendorff and Einsiedel with gentleness, intelligence, fancy and wit, and how Dalberg too brought flowers, less fair, but full of good will.

The tone of these lines is characteristic. Many of the pieces accepted for the *Journal* are artless first efforts, of ladies eager to keep up, as well as they can, relying on the protection of anonymity—for nothing is signed—with the gifted leaders of this small society. Nothing could show more clearly how taste and ideas spread by imitation in a well-defined social group. A refined secular humanism is here the order of the day, similar to that which is reflected, in an idealised form, in the first act of *Tasso*, a life lifted as high as possible above its material and animal foundations by man's imagination and capacity for free ideas. Goethe's ode, later entitled *Meine Göttin*, in No. 5 (September 1781), celebrates the most precious gift of the gods to man, imagination, called here the favourite daughter of Jove. It is our capacity to conceive images and ideas of things and events not immediately present to our senses that makes us free from the yoke of necessity, of strict determinism:

Hingehen die armen	Andern Geschlechter
Der kinderreichen	Lebendigen Erde,
In dunkelm Genuß	Und trübem Leiden
Des augenblicklichen	Beschränkten Lebens,
Gebeugt vom Joche	Der Notdurft.*

Goethe's second ode, in No. 40 (December 1783), later called *Das Göttliche*, is the complementary celebration of the application of man's ideas of the good, the true and the beautiful to life. Imagination, given free rein, is unpredictable, 'eine Törin', and to the poet in romantic mood, wisdom will have something 'stepmotherly' about it. He will rely rather on imagination's elder sister, the comforter, Hope. But when he thinks soberly of his position in nature, he will feel that man's surest resource is to be found in his intuitions of goodness and beauty, and those of his forebears, still remembered, thanks to a continuous civilisation, and tested out, as to their truth, in actual living. The divine does not reveal itself in any other shape, and only the action of good

* The other wretched races of the fecund living earth pass their days in the stupefied enjoyment and miserable endurance of the passing moment's limited life, bowed beneath the yoke of necessity.

men makes us capable of imagining absolute goodness. Nature is indifferent, morally neutral. The animals, and the animal in man, are slaves of necessity.

Nur allein der Mensch	Vermag das unmögliche
Er unterscheidet	Wählet und richtet
Er kann dem Augenblick	Dauer verleihen.
Er allein darf	Dem Guten lohnen
Den Bösen strafen	Heilen und retten
Alles irrende schweifende	Nützlich verbinden.*

During the three years covered by the *Tiefurt Journal*, mid-1781 to mid-1784, the incredibly many-sided author of these lines, in the busiest period of his official activity, so busy that he felt himself, as he wrote to Kestner (30 May 1781), 'more of a serf every day', was steadily advancing, as we shall see, in his knowledge of botany, geology, mineralogy, and comparative anatomy. By August 1783 he had drawn near to Herder again, after a year of estrangement, and found Herder's ideas on science, in its relation to religion and philosophy, so close to his own that he was able to co-operate with him most fruitfully while Herder was writing his *Ideen*. In 1782 Goethe had exchanged several outspoken letters on religion with Lavater, whom he had till now greatly liked as a man, though he had never seen eye to eye with him about Christianity. Lavater's *Pilatus* made him realise that he was, in relation to Lavater, a 'decided non-Christian', but he defended his humanism as just as sincere a conviction as Lavater's, to him, superstitious and one-sided Christianity, and made it clear that he regarded all religions as different human ways of thinking about existence, products of the self-healing power conferred on man by nature, in mental as in physical stresses. 'My plaster does not work with you, or yours with me; in our father's pharmacy there are many prescriptions' (4 October 1782).

It was a few months after this that the *Fragment* on Nature

---

* Man alone of all creatures can do the impossible. He distinguishes, makes choices and judgments, he can give lastingness to the moment.

He alone can reward the good, punish the wicked, heal and save, bringing into fruitful combination all that ranges at random.

appeared in No. 32 of the *Journal*. Whether it was actually written down by Goethe, or put together, after discussion with Goethe, by the young Swiss theologian Tobler, a recent visitor, whom he had first met through Lavater on his Swiss journey and found then rather immature, does not make much difference, as Goethe acknowledged the ideas as his own way of thinking. The manuscript is in the handwriting of his secretary Seidel, with corrections by himself. It seems extremely unlikely that the Swiss visitor could make of Goethe's conversation with him such a remarkable piece of poetical prose. It is the hymn to life of a creative genius, aware as few have ever been of all the possibilities of human experience, trusting nature's purposes, as fundamentally in tune with his own, for he is her child. It clearly owes something to Spinoza, the Spinoza who 'first impresses Goethe', as Matthew Arnold wrote in *Spinoza and the Bible*, and 'then composes' him, impresses by 'the grandeur of his view of nature', and composes by the moral lesson he draws from it. It owes perhaps more to the kind of 'enlightened' Christian belief that Goethe met with on all sides in his youth, much influenced by Shaftesbury and the Deists. With Lessing he believes that religion to be best which gives a man confidence amidst the trials of life, and he sees the heart of Christianity in the words ascribed to St John: 'Little children, love one another!'[10] For a modern scientist and a modern believer alike, his view of nature is excessively optimistic. Yet, like the 'Meditations' of Theocles in Part III of Shaftesbury's *Moralists*, later translated by Herder, of which it frequently reminds us, the *Fragment* carries the reader away, whenever he returns to it, with the wealth of suggestion contained in its evocation of 'deus sive natura' as a living and moving presence.

The opening lines state the theme on which the remainder is a series of variations rather than a logical development:

Nature! We are surrounded and embraced by her—powerless to step clear of her, and powerless to enter more deeply in. Without invitation or warning she takes us up into the whirl of her dance and moves on with us till we are weary and fall from her arms.

She creates ever new forms; what is there has not existed before, what has been will not come again—everything is new and yet the old ever recurs.

We live in the midst of her and are strangers to her. She speaks to us incessantly and does not betray to us her secret. We constantly work upon her and yet have no power over her.

She seems to have aimed at individuality in everything, and she has no regard for the individual. She builds always and destroys always and her workshop is inaccessible.

She lives in nothing but children, and the mother, where is she?— She is the only artist: from the simplest material she contrives the greatest of contrasts, without apparent effort she attains to the greatest perfection, the most precise definition, yet the outlines are always soft. Each of her works has its own being, each of her phenomena the most isolated conception, and yet everything makes up one thing.

[What is the place of man in nature?]

Men are all in her and she in all. With all she plays a friendly game and is pleased, the more one wins from her. She plays it with many and so secretly that she has ended the game before they notice it.

Even the most unnatural is nature. He who does not see her everywhere sees her nowhere aright. . . .

She sprays out her creatures from nothingness and does not tell them where they come from and whither they are going. They must simply run. *She* knows the course. . . .

Her spectacle is ever new, because she always creates new spectators. Life is her finest invention, and death is her device for having life in abundance. . . .

Her crown is love. Through it alone one comes near to her. She makes gulfs between all beings, and all try to consume each other. She has isolated everything in order to draw everything together. By a few drafts from the beaker of love she makes up for a life full of toil.

[And what is his own attitude to nature?]

She is kind. I praise her with all her works. She is wise and calm. No explanation can be wrenched from her, no gift extorted from her that she does not willingly give. She is cunning, but to a good purpose, and it is best to close one's eyes to her cunning. . . .

She has set me in, she will lead me out again too. I entrust myself to her. She may do her will with me. She will not hate her own handiwork. I have not spoken of her. Nay, what is true and what is false, it was all spoken by her. Hers is the blame for all, hers is the merit.

It may be doubted whether the *Journal de Paris* published any reflections of this quality, but Goethe's aphorisms remained unknown to the general public until they were printed in his *Nachgelassene Werke* in 1833. Five years before that he had come across them again, after nearly fifty years, and though he could not definitely remember writing them, agreed that they expressed his thought at the time. To Chancellor Müller he explained what further insight into nature he thought he had gained in the interval, laying special emphasis on his notions of 'Polarität' and 'Steigerung'. One can see in the essay, he said, 'the inclination to a kind of pantheism, in that an unfathomable, unconditioned, humorous, self-contradictory Being is thought of as the basis of all the phenomena of the world. As a playful handling of extremely serious thoughts it has its value.'

(iii) *Goethe's interest in science*

Goethe's nature studies had begun in his early days in Weimar with botany, he tells us in a late essay, much in the same way as botany itself, as a science, had arisen from the practical requirements of medicine.[12] Born and educated, as he had been, in a town, trained in languages, literature and law, he knew very little then about the country or natural history, though he had long delighted, as his poems show, in the beauty of natural sights. It was a great gain for him in going to Weimar to escape from city life indoors to country life in the open air. 'In the first winter I experienced the delight of shooting-expeditions in good company on horseback, and resting from our exertions in the evenings, we talked not only about sport, but a great deal about woods and forests and how they should be cared for.' He heard now about all kinds of trees, their uses and their habitat, and on his long rides through the Thuringian woods, already well maintained by trained foresters, he saw and understood more every day. He learned something too about the bearings of geology on forestry, and through various tasks in which the Duke enlisted his help, he constantly had occasion to extent this knowledge, to find out about good stone for repairs to buildings, and about trees and

shrubs for the gardens they improved at Belvedere and Weimar—
'weeping willows arrived from Frankfurt' is one of the first
entries in his Weimar diary, in March 1776.

Above all he was forced, as we have seen, to take up mineralogy
and geology seriously, in order to understand the problem of the
Ilmenau mines. In Weimar he could turn for help to Buchholz,
who needed a knowledge of botany and chemistry for his work as
doctor and apothecary, and who followed all advances in science
out of personal interest—he was the first in Weimar to experiment, in 1783–4, with hot-air balloons. Buchholz persuaded the
Duke to start a botanical garden, which Goethe, the factotum,
had of course to help lay out, and Linné's *Philosophia botanica*
became 'his daily study'. Expert advice could be had from the
University of Jena, where a *flora jenensis* had been compiled as
early as 1718. In September 1778 Goethe writes to Frau von
Stein: 'I have been in Jena, where stones and plants have brought
me into connection with men.' Every visit to Ilmenau brought
grist to his mill. From August 1776 he spoke, as we saw, of
God's world there as 'his green pasture', where he botanised,
geologised and sketched while the rest were shooting. A miner
tells us how eagerly, when they were doing their rounds together, Goethe one day searched for the place on a steep rock
face where a boulder he had noticed below, of granite combined
with a dark-blue rock, had come from. He ran over the slippery
mossy rocks and climbed on his companion's shoulders to reach
the spot where the two strata could be seen exposed.[13]

Every journey brought new insights, the winter excursion to
the Harz and the climbing of the Brocken in 1777, repeated visits
to the Wartburg, and above all the Swiss journey of 1779. We
have already noted the keen observation of the outer world that
marks his *Briefe aus der Schweiz*. Already little seems to escape his
eye as he studies the landscape before him, with the interest of a
geographer as much as a poet and artist. His descriptions of
mountain views are preceded by explanations of the geographical
position of the viewpoint, the structure of the mountain masses;
the changing rock formations and vegetation, the situation of

settlements, even cloud formations are noted, as they are even more thoroughly in his *Italian Journey*, but man, in this thinly populated region, seems to be dwarfed by 'the great objects of nature'.

Among other writings reflecting the growth of his natural-history studies may be mentioned a late essay, *Das Luisenfest*, describing how the redesigning of the Weimar park began, in 1778, with the construction of a 'hermitage' on the left bank of the Ilm, near the 'rock-steps' and wooden bridge that had been made a little earlier, to shorten Goethe's walk from the 'Garten-haus' to the town. The immediate occasion was the 'name-day' of the Duchess, to celebrate which she was greeted near the newly made hermit's hut, later called the 'Borkenhäuschen', by Secken-dorff, Goethe and several others, dressed as monks, with a little scene in verse, written by Seckendorff, and entertained with her companions to lunch in the open air.[14] From his first days in his Gartenhaus Goethe had busied himself with the garden there, and his letters tell us of the alterations he had made, the seeds he sowed and the trees he planted with his own hand that summer and for several years. Gradually, from 1778, the old formal garden just across the Ilm from the castle, the 'Stern', together with new land on both sides of the river, were transformed into an English garden, in excellent taste, apart from a few concessions, like the Hermitage, to the sentimentality that Goethe had satirised early in 1778 in Act IV of the *Triumph der Empfindsamkeit*. The landscape architects were Goethe and the Duke, taking as their immediate model the park at Dessau. The elaborate descriptions of the improvements to their grounds carried out by Eduard and Charlotte, in the early chapters of *Die Wahlverwandtschaften*, seem to indicate Goethe's continuing interest in such activities, and it is obvious that they would give him a wide knowledge of systematic botany.

But he did not rest content with that. 'Everything is new and yet the old ever recurs.' It was the antithesis between the One and the Many, the lasting forms persisting through all nature's changes, that particularly interested him from an early stage. The 'theorising' which, as he wrote later, 'we cannot avoid, whenever we look attentively into the world'[15] was directed with him especially to this problem. This is 'the keynote to the whole of his biological work'.[16] The branch of science in which this 'morphological' interest of his first produced results was comparative anatomy, to which he was led by his co-operation with Lavater, before he went to Weimar, in his 'physiognomical' investigations, the reading of character from the human head and face. Professor Loder in Jena introduced him systematically into the study of anatomy from 1781, and for two months in that winter Goethe passed on this knowledge in public lectures twice a week to the teachers and pupils, many of them adults, of the now flourishing School of Drawing in Weimar. Throughout the autumn and winter of 1783-4, Goethe was discussing the *Ideen* with Herder, and both Herder and Merck, with whom Goethe was in regular correspondence, drew his attention to the odd fact that according to the anatomists who had compared man's skull with that of monkeys and other animals, the middle portion of the upper jaw, carrying the upper incisors, is in most mammals a separate bone, bordered by sutures, but in human adults (though not in the embryo), the bones have grown together completely, leaving at most a faint trace of a suture in places. Comparative anatomists had not yet much interest in hidden correspondences, so-called 'homologies', even between embryo and adult forms, and in discussing man and the ape, the contemporary anatomists quoted so often by Herder in his *Ideen* (Books 3 and 4), Camper of Gröningen, and the younger men Blumenbach (Göttingen) and Sömmerring (Kassel), made much of this difference between the two species, in opposition to the many authors who were already stressing the similarities. Goethe determined to look into the matter for himself, seeking, as usual, to reconcile the antithetic elements in existence, and predisposed, as we saw in the *Natur-fragment*, 'to regard Nature as unified and directional, rather than inconstant and capricious'. 'It was from this viewpoint that his morphological work was developed', both in zoology and later in botany.[17]

He was soon examining animals' skulls wherever he could find them. From Eisenach, for instance, in June 1784, after he had made his discovery, he wrote to Frau von Stein: 'To my delight the elephant's skull from Kassel has arrived, and what I am looking for is clear beyond my expectations. I am keeping it hidden in my inmost closet, so that they won't think me mad. My landlady thinks it is porcelain in the huge packing-case.' He had come to Eisenach on Treasury business, to obtain the agreement of the Eisenach 'Committee of the Estates' to his financial proposals, but he was busy with many other things. He had brought Frau von Stein's youngest son, Fritz, who now lived with him, he wrote every day to Charlotte, he geologised in the hills—he tells Herder he has a new theory about the formation of the larger masses of rock—and he made some progress with *Wilhelm Meisters Theatralische Sendung*. In the letter to Knebel (17 November 1784) sent with the essay he had now written, he makes it quite clear that the sustaining interest he has in this inquiry is the desire to prove what Herder had suggested in the first part of the *Ideen zur Philosophie der Geschichte der Menschheit* (1784), that man is an animal, an animal with a difference, singled out for higher things, but formed by nature 'nach einem Hauptplasma der Organisation' along with the other animals. As Goethe puts it in this letter: 'And so every creature is only one note, one nuance of a great harmony, which must be studied as a single whole, or every individual part remains a dead letter.' The connection with his religious discussions with Lavater—and incidentally there is a reference to the newly invented balloon—is seen in his last sentence: 'Just as in ancient times, when men grovelled on the earth, it benefited them to have their thoughts directed towards heaven and to the spiritual, so now it is more wholesome that they should be brought back to earth and have the balloons they are tied to a little deflated.'

The anatomists to whom Goethe communicated his ideas— the same men, Camper, Blumenbach, Sömmering, to whom Herder constantly refers—did not for the most part accept them from him, though views had changed by the time Goethe published his essay in 1820. The question of Goethe's originality is complicated by the fact that a French anatomist, Vicq d'Azyr, had described the same 'homology' in a paper published in the same year, 1784, when Goethe made his discovery and wrote his essay. He had even communicated the gist of it orally to the Academy four years earlier. Goethe did not know of this, but he saw a book by the same author written in 1786 where the matter was mentioned, and seems to have thought, wrongly, that his own discovery had reached the Frenchman through Camper. Finding no response to his ideas, he held back his own essay till 1820.

The dispute between Anaxagoras and Thales, in the Classical Walpurgis Night scene in *Faust* Part II, on the geological history of the earth, probably seems to most readers one of the oddest and least appealing elements in a succession of mystifying episodes, but it reflects a private interest of its author that he had cultivated for half a century. We have seen how his duties in Ilmenau led him to find out all he could about mineralogy and geology, as well as about the technique of mining. The study of rocks soon became every bit as absorbing to him as that of plants and animals, and in this domain he was able for many years to enlist the help of a full-time assistant. Here too theory went along with observation and practical utilisation from the beginning, and to appreciate his achievement we have to think away the enormous additions to knowledge that have been made since that time. The Mosaic account of the creation of the world, though of course disputed, still held the field. Few had any inkling of what is now the basic assumption of geology and palaeontology, that the rocks have been formed in a series of stages extending over millions of years, and there was no exact knowledge yet about the age or the order in time of the various strata. Through ignorance of all this, Goethe could do little with the rich finds of extinct animals and of fossils already made in Thuringia, and now so admirably displayed in the Museum für Ur- und Frühgeschichte in Weimar, and he theorises on a quite insufficient basis, but he foresees correctly some future developments.[18]

As in botany, his first efforts were directed towards acquainting himself with actual specimens of all kinds of rocks, for he professed himself unable to learn anything from books. He called on many friends to help him, especially Merck, and later Knebel, whom he infected with his own interest. One of his first useful discoveries is reported in a letter to Merck in August 1778. It was a kind of stone he found in the castle ruins in Weimar, and soon tracked to its source, fine-grained and almost as suitable for the sculptor as marble. Next month he commissioned a bust of himself from Klauer as an experiment, and then a statue of little Fritz von Stein in the nude. This was the beginning of Klauer's successful career as a sculptor of portrait busts, and he was sent to copy the antiques in Mannheim for three months by way of training. The Swiss journey next year brought Goethe much new light. He collected specimens on all his trips to hilly regions and was always asking Merck, Knebel and even Sophie Laroche for particular items from their neighbourhood. Knebel joined him on his first holiday at Karlsbad in 1785, where he revelled in natural history. He took with him a handsome young fellow of twenty from a farm near Jena, whose grandfather, Adam Dietrich, had for many years supplied the Jena botanists with their specimens for lectures, and made his family into good systematic botanists. He himself had corresponded with the great Linné. On the way to Karlsbad, young Dietrich botanised in all the likely places, and handed in the plants as he found them to Goethe in his carriage, 'calling out in the manner of a herald their Linnean names, genus and species, with cheerful confidence, if sometimes with false quantities'. In Karlsbad itself he went out every morning at daybreak and brought back his finds to Goethe by the time he was taking the waters with his friends, who thus learned a great deal in an agreeable way, 'as the smart country boy in his short jacket displayed before them great bundles of herbs and flowers, giving them all names, of Greek, Latin and barbarous origin'.[19]

In geology Goethe's research assistant was the younger brother of C. G. Voigt, the able permanent official from the Department of Justice (Regierung) who began his long co-operation with

Goethe in 1783. J. C. W. Voigt was sent by Karl August for training at the Freiberg 'Academy of Mining' in Saxony, where the famous A. G. Werner had been professor since 1775. From Voigt, Goethe must have heard all about Werner's theories concerning the history of the earth's crust, the 'Neptunist' view that Goethe puts into the mouth of Thales:

> Nie war Natur und ihr lebendiges Fließen
> Auf Tag und Nacht und Stunden angewiesen.
> Sie bildet regelnd jegliche Gestalt,
> Und selbst im Großen ist es nicht Gewalt.*

Slow change under the influence of water, not volcanic cataclysms, as in the 'Vulcanist' hypothesis, is made the dominant factor. Voigt is first mentioned to Merck on 11 October 1780, together with George Batty, the young Englishman recently engaged as an expert in land drainage, from whom Goethe could learn a great deal about soils and erosion, and whom he repeatedly praises for his practical skill and common sense. In this letter Goethe says he has been devoting himself to mineralogy 'really passionately', and that in the last six months Voigt has rapidly surveyed for him the surface rocks from the highest point in the Thuringian Forest to the borders of Thuringia. He thinks that someone ought to write now a popular history of geology on the lines of Buffon's *Natural History*, for which he had the highest admiration. Soon he is planning such a 'novel', as he calls it, himself. He never wrote it, but his essay *Über den Granit* (1784) may be taken as showing the kind of thing he had in mind.

It is rather like the *Naturfragment*, eloquent and imaginative reflections on the paradox that 'the highest and the deepest' on this earth is granite, and the analogies thereby suggested to a poet whose theme has been 'the human heart, the newest, most complex, restless, variable, agitable part of creation'. How has life developed on an earth founded on granite?

---

* Never was nature and her living flow restricted to day and night and a matter of hours. She shapes and controls forms of every kind, and even on the grandest scale nothing needs force.

This crag, I say to myself, stood up steeper, more jagged, higher into the clouds, when this mountain-top was still a sea-begirt isle in the old waters; round it roared the spirit, that brooded over the waters, and in their vast womb the higher mountains formed themselves out of the ruins of the original mountain-mass, and from their ruins and the remains of their own inhabitants came the later and more distant mountains. Already moss begins to produce itself, already the shell-protected inhabitants of the sea move less frequently, the water-level sinks, the higher mountains become green, everything begins to teem with life.

Geology, clearly, had still a long way to go, and an enthusiastic amateur like Goethe could not contribute very much to the slow accumulation of accurate information and the patient, dispassion-ate analysis through which alone genuinely scientific results were achieved, but he continued all his life to occupy himself with the subject, and on a wall of his bedroom hung at his death the new geological time-chart from England, by de la Beche. Some experts trace ideas of Charles Lyell's epoch-making *Principles of Geology* (1838) back through the Gotha scholar K. E. A. von Hoff to Goethe.[20]

The effect of Goethe's lively interest in natural history and science on his friends at Weimar was soon plain. Herder shared it, in his more bookish way. Knebel, who left Weimar in 1780 for a few years, when Prince Konstantin needed him no longer, actively co-operated with Goethe, as we have seen, and several others were affected, especially the Duke himself, who maintained and de-veloped this interest to the end of his life. The atmosphere Schiller found in Weimar, on his first visit in 1787, would be inexplicable without this particular development, as he clearly saw. As he wrote to Körner (12 August, 1787), all Goethe's friends were like him in their distaste for metaphysical speculation. 'They would rather collect plants or study mineralogy than involve themselves in empty demonstrations.' It was not only in Weimar, of course, that people were to be found who followed eagerly the advance of science. Such an interest was typical of the Age of the Enlightenment and very widespread in Europe. But a serious and active pursuit of scientific knowledge was not at all common at German courts. Without these beginnings in Weimar, it is unlikely in the extreme that such rapid progress would have been made, after Goethe's return from Italy, with the development of the scientific institutes and museums in the University of Jena.

(iv) *Painting and drawing*

It is hardly necessary to add that in a circle where the personalities whose activities we have followed in the amateur theatre were leading figures, literature, art and music were by no means neglected, but this side of Weimar life is well known and there is no need to insist on it. Goethe's influence on music was limited to his 'Singspiele'. In painting and sculpture it was to be far greater after the Italian journey, but it was already considerable. He had been friendly with painters and had an eye for painting since his boyhood in Frankfurt, he had taken lessons in drawing with Oeser and in etching with Stock in Leipzig, and continued in Weimar to draw portraits and landscapes when he could find time, though often discouraged by his lack of technical skill. He had steadily collected engravings, especially Dürer and the Netherlands school, as well as plaster casts and drawings, making much use of Merck's many connections, both for himself and the Duke. He found two or three artists already established in Weimar, whom we have noticed in connection with the theatre—Kraus in particular, the portrait painter Heinsius, and Schuhmann, and he had introduced Oeser to the notice of Anna Amalia and the Duke, who asked him over from Leipzig for a few weeks every summer from 1776 to 1785, to paint a ceiling, or a backcloth, design a table or a garden seat, and give them his pleasant company. There were several other amateur artists besides Goethe, chiefly among the ladies. Corona Schröter was the most accomplished, but Anna Amalia herself, Frau von Stein, Frl. von Wöllwarth and Goethe's colleague Schnauss, also drew and painted. They were among the supporters of the School of Drawing, first suggested by Bertuch in 1774 and gradually brought into existence in the next few years. G. M. Kraus was engaged as teacher, at 400 talers a year, in the spring of 1776, and provided with a room for his classes. From 1781 they had a better room to meet in, in the old Rotes Schloss, and began to hold an annual exhibition of work. It was in this winter that Goethe lectured there, as we saw. In January the room was crowded to the door. All the professional painters and G. M. Klauer, the court sculptor, gave lessons there. Klauer could achieve a good likeness in portrait busts, and soon plaster casts of the Weimar celebrities could be sent anywhere in Germany. By the end of the 1780's Klauer was also producing terra-cotta figures of classical subjects, garden vases and so forth, in imitation of those earlier imported from Messrs Coade in London, probably at Bertuch's suggestion, for these artistic developments were all cleverly used by him for his 'Industrie-Comptoir' and his *Journal des Luxus und der Moden*, as we shall see.

Goethe's taste in art, as in literature, had by 1781 moved on from that of his Sturm und Drang days. There is particularly interesting evidence of this change in a long letter he wrote on 21 June 1781 to his old friend Friedrich (Maler) Müller, whom he and some of the Weimar court had been helping to support in Rome for two or three years already. He had now sent some of his work, which was found far too literary in Weimar, and lacking in technical competence, 'a mere stammering in paint'. Goethe advises him to give up over-dramatised subjects and learn to draw. Goethe found Tischbein far more promising, for whom he put in a good word with the Duke of Gotha. Müller had called himself 'Painter' prematurely, he wrote to Merck. For Goethe's general support of the interests of the arts in Weimar there is good evidence in a letter to Herder, commenting on his sermon at the thanksgiving for the birth of a son to the Duke and Duchess in February 1783. Herder drew a bright picture of the benefits they hoped the heir to the duchy would confer upon his country in due time, and urged him to remember then his duty to make his subjects happy and prosperous, rather than to indulge his passion for beauty. There are passions far less socially desirable than this, Goethe suggests, that are commonly indulged by the rich and powerful. 'Hounds, horses, shooting, gaming, banquets, clothes and diamonds, what capital sums are put into these and what a high rate of interest they demand in time and money, without any refreshment to the spirit, which is procurable at far less expense through the gifts of the muses.'

3. GOETHE AND FRAU VON STEIN

From the abundant records bearing on Goethe's external life in the first Weimar decade so much information can be gained that the historian's chief difficulty is to select and arrange his material. A purely chronological narrative like Düntzer's *Goethe und Karl August* tends to become so choked with facts as to be almost unreadable, while an account that deals with the various branches of Goethe's activity in turn, though gaining in clarity and continuity, may fail to convey what his life was like from day to day. Of a limited period we may, as a corrective, obtain a synthetic view by reading stretches of Goethe's diary, or diary-letters like the one written to Auguste zu Stolberg, 17–24 May 1776, or by studies of a single busy month such as Professor W. Flach has given us for February 1779.[21] The diary is a series of often cryptic notes, sometimes with gaps of months between entries, jotted down by Goethe in seven cheap, paper-covered calendars or desk-diaries, from 1776 to 1782. Reading these private scribblings in Goethe's hand, in unfaded black ink, one has the sensation of being close to him in his personal life, but to enter into it in imagination is even more difficult than to form a clear picture of his multifarious activities.

What are we to think, for instance, of the very foundation of his inner life, as he always insists, his relationship with Frau von Stein? It has been described and interpreted so often and so variously that many of his greatest admirers can see the 'Charlotte period' only as in a glass darkly. We know there is something there that is of the utmost importance for the understanding of his life, but in spite of the 1,800 letters Charlotte preserved so carefully, it remains unreal, a chapter in a novel that has not quite come off. To dispute her influence on him and on much of his greatest work, her significance through this friendship for the whole development of Weimar, would be to go against all the evidence. Goethe might well have left Weimar for good, it seems clear, when, after four or five years, the novelty of his situation had worn off, and in moments of depression he was filled with a sense of frustration.

> Gewiß, ich wäre schon so ferne, ferne,
> So weit die Welt nur offen liegt, gegangen,
> Bezwängen mich nicht übermächtige Sterne,
> Die mein Geschick an deines angehangen.*

So he wrote in the well-known poem from Brunswick on 24 August 1784, and he said the same repeatedly in prose (letters of 8 July 1781, 24 December 1782, and 23 November 1783, for instance). In the self-portrait already mentioned, written about 1797, Goethe sees as the centre and the basis of his existence an 'impulse towards poetic creation ('poetischer Bildungstrieb') that is always active, whether directed inwards or outwards'. If we accept this description as even a close approximation to the truth about Goethe's innermost nature, as we surely must, it is hardly conceivable that such a man could accept for long a situation in which compositions on which he was well started, like the early *Wilhelm Meister* or *Tasso*, were constantly interrupted by the empty distractions of court life, with which the letters to Frau von Stein frequently express his impatience, by boring missions to neighbouring small capitals and by the endless series of conferences and discussions on the domestic problems of Weimar in which his duties on the Council involved him. Something must be allowed, of course, for the habit which he had already acquired, of allowing his profounder works a long period of slow gestation. Even with unlimited leisure, he might not have completed *Faust* or *Die Geheimnisse* for some considerable time. On the other hand, this habit itself may have been in part the

---

* I would in truth long since have gone far, far away, to the very confines of the earth, if all too potent stars had not controlled me, linking my fate with yours.

result of the frequent interruptions he experienced. Controlled impatience with them is one of the most striking themes in his letters to Charlotte. His head, he says in one, is like a mill where many processes are going on at once. Then, changing the metaphor, he speaks of diverting the waters from ornamental fountains and cascades, and making them turn mills and water the fields, though from time to time, while he is not looking, an evil genius will pull out the bung and send them leaping and splashing. 'And when I think I am sitting on my nag and doing my dutiful round, the creature under me is suddenly transformed, acquires mettle and wings and runs away with me.'[22] Next day, he sent to Charlotte the ode to Imagination, *Meine Göttin*, in its first form. Or after finishing a chapter of *Wilhem Meister* he writes: 'It gave me a good hour. I am really born to be a writer. It gives me greater pleasure than ever when I feel I have written something well.'[23]

These clear indications that only Charlotte kept Goethe in Weimar, taken with the assurances of his complete devotion in every letter and poem, make it very difficult for us to accept Karl August's view of her, as 'no great light', though we can well believe that she never appealed to *him*. In the absence of her letters to Goethe, we tend to see only the reflection of her in his mind, and some of the best interpreters of Goethe, like Gundolf, maintain that that is all we need and should ask for. 'We are not concerned with how Charlotte von Stein "really" was, but with what Goethe looked for, found and saw in her. . . . She lives only through what she was for Goethe and what Goethe has eternalised in her.' While acknowledging much force in this argument, Walter Hof, in a recent valuable study, rightly insists that 'an *œuvre* like Goethe's, that is in a quite special sense and degree *Erlebnisdichtung*, the concentrated essence of actual personal experience, cannot be understood at all without reference to biographical reality, though indeed it cannot be understood from this alone.'[24] It is possible, he claims, from what we know of Charlotte's life, from her letters to others than Goethe and from what her friends tell us about her, to draw a portrait of her that is more convincing than any of the three main interpretations that have so far been advanced. The first, a parallel to the Kaulbach paintings of Weimar already mentioned and dating from the same nostalgic age, is the extreme of idealisation, derived from Goethe's letters and the two 'Charlotte' plays, *Iphigenie* and *Tasso*. Here she is the incarnation of all that is best in German womanhood, the 'edle Frau', a German Beatrice, who leads the morally immature young poet to the pure heights of Humanity. The second, by a natural reaction in an age of socialism and naturalism, sees her as the vain, shallow society lady, under-sexed and with merely pretensions to taste, who basks in his reflected glory and gives him nothing in return—though on this point there are two schools of thought. Serious Goethe scholars in this century usually take a middle line and represent her, to use Günther Müller's words, as

a delicate, charming woman, not in the first bloom of youth, decidedly a product of the age of sentiment, but a ready talker and socially most adroit. In her marriage with a robust country squire she had taken refuge in inwardness, had borne the death of four children with religious submission tinged with pietism and, however well she performed her social duties at court, her heart and soul were not in the life of this world but turned towards spiritual joys and consolations. She possessed the power of entering into other people's individuality, without giving up herself in the process.[25]

It is a psychologically acceptable thesis, Walter Hof admits, that Goethe, however conscious he might be of his indebtedness to Charlotte for her part in clearing up his youthful confusion of feeling, should feel the need, at the mature age of thirty-eight, of leading the life of a complete man of flesh and blood and so of 'shaking off the bonds of an anaemic spiritualism', to use Max Hecker's phrase. But can one truly speak of 'anaemic spiritualism' in either Goethe or Charlotte? The characters he created before the breach with her are surely more full-blooded than those in the later books of *Wilhelm Meisters Lehrjahre* and in the plays of the 'nineties? And Charlotte was in reality, he maintains, neither excessively etherial nor deeply religious. He quotes some evidence that she was not prim and prudish, that *naturalia*, for instance, were not for her *turpia*, and that she genuinely liked and felt she could live with Goethe's mother, when she met her in 1789, a hearty old hedonist with nothing etherial about her. Charlotte had been religiously brought up, of course, like everyone else in her family, but in maturity she showed no sign of Pietistic fervour, as far as we know, but was certainly tolerant and probably agnostically inclined. She was not a church-goer, except on her estate, for diplomatic reasons. She read Spinoza with Goethe and took down from his dictation, at the time of his controversy with Lavater and Jacobi about religion, in 1784 or 1785, the *Philosophical Study*[26] which is so clearly directed against the self-satisfaction of the orthodox, and the references to these matters in his letters to her are as outspoken as one would expect in letters to a correspondent who does not require to be spared. Charlotte hoped for a future life, as Goethe himself did, and in letters in her later years often speaks of looking up to the stars and longing for 'another planet', but this too was common form in her time, even amongst rationalists.

What Hof regards as central in Charlotte is the strength of her moral convictions and her directness in expressing them. She was spoken of by her friends as a strong and independent character, sometimes embarrassingly outspoken, but generally well-liked. She did not look on women as weak and inferior creatures and had nothing of the clinging or coquettish about her. Though she was considered excellent company, and sometimes, to judge by what Stolberg tells us (p. 81, above), was willing to fall in good-humouredly with rather extravagant ideas of Anna Amalia, for instance, whom she did not really like nearly so well as her much quieter daughter-in-law, her attitude was marked by moral dignity combined with outspoken frankness. The fullest description of her character, written by the shrewd Knebel in 1788 (18 April) in a letter to his sister, not long before the breach with Goethe, runs as follows:

Sincere right feeling, in one of a natural, serene disposition, not given to passion, aided by her own effort and the influence of the distinguished people she has known, which reinforced her native desire to learn, has made her into the kind of personality that is not likely to recur very readily in Germany. She is completely unpretentious and unaffected, straightforward, natural, open, not too serious and not too gay, not given to enthusiasm and yet capable of warm intellectual interest. Everything sensible and humane arouses her sympathy, she is well read and has a fine sense, and even some skill, in art.

A little later (11 October 1788) he adds: 'She is a rare good woman and really lives wholly in an attitude of clarity, which in her, with her sensitive, fine nature, takes the place of warmth. She lives really in the understanding and yet makes no claim to understanding.' About a year before this Schiller had conveyed very much the same impression of her to Körner (12 August 1787). He could quite understand Goethe's attachment to her, though he does not think she has ever been a beauty. 'Her features have a gentle seriousness and a quite peculiar openness. Good sense, feeling and sincerity belong to her nature.'

The resemblance between the Charlotte known to Knebel and Schiller and the Princess drawn in Goethe's *Tasso*, which did not appear until 1790, is striking, though in the play Goethe brings her before us in a moving human situation, and does not merely describe her. 'Tell me about this evening, for with the evening and morning clouds my soul hastens to you', we read in a letter from Goethe (24 April 1781), to which there are dozens of parallels, making it clear that every free evening belonged to Charlotte and that he associated the thought of her particularly with the sight of the morning and evening sky. The speech of the Princess to Leonore in Act III (ll. 1851 ff.) expresses exactly what must have been the feeling of Charlotte in the winter of 1788–9, when he was writing that act, with lines like these:

> Wie schön befriedigt fühlte sich der Wunsch,
> Mit ihm zu sein an jedem heitren Abend!
> Wie mehrte sich im Umgang das Verlangen,
> Sich mehr zu kennen, mehr sich zu verstehn!*

---

* How beautifully I felt my wishes satisfied to be with him on every clear evening! How our longing grew, the more we saw of each other, to know and understand each other better!

which remind us again of the picture of lovers looking together on the setting sun in *Der Bräutigam*, written at Dornburg a year after Charlotte's death. But quite apart from the numerous situations which recall experiences in their years together, the character and the thought of the Princess seem to be closely modelled on the Charlotte who meets us in her friends' descriptions and in the letters we have from her later years. 'From all this evidence we gain the impression of a quiet but strong nature of great openness and directness, trustworthiness and constancy, one clearly cool rather than passionate, sensible rather than sentimental, feeling things deeply but not lightly betraying her feelings, so that their intensity came as a surprise at decisive moments.'[27] The conception of the dreamy, sentimental, pious Charlotte comes entirely from a single letter of Zimmermann to Lavater, one man of feeling to another. Zimmermann had only met her taking the waters at Pyrmont in 1773 and the following year, but Knebel, when he described her, had known her well for fourteen years.

Walter Hof speaks of Charlotte's strong moral views, her view of love between superior people as involving for each partner the obligation 'to become continually better for the sake of the other', her insistence on lifelong loyalty, as 'an aristocratic ethic that had become second nature to her', but it was certainly not the ethic of the aristocracy in her own day, in Germany, France or England. The normal court view of sexual ethics, at least, was that of the male, as it is put, for instance, by Lord Chesterfield, who advised his son to adopt towards women an attitude of very carefully concealed contempt. 'Women are but children of a larger growth; they have an entertaining tattle and sometimes wit; but for solid, reasoning good-sense, I never in my life knew one that had it.... A man of sense only trifles with them, plays with them, humours and flatters them, as he does a sprightly, forward child; but he neither consults them about, nor trusts them with, serious matters.' In good society, it is necessary to please them, because of their great influence, and this can always be done by exploiting their love of flattery, praising their looks, if they are not too ugly, and their intelligence, if they are. Nothing could be further from this attitude than the tender solicitude and unselfish devotion expressed in every line of Goethe's letters and poems to Frau von Stein, a devotion which is for years rewarded only by her friendship and, until 1781, not even by the assurance of her own love for him. Immediately after he has sent on 14 April 1776 the first and greatest of his poems to her, 'Warum gabst du uns die tiefen Blicke', in which he says they see as clearly into each other's hearts as if she had been in an earlier existence his sister or his wife, we find him writing 'Adieu, dear sister, as it must be so', evidently in response to a reproof for using the word 'wife' so lightly, and a fortnight later we read: 'You are right to make me into a saint, that is, to keep me at a distance from your heart.' He is to show the genuineness of his love by renunciation, to become a saint of love.

This is of course only 'aristocratic' in being the closest approach to be found in a modern poet to the courtly love of the troubadours and the Minnesang, which was a secularisation, it would seem, though the point is disputed, of religious adoration for the Virgin, the transfer of this emotion to a mortal lady. It was in this way that a code of romantic love was first established in literature, though not in the forms of literature that closely reflected real life. Goethe himself, the author of *Werther*, was clearly prepared, as no one else in Germany was likely to be, to play his role, for that novel had revealed him as profoundly versed in the religion of love, in the modern form worked out by earlier eighteenth-century novelists, above all by Richardson and Rousseau. In England, where the passions were cooler than in the Latin countries, young women had since Elizabethan days been less closely shepherded before marriage than they were further south, and by the eighteenth century, though free choice of a partner was still exceptional, it had come to be favoured, especially among the middle class, by the rise of economic individualism.[28] The type of family life that we now regard as normal, what Durkheim calls the 'conjugal family', was at least common enough to make it a not impossible model for the novelist, writing now for a much larger public, including a high proportion of women. They liked to hear about a young man and woman who had married for love and established themselves in total independence of their parents, unconfined by the various ties and obligations of kinship that were so strong in the older, patriarchal kind of family, the kind that survived in the 'joint families' of the Russian peasantry, for instance, into the present century. It was delightful to hear of couples who had been able to follow their hearts as individuals, unhampered by differences of social class or religion or country, the three irrational factors that all the advanced groups, the Freemasons, for example, were trying to counteract.

The model family of the novelists, founded on romantic love, was not only happy, but virtuous, and here the ideas of Puritanism are important. Protestantism generally tended to idealise the state of marriage, and Puritanism in particular stressed the spiritual values in marriage, and still more the wickedness of sexual relations outside it. This attitude towards the strongest natural instinct can be traced back as far as St Paul, of course, the denial of the flesh in the interest of the spirit. The attachment of the highest value therefore to celibacy had been quite central in the Catholic ethic, and even in Protestantism, in spite of its rejection of celibacy for the priesthood, the mortification of the flesh inevitably remained the great test of spirituality and, following the usual pattern of secularisation, it became for many people an end in itself, quite apart from the idea of salvation. Changes in social attitudes concerning matters that have as many ramifications as these cannot be traced to any one source. The ever-growing refinement of manners was accompanied by the spread of humaner attitudes, the moderation of crude instinctive urges through feelings for others, imaginative sympathy, forces which had always been at work, we may surely presume, in happy marriages under any system. Why else do Hector and Andromache, for instance, become symbols of marital tenderness more moving than any biblical couple? In Richardson's day the age-old feeling of a small minority about the relations of man and woman, an application of the basic idea of Christianity, the respect for personality, had become sufficiently widespread, especially no doubt among women, to give his masterly presentation of it in living characters great popular appeal. The biological aspect of marriage is played down, the perfection of love is seen in friendship between man and wife, and nice girls are allowed so little expression of feeling towards their admirers, until they are safely married, that they may appear to us rather ambiguous characters.

The point of this excursus is to suggest that an important source of Charlotte's notions about love was her novel-reading, and possibly her reading of Klopstock, Gessner, and other German poets who expressed similar ideas about a spiritualised love of woman, but of this we have no direct evidence. Her correspondence with Zimmermann, before she met Goethe, is much concerned with *Werther*, reading which had depressed her for a whole week, because of its apparent claim of unlimited licence for 'große Geister', its rejection of any attempt to control powerful passions as a sign of Philistine timidity. When she expressed her wish to meet the author of this book Zimmermann warned her that he might be dangerous company. Before *Werther* she must have read *La nouvelle Héloïse*, where Richardson's influence is clear, and she had no doubt read something of Richardson himself. In Rousseau's novel her attention must certainly have been arrested by the question in which Julie gives classical expression to the new 'decarnalisation' of love, when she says to St Preux: 'Homme sensuel, ne sauras-tu jamais aimer?' (2nde partie, lettre 15).

In any case, it is certain that uncontrolled passion and violence annoyed her in men. That is why later she detested Napoleon, for instance, and at first she was shocked by the impulsive, wild ways of Goethe, genius though he might be. This was not merely her aristocratic ethic, the reaction of a former lady-in-waiting and the daughter of Hofmarschall von Schardt—a figure of fun in Weimar, at least in his old age. There was something of that in it, but something too perhaps of the Scottish reticence of her mother's family—her mother's maiden name was Irving, and her grandfather, Consistory Councillor Irving in Berlin, was connected with the Irvings of Drum in Aberdeenshire. In any case,

traditional aristocratic restraint forbade the too open expression
of emotion, between man and wife in public, for example, just as,
in Lord Chesterfield's *Letters to his Son*, laughter and swearing
are alike condemned as ungentlemanly. From what Goethe puts
into the mouth of Serlo in *Wilhelm Meisters Lehrjahre*, about the
manners of a gentleman, we see what Goethe learned in his first
years at Weimar, largely, no doubt, from Charlotte, who served
as what Chesterfield would have called his 'décrotteuse'. The
manners of a gentleman, Serlo says, are difficult to imitate because
they are mainly negative, and the result of long practice. A
gentleman does not strike dignified attitudes; he simply avoids
any suggestion of the vulgar. He never forgets himself, he is
never hurried or embarrassed or carried away by enthusiasm (as
Wilhelm is, for instance, before the Prince). By self-control he
has learnt never to betray his feelings. Even to wear court dress
as it should be worn, he must be careful how he moves and what
he touches, while giving himself the appearance of perfect ease.

Self-control, the all-importance of the inner life, and a certain
'ethical purism', as Barker Fairley calls it, these are the things
that Goethe learned from Frau von Stein. Fairley has well
analysed the expression we find in *Iphigenie* and *Tasso* of these,
for Goethe, new ideals, and it is not necessary to repeat what he
says. Summing up, he writes: 'Goethe, we discover, has no
secondary source of inspiration at this stage; the only constituent
poetry that comes from him in these years, or as the result of
these years, is what comes deviously by way of Charlotte, all
curbed and contained by her traditions and bearing, as it were,
her invisible signature.' Erich Trunz describes in a similar way
the impression we receive from the shorter poems of this period,
as well as from *Iphigenie*. 'The man, young, devoted to the things
of the mind, but still groping his way towards an understanding
of himself and the world, is brought nearer to the best that is
possible for him by the harmony, the perfection and understanding sympathy of the woman; the sick man, conscious of guilt, is
healed and purged—this is the Orestes theme. It is a quite special
form of love, which Goethe held at this time to be the one and

only kind possible for a modern man of thought and feeling.'[29] When Goethe had known Charlotte only a few months he published in the *Deutscher Merkur* the original version of *Jägers Abendlied*, in which the Jäger, Goethe on one of his innumerable shoots with the Duke, suddenly thinks of someone 'still and mild', who can only be Charlotte, and not Lili Schönemann, as used to be said. She may not be thinking of him at all, he muses, birds of passage as he no doubt is for her, a man 'who will never find calm or rest in all the world', but to whom thoughts of her, like the sight of the moon in the sky, bring peace and quiet of mind:

> Und, ach, mein schnell verrauschend Bild
> Stellt sich dir's nicht einmal?
>
> Des Menschen, der in aller Welt
> Nie findet Ruh noch Rast,
> Dem wie zu Hause so im Feld
> Sein Herze schwillt zur Last.
>
> Mir ist es, denk ich nur an dich,
> Als säh' den Mond ich an;
> Ein stiller Friede kommt auf mich,
> Weiß nicht, wie mir getan.*

It is the germ of the much-discussed *An den Mond*, another poem that the revision for the collected edition in 1788 or 1789 made more complex and less transparently autobiographical.

There is perhaps more continuity in one respect at least, however, between the 'Charlotte' period and what followed than Fairley allows, and that is in Goethe's pursuit of what he calls 'Bildung', the inward pursuit of perfection. It is never again so directly described in ethical terms as in the diary and some letters of these years before Italy, it is broadened and aestheticised, partly under the influence of Schiller, but the conception of the individual's responsibility for his own inner development, his duty to make and re-make himself, remains constant. We have mentioned

---

* And does my fleeting image, alas, not even appear to you? the image of one who in all the world will never find calm or rest, whose heart is full to bursting, at home or in the fields. I feel, whenever I think of you, as if I were gazing at the moon. Stillness and peace come over me, I know not how.

Charlotte's view, expressed in several later letters, that it was incumbent on cultivated lovers 'to become continually better' for each other's sake, to keep each other up to the mark, as we should now say. It was a common idea at that time, when we find mutual self-improvement as a conscious aim in friendships both between people of the same and of different sexes. A well-known example between men is the friendship between Schiller and Körner, as we shall find. Between man and woman, the most striking parallel to that between Goethe and Charlotte is to be found in the life of Princess Gallitzin, the centre, in the second half of her life, of a small Catholic group in Münster who dedicated themselves to the good life and to good works, in a way which in some respects resembles the pursuit of secular humanism in Weimar.

The Princess, a more distinguished person in her own right than Frau von Stein, cultivated a high-minded friendship with the Dutch civil servant and amateur of art and philosophy, Franz Hemsterhuis, and then with Franz von Fürstenberg, the statesman who ably administered the affairs of the small ecclesiastical state of Münster for the Archbishop of Cologne. Hemsterhuis was a good Greek scholar, a great admirer of Plato, who in his *Lettres sur les désirs* expressed ideas that are basically very similar to those we have found in Shaftesbury, in language that drew both on Plato and Newton. It was he who spoke of love, of man and of God, as 'an eternal approach' hindered by the body, and coined the phrase, beloved of Herder and the Romantics, about love seeking God, but never reaching Him in mortal life, 'like the hyperbola and its asymptote'. In Münster the Princess returned gradually to the beliefs in which she had been educated, and accompanied by her two distinguished friends, she visited Goethe in Weimar in 1785, before she was quite firm in the faith, having greatly admired his *Iphigenie*, lent to her in manuscript by Jacobi. Greatly struck by her intelligence and character, Goethe wrote soon after her return suggesting an exchange of letters, that he might open up his whole mind to her—a surprising proposal, in view of his still unbroken commitment to Frau von Stein, and one which perhaps indicates a certain cooling off even before Italy—but the Princess apparently feared the lure of his secularism too much to fall in with his suggestion, though sorely tempted. It was only after his return visit in 1792, described fully in *Die Kampagne in Frankreich*, that she exchanged some very interesting letters with him, from which it is clear that they had a great liking and respect for each other, in spite of their different religious beliefs. The Princess had come to look on her attempts at self-improvement as vanity, under the influence of her recovered belief, but also in a marked degree of the highly unconventional and unorthodox Protestant Hamann, of whom she saw a great deal in the last months of his life, and who was buried in her garden. She and her circle form a most instructive contrast to Goethe and Weimar, but the parallel at certain stages is also close.[30]

The mention of a possible cooling-off in Goethe's love for Frau von Stein needs to be supplemented by some reference, however brief, to the later history of this 'friendship of souls', which naturally had its all-too-human side. Since the first publication (by Schöll) of Goethe's letters to Frau von Stein, over a century ago (1848–51), this has been a favourite theme with German writers. Schöll, now permitted at last by the Stein family to publish the letters, and Charlotte's play *Dido*, took a very idealistic view of her in his annotations, but Lewes in 1855 was much more down to earth. For him Charlotte's conduct to Goethe 'was not straightforward in the beginning', for she led him on coquettishly, 'and ungenerous towards the close'. He clearly implies that she had been his mistress, and now 'she was five-and-forty to him, as to others'. These two views persist to this day, though those who choose to write about this subject, often women, tend to agree rather with Schöll.

It is hard for us now to imagine how Goethe appeared to his readers before the letters lifted the veil from his private life, and to read the letters rightly we must not forget, of course, that they *were* private, though it was known to the Weimar circle, as Schiller's letter to Körner (12 August 1787) quoted above makes clear, that there was a close, but according to all that Schiller heard, quite innocent friendship between Goethe and Charlotte von Stein. There is no evidence that he changed his opinion, though his own wife had been an intimate friend of Charlotte while Goethe was in Italy. Even Schiller's letter was not published until 1847, so when Victor Hehn wrote his remarkable lectures on Goethe's poetry in 1848, he did not know who 'Lida' was, and could only guess that she had 'belonged to the highest circles'. He saw clearly, however, that she 'helped to bring about the inner purification of the poet', that 'her influence, her love, contributed towards shaping the artist in him, making him wise and happy and strengthening the humane feeling about questions of conduct which attracts us in his whole being and character'.

That still remains the essence of the matter and is not questioned by anyone, but there is much difference of opinion about the exact nature of the relations between the lovers after the spring of 1781, when Charlotte evidently at least confessed her own love for Goethe, and varying interpretations are offered of Goethe's flight to Italy, and of the behaviour of both of them on his return. The more modern biographers tend to be very reticent about all this. Among the older books, that by Edmund Hoefer (*Goethe und Charlotte von Stein*, Stuttgart, 1878) argues persuasively that 'the pair lived from 1781 in a genuine marriage, though not under one roof'. Walter Hof seems to leave the question open. On 12 March 1781 Goethe certainly wrote to Charlotte: 'I can no longer write "Sie", just as for a long time I could not say "du"', and this is in keeping with a whole series of letters about this time which are prose poems of happy love with few parallels in any literature. Hoefer comments that the 'du' of the earliest letters of 1776, soon discontinued, had been in the easy familiar tone that the Sturm und Drang Goethe adopted with all his friends, but from 1781 it was 'the natural and necessary expression of the fullest assurance of love and heartfelt unity, such as husband and wife and members of a family use to each other', and Walter Hof finds these later letters true love-letters, compared with the earlier 'friendly letters of a man who thinks himself in love'. The lovers exchanged rings at this time, not plain wedding rings, of course, and Goethe evidently made a promise or vow never to leave Charlotte, and expressed the hope that they and young Fritz Stein, whom he took into his house about now, would spend all their lives together. The vow is mentioned bitterly later by Charlotte in a letter to Fritz and in her lamentable tragedy, written in 1794.

It is difficult, certainly, for us post-Freudians to believe that a woman would show signs, as Charlotte did after the breach, of a jealousy so uncontrollable, if her relations with the offending man had never been more than Platonic. If that was so, was not Goethe justified in asking, in the letter of 1 June 1789, 'Who is the loser through this relationship (with Christiane)? Who lays claim to the feelings I entertain for the poor creature? or the hours that I spend with her?' We are unpleasantly reminded, perhaps, of the egotism of an eighteenth-century gentleman like Boswell, who might have written in this tone to his Dutch friend Zélide, the 'metaphysician and mathematician', about one of those encounters he considered necessary 'for health'. But we recognise Iphigenie, alas, no longer in the woman whose behaviour Goethe describes as follows: 'If I was in the mood to talk, you silenced me, if I told you about what I had seen, you accused me of indifference, if I did anything for friends, of coldness and neglect. You watched every change in my features, found fault with my movements, my whole way of being, and made me constantly ill at ease. How could there be full trust and openness between us, when you deliberately indulged your temper and thrust me away?'

It is even more difficult, however, to imagine the woman who wrote the cool and sensible letters to Knebel, of which we have dozens, making secret rendezvous with Goethe in his garden-house, or getting the servants out of the way at home, yet never giving rise to the slightest gossip, in a small town that loved nothing better. For all through these letters, both before and after the breach with Goethe, the impression Charlotte makes is that of the 'rare good woman' and 'sensitive fine nature' that Knebel saw in her, and we seem forced to conclude after all that her anger resulted from her intense disappointment at the break-down of a most rare relationship, one that came more naturally to her, in whom we may well believe that all interest in physical intimacies had been lost in the duties of a loveless marriage, than in the still young man who was soon to write the *Roman Elegies*.

From Charlotte's letter to Knebel on 15 November 1789, after the bitter exchanges with Goethe of which Knebel knew nothing, we see that love remained for her something of which men were seldom capable. 'I do not doubt', she said, 'that Fritz will follow in time your good advice on how to fall in love. But as the unprejudiced friend of women that you are'—Knebel seemed a confirmed bachelor—'you should also write an essay to prove that our sex should never return men's love! My reason is, that men can never do more than "fall in love" (sich verlieben), for the word is a fitting expression of something that wastes itself, like *ver*spielen, *ver*schmausen and so on (to waste in gaming, in feasting), and not of something enduring like "love", the charac-teristic of *our* way of feeling.' This is Iphigenie again, or rather Tasso's Princess:

> Wenn's Männer gäbe, die ein weiblich Herz
> Zu schätzen wüßten, die erkennen möchten,
> Welch einen holden Schatz von Treu und Liebe
> Der Busen einer Frau bewahren kann. (II, 1)*

and the final version of *An den Mond* sounds like a lament of both partners for something that could not be maintained and yet, to their sorrow, never forgotten.

On any reading of the evidence, Goethe shows marks of the indecision and weakness that often accompany the artistic tem-perament, a refusal to face facts and a tendency to drift, but Charlotte was certainly very demanding after 1781, and it was she who was the more easily moved to jealousy. In the fine poem printed as *An Lida* in 1789 Goethe had originally written, in the version sent as a letter from Gotha in October 1781,

---

* If there were men who could rightly value a woman's heart, and see what a fair treasure of loyalty and love her bosom can hold secure.

Den einzigen, Lotte, welchen du lieben kannst,
Forderst du ganz für dich,*

and numerous other letters strike the same note. Why, we ask ourselves, did Charlotte not make a clean break with her husband, who had played no part in her life for many years, and after a divorce, which could easily have been obtained in Weimar, marry Goethe? It was perhaps her innate conservatism that prevented her, as Hof suggests, or perhaps, he says, she still felt that Goethe did not really want it, that he still wished, as Valéry puts it, 'to keep his future open'. Anyhow, alongside repeated assurances of devotion in the letters, there are many hints of disagreement, and it is clear that among Goethe's many motives for his flight to Italy his relationship with Charlotte was one. He refers to it later (to Karl August, 1 October 1788) as unnatural, whether because of the differences we have mentioned or, on the other interpretation, because he was not in the full sense Charlotte's lover. 'She was probably no more trying in her conduct towards Goethe', in Hof's view, 'and no more jealous than any woman who is deeply in love.' It was also merely human, Hof continues, 'if she would have liked to have him always by her side, whereas he felt that his love suffered through this monotony, and that a temporary parting would only give them more joy in each other on coming together again'.

In any case, the manner of his departure for Italy, without consulting her beforehand, and his extraordinary letter of 1 June 1789, culminating in the suggestion that, as he had always told her, she would be healthier and better-tempered if she abstained from coffee, are not easily defensible, any more than Charlotte's undignified and sometimes spiteful references to Goethe and Christiane after the breach, her total incomprehension of his writings and studies in Italy and the ineptitudes of her play *Dido*, in which Goethe appears as 'Ogon', a heartless and ridiculous Don Juan, in whose speeches actual phrases from the letters are parodied. Goethe's letter defending himself reflects only too clearly the sad deterioration in their feelings for each other, and it lasted many years, though they were finally reconciled. It was

* The only man, Lotte, whom you can love, you claim wholly for yourself.

evoked by a written outburst from Charlotte, left behind for him
a month earlier on her departure for Ems, when she had heard at
last through Fritz of Goethe's liaison with Christiane Vulpius,
which had begun on 13 July in the preceding year. It is possible,
Hof thinks, that Goethe would not have surrendered to a passing
impulse if Charlotte, in her anger at his presumed neglect of her
in going to Italy, had not at their first meeting on his return
shown more interest in her pet dog than in anything he tried to
tell her about his 'rebirth' in Italy, though later he was chivalrous
enough to say that he had always looked upon Christiane (his
'little Eroticon' at first) as his wife. Goethe had no doubt come
back from Italy with a pagan view of love. It fits in well with his
praise to Charlotte from there of 'people who are happy because
they are whole', with his learning to accept everything in life
and art as part of the natural world, the return to concreteness from
the transcendental on which Barker Fairley rightly insists so
strongly. But as he also says, while it is easy to dispose of the
new affair 'as part of the setting for the *Roman Elegies*, and so to
let it be seen for the time being in an idealised light, there can be
no doubt that it was not long before Goethe found it embarrassing', and that Karl August was not far wrong when he declared,
late in life, that Christiane 'had alienated Goethe from society and
spoilt everything'. We shall find Goethe's own considered view
of the two kinds of love in the *Tabulae votivae* (see pp. 343 f.).
Finally, years after Christiane's death, advising a young schoolmaster about marriage, he wrote: 'All the evils we endure, living
within the law, do not make up a thousandth part of those we
must contend with if we proceed outside and alongside the law,
or perhaps in contravention of law and custom, feeling within us
all the time the need to remain in harmony with the moral order
of the world' (7 November 1821).

3. GOETHE'S INNER LIFE

Before examining Herder's thought at the time when he was in
almost daily consultation with Goethe about his *Ideen*, which is
much concerned both with Bildung (cultivation) and Kultur

(civilisation) in the search for the roots of 'Humanität', let us look at some typical passages dealing with self-improvement in Goethe's diary and letters in the years just preceding his renewed intimacy with Herder. The diary extends, with gaps, from March 1776 to June 1782, but the passages we are concerned with occur only in the middle portion, roughly between November 1777 and May 1780, beginning just before the *Harzreise im Winter* and the visit to the hypochondriac Plessing, that was followed in January 1778 by the shock of the suicide of Christel Lassberg in the Ilm near the Gartenhaus, reflected, according to some interpretations, in Goethe's poem *An den Mond*. Before and after these dates the entries are almost all very brief records of external events, at first a succession of social engagements and short journeys, and in the last years official conferences and engagements. This diary, fortunately preserved when so many of his private papers were destroyed by Goethe, is as we have already seen the source of much of our knowledge of his early years in Weimar.

The first of the meditative soliloquies is written on a piece of paper stuck into the diary and reminds us of the poem *To Fate*, of August 1776, already quoted (p. 78). Fate has transformed his outer life as if he were a character in a fairy-tale. 'Let me now, fresh and alert, enjoy clarity (Reinheit)', he prays, and he continues: 'The first rays of the sun, on 14 November (1777), signal Yes and Amen.' The usual alternation of depression and elation is recorded on the Harz journey that follows, both in the diary and in diary letters to Charlotte. He envies the uncomplicated minds of the working people he meets on his journey, and still records days when 'Reinheit' was achieved. In February 1778, after open-air days skating, he is in a confident mood 'of almost too great clarity'. It is just after the production of *Der Triumph der Empfindsamkeit*, and he feels that he sees his own position and conditions in Weimar more clearly, even adding: 'Calm, and anticipation of wisdom. Continued pleasure in good management, saving, avoiding debts. Welcome calm in my domestic affairs compared with last year. More definite feeling of limitation and thereby of true expansion.' In April he is 'vegetating, calm and clear', enjoying himself in his garden and superintending the improvements in the park, but is still visited by 'a thousand thoughts about our affairs and our fate'. He records the Duke's restlessness, and their fears of a possible war, but after that there is nothing of note until he speaks of a discussion with the Duke on 14 December and the difference in their views about the maintenance of law and order. He seems to show here increasing realism, considering it a waste of time to try to correct defects in men and circumstances that are past correction. Next day Knebel, in a talk with him, tells him how his situation appears to outsiders. Goethe is not looking forward to his work on the Military Commission, but encourages himself with the thought that calm and straightforwardness will see him through. This new. commitment is much on his mind in January 1779, too, and now he mentions for the first time a 'plan for this year' that he has drawn up, after tidying old papers on 2 January. The Military Commission is evidently very tedious, but official work, he notes, is good for his peace of mind. 'There is nothing more wretched than the state of a man living in comfort without work, he loses his taste for the fairest gifts of life.' Text-books and history are both equally useless to the man of action, and what presumption it is to pray for wisdom! The Gods have denied this to man, once and for all, giving him at best cunning to protect himself, as a cat has its claws. Then, on a lower plane, he notes how much better he is for watering down his wine ('drinking half wine'), the most beneficial change in his habits since he left off drinking coffee, which he did apparently a year or two earlier.

Complaints about his difficulties with the Duke recur in February, but on the fourteenth, after the note 'Began to dictate *Iphigenie*', he writes: 'In recent weeks I have mostly been trying to keep on top of my affairs, and to be firm and calm whatever happens.' Merck's visit in July is another occasion for a review of his position. 'The only man who fully understands' what Goethe is doing, and how, gives him renewed courage. His chief trouble is that all the men around him, except the Duke, are incapable of growing, 'like wooden dolls, finished except perhaps for a lick of paint'. Next day (14 July) he reflects again on the ease with which practical men who know their job, like Batty, take the right course of action, and how difficult it is for him. On 15 July, after a fire at Apolda, similar thoughts come again. 'Human misery is coming to be as familiar to me as the fire in the grate. But I will not give up my ideas and will wrestle (like Jacob) with the unknown angel, even if he put my thigh out of joint. No one knows what I am doing and with how many enemies I am contending, to accomplish so little. As I struggle and fight and labour I beseech you not to laugh, you gods who look on. Smile at most, and help me!'

The most revealing passage of all is the entry for 7 August 1779, when his thirtieth birthday is approaching and he is soon to set out with the Duke on the journey to Switzerland. He goes through his papers, burns a mass of old letters, and looking back on his life, is struck by

youth's confusion, restless energy and thirst for knowledge, groping in all directions for satisfaction. How I delighted in mysteries, obscure, purely imaginary situations. What a dabbler I was in scholarship, soon letting things drop. The sort of self-satisfied modesty in everything I wrote then. My vacillation and lack of direction in things human and divine. How little has been accomplished, how little adequate thinking and writing, how many days have gone in emotion and shadow-passion that was a waste of time, how little of it has been of any good to me, so that, with half my life over, I seem to have got nowhere, but stand there, like a man just saved from drowning, who feels the welcome sun beginning to dry him. The time I have spent in the busy world, since October 75, I don't yet care to sum up. God help us on and give us light, that we may less often stand in our own way, make us to do what is needful from morning till night and give us clear perception of the consequences of things, so that we may not be like people who complain all day of headache and take medicine for it, and every evening drink too much wine. May the idea of clarity (des Reinen) extend even to each morsel that I put into my mouth, and become brighter in me every day.

These are prosaic reflections for the author of *Iphigenie*, especially if we compare them with, say, *Hälfte des Lebens*, but how much more promise they hold out for the future than poor

Hölderlin's tragic poem! Goethe is evidently not quite comfortable in talking about himself in this direct way, and he does
it seldom. A little later, speaking about his state of mind on being
made a Geheimer Rat, he writes (6 September) that it is not
fitting to put down these personal feelings on paper for oneself,
and in general this diary, like his later ones, looks outwards
rather than within. But there are one or two more introspective
passages before the diaries cease. In January 1780 Goethe is busy
picking up the threads again after the Swiss journey, and there is
no mention of another stocktaking, but by the end of February
things are going smoothly again and he makes a remark that is
important for his general way of thinking: 'I see in this too that
I have been wasting effort in trying to learn the whole by starting
with the details; I have always only been able to work my way
out into the details from a general conception of the whole.'
Finally, on 13 May, realising that even more is likely to be
demanded of him in Weimar, he writes:

I am training myself and making all preparations. In my present circle
there is hardly anything to hinder me outside myself. Within me there
is much. Human weaknesses are truly tapeworms: you may tear a bit
off, but the main trunk always remains. But I will be master! Only one
who entirely denies himself deserves to rule, and can rule. . . .[31] I am
coming gradually to have a feeling of general confidence, and God grant
that I may gain it, not in the easy way, but in the way I wish. What a
burden I bear in myself and others no one can see. The best thing is the
quietness, protected from the world, in which I live and grow, winning
for myself what they cannot take from me with fire or with sword.

It was on 6 September of this year, in the wooden hut on the
Kickelhahn above Ilmenau, a favourite retreat, that he wrote *Über
allen Gipfeln ist Ruh*. On a single day in March in the previous
year, he had written the whole of the fourth act of *Iphigenie* near
here, on the Schwalbenstein.

When the diary fails us, there is much to be learnt from Goethe's
letters, especially those to Lavater and Jacobi, with whom he
discussed religious questions. The diary had shown him aiming
at self-mastery chiefly in relation to his official duties. In the

letters the emphasis is on the ethical, and several passages outline a
kind of secular humanism similar to that conveyed by the poem
Das Göttliche. Goethe had joined the Weimar Freemasons' Lodge
early in 1780, for social reasons, according to the letter he wrote
then to Fritsch, the Grand Master of the Lodge 'Amalia', and
though he soon found the rites tedious, he was fully in sympathy
with the humanitarian aims of the society, as they had recently
been formulated for instance by Lessing in *Ernst und Falk*. The
lodge was closed down in 1783, and only reopened in 1808, as a
means of resisting Napoleon, when Goethe joined it again for a
few years. When his son was admitted in 1815, he wrote the fine
poem *Symbolum*, beloved of Carlyle, using Masonic symbolism
to convey his own view of life. The well-known letter to Lavater,
in September 1780, indicates how seriously he now thought about
a man's duty towards himself.

The daily task that is assigned to me, [he says] that becomes easier and
harder for me every day, demands my attention waking and dreaming.
This duty becomes dearer to me daily, and in this I should like to prove
the equal of the greatest men, and in nothing greater. This desire, to
raise the pyramid of my existence, the base of which is given and
founded for me, as high as possible into the air, outweighs everything
else and hardly allows of a moment's forgetfulness. I have no time to
lose, I am already well on in life, and fate may break me off in the
middle, and the Babylonian tower will remain blunt and unfinished.
At least they shall say: it was boldly planned, and if I live, I hope with
God's help to have strength to finish it.

And he goes on: 'Besides, the talisman of that rare love, with
which Frau von Stein gives savour to my life, is of great
help. She has gradually taken the place of my mother, sister
and sweethearts, and a bond has been woven like the bonds of
nature.'

In 1781 and 1782 there follow the deeply serious letters already
referred to, directed against Lavater's 'exclusive intolerance'.
Goethe appeals to the authority of 'the aristocracy established by
God, as I see it . . . whom we worship as sons of God in ourselves
and all his children'. He had not changed his views since his first

outspoken letter to Lavater and Pfenninger (26 April 1774), when
he had included in the list of these 'aristocrats' Moses, the prophets, evangelists, apostles, Spinoza and Machiavelli. The name
of Spinoza is mentioned repeatedly, especially in 1784 and 1785.
In November 1782 he told Knebel he was arranging all his papers
and correspondence for the last ten years and trying to see this
whole period as one looks down from a hill on the valley through
which one has walked. He was seeing no one, except on business,
apart from those who came to his weekly 'at home', Frau von
Stein in the evenings, and the Dowager Duchess occasionally.
The Duke, he said, 'lived now for riding and shooting'. 'And so
I am beginnning', he went on, 'to live for myself and to recognise
myself again.' He had lost his illusions about transforming
Weimar, in accordance with his ideals and those of his friends,
'giving those heavenly jewels a setting in the crowns of these
princes', and he is the happier for it. The Geheime Rat in him
and his other self lead separate existences, though at the very
centre of him the threads of his social, political, moral and poetical
life are tied in a hidden knot. He tells Knebel, now living in
Ansbach, of the various interests described above, and says 'the
whole of natural history surrounds me like Bacon's great Solomon's Hall (in the *New Atlantis*), about which Herder and
Nicolai are disputing'.[32] This is evidently quite a different Goethe
from the careless young genius of 1775, one given now to lonely
brooding over himself and the world. A week before this he had
written to Jacobi, with whom he had lost touch for some years
because of his disrespectful reception of *Woldemar*, and told him
how glad he was again to have his confidence, for he had lived
through difficult years.

If you see a glowing mass of iron from the furnace, you do not think
there is so much slag in it as comes to light when it has been under the
great hammer. Then the impurities come away that the fire itself had
not removed, and run and fly out in glowing drops and sparks, leaving
the clean ore in the workman's tongs. It seems as if this mighty hammer
was needed to free my nature of all its slag and make my heart clean.
And yet, how many defects manage to hide in it still.

Looking back, he felt that he 'understood himself and what he ought to do less than ever', a note to Charlotte on this same 17 November says. Before despatching the Jacobi letter, he sent it to her too, as the keeper of his conscience.

In passages like these we see Goethe as he sees himself in graver moments, the thoughtful young man he draws in *Ilmenau*, the stranger, held fast by friendship, who doubts whether his influence has been good:

> Ich brachte reines Feuer vom Altar;
> Was ich entzündet, ist nicht reine Flamme.*

There is no sudden change of tone between letters such as we have quoted and the letters Goethe wrote home from Italy. His development in character, as in knowledge, was continuous, and from the early 'eighties conscious effort in accordance with a clearly conceived ideal plays a very important part. The ideal is the 'reine Menschlichkeit' implied already in the prose *Iphigenie*. It is a view of human nature that is fully aware, on the one hand, of the dark passions, lust for power, jealousy, a cruelty unmoved by consideration for even the closest kinship, and on the other, of human sympathy and unselfish love, capable of rising to the heights of saintliness, if it has had time to develop, in a tradition handed on for generations in a cult. The closer men approach to this ideal, the more truly human they are, so that it can be described as 'pure' humanity, human feeling freed from its 'slag'. The purification is effected in gifted individuals by experience of life, though before great advances can be made, successive separate intuitions pointing in the same direction must accumulate, by being handed on in words or symbols of some kind, to form the basis of a civilisation. Then apparent miracles are possible, like Iphigenie's successful appeal to King Thoas, for those who possess this insight have an increased trust in life and in their fellows, which they can communicate to others by a kind of infection. To the end of his life Goethe believed that God 'is

* I brought pure fire from the altar; what I have kindled is not pure flame.

continually active in higher natures, to lead on those with lesser powers'. These are the last words of Goethe quoted by Ecker-mann in the third part of his *Conversations*. He could not conceive God as a Being apart from the world, responsible only for its first creation and for pushing it round, as it were, from outside. He had not been idle since the six days of creation but had revealed Himself repeatedly, not only in prophets and teachers, but in artists and scholars too, as well as in His own works in nature, as Goethe was never tired of saying. This is a mythical way of expressing a kind of humanism which, while rejecting the idea of a special revelation and making use poetically of many different mythologies at different times, was yet not guilty of spiritual pride. Goethe could not think of the work of even a Mozart, a Raphael or a Shakespeare, to quote the last Eckermann con-versation again, as 'completely of this earth, and nothing more than a product of purely human forces'. Creation was going on continually, both in nature and in man, and there was a mystery about it which, though it could be dispelled in part by study, always retained something which we must be content to regard 'with quiet reverence'.

If Goethe had written the religious epic which he planned in the summer of 1784, in response, it would seem, to suggestions from Herder or Charlotte von Stein, to whom he sent the beginning of the 'promised' poem on 8 August, we should have a more direct reflection of the religious humanism towards which Goethe was feeling his way in those years before the Italian journey than either in *Iphigenie* or in *Wilhelm Meister*. That he attempted it at all shows that he was concerned, as Herder was, about the effects on society of the waning of the old faith. The poem *Zueignung* was written as the invocation of the muse, traditional in the great epics, and in it we see the poet persuaded to share with others his view of religious truth, even if it is in advance of his time, and not, now that he had shed some of his youthful illusions, to 'bury his talent' and 'live for himself', as we have found him wishing to do two years before this (p. 177). In this year he was, as his letters show, in close touch with other friends besides Herder whose interests were above all in religion, with Lavater and Jacobi, for example, defending his views to them and discussing Hamann, Hemsterhuis and above all Spinoza, whom he was reading with Herder and Frau von Stein, at the same time as he was pursuing eagerly his scientific hobbies, osteology, geology and botany, and delighting Herder with specimens of the 'harmonies of nature', while Herder was writing the Second Part of his *Ideen*. Goethe soon found that he had taken on an impossibly difficult task. It was, in effect, to express in poetry 'the lasting meaning that lies in all religious doctrine from the beginning till now', to use George Eliot's words. The winter produced nothing, and in the next spring, even when he tried to 'command poetry' and write two stanzas a day in a calendar, a procedure which shows how different this poem was from most of his work, a task imposed from without, in fact, he found himself unable to continue. Forty-four stanzas were published as a fragment in 1789, and the *Dedication* was used first for the Göschen edition of the collected works, and later for the poems alone.

The Mysteries had always been intended as an esoteric work for a few friends like Herder and Charlotte von Stein, and the ordinary reader could make little of it. Goethe wrote a valuable note on his intentions, however, in response to an appeal from some Königsberg students in 1816. There has been much discussion about details, especially the use possibly made by Goethe of seventeenth-century writings about a certain Christian Rosenkreuz, and an order he is supposed to have founded, like the secret societies Goethe knew in his own day, the Freemasons, Illuminati, etc., which had an astonishing vogue because they met a real need of the time.[33] The first thing that a modern reader notices in the fragment is a certain resemblance to the story of *Parzival*, of which Myller's edition had indeed appeared early in 1784, but can hardly have been known to Goethe, who never mentions the epic anywhere. It has been suggested, however, that Wieland, who read Wolfram and wrote an *Essay on Parzival* while in Zürich, may have been reminded of its theme by hearing

of Myller's edition, and discussed it with Goethe.[34] The aim of
Goethe's poem is quite clear without any commentary, from the
fragment and his summary of 1816. Using the familiar symbols
of Freemasonry and so on, he meant to suggest essentially the
same convictions about the emergence of 'Humanität' as was
voiced by Herder in the works we are about to discuss, the idea
that 'God does not exercise influence on earth except through
chosen outstanding men',[35] the idea to which Goethe held fast, as
we have seen, until the end of his life. Here then is part of his
synopsis:

I may assume that the reader is familiar with the poem itself, but I will
just mention this. It will be remembered that a young member of a
sacred order, lost in a mountainous region, at last comes upon a
splendid building in a pleasant valley that seems to be inhabited by
mysterious pious men. He finds there twelve knights who, after leading
adventurous lives, full of toil, suffering and danger, have at last undertaken to live here and serve God in quiet retirement. A thirteenth,
whom they recognise as their Superior, is just about to leave them, we
are not told how. But he had begun in the last days to tell the story of
his life, and the newly arrived spiritual brother is well received and
briefly informed of this story.

And now to communicate my further intentions and the general
plan, and so the aim of the poem, I will reveal that the reader was to
be led through a kind of imaginary Montserrat, and after passing
through the various regions of mountain, rock and crag was presently
to reach broad and happy plains. Each of these knights and monks
would have been visited in his dwelling-place and it would have been
clear from observing the climatic and national differences that men of
the highest excellence from all ends of the earth come together here,
where each of them worships God in retirement in his own special
way.

Going the rounds with Brother Mark the reader would have remarked that it was intended to illustrate the very different ways of
thinking and feeling that develop or are impressed upon man through
atmosphere, region, race, needs and habits, in these chosen individuals
in the one place, and to show how, though separately imperfect, they
strive in their communal life for perfection. To make this possible,
they have gathered round a man who bears the name Humanus, a
course upon which they would not have embarked unless they all felt a

similarity and an attraction to him in themselves. Unexpectedly this mediator is now about to depart from them, and as much overwhelmed as edified, they hear the history of his past experiences. It is not narrated by him, however, but each of the twelve, with all of whom he has come into contact in the course of time, can give news and information about one part of this great life.

Here now it would have been discovered that every particular religion has experienced a moment of highest excellence of blossom and fruit, when it approached that supreme leader and mediator, and even became completely united with him. These epochs were to appear embodied and perpetuated in those twelve representatives, so that every kind of homage paid to God and virtue, however strange the forms it might assume, would have been found worthy of all honour and love. And now, after a long sojourn together, Humanus could well depart from them, because his spirit had become embodied in them all, was shared by them all and needed no longer to be clothed in an individual earthly form. . . .

If the whole of this action takes place in Holy Week, and if the chief symbol of this society is a cross entwined with roses, it will easily be realised that the eternal continuance of the enhancement of the human lot of which Easter gives assurance would have been revealed for our consolation at the departure of Humanus also.

It is in *Die Geheimnisse* that the often-quoted lines about renunciation occur, introducing the picture of the willingly accepted asceticism of the youth of Humanus, a vision of saintly self-forgetfulness in a man, exceeding even that of Iphigenie, and even more clearly opposed to the defiant attitudes of Faust and Prometheus:

> Von der Gewalt, die alle Wesen bindet
> Befreit der Mensch sich, der sich überwindet.*

The 'Entsagung' of Goethe's later years is a different matter, not one of overcoming one's desires, but of canalising them. It is no accident that the portrait of Humanus remained unfinished, for the kind of ethical feeling embodied in it was, it would seem, not wholly Goethe's own, but in large part a reflection of that of

---

* The man who overcomes himself is delivered from the force that binds all creatures.

Frau von Stein, whose toleration came far more than did his from the wish to hold on to an old-established order. His, on the other hand, was fundamentally aesthetic, akin to Herder's acceptance as valuable of every way of life that 'had its centre of happiness within itself'.

CHAPTER IV

WEIMAR THEORIES OF CULTURE

I. HERDER

WEIMAR Humanism (Humanität) or Classicism, the temper of the mature works of Herder, Goethe and Schiller, was a plant of slow growth. Even as far as Goethe is concerned, it was not wholly the result of the journey to Italy. The acceptance of the Greeks as the perfection of human development goes back, as we have seen, at least as far as Shaftesbury. It is his view already that the training of the modern 'virtuoso' should be in the hands of a philosopher, not a theologian, and that 'the taste of beauty and the relish of what is decent, just and amiable' should be gradually formed in the pupil by the presentation to him of 'right models', with which before him he may become the 'architect of his own life and fortune'. The supreme model is the 'kalos kai agathos' of the Greeks. We have seen how much Wieland's educational philosophy owed to Shaftesbury and how frequently he chose a Greek setting for his novels and 'Singspiele', though his interpretation of Greek life and thought combined with the notion of 'man as his own second creator' a great deal that is pure rococo. To the young Goethe a work like *Alceste* had seemed to trivialise the Greeks, although it was a one-sidedly Sturm und Drang point of view from which he criticised Wieland, when he claimed, for instance, that the young Admetus in Euripides, with whose conduct Wieland found himself unable to sympathise, was perfectly justified in wanting to live for ever. It is true, Goethe says, that he knew Alcestis was to die for him, and never thought of refusing her sacrifice, but he was a king, and young and happy, and his conduct was quite natural. The abstract notions of human dignity that Goethe ridicules in his skit against Wieland were something for which he only gained an understanding himself

7   HERDER

later, in Weimar when, as we have just seen, he conceived his Humanus in an attitude entirely opposed to that of the naïvely selfish Admetus.

The first to open Goethe's eyes to the greatness of the Greeks had been Herder, the first man of outstanding intellectual powers and real originality as a critic whom he had met. It was through him that Goethe began to read Homer in the original, having till then known little about the Greeks, and now, as Herder says, 'all (Greek) heroes became for him so many handsome storks, wading long-legged and free'. Inspired himself by Lowth's appreciation of the poetry of the Old Testament, by Winckelmann and Lessing and Hamann in their approach to literature, language and art, by Bishop Percy on the folk-ballad, and so on, Herder made Goethe aware of the limitations of the rococo conception of the Greeks and of literature in general. Most important of all was his master-idea of the uniqueness of the human personality, always different and always interacting with a changing environment, so that even Homer, though the greatest Greek poet, was not a norm for other ages. But in him, as in Shakespeare, or the Hebrew prophets, there was a poetic quality which Herder also found in folk-songs of all nations, because 'the gift of poetry was one granted to certain people in all nations everywhere, and not the prerogative of a few elegant men of cultivation', as Goethe sums up his message in *Dichtung und Wahrheit*. This is the essence of the Sturm und Drang view of poetry. A singer must have a natural voice, which no amount of training can supply. In their insistence on the natural gift required for writing, as for any great accomplishment, the 'Natural Geniuses' tended to neglect technique and tradition, everything which hindered free self-expression, and to sacrifice everything to the effect of spontaneity, but Goethe had been writing verse too long to fall into that error in practice, though in theory he spoke much of 'creative power' and 'inner urge' and so on, because so much of his best work seemed to be a product of his unconscious mind. It was a mind trained however by long practice and by the habit of self-criticism. In the letter to Herder from Wetzlar in

July 1772, in which Goethe says the Greeks are now his sole study, though he finds in Pindar authority for thinking that 'he in whom the head is everything is a wretched man', he also finds in him the idea of mastery, and he describes the charioteer driving four fresh horses as the very image of it. Herder had above all pricked the bubble of his boyish self-conceit and given him new standards of excellence.

Goethe at twenty-one in Strassburg had borne with admirable good-humour Herder's perpetual fault-finding and sarcasm, for a difference of five years in age counted for a great deal at that stage and every hour with Herder taught him something new about literature and life. He must have realised even then that the older man's prickliness was not entirely due to the pain caused by his eye-operation, but came partly from inner conflicts. His fierce rejection of French rococo art and poetry, with all their grace and elegance, reflected in part the resentment against everything that pertained to the aristocracy felt by one who saw himself as one of the under-privileged. Yet the poor schoolmaster's son from Mohrungen in East Prussia had not received such bad treatment from his patrons. Winckelmann, Heyne, Fichte and many another poor boy who rose out of his own class through intellectual ability—for the number who did so was surprisingly large—suffered at least as much without becoming permanently soured. But Herder's mental conflict had another source as well. His nerves had not stood the strain of the study of medicine, for which his first patron, a Russian military doctor had taken him to Königsberg, and he had naturally transferred himself to the poor man's faculty, theology, towards which his Pietistic upbringing had given him a leaning. But the philosophical and literary studies which he eagerly pursued at the same time aroused in him doubts about the intellectual and historical foundations of Christian belief, so that when he wrote to Kant, for instance, from Riga, on being congratulated by his former teacher on his first publication, the *Fragments*, he said that he had entered the Church simply because he knew that, as society was constituted in Germany, he would in this way be in the best position to promote the spread of cultivation and common sense among ordinary people, and he mentioned Shaftesbury, the Deist, as his principal model. In the sermons he preached as Assistant at the two churches in the suburbs of Riga, combining this occasional duty with his main task as a master at the Domschule, he had great success, as he tells Kant, with 'the most receptive part of the public, ladies and younger men'. He interpreted the doctrine of salvation in a purely ethical way and revelation as involving human agency only. Jesus was for him a man, influenced by the current ideas of his time, and prayer was a means of improving the character and directing the mind towards nobler thoughts. An enthusiastic moralism was in fact the heart of his religion.[1]

Herder was still under twenty-five when he left Riga on a sudden impulse, ill at ease and inwardly unsure in spite of a greater public success than he was ever to enjoy again. His private diary, begun on his two months' sea voyage to Nantes, and finished on his arrival, reveals him brooding over his past life and making ambitious plans for his future literary work and practical activities in the field of education. He had hopes of becoming headmaster of the Lyzeum, the grammar school at Riga, and from this centre reforming the educational system of the backward province of Livonia. He would try to understand man and human conduct, psychologically and scientifically, he would look for evidence in the history of all times, and he would apply this knowledge to the improvement of the present age, which contained the germs of a development just as promising as that of any of the famous civilisations of the past. His later career gave evidence at every stage of a similar combination of scholarly and practical ambitions, of self-questioning introspection and confident didacticism.

A short stay in France, a leisurely journey through north Germany, leading to meetings with Lessing and other writers, before taking up a tutorship he had accepted in the hope of further travels, and a few months in this post took up the next year. The large party accompanying the son of the Prince-Bishop of Lübeck, Herder's princely pupil, on his grand tour had now reached

Strassburg, after long halts in interesting German towns, including Darmstadt, where Herder met his future wife, in the sentimental circle well known to Goethe soon afterwards. In Strassburg Herder asked to be released from his tutorship, mainly in order to undergo an operation by a good surgeon there. Goethe's first meeting with him followed, in the circumstances so vividly recorded in the tenth book of *Dichtung und Wahrheit*. Goethe describes this chance acquaintanceship with Herder as the most important thing that happened to him in Strassburg, a turning-point in his life. Herder seemed to release new powers in him with his conception of poetic genius, Shaftesbury's notion of the poet as a creator, 'a second Prometheus', deepened by Hamann's mystical teaching, 'that language is God made manifest in the Word, the Word communicated ever anew, on the one hand in nature and man's efforts to understand her throughout history, and on the other in the commentary to all things provided by the Bible'.[2] Goethe had a foretaste in these few weeks of everything that Herder gradually elaborated later in his writings, he says, all Herder's seminal ideas were handed on to him, linking up with his own rich but unsystematic thought about literature and life.

The essence of it all we may call secular humanism, the belief in the positive creative power of man in a civilised society, where the insight of gifted individuals has been preserved and handed on in symbolic form. In spite of many differences that developed between Goethe and Herder later, this belief held them together and made a most fruitful co-operation possible while Herder was writing his central work, the *Ideen*, and it is this belief which Goethe once more expressed to Eckermann, as we have seen, almost on his deathbed. It comes out clearly already in Herder's Shakespeare essay in *Von deutscher Art und Kunst* (1773), many leading ideas of which are already to be found in Goethe's *Zum Schäkespears Tag* (1771), proving that Herder had discussed them with him in Strassburg. For Herder, as Gillies says,

Shakespearian drama is fundamentally an interpretation of the world. .... When Herder states, therefore, that he loses all idea of theatre and wings and actors when reading Shakespeare ... he merely means this, that his attention is monopolised by the manifestation of the world-process with which he is presented—the 'Blätter aus dem Buch der Begebenheiten, der Vorsehung, der Welt'. It is thus clear why Shakespeare, with Homer and Ossian, is linked with Moses, Mahomet and Prometheus in Herder's mind. Creative genius is not exclusively poetical.

In the thirteen years that elapsed between the conversations in the darkened room in Strassburg and the beginning of the ten years of renewed intimacy that followed Goethe's invitation to the Herders, on 28 August 1783, to celebrate with him his own birthday and that of their nine-year-old son Gottfried, Goethe's brilliant gifts as a writer had won for him fame and a position of some distinction, and Herder, after five disappointing years as court preacher to the Count of Schaumburg-Lippe at Bückeburg, had been persuaded, in spite of offers from the University of Göttingen, to join Goethe in Weimar, early in 1776, as the head of the clergy in the state. Both in Bückeburg and in Weimar, what had chiefly recommended him to the ruler who had appointed him had been his open-mindedness and his literary distinction, but in both places, the clergy and consistory court had for the most part proved to have much more orthodox views than his. Ever since his boyhood reading of Arndt's *Vom wahren Christentum* Herder had been accustomed to look upon his own intuitive individual interpretation of God's word as the ultimate appeal in religion. Faust 'translating' St John, and telling him, in effect, what he must have meant, in accordance with the promptings, at that moment, of his own deepest feeling, has more than once reminded Herder scholars of Herder's attitude to religious authority, though it might perhaps equally well be applied to Luther himself as a translator, or to scores of later German theologians. For a year or two in Bückeburg, where the fragile, Pietistic Countess so much needed his ministrations, he seems to have been more than usually devout, and he certainly tried hard to avoid any appearance of unorthodoxy in the *Erläuterungen zum Neuen Testament*, begun in 1773, when he had heard there were prospects of a professorship being offered to him in Göttingen. Yet even here he shows himself to share the central conviction of the Enlightenment, that man is good, not the slave of original sin, and this in spite of the attack in the *An Prediger, 15 Provinzialblätter*, written at the same time, on the leading rationalist theologian, J. J. Spalding, the translator of Shaftesbury, and one whom he had singled out for praise in his first essays for the humanity of his preaching.

In its commentary on the doctrine of salvation, Professor R. T. Clark points out, the *Erläuterungen* puts forward something very like the point of view of the Freemasons—Herder had belonged to the brotherhood since 1766—one similar in its relativity to that of Lessing later, in his *Nathan der Weise*. There is no mention of vicarious redemption. Clark concludes, in fact, that Hermann Hettner is right (in spite of Rudolf Haym's caveat) is asserting that at Bückeburg 'he subjected his bold and free thoughts to deceptive coverings and obscurations, of which he was guilty many times throughout his life in the tormenting conflict between his office and his convictions', and he continues: 'Hettner's thesis explains much that cannot otherwise be explained, and although Herder was at no time an atheist or agnostic, he was likewise at no time after 1764 a believer in the majority of the doctrines of his own church or any other.'[3]

Hettner quotes from a draft of 1768, when Herder was already pursuing the studies into the history of religion which led to his famous but obscure *Älteste Urkunde des Menschengeschlechts* (1773, 1776), a passage which illustrates well his position between the orthodox, whose religious emotions he shared, and the Rationalists, whose historical criticism he accepted, if it stood up to his severe tests. He was convinced, like George Eliot later, that there had been some truth in all religions from the beginning, but a truth expressed in poetical language, easily misunderstood. The draft in question deals with the *Origin and Transmission of the first Religious Notions*. Following Hume, Herder sees the origin of religion in fear and superstition, but this first stage was followed, he maintains, by a second, when men were concerned above all with answering questions about the origins of the world and of their own nation, and appealed to the wisdom of their fathers, to tradition and myth.

These theological traditions were inevitably as national as anything can be. Everyone spoke from the mouth of his fathers; his vision was that of the world he lived in; he sought explanations of those things around him that seemed the most remarkable, and in the way that fitted in best with his climate, his nation, his form of society; he thought according to his own interests, and the temper and language and manners of his people. A picture of the world, the human race and particular people was constructed following ideas of his time, his nation, his civilisation; it was national and local in matters great and small. The Scandinavian built his world out of giants; the Iroquee made tortoises and otters, the Indian, elephants, into machines producing that which he wanted to explain to himself; antiquarian writings and travel-books are full of such sagas and traditions, of local poems and national tales. And everywhere these age-old theological-philosophical-historical national traditions are clothed in a language of the senses, full of images and appealing to the curiosity of the common people, satisfying their imagination, directing their impulses, delighting their ear. Nay, they became complete poems; for at a time when one can hardly imagine any art of letters and writing to have existed, the voice of tradition had to preserve them.[4]

The religions, like the literatures of mankind, were for Herder, then, keys to the history of the human mind, the great poet was a species of prophet, and the only difference between Herder's studies in religion and those in literature is one of emphasis. In both he was tracing the history of man. 'Poetry', he wrote in 1774, 'was originally theology, and the noblest, greatest poetry will, like music, always remain in essence theology. Singers and prophets, the sublimest poets of the Old Testament, went to holy fire for their flames. The oldest, most venerable heathen poets, lawgivers, fathers and educators of mankind, Orpheus and Epimenodes, sang of the gods and enraptured the world.'[5] Goethe and Schiller, we shall find, took an equally lofty view of the function of the poet, as the voice of human genius at its highest. 'The poet alone is the true man', wrote Schiller, and Goethe makes the poet in the 'Vorspiel auf dem Theater' in *Faust* end a passage all in this strain with the lines

Wer sichert den Olymp, vereinet Götter?
Des Menschen Kraft, im Dichter offenbart.*

These are typically Pre-Romantic views, first encountered in England in the middle of the eighteenth century, in Joseph Warton and Edward Young, proclaimed with great conviction by all the great Weimar writers and still more emphatically by some of the German Romantics, and praised in these German writers, especially Goethe, by Carlyle, as 'the beautiful, the religious wisdom, which may still, with something of its old impressiveness, speak to the whole soul', a spirituality without superstition.

(i) 'Auch eine Philosophie'

For our present purpose, to describe briefly the influence of Herder on Weimar humanism, and the effect of his life in Weimar on his thought, two of his works are of particular interest, *Auch eine Philosophie der Geschichte zur Bildung der Menschheit*, written in Bückeburg and published in 1774, and the *Ideen zu einer Philosophie der Geschichte der Menschheit*, begun in response to a request from the publisher for a revised edition of the former work. The *Ideen* appeared in four parts, in 1784, 1785, 1787 and 1791. They carried the story of man's development down to the Middle Ages. A fifth part was planned but never written, though the *Briefe zu Beförderung der Humanität* to some extent takes its place. The conversations on Spinoza, with the title *Gott* (1787), belong to the same complex. They expound the metaphysical views that are implied in the later books of the *Ideen* and sum up the results, as Herder sees them, of the Spinoza controversy initiated by Fritz Jacobi in 1785. Goethe took the greatest possible interest in all this work both before and during his Italian journey, Herder exchanged ideas with him freely about it, and some of it may almost be regarded as an agreed statement of the two authors' views on man's nature, history and place in a world which is 'the living garment of God'.

* Who secures Olympus, unites the gods?
The power of man, revealed in the poet.

There are signs of an uneasy compromise between liberal and orthodox ideas in *Auch eine Philosophie*, an obviously immature and hurriedly written work, but we also find there, clearly formulated and applied to whole civilisations, the 'historicist' conception already evident in the Shakespeare essay, and in fact in Herder's first essays, the *Fragments*, the notion that if poetry, as Hamann said, is the 'mother-tongue of mankind', good poetry is not to be expected only from, say, the Greeks. It may arise anywhere where the natural conditions that determine its growth are favourable. English classical scholars had begun to approach Homer 'sociologically' in this way, from the observations made in their archaeological investigations in Mediterranean countries. Herder generalised further, and said that different geographical, political and cultural conditions will always produce different kinds of art and poetry, so that the drama, for instance, came into being in Greece in a form that it could not take in the north. In the same way he says now in *Auch eine Philosophie* that no civilisation, even that of the Greeks, is to be regarded as perfect, and a model for all time. Each is unique, just as individual men are, in some respects superior, in some inferior, to others, and each goes through a cycle of development as plants and animals do, responding, as they do, to its environment and changing with time.

There is a characteristic difference between the approach to Homer of Robert Wood, the traveller and scholar, and the stay-at-home but immensely learned Herder. 'If we would do the poet justice, we should approach as near as possible to the time and place, when and where he wrote', says Wood, in the preface to his *Essay on the Original Genius and Writings of Homer* (1769). With two friends, he had accordingly 'read the *Iliad* and the *Odyssey* in the countries where Achilles fought, where Ulysses travelled and where Homer sung', and in his *Essay* tried to 'illustrate Homer's writings and his country from each other', finding in the manners of Homer's heroes something very like what he had observed in the patriarchal society of the nomadic Arabs he encountered on his journey to Palmyra and Baalbec, the subject of his first book. Herder had avidly absorbed the vivid detail supplied by such travellers and constructed for himself, with hints from Montesquieu and other students of society, a mental picture of early civilisations, one which strikes us now as far too sketchy and schematic to be convincing, and too obviously coloured by the author's personal prejudices to be trustworthy, and which yet conveys much of the essential character of each in a memorable outline. Herder always communicates to the reader his feeling that, however different these earlier ways of life were from our own, they were all good in their own way and can still be understood, if we give ourselves the trouble of learning about the physical as well as the mental factors involved. It is the height of absurdity to imagine that it has been reserved for us alone to establish a reasonable and satisfying form of society. Yet this is precisely the attitude that Herder found to have been adopted by almost all the acknowledged authorities of his time, by John Millar in his *Origin of the Distinction of Ranks in Society* (1771), for example, reviewed by Herder in 1772, and by Isaak Iselin in his *Philosophische Mutmaßungen über die Geschichte der Menschheit* (1764), the chief target for his ridicule in *Auch eine Philosophie*. Iselin was the liberal and enlightened citizen of Bâle who had been ready to help Wieland with his projected school, it will be remembered, and was a friend of all progressive causes, a co-founder of the idealistic 'Helvetische Gesellschaft' (1762), which drew so many 'patriots' together, Bodmer, Lavater, J. K. Bluntschli, Pestalozzi and others, in the best spirit of the Enlightenment, in the pursuit of 'perfection' and 'virtue'. He was full of Rousseauistic ideas, like all these eighteenth-century Swiss liberals, and adopted Rousseau's terminology for the successive stages of humanity's history, speaking of a first, savage, stage as the childhood of man, the second, barbaric, stage as his youth and the third, civilised, stage as his manhood. In each successive stage, according to Iselin, new faculties ripened in man, so that from a creature of sense he gradually became one endowed with will and reason.

Herder uses a revised version of this scheme, perhaps with ironical intent, in which the final stage is decrepitude. For him the childhood of man is illustrated by the early civilisations of the Middle East, with their patriarchal society for which 'religion was the element in which all lived and moved'.[6] He is thinking here particularly of the ancient Hebrews, as they appear in the Old Testament. From this stage 'Providence led the thread of development further—down from the Euphrates, Oxus and Ganges to the Nile and to the Phoenician coasts'.[7] In Egypt a part of the boyhood of mankind was lived out by tillers of the soil, who developed new arts and a system of law. 'The child had grown out of its winged costume; the boy now sat on the school bench and learned order, diligence, the habits of a citizen.' The Phoenicians, 'the boy grown older, who ran around', took 'the remains of ancient wisdom and skill' to Greece, which is for Herder the happy adolescence of the world's history, on which it later looked back as on a golden age. This youth 'despised the coarse arts of labour, as he did merely barbarous splendour and pastoral simplicity; but he plucked from everything the flowers of a new fair nature, turning craftsmanship into art', and so on.[8] Yet

the human vessel is not capable of perfection, it must always leave something behind as it moves forward. Greece moved forward: Egyptian industry and administration could not help them, because they had not behind them an Egypt and a Nile—Phoenician skill in commerce could not help them, because they lacked a Lebanon and an India. The time was past for oriental education. Enough! It became what it did, Greece! Origin and model of all beauty, grace and simplicity, youthful blossom of the human race. Would that it could have lasted for ever![9]

With equal eloquence Herder praises Rome, 'the manhood of human powers and efforts', strong in its courage, integrity, magnanimity, justice, raising the arts of government, war and law-making to unprecedented heights, but leaving the fine arts and the accomplishments of youth, as Virgil said, to the Greeks, in its overmastering desire for empire. He knows how impossible it is to put into words the unique qualities of any nation, as of any individual man, but the attempt can remind us what folly it is to imagine, as some of his contemporaries seem to him to do, that they have inherited all the capabilities of these ancient peoples, because they know about them, that 'they need only time and opportunity to transform into actuality the capacity they feel in themselves to become like an ancient patriarch, a Greek or a Roman'. That is the illusion of intellectualists. Time and place are our masters. 'We can make ourselves only into that for which time, climate, our needs, the world, fate provide the occasion', closing at the same time other possible lines of development. 'A patriarch cannot be a Roman hero, nor a Greek athlete a seafaring merchant, nor can a Roman be a 'typical Roman' at just any point in Rome's history. All civilisations have their period of growth, of flowering and of decay, no two moments in the world are the same, and therefore Egyptians, Romans and Greeks were not the same at all periods in their history. But 'each nation has its centre of happiness within itself, as every ball its centre of gravity'; it is 'immediate to God', as Ranke was to say later. It is therefore blessed with blindness and insensibility for what is incompatible with its nature. Its prejudices are good, in their proper season, for they make for happiness. It is folly to imagine that all things are possible at all times, and to judge remote times and places by our own contemporary standards.[10]

There are the germs of a dangerous relativity in all this, but also a most refreshing realism and penetration, most salutary for what Schiller's Karl Moor calls 'an ink-splashing century'. In the treatment of medieval and modern times Herder's prejudices are more apparent. To explain the big movements of history he still has to bring in Providence. He does not accept what he implies to be the current belief in inevitable progress, as measured by individual happiness, but there is a stream of history, a general movement, in which he finds continuity, progression (Fortgang), though he repeats that 'each age has the centre of its happiness in itself. The youth is not happier than the innocent contented child, nor the tranquil old man unhappier than the restlessly active man in his prime.' How strange and admirable was the way of Providence with the Romans in their decadence! A new Man was born in the north, Germanic and Slavonic tribes and Huns swept over the Empire and remade Europe, bringing nature instead of the arts, sound northern sense instead of the sciences, a strong and good, though wild way of life instead of over-refinement. This is the kind of strain in Herder that makes him one of the ancestors of the Nordic theorists of recent times. In his view of literature he was inclined to equate the primitive with the good, and his picture of the barbarian invaders is derived from Mallet's *Nordic Antiquities*, the source of much of the Bardic enthusiasm of Klopstock and others, as well as from Ossian and the Norse sagas. Into the 'seething mixture of northern and southern juices' he makes Providence throw, as additional ferment, the Christian religion, 'for better or for worse'.[11] This he interprets as an essentially universalistic religion, not, like all earlier faiths, a national one, and the chief point he makes about it in a rather brief discussion is that in every century, so-called 'Christianity' has taken on the colour of the times. He hurries over the Dark Ages, not making them into a separate medieval period in its own right, but one of transition, but he will have none of the denigration of them practised, he says, by Voltaire, Hume, Robertson and Iselin, in favour of their own 'century of light'. Instead he draws an idealised sketch of them as another primitive age, strongly contrasted with the really decadent period, the 'old age' of humanity, the eighteenth century.

The greater part of this second section is a sustained diatribe against those who have described the age he lives in as 'the summit of human culture'. For him it is a caricature of true culture, both in respect of the cultivation of the individual and of the civilisation of national groups. It has not, in the first place, made itself, as it imagines, by the free exercise of reason. Its present state is the result of a series of accidents, of trifling events that had unforeseen consequences. The only real achievement in modern times is the invention of a number of machines, from the printing press, artillery and the mariner's compass onwards. In everything he sees signs of a parallel mechanisation. In the system of government, it is over-centralisation, absolutism, based on military power. Philosophy has become an elaborate technique, of no practical use. In the arts everyone can argue endlessly, but no one can use a paint brush or a chisel. In social intercourse there is wit and polish, but only the aping of true humanity and virtue. A capacity for abstract thought is not, as the rationalists imagine, the acme of culture. It results rather (as we should say now) in rootlessness. A man will claim to love mankind, whole nations, even his enemies, but will be cold to his father, mother and children. True progress in culture does not come from study or legislation, or elaborate cultural institutions—these academies and picture-galleries serve for the glorification of princes and little else, and educational systems have less effect than the home or the workshop. 'The great divine task of cultivating humanity' proceeds through the combination of thousands of imperceptible changes, which only Providence can bring about. And once more, with heavy irony, Herder speaks of the blessings spread abroad by our missions (accompanied by brandy and vice), our commerce, our art of government (based on fear and cupidity), our social life, our wars for the balance of power, our refined manners, our good taste à la française, our philosophy, our encyclopedias, our biblical criticism.

These pages may be regarded as an ill-tempered outburst from a disappointed man, and so in part they were, but no one can fail to notice points that anticipate many later criticisms of modern culture, from Burke to our own day. There is much too that might be paralleled in other writers of Herder's time. The attitude he takes to the French is like that of Goethe in Strassburg, as he describes it in *Dichtung und Wahrheit*. Voltaire, and French literature and art of his time, he looks upon as 'bejahrt und vornehm', senile and genteel. That is a reaction to France's seldom disputed pre-eminence and her disdain for German writers, as well as the expression of a genuine national difference in temperament. The praise of the Middle Ages at the expense of the present recalls Justus Möser, the author of the *Patriotische Phantasien*, whose essays in a local newspaper Herder brought to Goethe's notice. They express a cultural conservatism not unlike

Burke's, and a sturdy common sense. Herder is, however, much more outspoken, and probably unique in the Germany of his time for a criticism of social and political abuses on the basis of a new conception of culture as a whole. Here he reminds us strongly of what was to follow in England in the early nineteenth century from Coleridge, Carlyle, Matthew Arnold and other literary men who were severe critics of contemporary civilisation, as Mr Raymond Williams has shown us in his *Culture and Society*. There is, however, one big difference already mentioned between Herder and these writers, as Mr Williams sees them. It is not a new industrialism that Herder criticises in the name of culture. The exploitation of colonial peoples is mentioned, and some references are made to trade, but industrialism is something with which Herder was not acquainted. He is concerned with the pre-capitalistic form of society he knew, but still more with philosophy and the fine arts, religion and ethics, and this remains true on the whole of all the Weimar writers.

(ii) '*Ideen*'. First Part

In the preface to the *Ideen zu einer Philosophie der Geschichte der Menschheit* Herder treats his earlier work as a provisional sketch, which he seems to think has been taken too seriously, especially his 'allegorical' use of the words 'childhood', 'youth' and so on. Far more is needed for a real history of culture, such as he now has in view, and more still for a philosophical interpretation of human history. It is misleading, he thinks, to use the word culture of whole peoples and ages, for 'how few in a cultivated people are cultivated?', yet there is no people on earth without some culture. Altogether, it is the vaguest of words, yet he must use it if he is to find some common measure for the various kinds of happiness that different peoples have attained to in the infinitely various conditions of life. He shows how close he is to Goethe's general point of view when he writes: 'Anyone who is looking for merely metaphysical speculations can find them more directly; I think however that, cut off from experiences and analogies of nature, they are a journey by air that seldom leads to its destination'. The last remark is, incidentally, another reference to the first balloon flights. 'The course of God in nature,' he goes on, reminding us now of Shaftesbury and the Deists, 'the thoughts that the Eternal manifested to us by deeds in the succession of His works: they are the sacred book whose characters I, less than an apprentice, but zealously devoted, have spelt out and will spell out.' It is with devout intent that Herder studies nature and history then, and until the end of the Second Part, he continues to speak of Providence as the moving force behind history, though with more and more insistence on what man has done for himself, with the powers with which he was endowed at the creation. Then in the Third Part, written together with his Spinoza book, *Gott*, he omits all mention of Providence and rejects the idea of final causes.

The First Part is begun entirely in the spirit of the scientist. Without any reference to the biblical creation story, Herder does his best to reconstruct, from the very inadequate scientific knowledge of his time, 'the first beginnings of the water-earth and the organic life that developed on it from the earliest times'—so Goethe sums up the subject of his 'daily discussions' with him.[12] Herder leads up to this with a brief description of the position of the earth, a medium-sized planet, in the solar system. Plants and animals were created before man, and he 'appeared upon an inhabited earth. All the elements, swamps and streams, sand and air were filled or being filled with creatures, and he had to establish his dominant position by his God-given cunning and strength. How he did this is the history of his culture, in which the most primitive peoples have a share. It is the most interesting part of human history'.[13] Man had to learn from his fellow-creatures and adapt himself to his surroundings, so 'the history of his culture is largely zoological and geographical'. The first three books of Part I are concerned with these aspects and culminate in a comparison between man and the nearest animals.

Man walks upright and is 'organised to be capable of reason'. There is a mention of the intermaxillary bone here (early in Book

4), but no distinction is drawn between man and monkey with regard to it. Man's supreme gift is speech, which nature seems to be working up to in the animals. Through speech the dormant reason in man is awakened. The child is gradually taught to reason and to use his freedom, as he is taught to walk upright. All these finer capacities of man can be called his 'humanity' (Humanität), and 'man is made for humanity and religion'. 'Religion is man's humanity at its highest.'[14] From this point in the fourth book the Protestant minister in Herder takes over, and assures us that man is made for the hope of immortality. The fifth book is devoted to arguments supporting this belief. 'From stone to crystal, from crystal to metal, from metal to the plant creation, from plants to animals, from these to man we have seen continually higher forms of organisation, and with the form we have seen the powers and impulses of each branch of creation grow more manifold, so that in the end they all unite in the figure of man, so far as this can contain them. At man the series stops.' The 'powers' (Kräfte) are thought of as controlling forces within living things, what Goethe calls by Aristotle's term 'enteleche'. Herder is consistent, and maintains that when a flower dies, this principle within it does not, and in the same way the soul of man does not die with the body. We cannot imagine, he says, that a principle that is there one minute is gone the next.[15] In spite of Priestley and all the other opponents of such a 'spiritualism', who ask where pure spirit is to be found in nature, Herder produces one analogy after another to suggest that the Creator who put the controlling 'power' into his body 'will not lack a medium in the great complex of nature to lead it out, and must he not do so, since he introduced it just as miraculously to this organic home, clearly that it might be formed into something higher?' 'When man has come to the end of the chain of earthly organisation as its highest and final link, he begins by so doing the chain of a higher order of creatures as its lowest link, and so he is probably the middle ring between two connected systems of creation.'[16] The words of the practised preacher flow, expressing age-old emotions, but there is no clear thought behind them. To

Kant, who reviewed this first volume of the *Ideen* in the first week's issues of the new *Allgemeine Literaturzeitung*, the important review started in Jena in 1785, this about invisible forces producing organisation was 'very dogmatic metaphysics', in spite of Herder's repudiation of metaphysics, 'an attempt to explain what one does not understand by means of what one understands still less'. Herder, who had not liked the first of Kant's *Critiques* when it appeared in 1781, had from now on not a good word to say for his old teacher, and certainly the review was unnecessarily sharp.

(iii) '*Ideen*'. Second Part

The Second Part of the *Ideen* is concerned with the varieties of peoples and of physical types on the earth, and the underlying unity that can be found in this variety. Peoples are classified in Book 6 geographically, though the third chapter deals with an ill-defined 'region of handsome (schöngebildet) peoples', a very unscientific category by modern standards, reflecting no doubt the confusion spoken of by Goethe later as prevailing in scholars' minds at this time, when there were great disputes as to whether beauty was an objective quality or not.[17] The Mediterranean lands, needless to say, are the home of the most handsome peoples of all. The book is based on Herder's wide acquaintance with travel literature. In the next book he moves away from particulars to generalisation, pointing out what is specifically human in all these varied types, and how man has succeeded everywhere in acclimatising himself. There are common inherent qualities and powers in man, called here 'genetische Kraft', that are modified by the influence of climate. The possibilities of distinguishable varieties resulting from this interaction are so great that Herder dislikes the rigid classification into a few main races that has been attempted, and prefers to speak always of peoples, each a social unit with its own language. In all such changes of the type he sees the wisdom of nature, another expression for the hand of Providence, and in them all, 'love is the greatest of the goddesses'.[18] It is loveless marriages that produce degenerates. After the physical characteristics of man, Herder deals with the mental, attempting in Book 8 a comparative psychology of the peoples of the earth, describing the range of their senses, their imagination, their intelligence, their feelings and impulses. He sees here too the interaction of innate powers and environment, but environment includes a man's neighbours and the traditions of his society. In describing these traditions, Herder does not conceal his own sympathies, and many of his statements involve hidden assumptions, usually liberal and optimistic, though distinctly influenced by Rousseau. The patriarchal simplicity of nomadic peoples appeals to him greatly. He must admit the supreme importance of the change to a settled agriculture, but before long, 'the soil does not belong to man, but man to the soil', and he has lost his old freedom for good.[19] Repeatedly Herder shows his democratic spirit, in the sense that he refers to every kind of despotism with scorn. The only natural society for him is the family. As in his *Travel Diary*, he praises a simple, active life, in direct touch with external reality. 'Do not believe that happiness is to be found through an untimely, excessive refinement or cultivation (Ausbildung).... Woe to the wretched man, who can only find pleasure in life by racking his brains!'[20] For the unspoilt man, life in itself is good, and a sufficient end in itself. He is by nature peaceful and well disposed towards his neighbour. He can find his happiness in the present. It is nonsense, Herder thinks, to say that 'man is made for an infinite expansion of his powers, for a progressive widening of his feelings and influence, or finally, that he is made for the state, as the goal his race is making for, so that all his generations really only exist for the sake of the last one, that it may triumph, enthroned on the scaffolding left behind by all its vanished predecessors'.[21]

It is not easy to disentangle all the ideas and feelings implicit in a passage like this. There is first of all the 'historicist' notion already discussed, that every age and people, and every stage in a man's individual life, has its own unique value. What Herder stresses here, however, is happiness, and one has the impression that he is thinking of his own experience, as in the *Travel Diary*, and urging himself to live more in the present, not to neglect, lost in longing for the unattainable, the opportunities of happiness that it offers. He seems to be free, for the moment, from the 'Schwärmerei' which had marked the last books of Part I. At the same time Herder is criticising ideas put forward in an article by Kant, 'Idea for a Universal History with Cosmopolitan Intent', which had appeared in the *Berliner Monatsschrift* a few months before Kant wrote the review of the first volume of the *Ideen*. In the article Kant had asked himself whether any 'intention of nature' could be discovered in human history. If this intention were that man's powers should be developed to their fullest extent, the development could only happen in the course of many generations, and only if each could hand on its knowledge to the next. At the end of this cultural progression Kant envisaged a form of society constituted with perfect justice, in which the freedom of each citizen would be limited only by the freedom of all others. This could never happen unless the separate nations came together in a League of Nations founded on reason. In the light of our own experience, after nearly two centuries more of national conflicts, Kant's ideas seem very much more in accord with the facts of political history than Herder's, but Herder had a horror of interfering despotic states and organisations, bred in him as an individual in his own youth in Prussia, and his national feeling was confined to matters of culture.

In spite of his objections in Book 8 to Kant's view, 'that man is made for an infinite expansion of his powers', Herder devotes Book 9 to the theme of the continuity of culture, for what he cannot accept in the rationalist philosophy is the idea that reason is 'independent of senses and organs', and that a man 'produces everything out of himself' by the exercise of pure infallible reason. Herder is not the abstract type of thinker who aims at producing a long argument by purely logical deduction from a single statement regarded as axiomatic, like Fichte, for instance, in his *Über die Bestimmung des Gelehrten*. Here Fichte begins with a lecture 'On the Mission of Man in Himself', where he says: 'I must start from something positive, and as I cannot here (in a public lecture) take as my starting-point the absolute positive, the thesis "I am", I must set up as hypothesis a thesis which is ineradicable from human feeling, which results from the whole of philosophy, and of which a strict proof can be given, the thesis: As certainly as man possesses reason, he is his own aim, i.e., he does not exist because something else is to be.' From this he proves that man's mission is a ceaseless striving after perfection, or 'Bildung'.

Herder relies on his own individual experience, he allows for non-logical elements in thought, and he insists on every man's debt to the inherited civilisation in which he has been nurtured, and without which he would be a barbarian.

No man gives birth to himself, and he is just as little self-born in the use of his intellectual powers. Not only the germ of our inner disposition is inherited, like our physical formation, but every development of this germ depends on the destiny that planted us at this place or at that, and disposed around us, according to the time and our years, the means for our cultivation. Even eye and ear had to learn to see and hear, and everyone must realise how artificially the supreme tool of our thought, language, was acquired. Clearly nature has arranged our whole make-up, and the length and character of the successive stages of our life, to depend on this help from others.

The body is like an instrument, that even the ablest of us must learn to play during our prolonged childhood and adolescence. 'Reason is the aggregate of what our mind has learnt by observation and practice', observation of our elders, who had acquired their skill in the same way, so that when, as the result of much effort, we have mastered the instrument given to us, we owe our education in reality to the whole species.[22]

Here we have therefore the principle behind the history of human development, without which there would be no such history. If man received everything from himself, and developed it in isolation from external objects, a history of *man* would be possible, but not of *men*, not of their whole race. But since our specific character is to be found in the fact that, born almost without instinct, we are only trained up to humanity by lifelong practice, both the perfectibility and the corruptibility of our species depending on this, it follows that the history of human development is necessarily a whole, that is, a chain of sociability and cultural tradition from the first to the last link. There is therefore such a thing as the education of the human race, just because every man only becomes a man through education, and the whole race only lives in this chain of individuals.[23]

Strictly speaking, Herder points out, it is the individuals, in successive generations, who constitute the race, and who are educated, the race being an abstraction, a thing with which no one can be personally acquainted as he can with individual men, and on which it is useless to heap up every kind of perfection. But it is equally misleading to think of an individual as completely self-sufficient. 'The whole complex of humanity in him is connected by a mental genesis, education, with his parents, teachers, friends, with all the circumstances in the course of his life, and so with his people and its fathers, in fact finally with the whole chain of the human race that, through any one of its links, affected one of his mental powers.'[24]

Herder's theory of the growth and transmission of culture is for us now one of the most interesting and valuable features in his *Ideen*, essentially sound, though sometimes associated by him with a teleological conception of history apparently abandoned later, under the influence of Spinoza. After the passage just quoted Herder reverts to the thought of Providence working out its purpose in human history, for instance by providing so much variety in man's habitat. Then he continues his analysis of the cultural process. It involves two main factors, he says, tradition and 'organic powers'. Traditions can only be handed down, preserved and added to by living creatures, endowed with certain powers which he does not specify at this point. 'The imitator must have the power of receiving what can be and is communicated, and transforming it, as he does the food he lives on, into his own nature.' This is a sort of 'second genesis of man, which continues throughout his life'. It does not matter whether we call it 'culture', using a metaphor from the cultivation of the soil, or 'enlightenment', from the image of light. In any case, 'the chain of culture and enlightenment reaches to the ends of the earth.'[25] Herder extends the meaning of the words here so that they cover not only the higher stages but also the beginnings of culture, and we arrive very nearly at the modern anthropological use of the word. 'The native of California and Terra del Fuego too learned to make and use bows and arrows. He has language and ideas, skills and arts, that he learned as we learned ours. To this extent he was really cultivated and enlightened, though only in the lowest degree. The difference between enlightened and unenlightened, cultivated and uncultivated peoples is therefore not absolute, but a matter of degree.' Any standard we may adopt will be arbitrary, but everywhere we find 'the tradition of an education to some form of human happiness and way of living'.

If man has been given capacities that can be so developed, must it not be God's fatherly intention, the preacher in Herder continues, that they should be used in due time? And is it not true here too, that all His means are ends, all His ends means to higher ends? 'So what every man is and can be, that must be the purpose of the human race. And what is this? Humanity and happiness at this place, in this degree, as this and no other link in the chain of cultivation that extends throughout the whole race.' At whatever stage a man finds himself, he has something to live for in action, that will bring him contentment. At every stage, further, he has good grounds for humility. If he is proud of his reason, let him remember what depths of inhumanity have been reached on earth by single men, by nations and often by an associated series of nations, when they have descended, for instance, even to cannibalism. Everything depends on the tradition in which he is nurtured, and all forms of human behaviour have been tried out somewhere or other. But 'all vice and atrocities exhaust themselves in history, till at last here and there a nobler form of human thought and virtue appears. . . . God does not exert his power on earth except through chosen, superior men. . . . The body moulders in the grave, a man's name is soon forgotten. Only by being incorporated in the voice of God, the tradition of culture, can we live on as an anonymous influence in the minds of our fellows.'[26]

It is only in the chain of culture that Herder finds a meaning in history, an expression of the Creator's will. 'The perishable form and the imperfection of all human works are also part of the plan of the Creator. Folly had to appear for wisdom to overcome it, fragility, even of the finest things made, was inseparable from their matter, so that on their ruins men should make new efforts to build or improve, for all of us here are in a place of training', and it is only heightened powers that we take with us out of the world. Herder is no longer troubled by the thought of the mutability of all earthly things. The noble plant of 'Humanität' could only grow amid storms. Revolutions do not dismay him. They are as necessary to our race as the waves to the rolling river, that it may not become a swamp. This is still a religious conception of progress, and for those who do not accept his premise of a wise Providence, its optimism will seem rather facile, though his general conception of the movement of history is more acceptable than the obviously mythical presentation in *Auch eine Philosophie* of the history of humanity as an organic sequence, beginning with childhood and ending, in his own age, with senility. Herder is beginning to have a clear understanding of the means by which culture is transmitted, the 'how', but he always asks insistently 'why?' He describes a chain of cause and effect, but he views it at one time from behind, as it were, stressing the influence of milieu and inherited tradition, and at another from in front, explaining the process as one foreseen and planned by God for the attainment of a certain end.

In the second chapter of Book 9 Herder continues his analysis of the means by which culture is transmitted, in an excellent description of the all-important part played by language in social evolution. This is a branch of cultural history in which he had long been at home, though it cannot be said that his views had gained in consistency since his brilliant prize-essay *On the Origin of Language*, written in Strassburg late in 1770. Here he had rejected both the theory of the Divine origin of language and that of its deliberate invention by individual men, and suggested a gradual evolution from involuntary expressions of emotion. Now, however, it seems that he no longer believes in the natural origin of reason and language, which he had formerly represented as growing alongside each other. He realises so fully what a miraculous gift language is that he leaves its origin shrouded in mystery and speaks of 'this miracle of a Divine intervention'.[27] But he is clear and convincing on the part played by language in the growth of culture. It is only through language that men are capable of 'free ideas', ideas of things and events not physically present to the senses. Herder does not say this quite explicitly, but something very like it is implied when he writes:

A people has no idea, for which it has no word. However intently we look at something, we have only a vague feeling about it until our mind finds a distinguishing feature and incorporates it through a word in our memory, our power of recollection, our understanding—and finally in the understanding of men (in general), in tradition. Pure reason on earth without language is a utopia. It is the same with the passions of the heart and with all social emotions. Only language has made man human, by enclosing the vast flood of his feeling behind dams, and setting up reasonable memorials to it through words. It w s not the lyre of Amphion that erected towns, it was no magic wand that turned deserts into gardens. Language did it, the great social educator of man.[28]

How miraculous, yet how imperfect a tool is language! 'No language expresses things, but only names', Herder goes on, straying from his central theme to discuss the problem of knowledge. We think in language by means of quite arbitrary symbols. 'If we thought things, instead of abstracted characteristics, and if we expressed the nature of things, instead of using arbitrary signs, then farewell, error and opinion, we are in the land of truth.' The point of this excursus is to discredit metaphysical speculation, and Goethe will have thoroughly approved of the statement that 'He who does not trust his senses is a fool, and must become an empty speculator'.[29] As Mephistopheles was to say to Faust:

Ich sag' es dir: ein Kerl, der spekuliert,
Ist wie ein Tier, auf dürrer Heide

Von einem bösen Geist im Kreis herum geführt,
Und rings umher liegt schöne grüne Weide.*

Because language is so intimately associated with the growth of civilisation, a'philosophical comparison of languages', Herder suggests, would throw much light on history and national characteristics. This is the germ from which grew, among other things, the extensive researches of Wilhelm von Humboldt into language, and the 'Idealistische Sprachwissenschaft' of Karl Vossler and others in our own century.

Returning to his theoretical consideration of the growth of culture, Herder discusses in the third chapter of Book 9 the development of the sciences and arts, which would have been impossible without language. The truly divine in man, his characteristic prerogative, is his power to observe and record, the basis of all invention and science. No age, however advanced, should forget its immense debt to the untold ages that preceded it.

Vain is the boasting we hear so often from the rabble of Europe of its superiority in enlightenment, art and science to the other three continents. . . . Wretched creature, did you invent anything of these arts? Have you any thoughts of your own as you absorb all these traditions? That you have acquired those arts is a mechanical accomplishment; you have sucked in the sap of knowledge like a sponge that happened to grow in this moist place. If you sail a ship of war to Tahiti, or fire a cannon in the Hebrides, you are no wiser or cleverer than the Hebridean or Tahitian, who skilfully steers his boat and built it with his own hands. This is what all savage peoples vaguely felt as soon as they came into contact with Europeans.[30]

The comparison between Europeans and less civilised peoples leads Herder to Rousseau's famous paradox about the arts and sciences, which he modifies however into an inquiry about the degree of *happiness* conferred on man by the arts and sciences, as he has all through tended to consider the civilisation of each age and people as its own peculiar way of finding contentment.

* I tell you this: a fellow who speculates is like a poor beast that an evil spirit leads round in circles on a patch of dried-up heath, when all around lies fair green pasture.

Progress in the discovery of labour-saving tools and machines is undeniable, and with it has gone an increasing dependence of men on their neighbours, but men are not more contented because of the greater complexity of their life, rather the reverse. He illustrates the potentialities both for good and evil of scientific discoveries, not to be foreseen at the time when they are made, from the invention of gunpowder, which may still, he is bold enough to say, be the means of dethroning many a despot.[31]

Law and order are clearly a most important feature in any civilisation, so Herder cannot avoid the discussion of forms of government, a ticklish subject, even in a minor German state, in the decade preceding the French Revolution. 'Some sections of this Part', Herder wrote to Hamann, 'have given me a dreadful amount of trouble and still do not satisfy me, especially the *caput mortuum* of government, on which, as Herr Immanuel and the public for Universal History will have it, the whole of this wretched history depends. After condemning my first essay *ad carceres* myself, I gave the second to our friend Goethe for ministerial censorship, and he returned it to me with the comforting assurance, that not a word of it could really be allowed to stand.' We do not know what has survived into the final version of the one that was shown to Goethe, but the chapter as published is one of the least satisfactory in the whole work. It is evident from it that Herder had no liking for princes, but also that he had only the vaguest ideas about what governments can and should do. On the first point a cancelled passage is more explicit than the final text: 'The more the classes mix, the more rulers come down from their thrones and show themselves without their regalia, the more quickly and clearly will even those who are most deluded realise, that the ruler is not a god.'[32] Hereditary monarchs seem to Herder a complete anachronism. It is only by the rarest of accidents that they are in any way outstanding as men, he thinks, and their time-worn rights were won by some ancestor only by conquest, by war. They are all, for him, despots, and history is 'a sad picture of man-hunts and conquest. Every little boundary, every new age is written into the book of time with the blood of the sacrificed and the tears of the oppressed.' Under the yoke of despotism, the marrow is squeezed out of the bones of even the finest people, it grows accustomed to deceit, flattery and luxury, and ends by kissing its chains and twisting garlands round them.[33]

The vehemence of Herder's denunciation is partly to be explained from his memories of his Prussian home, no doubt, but he draws no distinction between constitutional and other monarchies and discusses no form of government except (*a*) the family organisation that he imagines as prevailing in the earliest societies, the state of nature, and (*b*) the rule of freely elected leaders for a limited time among food-gathering tribes and nomads, which he calls the second stage of natural government, hereditary kingship being the third and last form mentioned. He shows no appreciation at all of the functions of government, not even mentioning defence, the making and administration of law or any kind of economic guidance, and his general position seems to be closer to philosophical anarchism than to liberalism. There is a very marked contrast between his one-sided rhetoric and the closely argued reply of Egmont to Alba in the fourth act of Goethe's play, written when Goethe had many years' experience of responsible administration behind him. Like most German intellectuals of his day, Herder had no real interest in politics and no understanding of its problems. Kant showed himself in this respect greatly superior to him in the already mentioned article of 1784, the 'Idea for a Universal History', which Herder here again attacks, without mentioning any names. Man is not, for Herder, 'an animal that needs a master'; the reverse is true, that if he needs a master he is not truly a man. Only our animal vices and passions need to be controlled, and mature men, formed to true 'humanity' by inherited traditions, can do that for themselves.[34] Kant takes a much more pessimistic view of the political animal, being nearer in this to Hobbes. It is the experience of conflict that teaches man to be reasonable, but very, very slowly, and that is why Kant attaches so much value to a society ruled with perfect justice, and sees no hope of it coming into being until men are citizens, not of a national state, but of the world, when a world order has been established. This is for him the goal of civilisation, a goal to which, as he says in his review of Herder's Second Part, the existence of an isolated, happy, ignorant Tahiti brings mankind no nearer, so that, for him, the purpose of Providence in bringing it into being would not be apparent.

With religion, the final element in the cultural tradition discussed here by Herder, he is on more familiar ground. It is the oldest and most sacred tradition on earth, and there has never been any culture worthy of the name without a religious basis. Like language and reason, it has been handed down by tradition, through the use of symbols, by which Herder seems to mean here verbal symbols, of which many become meaningless, he says, in the course of a few generations. The history of even the most advanced peoples shows that all their culture began in religion, and we cannot imagine a stage at which man was a monster before he became human. 'No, beneficent Deity, Thou didst not abandon the creature Thou hadst made to that murderous chaos. To the beasts Thou gavest instinct, in the soul of man Thou didst implant Thine image, religion and humanity: the contours of the statue are there, deep in the dark marble, but it cannot form itself, carve itself out, unassisted. Tradition and instruction, reason and experience were meant to do this, and Thou didst not leave man without means to this end.'[35] This seems to be the Hellenistic idea of self-cultivation—the image of the statue in the block comes from a late work of Plotinus—to which Herder gives a theological twist. As M. Marrou says: 'Se faire soi-même; dégager de l'enfant qu'on a d'abord été, de l'être mal dégrossi qu'on risque de demeurer, l'homme pleinement homme dont on entrevoit la figure idéale, telle est l'œuvre de toute la vie, l'œuvre unique à laquelle cette vie puisse être noblement consacrée.'[36] For Herder, the ideal towards which the humanist strives in cultivation is the image of Himself planted by God within man. The inner disposition towards 'Humanität' is found, he says, in all races and times. Signs of it are for example the idea of justice and of social

rights, monogamy, paternal and maternal love, respect for bene-
factors and friends, and even the dim feeling that an all-powerful
and beneficent Being exists—a list that would hardly be accepted
by modern anthropologists. 'The kingdom of these dispositions
and their development is the real City of God on earth, of which
all men are citizens, but according to very different classes and
degrees.'[37]

(iv) 'Ideen'. Third Part

The last book of Part II discusses a speculative subject dear to
Herder from his biblical studies, the question of the original home
of mankind, then in Parts III and IV of the *Ideen* Herder deals
more or less chronologically with the universal history of civilisation, beginning with the ancient Chinese and ending with the
medieval town. Herder's treatment of this vast subject is necessarily very sketchy. As a source of information these parts of his
work have, of course, long been superseded, but for their time
they were a considerable feat of learning, and much can be
learned about Herder's view of life and of man from his selection
of topics, the recurring emphasis laid on certain aspects of history,
and the general observations introduced at intervals on the
'philosophy' of history suggested by each civilisation in turn. It
is a summary characterisation that Herder gives us of the various
types of culture thrown up in different times and places, illustrated
from chosen episodes, and coloured throughout by his own rather
crotchetty personality.

Having found the original home of mankind in the mountainous
regions of Asia, Herder thinks of the regions south of these
mountains as the natural seat of the earliest states and empires of
men, and of these he discusses quite briefly China and Japan,
Tibet and India, mainly from an ethical and religious point of
view. His general observations, in chapter v, are concerned with
the importance of a priestly and learned class in the development
of a civilisation. It is not necessary, however, for a whole people
to be enlightened for it to count as civilised for him. It is enough
if they have 'the notions and virtues that they need for their work

and the happy wellbeing of their life'. Every way of life has its own compensations, even in the unchanging east.

Babylonians, Assyrians, Chaldeans, Medes and Persians take up two short chapters, the Jews another, a very critical survey of their chequered history, not once referring to the hand of Providence, and explaining the survival of the Jews in all their later trials as just as natural as that of the 'Brahmans, Parsees and Gypsies'. The dignity and sublimity of the Old Testament is given the highest praise, but Herder regrets the mischief that has been caused in scholarship by regarding the Mosaic account of the Creation and the Flood as historical. In the chapter on the Phoenicians and Carthage, a comment is made which comes again several times, when Herder contrasts these trading peoples with the military empires on the Tigris and Euphrates. 'The conqueror conquers for himself: the trading nation serves itself and other peoples also. It makes its goods, industry, science and scholarship equally accessible to a whole section of the earth, and must therefore involuntarily help to spread Humanity.'[38] The behaviour of modern colonising powers, who 'made slaves, preached the cross and exterminated', is also contrasted unfavourably with that of the Phoenicians. Egyptology has made such strides since Herder's day that his chapter on Egypt seems particularly thin, and the review which follows of the philosophical results of his examination of the early civilisation of Asia is rather commonplace too. The main law of history that it suggests to him is that in every corner of the globe, everything happens that can happen, given the governing factors of the situation and needs of the place, the circumstances and opportunities of the time, and the inborn or acquired character of the peoples. It is his sense of the unlimited possibilities of nature and history that he puts into often repeated phrases like 'Everything that can be, is; everything that can develop, develops; if not today, then tomorrow.'[39] The other side to this is that everything passes away; 'Death is her device for having more life', as Goethe had said. Tradition, maintained by education, was the counter-measure of the early civilisations, but it became only too easily 'true opium of the mind'.[40]

Very little was known, Herder admits, about the ancient east in comparison with the abundant light that had been shed on Greece and Rome, to which he now turns, giving to each a whole book, one consisting of seven, the other of six chapters. The geography and ethnology, language, mythology and literature, the plastic arts and music, ethics and politics, science and scholarship of Greece are soberly described, with full recognition of Greek achievements, but in a scientific, sociological spirit without the rhapsodical note struck by so many of Herder's contemporaries, from Winckelmann on. Even so he sees the drama, the dance, poetry and music of Greece as those of 'an age of youthful elation', 'in a happy clime', perfect of their kind and inimitable, unapproachable by the moderns. He insists, for instance, on the severity of the Greeks to their captives and colonies, their endless raids and wars, the heavy burden of service that fell on the citizen, the corruption of manners that accompanied their male friendships, and other shadows in the picture, but he is filled with admiration for the patriotism of Sparta, the enlightenment of Athens, the extraordinary accomplishments in both places of men born into a fine tradition combining their forces in freedom. After recounting the stages he discerns in Greek history, he draws philosophical conclusions from his study of Greece. Again he dwells on the combination of national traditions, in a particular time and place, to produce a unique brand of civilisation, but one in which he sees nothing mysterious or superhuman. 'The whole of human history is purely a natural history of human powers, actions and impulses governed by place and time.'[41] Quite in the spirit of Goethe at this time, he wants the historian to try to see just what is 'there', and not to read into the events he records 'hidden special intentions of a plan of things unknown to us, or even the magic influence of invisible spirits', which we would not now think of in contemplating nature. 'Fate reveals its intentions through what happens and how it happens; the writer contemplating history develops these intentions simply from what is there and shows itself in its full extent.' There are purely natural causes for everything that happens, even for the flowering of a great civilisation, which grows out of the life of a people, but cannot live for ever, however admirable. It cannot keep a state alive either. States, to live long, must be solidly based on 'humanity, that is, on reason and fairness'.[42]

Herder was temperamentally less well fitted to appreciate 'the grandeur that was Rome' than 'the glory that was Greece', and he had not yet visited Italy. As Goethe remarked when he read this Third Part of the *Ideen* in Rome itself, although he was entirely delighted with the book, especially with the section on Greece, he missed in the Roman section 'etwas Körperlichkeit', the feeling for Roman greatness which is inspired by monuments like the Colosseum, and to which Wilhelm von Humboldt was to give such eloquent expression in his letters to Goethe, especially the famous one of 23 August 1804. There is for Herder a fundamental inhumanity in the Romans, as a nation of conquerors, which outweighs his admiration for their courage and political sagacity, and makes him regret that Latin is still so much more favoured than Greek in the education of the young, so that 'on the blood-soaked soil of Roman splendour we move as in a shrine of classical learning and surviving ancient works of art'.[43] He brings out well 'the peculiar character of Roman history and eloquence, law and religion, philosophy and language: all breathe a spirit of action and political power, a manly, bold courage, combined with cunning and the urbanity of the citizen'.[44] How different they are from their Chinese or Jewish counterparts, or even from Greece, Sparta not excluded! He sees that 'without the narrow stern *constitution* of their state the greatest part of the much-lauded Roman virtue is inexplicable; it disappeared when this fell.'[45] He understands how education, family tradition among the aristocracy, and civic spirit embodied in laws and institutions, worked together in the days of Rome's greatness to produce a pride and confidence in their country that nothing could shake, but he never forgets his ethical standpoint. 'The Romans, who want to bring light to the world, first make a night of devastation wherever they go.'[46] He sees the decline of the Roman empire as the nemesis resulting from flaws that were there from the beginning, an inherent disharmony between senate, nobility and citizens, between Rome's constitution as a city and its task of ruling an empire. Further factors were its dependence on slave-labour, the lure of luxury, and above all, the mania for conquest. Rome's fall is an object-lesson for the would-be new Romans of Europe.

A short chapter is enough for Rome's contribution to general civilisation, particularly in law, eloquence and history, and then Herder returns to general reflections on the fate of Rome and again the question of Providence. Viewing Roman history with the impartiality of the natural scientist, as one should, it is impossible to believe that all this shedding of blood was the working out of a special secret plan of Providence. It would be like thinking that a ship must sink that a single pearl might be found, or a thousand men perish that from their ashes a few flowers might grow, to be scattered by the winds. Nor was it to prepare the way for the spread of Christianity that Rome rose and fell, and what influence it had on Christianity was evil. 'The philosophy of ends', he sums up, revealing clearly the Spinozist inspiration of this book, 'has brought no advantages to natural science, but has fobbed off its adherents with specious illusions instead of genuine research; how much more will this be true of human history, with its thousands of ends and interconnections. We must therefore refrain from imagining that the Romans appeared in the procession of the ages, in order as in a human picture to form a more perfect link in the chain of culture than the Greeks had been.' Each of these nations, like all others, had its own peculiar merits and defects, which we should study in their natural background. 'The work of Providence proceeds on its eternal course according to great general laws', that is, in effect, Providence is now another name for the laws of nature.[47]

The last book of Part III of the *Ideen* is given over entirely to grappling with the fundamental problem for Herder, the meaning of history. It begins with a gloomy account of the story of man as it appears to the naturalist that Herder is trying to be. It is much as Voltaire might have seen it in his more sceptical moments.

Everything passes, everything changes, mind no less than body because mind depends on body. There is no progress in history, culture is handed on and diffused but never reaches perfection. Human nature remains unchanged. Like Sisyphus rolling his stone, each generation must relearn the same old lessons, and Herder asks: If history has no goal, why did God impose this toil on us, without our consent? Why were we born into a world where power and cunning are always victorious? How much more difficult it is to see the hand of God in history than in nature, yet if He exists, He should be evident to us in both, if we use the powers He has given us.[49]

Herder begins his answer with his old assurance (what scholars call the 'Individualitätsgedanke'), that 'the purpose of a thing that is not a mere dead means, must lie in itself.'[50] He cannot conceive of a God who would create us to strive for some perfection outside ourselves, that we should never reach. To be kept constantly striving (like Faust), without attaining any end, is not for Herder a good, but we are not reduced to this explanation. 'We know of nothing higher than the humanity (Humanität) found in man. Even where we imagine angels or Gods, we think of them as ideal, higher men.'[51] This is exactly what Goethe had written in *Das Göttliche*:

Heil den unbekannten höhern Wesen / Die wir ahnen! Ihnen gleiche der Mensch. / Sein Beispiel lehr uns / Jene glauben.*

The purpose or end of human nature, Herder believes, is to bring forth this 'Humanität', and to this end God has placed the fate of our race in its own hands. Herder recapitulates his findings in the first three Parts, to the effect that all in man makes for 'Humanität', his physical and mental make-up, his social and political institutions, technical and economic achievements, ethical and religious development, even his wars and treaties. Whatever good is done in history is done, therefore, for 'Humanität', whatever is evil and foolish, against it, so that man cannot imagine any other

* Hail to the unknown higher beings of whom our hearts tell us! Let man be like them! Let his example teach us to believe in them.

goal for all his earthly activities than lies in the mixed nature with which God endowed him at the creation, when He said to him: 'Be my image, a God on earth . . . and all my sacred eternal laws of nature will help you.'[52]

Natural laws or uniformities may be discovered in human history as in nature itself, Herder claims, revealing equally clearly a Divine intention. Order in the universe was born out of chaos, and the earth became habitable, nature established a balance among its creatures, and this same tendency towards order must lie in men too, and be manifest in history. Fewer men are born to destroy than to preserve, for instance, just as among animals there are fewer lions than lambs. Wild animals die out with the advance of civilisation, man's wild passions grow weaker. It is the same with nations as with men. No cultivated empire has arisen in Europe since the fall of Rome that has built up its whole structure on war and conquest. (Johannes von Müller, in his edition of Herder's works, adds a footnote: 'The reader should remember that this book appeared in 1787.' We could add further notes now.) A peaceful balance has been reached, and even trade rivalries seem likely to be moderated by common consent.[53]

The general growth of humane feeling in Herder's age excuses his optimism, but his arguments no longer convince us, any more than his belief in the inevitable good that will follow from improving techniques, in the tendency of war to make itself impossible, or of merchants to become more honest because deceit never pays. This idea of the inevitable establishment of equilibrium after a period of unbalance is a relic of Shaftesbury's philosophy, according to Meinecke, and it brings Herder often close to those over-optimistic views of the Enlightenment on which he had poured scorn in *Auch eine Philosophie*. Some sort of self-corrective tendency there must be, of course, in a world that somehow maintains itself in being, but as Meinecke says, 'the real rhythm of the movement of history is too complex and too ambiguous for the simple formula of Herder's balance theory to be applicable to it everywhere. This theory arose more out of an ethical need, thirsting for immediate satisfaction, than from the pursuit of knowledge in its purest form.'[54]

The same friendly critic finds, as everyone must, a fatal ambiguity in the central notion of 'Humanität'. Herder's aim was to present the history of Mankind as part of the total process of nature and to explain every step in it genetically. But his conception of nature was never free from theological, metaphysical ideas, ideas necessary to him as a man 'to whom the Germany of his day and its political and social conditions were painfully repugnant'. The tension between the contemplative activity of the historian, further stimulated by Goethe's effort to see nature as it really was, and the ethical striving of the preacher and educator, is reflected in the varying impressions the reader receives of 'Humanität'. Sometimes it is a *natural tendency* in man to draw continually closer to perfect humanity, to reveal the immanent deity Herder sees in him as in all nature; sometimes an *absolute ethical ideal*, in the light of which the power-state, for instance, is condemned. As he grew older the ethical emphasis and the criticism of his own time became still more marked, with the result that while he inspired, on the one hand, the 'historicism' of Ranke, with its convincing fusion of the individual and the general, its presentation of all the generations of humanity as equally justified before God, it encouraged also the pragmatic, moralising histories of Schlosser and Rotteck.

A similar dualism in Herder's treatment of nationality makes him seem, to Rohan Butler, for instance, to have been a forerunner of the Nazis, because of his feeling for the uniqueness of every people and his praise of German virtues in particular, especially in remoter ages, though in other respects he is a pacifist anarchist. The highly organised military state, whether in Prussia or anywhere else, is condemned by him, even excessively, and any kind of aggression is for him the very height of inhumanity.

Herder was trying to combine so many possible approaches to history in his *Ideen* that he almost inevitably failed at one point or another to reconcile them with each other. The *Ideen*, as Meinecke says, is a mighty sea of a work, always moved by current and counter-current at the same time. There is first the disposition habitual with Herder since his earliest essays on literature, to 'feel his way' into every individual phase of the historical process—into the general spirit of an age or a people, certainly, rather than into personalities; in this respect he is almost the antithesis of Carlyle, with his hero-worship. The very word 'Einfühlung' is his invention. This we may regard as a mainly *aesthetic* approach. Then there is the search for the 'genetic', the idea of the gradual development of all things according to natural laws. Even in the history of human society he looks for recurrent uniformities, and though some of the 'laws' propounded in the 15th book of the *Ideen* are not unlike the 'pragmatic maxims' castigated by Faust as he talks to Wagner, it is undeniable that Herder is the first German sociologist of note. This approach is dictated by *intellectual* needs, the desire for consistency and order in his thought.

A third approach, often encroaching on the second, proceeds from his strong *ethical* convictions, his pedagogical instinct, clear already in the *Reisetagebuch*. His conception of 'Humanität' as consisting principally in reason and fairness (Vernunft und Billigkeit), the often-repeated formula, shows that he shared the general view of his age that man rises above nature, above the beasts, chiefly through his ethical capacity. It is surprising that Herder did not include the sense of beauty among the specifically human qualities, for it counts heavily in his appreciation of culture, but Rudolf Lehmann reminds us that there is a large element of the aesthetic in Herder's notion of morality itself, influenced strongly, as it was, by Shaftesbury. Moral conduct is a harmony, resulting from control by reason and good example, but acquiring beauty, immediate appeal, in its perfection. The fourth chapter of Book 15, which prophesies the continual spread of reason and fairness among men, from the very laws of their nature, ends, as Lehmann points out, with a sentence which is pure Shaftesbury: 'As in thinking of the creation we call to mind first the *power* that brought forth chaos, and the *wisdom* and harmonious *goodness* that reduced it to order, so the order of nature in the human race develops first crude forces. Disorder itself must lead them to the path of reason, and the more fully reason completes its work, the more clearly it perceives that only *goodness* confers on this work lastingness, perfection and beauty.'[55]

Herder's ethical views bear also the imprint of his own experience and habit of life in an unpolitical age and country. In his maturity, at least, it is quiet family life that is the norm for his view of the good, as it was Goethe's and Schiller's. The values of inwardness are to the fore in it, but political action, adventure and heroism are praised as virtues only for earlier ages.

Herder's preaching, as we have seen, had always been 'rein menschlich', but however unorthodox, he was still a Lutheran minister, and had to reconcile the three approaches to history with his Christian beliefs. The increasing secularisation of his views is reflected in the *Ideen* from volume to volume, as has been seen. In Part III there is no longer any mention of the life to come as the goal for which man is made, as in Part II. The goal of life is spoken of as entirely on this earth. The one reference to the earlier view comes right at the end of Part III:

It is a beautiful dream, that of the future life, when we think of our-selves as enjoying the friendship of all the wise and the good who have ever worked for humanity, and who, as sweet reward after the accomplishment of their labours entered the better land. But in a certain measure history already throws open to us these delightful arbours for converse and intercourse with the men of sense and virtue of so many ages. Here Plato stands before me; there I hear the friendly questions of Socrates and share his final fate. When Marcus Aurelius communes in secret with his heart, he speaks with mine too, and poor Epictetus gives orders more imperatively than a king. The tortured Cicero, the unhappy Boethius speak to me, confiding to me the circumstances of their life, the grief and the comfort of their soul.[56]

This sounds very like a repudiation of the earlier view, and its replacement in part by the thought that already in this life one may in a sense enter a timeless world and hold communion with the great minds of all ages through literature. The culture of the individual (Bildung) has become a substitute for salvation, a salvation itself conceived in terms reminiscent as much of Greek ideas as of Christian. It is consistent with this view that in the sections on Christianity in the Fourth Part (1790) no mention is made of the doctrine of redemption, Christ is spoken of throughout as a man and the 'Kingdom of God' of which He spoke is interpreted as an ideal community on earth. The religion of Christ Himself is distinguished from the Christian religion that grew up after Christ's death, which is made responsible in the course of its history down to the Middle Ages for as much evil as good, especially, of course, when it became a state religion. Though Herder is so completely 'enlightened' he remains a Protestant in his opposition to everything Roman Catholic—monasticism, papal authority and so on. Gibbon's *Decline and Fall* is referred to in a footnote, along with Hume and Robertson, as a 'finished masterpiece'.

(v) '*Gott*'

The religious position at which Herder had arrived when writing the Third Part of the *Ideen* is explained by him in the short book *God*, written about the same time. It was a view very largely shared by Goethe, and reached by repeated discussion between them during their period of closest friendship, before Goethe left for Italy, when they read Spinoza together and with Frau von Stein, and found in him or through him new understanding, the one of nature and the other of history. Herder interpreted Spinoza as a great religious leader whose message confirmed that of Christianity, as he understood it. With a copy of the *Ethics* in the Latin original, to be passed on to Goethe, he sent to Frau von Stein in 1784 on Christmas Day, which was also her birthday, some rather involved distichs expressing the hope that his two friends might always in future associate Spinoza, the sage whom Charlotte already made it a pleasure for Goethe to study, with thoughts of Christmas and of Christ:

'Und Spinoza sei euch immer der heilige Christ'.

Goethe's approach to Spinoza in the second period of his Spinoza studies was a different one, that of a poet and a lover of natural history. As Erich Franz says: 'Everywhere in his writings and poetry of that time we meet with the clear distinction, following Spinoza, between a relative and an absolute view of the universe. In particular . . . anthropomorphic ideas are rejected.' Further, 'Spinoza's doctrine about the conquest of the emotions is applied by Goethe to his own relationship to poetry. . . . A man is made restless and unhappy by the surge of obscure feelings within him. As soon as he can form a clear and definite idea of things, the spell is broken.' Spinoza's notion of the freedom attained through intellectual clarity is equated by Goethe with his habit of mastering his experience by a poetic 'confession'.[57]

Yet the two writers felt themselves to be agreed in essentials, so that Goethe could greet Herder's book with enthusiasm, when it reached him in Rome on his birthday in 1787. K. P. Moritz too found it most helpful: 'It seems as if this is just the work that was needed to be the keystone of his thoughts, which always tended to fall apart.' Goethe is encouraged by it in his scientific studies; he uses Herder's key phrase 'the One and the All' (ἓν καὶ πᾶν) to describe the discovery of the 'Urpflanze' that he has just made.[58] After he has had the book for two months another letter gives some reasons for his admiration of it. It is a book that will clear the minds of those who have themselves thought about these questions, as he has. Others may find nothing in it. Goethe tries to make clear what he feels about it by comparing it to the elaborate tackle, Archimedean screws, etc., required to lift immense weights, as opposed to the simple lever that serves the stone-mason; and he goes on:

When Lavater uses his whole strength, to make a fairy-tale true; when Jacobi strains his powers, to deify a hollow feeling such as children's brains may have, when Claudius tries to make a humble messenger ('Fussbote', i.e. his periodical, the *Wandsbecker Bote*) into an evangelist, it is evident that they must detest anything that opens up the depths of nature to our sight. Would the first get away with declaring 'Everything that lives, lives through something outside itself'? Would the second not be ashamed of the confusion of ideas, the mixing up of the words *Knowledge* and *Belief*, *Tradition* and *Experience?* Would not the third have to take himself less seriously, if they were not all so busily engaged in setting up chairs round the Throne of the Lamb, if they did not so anxiously avoid coming down to the firm ground of nature, where everyone is simply what he is and all of us have the same claims? [59]

The Third Part of Herder's *Ideen*, on the other hand, Goethe goes on, could not have been written without the conception of God and the world that his *Gott* now reveals. He himself has long had some such notions of reality, his Archimedean screw, but the others can keep to their levers if they please. This passage suggests that what united three so different minds as those of Goethe, Herder and Moritz was perhaps most of all their opposition to current orthodoxy, and the violence done to common sense, as they thought, by so many of its apologists.

Reading Herder's *Gott* now, it is difficult to understand Goethe's warm welcome for it, though his likening of it, in the passage quoted, to a dish rather than to food, something which will help those who have much of their own to put into it, is a clue. Its dialogue form reminds us immediately of Shaftesbury. Even the Greek names and the vaguely suggested landscape setting are from the same model, but little use is made of the possibilities of the form, because, after the first conversation, Philolaus and Theophron have no real argument with each other and become colourless media for the expression of Herder's views. The preface tells us that the original title was *Spinoza, Shaftesbury, Leibniz*, and that the work went back ten or twelve years. In the second edition Herder added a free translation in Alcaic stanzas, with the title *Hymn to Nature*, of Shaftesbury's prose meditations put into the mouth of Theocles in *The Moralists* (III, section 1).

In the first dialogue Philolaus is persuaded by Theophron to read Spinoza himself, instead of accepting current criticism of him, and he is surprised to find that the alleged atheist must have been something like a saint. The second dialogue is hard going, dealing as it does with the relation between Spinoza, Descartes and Leibniz in their view of matter. The most interesting feature is a characteristic suggestion of a way round the Cartesian and Spinozistic dualism of mind and matter, thought and extension, through introducing the notion of 'organic powers', a phrase much used in the *Ideen*. This is a bold revision, not an explanation, of Spinoza. At the end of the dialogue, as elsewhere at intervals, oriental and other mystical and poetic reflections about the nature of God are quoted for illustration, it being implied that they all mean the same thing. In the third dialogue, the laws of physics are used as examples of the 'wise necessity' manifest in all creation, and Spinoza's rejection of final causes is discussed at length and affirmed. To repeat the thought-processes of God by discovering the laws of nature is the supreme aim of scientist and sage. The fourth dialogue brings in Lessing, as reported by Jacobi, to support the conception of an immanent God, not one 'der nur von Außen stieße', in Goethe's phrase, and the idea of a personal God, that of human freedom, and the proofs for the existence of God are discussed. Finally in the fifth dialogue the two men are joined by Theano, in whom Haym sees traits of Karoline Herder. In livelier vein she points to the contemplation of nature as sufficient proof of God, and a number of themes now familiar to us in Herder are heard again, Shaftesbury's notion of the beautiful soul (XVI, 535), immortality through the provision of new organs for the soul (548), the key conception of the organic (545) as the means by which Divine power, wisdom and goodness reveal themselves in the world, and combined with it the apparently neo-Platonic notion expressed in such phrases as: 'All forces exist that could exist' (542), or 'everything is connected and everything possible exists' (548), or 'everything exists in the world that can exist' (558). Further we find Shaftesbury's notion of an advance from chaos to order, 'an inward increase in number and beauty of the forces (of nature), in wider areas, according to rules of harmony and order ever more closely observed' (568). When Theano points to forms of life that prey on others, she is reminded that but for this apparent death, everything in creation would be true death, i.e. a stagnant calm (träge

Ruhe), 'a desolate realm of shades, in which all active existence had died' (563)—a reflection close to Goethe's in the 'Nature' essay, with which we have suggested a parallel in Shaftesbury. The problem of evil and suffering, however, is never really faced: 'All evil is negative, but we call evil what is really a limitation, an opposition, a transition, and none of these three deserve this name' (570). 'The faults of men too are for an understanding spirit good: for the more understanding he is, the more clearly they will appear to him as faults, and help him therefore, as contrasts, to further light, to purer goodness and truth' (571)—but what about those afflicted with these 'faults'? Is it enough, one asks, that they should be walking sermons to the virtuous?

With the real Spinoza, the experts agree, this work has very little to do, but it is revealing as a statement of Herder's eclectic religious philosophy just before the French Revolution. Through the dialogue form he intended, as the preface shows, to present certain views that suggested themselves to him as he pondered over Spinoza, Leibniz and Shaftesbury, without committing himself finally to any of them. What is put forward here does not go beyond a mild Deism, closest to Shaftesbury of the three teachers mentioned, an optimistic nature-worship in the main, too vague and superficial to provide anything but a fair-weather philosophy. There is of course nothing specifically Christian about it at all and it contains no reference to Christ or any Christian doctrine.

(vi) 'Ideen'. Fourth Part

The Fourth Part of the *Ideen* adds nothing essentially new to Herder's theory of culture, though it illustrates certain features more fully, particularly in his attitude to the early Church and to the Middle Ages. There is less general reflection than in Part III, and much wide-ranging narrative, remarkable for the learning and the imaginative grasp of universal history displayed. Herder deals in it principally with northern Europe from the Dark Ages to the Crusades, but he is fully alive to external influences, especially that of the Arabs, and one of the five books is devoted to the origins and the spread of Christianity. The general ideas and the personal likes and dislikes already mentioned are much in evidence. The continuity of civilisation is frequently illustrated, as when Herder writes: 'Of itself no people in Europe has risen to civilisation. Each has rather tried to hold on to its old barbarous manners as long as ever it could'—as is understandable in view of the geographical conditions and their need of strong military institutions. 'The whole civilisation of north-eastern and western Europe is a growth from Roman, Greek and Arabian seed,' and what the Romans had failed to do by conquest had to be done by the spiritual conquest made by a foreign creed.

Herder prefaces his account of Christianity with a stanza (from memory?) from Goethe's unfinished *Die Geheimnisse*, which had been begun as a result of Goethe's talks with him about the *Ideen*, in 1784. The coolness of his attitude to early and medieval Christianity is that of a man of strongly Protestant upbringing in a free-thinking century, but some of the interpretations and omissions are surprising all the same in one of Herder's cloth. Christianity was founded, he writes, by a man of the people— born of a virgin, certainly, he says somewhere incidentally, but not, apparently, divine, and possessed by the mission to found a heavenly kingdom on earth at what he speaks of as his second coming, to 'form (bilden) men of God'. His few recorded sayings are full of 'Humanität', he showed it in his whole way of life and through his death. Herder distinguishes, as we have seen, like Lessing and most of the Enlightened, between the religion preached by Jesus, his 'living plan for the welfare of man', a 'Christianity of attitude and action' (Goethe to Eckermann, 11 March 1832), and the religion of belief in Him, Goethe's 'Christianity of the World and of Faith', 'an unthinking worship of his person and his cross'. The time was ripe for a universal religion. The miraculous features in the Christian story are put down to 'pious deceit', and even its moral code is admired with a certain reserve. In Herder here we find for instance the phrase about the danger of 'human society becoming a great hospital',[60] which may well strike readers who come across it in Goethe's *Italian Journey* as an anticipation of Nietzsche's rejection of Christian pity. Goethe apparently used it first, in a letter of 1787, before he received the Third Part of the *Ideen*.[61] On Herder's next page we read: 'It became (in the Church) a Christian virtue to renounce the use of one's reason and to follow, instead of one's own convictions, the authority of another's opinion.' Herder is not only opposed to the principle of Church authority, but to the formulation of belief in creeds and to any kind of monasticism. He thinks that Gibbon judges Christianity very charitably and defends him against his English critics.

Herder gives a full and sympathetic account of the migrations of Germanic tribes and of the early Germanic kingdoms, culminating in an admiring description of Charles the Great. The exploits of the Viking age also clearly appeal to his imagination. The medieval German Empire, on the other hand, is very briefly discussed and praise is reserved for the peaceful work of the cities and one or two monasteries, German women receiving special mention for their domestic virtues. In a few general reflections on the German kingdoms in Europe the tradition of court pomp and ceremony is traced back to Tartar Khans. The development of the Papacy and Church domination of life is depicted in dark colours, apart from the grudging admission that Christian sympathy for the poor and afflicted always wrought good under any form of state organisation, and that much benefit resulted, at least indirectly, from the work of the monasteries, for scholarship, morals, order and humane feeling. But Herder thinks that the universal use of Latin was a hindrance to the development of the native cultures, though, as we saw, he had elsewhere stressed the indispensable role of the civilisation of the ancients in the development of northern Europe. Finally, he has hardly a good word to say for the influence of the Crusades on civilisation, but recognises fully the civilising role of the Arabs. Summing up, he says: 'The Roman Church deserves praise as a counter-weight (to barbarous impulses); as primary and lasting motive force, it would have turned Europe into a Tibetan Church state.' Knights and clerics fortunately gave way finally in importance to the third estate, of scholars, useful workers and craftsmen.

(vii) The 'Humanitätsbriefe'

The Fourth Part is an uneven, highly subjective piece of writing, and it seems clear that, as usual, Herder was losing interest in the full working out of his ambitious plans. At any rate, the projected Fifth Part was never written, but after the French Revolution Herder produced a long series of articles in the form of letters, published in twelve 'Collections' between 1793 and 1797, on the central theme of 'Humanität', which to some extent take the place of the missing Part, in that they take the examination of the growth of 'Humanität' down to his own times, though quite unsystematically. Few judgments are revised and on the whole the Humanitätsbriefe add little of substance to Herder's theory of culture, though they illustrate some aspects of it more fully.

In Weimar, the French Revolution was greeted with enthusiasm by Wieland, Herder and Knebel. Wieland commented on each month's news in his Merkur, with good sense and moderation, like a wise uncle who had thought all these things out already in works like Der goldene Spiegel. He continued hopeful for about two years, until the death of Mirabeau, and still allowed articles for and against the Revolution to appear in his monthly, but took himself a more and more legitimist line, insisting that only reasonable reform, and particularly the efforts of individuals to be better and more rational men, could improve the lot of mankind. Herder's faith in the revolutionary leaders lasted a little longer, until the execution of Louis XVI in January 1793, but during that time he expressed more radical views than Wieland in private correspondence and in the first, unprinted version of the 'First Collection' of the Humanitätsbriefe, written in 1792. Here he was more concerned with current politics than in any previous work, though he took care to express his ideas in the form of a correspondence between friends of different shades of opinion, so that he could not be pinned down to any one view. The Spirit of the

Times was disposing of feudalism and class privileges, he makes one of his mouthpieces declare, and bringing into being again a real *Volk*, such as Herder had long believed to have existed in simpler ages.[62] The original letter 17 probably comes nearest to his own view of the Revolution at this time, and here he rates it as equal in importance to the introduction of Christianity, to the Migrations of Peoples, the Renaissance and the Reformation. The Crusades and the Thirty Years War he puts lower. The apparent evil in this great event will be turned to good by a higher power. As for Germany, if its thousand governments are as just and kindly as everyone is now saying, it has nothing to fear. Has the Papal Court, he adds ironically, not done it the honour of calling it 'The Land of Obedience'?[63]

What was actually published was a much milder version, written after the Terror, when Herder swung violently away from his earlier view. Much of the first version was discarded and the rest was given a more general treatment. The reader has the impression that Herder was losing his grip. He relies far too much on copious quotation from writings by well-known personalities, mainly from modern times, who in his view have contributed to the growth of 'Humanität', first Benjamin Franklin and Frederick the Great, who is compared with Joseph II and represented in a surprisingly favourable light, in view of Herder's earlier pronouncements about the power-state, and Prussia in particular. He makes the most of humane sentiments in Frederick's letters, and of his literary and philosophical interests, but he does not now stress his hostility to German literature and says nothing about the many inhumane features in his view of life and his system of government—his contempt for the general mass of mankind, his treatment of even high officials as mere tools, his deliberate acts of aggression. The spread of 'Humanität' in forms of government seems to be the general theme intended for this first group of letters, but republicanism and benevolent despotism find equal favour in Herder's eyes, perhaps because both are far removed from the rule of the self-indulgent petty princes he has so frequently criticised.

The models of humanity cited later are chiefly men of letters and philosophers, though they include Comenius, Machiavelli, Grotius, Montesquieu, Rousseau and Kant, all important for contributions to political theory, as well as Leibniz, Lessing and a few obscurer figures. Herder is interested in all efforts that have been made to break down the barriers between nations, social classes and religions, and he naturally quotes liberally, for instance, from Lessing's dialogues on Freemasonry, *Ernst und Falk*, where the ideal of an 'invisible church' of enlightened individuals in all countries is so persuasively put forward. Repeatedly, too, Herder comes back to the question of how Germany itself can be made more truly humane. The power of literature, especially the literary drama, to encourage humane ways of thinking and feeling is illustrated from Lessing's *Emilia Galotti*, where an appeal is made to the deepest feelings of the audience about evils which are beyond the reach of the law.

The purpose of Herder's examination of so many models of humanity is apparently twofold, to encourage his readers to make themselves into better men, and to foster what he considers the right kind of national feeling. With the first aim in view he often recurs to the topic of 'Bildung' in the sense of self-improvement. 'Man has a will', he writes in No. 29. 'He is not just a mechanical link in the chain of nature. The spirit which controls nature is partly in him. . . . He should organise the things around him, and in particular his own actions, in accordance with the general principle of the world.'[64] To support this view, essentially still the same as he had put forward in the *Ideen* and *Gott*, of man's 'Gottähnlichkeit', he quotes from the stoic reflections of Marcus Aurelius. After some discussion of the best name for this humane ideal, he decides in favour of 'Humanität' and again tries to define it (No. 27). It is 'the character of our species; but it is only innate in us in germ (in Anlagen) and must really be added to us by education. We do not bring it all complete into the world; but in the world it should be the goal of our effort, the sum of our exercises and what we most value. . . . What is divine in our species is therefore *Bildung zur Humanität* (the capacity to train ourselves to 'Humanität'). . . .'[65] If we neglect it, we sink back into *brutality*. 'Humanity' is still a name partly for the qualities observed in man, partly for the highest qualities that should be his ideal, and the link is to be found in Herder's revised notion of Providence. God has put the seeds of excellence in man, and at the same time the urge to cultivate them to the full.

On the second point (nationality) he quotes criticisms of German over-readiness to imitate others, especially the French, revealing again his distaste for the French and his strong desire for cultural independence. But it is simply a cultural nationalism that he has in view, and he does not encourage the idea that his nation is superior to others, only that every nation has its own form of excellence (No. 42). 'Of all forms of pride I consider national pride, together with pride of birth and nobility, as the greatest of follies.'[66] He returns to this theme more than once, reprinting in No. 57, for instance, in a revised form a youthful essay with the title 'Have we still the public and fatherland of the Ancients?' He deals here with the German indifference towards German literature and the German theatre, and German lack of patriotism. Sparta and Rome are not held up as models, the dangers of national pride are insisted on, and any kind of aggression in its name is strongly condemned.[67] The Ninth of the Collections is entirely devoted to the advocacy of a purified patriotism, a fair and just attitude to other nations, and the condemnation of war, except in self-defence. He still rejects fiercely the 'Gallicomania, which for 100 years has kept whole classes of our society apart'—for the use of French has been a social shibboleth, 'a man to whom you spoke German was a *domestique*',[68] and rejoices in the measure of emancipation from excessive foreign influence which has been achieved by a series of middle-class German writers like Lessing, though he regrets that so many of them write now for 'Lesegesellschaften', subscription libraries, to which he attributes the worst of taste. 'France herself has tasted the results of the misuse of various principles of Rousseau, Voltaire, Helvetius; time has passed judgment on them and helped the onlookers to wiser views', but there is still much to learn from the French, and the Germans should continue to do so, just as they have profited infinitely from English writers.

We will continue on this modest course and not expect that people should understand and appreciate us. National fame is a snare and a delusion. At first it lures and encourages us, but when it has reached a certain pitch, it encloses the head in a brazen bandage. Incapable of taking in any new impressions from outside, the victim sees in the fog nothing but his own image. Heaven preserve us from national fame of this order. We are not yet (fully ourselves) and we know why, but we are making every effort, and will succeed.[61]

Almost every essay in the Tenth and last Collection makes clear the difference between what Herder has in mind and the national self-assertion which some of his writings have occasionally been used to justify. Taking up in No. 118 the topic of how to abolish war, one much discussed during the wars that shocked the conscience of Europe in the closing years of the century, after so long a peace, he introduces, under the heading *Zum ewigen Frieden*, the title of Kant's recent treatise, the story of the Delaware and Iroquese Indians and their 'grosse Friedensfrau'. *His* 'great-woman of peace', he says, is general fairness, active reason, in a word, 'humanity'.[70] War, where it is not enforced self-defence, but aggression, is an action unworthy of a beast. There is a false glory surrounding the names of conquering heroes and sly diplomatists that must be dispelled. True patriotism does not desire to interfere in other nations' affairs, but does its utmost to understand. Only a common feeling of decency among civilised peoples, and no rules or mechanisms, can ensure lasting peace. There is *no* 'best form of government'—every nation must work out the one appropriate to itself. It is not true (as Kant asserts) that there is an 'absolute evil' in mankind that would prevent this (No. 123). Man is essentially good. Christianity itself preaches pure humanity in his sense. The experience of wartime, we see, confirms Herder in all the old beliefs proclaimed in the *Ideen*.

2. GOETHE, 1785–1805

Herder's theory of culture was concerned above all, as we have seen, with the group, the people or nation and its 'Kultur' or civilisation, though he was fully aware both of the debt every civilisation owed to its predecessors, and of the insignificance of the contribution made by any one generation, in comparison with the immensity of its inheritance from the past. He naturally speaks frequently, in the *Ideen*, of the important role of education in the maintenance and extension of a civilisation and of the necessity for each individual to develop the full potentialities of his own nature by conscious effort, with the help of his fellows and the social inheritance. That this should be a man's chief aim in life is urged in the passage already quoted from the *Humanitäts-briefe*. The same message is proclaimed even more emphatically in *Tithon und Aurora*: 'We all bear an ideal within us of what we should be and are not; the slag (Schlacken) we discard, the form to which we should aspire, we all know.'[71] The 'slag' metaphor is exactly that used by Goethe in the letter quoted above (p. 177), and the whole reminds us of the Plotinian saying about the statue each should make of himself, which he had used in the *Ideen*.

In the Goethe of the middle years this notion of the duty of self-improvement is quite central, and it is to him more than to any other of the German classics that the ideal of the pursuit of 'allgemeine Bildung' owes the strong hold it obtained over the educated class. The work which did most to spread Goethe's ideas was of course the novel *Wilhelm Meister's Apprenticeship*, which came to be known as a novel of 'Bildung' and established itself as the supreme model for serious German novelists. But thoughts about 'Bildung' are scattered throughout Goethe's letters and works of the Weimar years, especially in the auto-biographical writings and the novels.

(i) *The effect of Italy*

The *Italian Journey* shows how eagerly Goethe continued in Italy the process of self-education which we have followed, particularly with regard to his scientific interests and ethical aspirations, for his first years in Weimar. A few examples only can be considered out of the abundant evidence to be found in the contemporary letters and journals which Goethe collected and wrote up, between 1814 and 1817, and again in 1829, into the record of his two happiest years. From first to last the reader is struck by Goethe's voracious but supremely intelligent appetite for experience, especially of nature and art. It is not the acquisition of what A. N. Whitehead calls 'inert knowledge' that makes a cultivated man. Goethe would have agreed with him when he calls 'a merely well-informed man the most useless bore on God's earth'. Facts are of no interest to him except in so far as they illustrate ideas. When Claude Bernard wrote in 1865 his still valuable *Introduction à l'étude de la médecine expérimentale*, which anticipates in some essentials the modern theory of scientific method as expounded, for example, by Karl Popper, he appealed to the authority of Goethe in support of his notion of experimental reasoning. This is for him 'the very reverse of scholastic reasoning. Scholasticism must always have a fixed and indubitable starting-point', from which conclusions are deduced by pure logic. We shall find examples of this method presently in Goethe's contemporary Fichte, and even to some extent in Schiller. For Bernard, 'there is no absolute truth apart from mathematical principles; in all natural phenomena the principles from which we start, like the conclusions which we reach, embody only relative truths. The experimenter's stumbling-block, then, consists in thinking that he knows what he does not know, and in taking for absolute, truths that are only relative. Hence, the unique and fundamental rule of scientific investigation is reduced to doubt, as great philosophers, moreover, have already proclaimed.' (English translation by H. C. Greene, p. 49.)

Bernard refers explicitly (p. 31) to Goethe's essay of 1792, *Der Versuch als Vermittler von Objekt und Subjekt*, and earlier (p. 12) he quotes Goethe to the effect that 'Experience disciplines man every day', adding the comment: 'But this is because man reasons accurately and experimentally about what he observes; otherwise he could not trust himself.' In Goethe's essay the point is not made so plainly, although we have from it the impression that Goethe is well on the way towards a true theory of method. He sees that scientific observation and experiment must be preceded by theorising, by a working hypothesis, and that man, being, as Bernard says, by nature proud and inclined to metaphysics, must constantly question his findings, but we are a little shaken to find that the intention of the essay is obviously to discredit Newton's theory of colour and to serve towards establishing his own, which he looked upon in the end with the affection of a fond and indulgent parent, and which everyone had to accept if they wished to be in his good books.

The opening paragraph of Goethe's essay admirably describes however that objective attitude of the naturalist towards his material which we find Goethe striving for in Italy. 'The true botanist', he writes, 'should not be moved either by the beauty or the usefulness of plants. He should examine their formation, their relationship towards the rest of the vegetable kingdom, and just as they are all encouraged to come out and are irradiated by the sun, so he too should look at and survey them all with the same calm eye, and take the standard for this investigation, the data for his judgment, not from himself, but from the circle of things that he is observing.' Yet brute facts are of no interest until they suggest hypotheses about their connection with what is already provisionally established.

It is only a hasty reader who finds the *Italian Journey* over-loaded with mere facts. What fills sympathetic minds with astonishment is Goethe's immense capacity for finding things interesting, because they all have a bearing on problems that have occupied his mind in the course of his varied duties and studies. The changes in the soil as he moves south through Bavaria, their geological causes and their agricultural results, naturally catch the eye of the friend of Batty and Voigt, for instance, but in the same way, because of their importance for his living interests, he notices the rocks and their structure, trees and plants and their variations in different habitats, cloud formations, weather and climate, and just as attentively, the villages and towns, their position, their plan and architecture, the people and their activities, the influence of the past on the present, and so on indefinitely. In Italy, besides nature and man, it is art above all that occupies his attention. His sympathies are not universal, but subject to the limitations imposed upon him by his previous experience and education in art. He came to Italy full of the ideas of Mengs, the classicistic painter, with his admiration for the Italian Renaissance painters, the nearest approach for him to ancient Greek art. Goethe too put Raphael highest among modern artists, and in architecture Palladio. He had no taste for the Baroque; even Michelangelo did not really satisfy him, nor did he show any interest in the Italian Primitives. The art of the Ancients that he saw consisted mainly of Roman copies of Greek statues in the museums, Winckelmann's material for his *History* and seen through his eyes. Goethe was not yet in a position to realise the difference between Roman and Greek architecture because so little was known about the latter. The few remains of Greek temples Goethe saw he seems to have found rather forbidding.

He is much influenced by his German artist friends in Rome, and the inner urge he feels, though discouraged by his lack of technical skill, to draw and paint, helps to make his art studies too a kind of experimental thinking. This life of free activity, spontaneously following his interests, fills him with a delight he has not experienced for years. In Rome (10 November 1786) he writes: 'I am living here now in a mood of calm and clarity such as I have not known for a long time.' He is trying to see things as they are and forget all preconceived ideas. 'Any one who seriously looks around him here and has eyes to see, must become solid, he must acquire a notion of solidity such as he has never had so vividly.' He feels as if he had never valued the things of this world so truly as now. He would like to stay for some time longer. 'I am not here to enjoy myself in my fashion; I want to occupy myself with the great objects that surround me, to learn and *develop* myself fully (mich ausbilden) before I am forty.' He had written earlier: 'It is in my nature to do reverence to the great and beautiful, willingly and with joy, and it is the most blessed of all feelings to be able to *develop* this capacity day by day, hour by hour, on such glorious objects' (17 September 1786). Soon he is speaking of the change wrought in him by this new experience as a rebirth, so much has had to be unlearned as well as learned, and he reverts to the already familiar image of the tower. 'I am like an architect who wanted to build a tower and had laid bad foundations; he finds it out in good time and gladly pulls down what he had raised' in order to build it more solidly. 'Along with my feeling for art, my moral sense is experiencing a great renewal' (20 December 1786).

This renewal is difficult to describe, but its reality is evident from all Goethe's later writings, as well as from what he says about it here. There is no such reversal of direction as might seem to be implied in the last quotation, for he had been developing along these lines since the beginning of the 'eighties, but he can move now so much more freely and quickly than he had been able to do in Weimar, with his many responsibilities there, that he only now fully realises the change in himself, though it had come about by the continual response of his whole being to particular demands of life. Repeatedly he speaks of his youth as lived in a world hidden from him by a mist, 'Da Nebel mir die Welt verhüllten' (*Faust*, I, 188), a mist of subjective imaginings about life. By middle age he has learned to see things as they are, he feels, and so, more than once, he thinks of himself as visited by truth herself as his muse, a figure he associates with the sun breaking through the morning mist (*Zueignung zu den Gedichten*), who hands to him 'the veil of poetry'. Seeing things as they are means for him not merely seeing them as they appear to the general run of people, in their public aspect, but understanding them, by linking them up in thought with all that he knows of the order of nature. So at one moment we find him declaring (23 August 1787): 'I am so far from the world now and from all worldly things that it seems very strange to me to read a newspaper. The shape (Gestalt) of this world passes away; I would like to occupy myself only with those aspects that are lasting

relationships, and so, following the teaching of . . . [Spinoza?],
gain access to eternity in the spirit.' Two months later (27
October 1787), after expressing his agreement with the conclusion
of the Third Part of Herder's *Ideen*, he says he has found in this
year that all really intelligent people come to the view 'that the
moment is all, and that the only thing a reasonable man can desire
for himself is that his life, as far as it depends on him, may contain
the greatest possible number of rationally occupied, happy
moments'.

The remarks of Herder with which he is expressing agreement
here are about the eternal order that Herder finds everywhere in
the labyrinth of history, as in nature, e.g.: 'All the works of God
have their foundations in themselves, and their beautiful connection with themselves: for they all maintain themselves within
their definite limits, contrary forces being brought to balance by
an inner power that guided them to order.'[72] A little later comes
the reflection, quoted above, about the 'beautiful dream' of
immortality and the possibility of escaping from time, even
during life, through literature and philosophy. It is not a 'carpe
diem' philosophy, then, that Goethe is preaching, but a concentration on the concrete here and now, as opposed to an
imagined future life, but a here and now seen 'in the light of
eternity', as illustrating the unchanging laws of nature and life.
The two passages quoted have essentially the same thing in view,
though we have to wait for the philosophical poems of his old
age, like *Dauer im Wechsel*, *Eins und Alles* and *Vermächtnis*,
to find the underlying thought more clearly stated. It is
perhaps expressed most beautifully in *Um Mitternacht*, in the
lines:

Bis dann zuletzt des vollen Mondes Helle
So klar und deutlich mir ins Finstere drang,
Auch der Gedanke willig, sinnig, schnelle
Sich ums Vergangene wie ums Künftige schlang; Um Mitternacht.*

* Till then at last the full moon's brightness lit up so clearly and distinctly all
my darkness, and thought too, willing, judicious, swift, wove itself around both
the past and the future, at midnight.

It is a thought habitual with Goethe from the Italian days on, and it enters into all his reflections on culture. For it is only the full mind that can live in the moment in this sense, 'the moment that is eternity' ('Der Augenblick ist Ewigkeit'—*Vermächtnis*), when the mind is aware that 'Das Ew'ge regt sich fort in allen'. This is the intellectual life in the fullest sense, the capacity for 'ideas' that, together with the power of human affection, still makes life worth living in extreme old age, when everything else has gone:

Mir bleibt genug! Es bleibt Idee und Liebe!* ('Die Jahre nahmen dir, du sagst, so vieles' in *W.Ö. Divan.*)

English readers, born into a very different tradition, which immediately suggests to them an attitude of humorous self-depreciation when they feel they are beginning to take themselves and life too seriously, naturally find some of Goethe's remarks in the *Italian Journey* a little portentous. Max Beerbohm has expressed their feeling wittily in his essay 'Quia Imperfectum' (in *And even now*). Goethe was conscious of being very German as a traveller, very like Winckelmann, he thought, in the seriousness with which he *studied* art and life (13 December 1786). He is for ever insisting that he is working hard, not just enjoying himself (20 December 1786, 14 September 1787), though it is a 'seriousness without dullness', which he enjoys in itself and because it will benefit his whole life (9 November 1786). His seriousness may sometimes be exaggerated to salve his conscience and to excuse to Frau von Stein his truancy from Weimar. He did not write to her about the Roman widow! A certain over-seriousness continued to be an ingredient in German 'Bildung' long after Goethe's time, but if art, for us, is primarily there to be enjoyed, there is no doubt that the German pursuit of 'Bildung' has also deepened our enjoyment, and the range of Goethe's response to experience makes Paul Valéry call him 'un monstre de compréhension et de force créatrice', 'un de nos meilleurs essais de nous rendre semblables à des dieux'.[73]

---

* I have enough. I have ideas and love.

To describe the advance Goethe made in knowledge and understanding in those two happy years in Italy is far beyond the scope
of our study. Even his *Italian Journey* only indicates a part of it.
But we may note some of the ways in which he continued there
the lines of investigation of which we have seen the beginnings
made in Weimar, usually prompted by some problem presented
to him by everyday life and work.

There was first the whole complex of his interests in the natural
sciences, particularly geology, botany and zoology. In the varied
landscapes of Italy, among the rich flora and fauna warmed by its
sun, he found new material, of course, wherever he went, and
was continually adding to his collections. In this he was not so
exceptional as one might think, for even in Europe, in that century
so eager for enlightenment, a serious traveller tended to regard
himself as something of an explorer, as the prefaces to some
famous books of travel indicate, Diderot's *Voyage en Hollande*,
for instance, or Nicolai's *Reisen*, the former demanding an
encyclopedic knowledge of his tourist, and the latter preparing
him for all contingencies with practical hints. Goethe had contacts, M. Michéa reminds us,[74] with the numerous Italian amateurs
of science, and he went on looking for evidence to confirm or
refute theories which he brought with him from Germany. In
geological matters he refers in the *Italian Journey* not only to the
the general guides (especially to Volkmann's *Historisch-kritische
Nachrichten von Italien*, Leipzig, 1770–1) but to special treatises
like that of the Swede Ferber, the Pole de Borch, and the Swiss
Bénédict de Saussure, whom he had visited. He finds nothing to
shake his belief in Weimar theories about the primary importance
of slow change through the action of water, rather than cataclysms
produced by volcanic fury.

The most striking new development in Goethe's scientific
thought was in the field of botany. His reflections in the fine
botanical garden at Padua (27 September 1786) show the way his
mind had long been working. The many plants new to him were
a great stimulus to thought, he found, 'and what is looking
(Beschauen) without thinking?' (experimental thinking), he goes

on. 'Here that thought comes to me with renewed force, that it might perhaps be possible to develop *all* forms of plant from one. Only in this way could we determine genera and species properly, instead of by the very arbitrary method, as it seems to me, employed up till now.' But so far he finds the problem offers insuperable difficulties. He reverts to it more than once; in Sicily, in the public garden at Palermo, with its lush growth of plants he had only known in hothouses, he felt he *must* be able to find 'die Urpflanze'—but by what criterion could he recognise it? (17 April 1787). In Naples, a month later, he writes to Herder that he is hot on the scent. 'The "Urpflanze" will be the strangest creation in the world, which nature herself will envy me. With this model and the key to it you will be able to invent plants *ad infinitum* which will necessarily be consistent, i.e. even if they never existed, they *could* exist . . . having an inner truth and necessity.' Commenting on this letter later in the *Italian Journey*, Goethe says he had realised that it is 'the part we call leaf that is the real Proteus, that could hide or reveal itself in all plant formations. Forwards and backwards the plant is always only leaf.' The various parts of the plant, that is, can be looked upon as all modifications of the one type of structure, the leaf, adapted to their particular function in the life of the plant by a process he calls 'metamorphosis' in the short treatise written on his return from Italy. Mrs Agnes Arber, who has written of Goethe's botanical researches with unusually sympathetic interest, reminds us that 'Goethe uses the term "leaf" (Blatt) for the member which undergoes successive changes, appearing in the guise of one lateral appendage after another. Goethe himself recognised that this terminology is unsatisfactory, since the word "leaf" is inseparably associated in daily usage with the foliage leaf, whereas, on this view, the foliage leaf has no more claim to be itself the typical "leaf" than has, for instance, the cotyledon or the stamen.' The theory at which he arrived in his attempt to understand the mechanism of metamorphosis, about the gradual elaboration and refinement of the sap in its course, 'may well be regarded as foreshadowing modern ideas upon the relation of chemistry and form. It has also been suggested that the process of metamorphosis, as visualised by Goethe, may be restated in twentieth-century terms by interpreting it on genic lines.' There is an obvious artificiality, she thinks, about his theory of the six alternating stages of expansion and contraction, 'but Goethe may have been dimly groping after a conception of periodic rhythm in the development of appendages at the growing apex'.

Mrs Arber admits serious inadequacies in Goethe's theory, and what she says about them is important for an understanding of Goethe's science in general. 'The artistic economy of his exposition', she says, 'was achieved at the expense of deliberate and ruthless exclusions, which to some extent reduce the significance of the work.' He discusses only annual plants, and only the metamorphosis of the appendicular organs of the stem in them. His was not

a full morphological interpretation, but merely a single step towards such an interpretation. He did not, however, see the matter in this light, but he treated his theory, of which he was enamoured, as having the finality of a work of art, rather than the provisional character of a work of science. . . .It was a defect in Goethe's amateur pursuit of science that he was too much attached to his personal notions and never attained the professional's hard-earned capacity for seeing his own work in due proportion in the general stream of thought.[75]

The truth of this criticism is even more clearly evident in regard to Goethe's *Theory of Colour*, as Sherrington has clearly shown.

For an understanding of the importance of these ideas in Goethe's thought about life and culture, the researches of M. René Michéa into the philosophical and scientific background, Goethe's known sources of information, are very helpful. The climate of philosophical opinion in which they grew owes most, as is generally agreed, to Leibniz, apart from Spinoza, although Goethe may not have received Leibniz's ideas at first-hand, but through intermediaries like the Swiss scientist, Bonnet. Leibniz, co-discoverer of the infinitesimal calculus, was intensely interested in the notion of continuity in nature. 'Continuity and discontinuity are for him two complementary aspects of reality', as

M. Michéa puts it. Nature is inconceivably rich in separate, individual creations, yet the connections between them are so close that if we had full knowledge we should hardly see any gaps in between, for there is continuity everywhere.

There is no void between the varied phenomena of the corporeal world....Beginning with ourselves and proceeding to the lowest things, it is a descent made by very small stages and through a continuous succession of things which differ very little from step to step. There are fish which have wings, and to which the air is not a foreign element, and there are birds which live in the water and have cold blood like fish. . . .There are animals which seem to have as much knowledge and reason as some animals called men; and the animal and vegetable are so close to each other, that if you take the most imperfect of the one and the most perfect of the other, you will hardly notice any great difference between them.

So it must be also, Leibniz thinks, in the series of beings between us and God's infinite perfection.[76]

A little further on he writes: 'Perhaps at some time or in some place in the universe, the kinds of animals are or were or will be more subject to change than they are at present among us, and several animals which have something of the cat about them, like the lion, the tiger and the lynx, might have been of one and the same race, and may be at present as it were subdivisions of the old species of cats.' Here, with the notion of the variability of species and the unity of the type, Leibniz comes much closer to modern ideas than most of the poets and philosophers in the seventeenth and eighteenth centuries presented in A. O. Lovejoy's well-known book, *The Great Chain of Being*,[77] like Pope, with his

> Vast chain of being! which from God began,
> Natures ethereal, human, angel, man,
> Beast, bird, fish, insect, what no eye can see,
> No glass can reach; from Infinite to thee,
> From thee to nothing.

Herder echoes this strain of thought in the phrase, repeated, we found, so often in the *Ideen*, about 'everything coming into being that could', which evidently expresses what Lovejoy calls 'the principle of plenitude', first propounded in the *Timaeus* of Plato and so on, his frequent references to the great chain of being, and his search for continuity of development in culture. In Buffon, so much admired by Goethe, the idea of continuity is also stressed. Nature proceeds 'by unknown gradations' and passes from species to species by 'imperceptible nuances'. For Bonnet, this idea, Michéa says, is the thread of Ariadne. Everything in the universe is connected, everything makes for the same end, as he shows by innumerable examples.

We have seen already how the desire to disprove an apparent discontinuity had led to Goethe's discovery of the intermaxillary bone. 'Every creature is only one tone, one nuance in a great harmony', he wrote to Knebel (17 November 1784), which we must study as a whole. It was on his second, much briefer stay in Italy in 1790, to anticipate a little, that Goethe, still applying the principle of continuity, was led, by the sight of a sheep's cranium in the Jewish cemetery on the Lido at Venice, to the idea that the bony covering of the brain has developed from a vertebra, each of which similarly encloses marrow. This is another instance of what he called 'metamorphosis' and was eventually written up into two essays (*Bedeutende Fördernis*, 1823; *Das Schädelgerüst*, 1824).

Goethe's ideas on metamorphosis in plants and animals are acknowledged by many, but not all, historians of science to have had a certain importance in themselves, but what is still more interesting in the history of ideas is to see them as one aspect of his general metaphysical outlook, and to see this in relation to its time. For purely metaphysical speculation he never displayed much interest. We have seen how he himself and many in Weimar influenced by him turned rather to geology or botany or some other concrete study of the world of nature, to Schiller's initial disgust. But metaphysical ideas were quite clearly implied even in this turning away from traditional metaphysics, and the notions of continuity and of order, for instance, that enter into all his biological studies, were as little invented by him as any of the eighteenth-century cultural achievements which Herder delighted in tracing back to centuries of accumulated tradition. Leibniz, Spinoza, Herder himself and probably a score of others had a share in them, but perhaps the deepest root of all was to be found in the religious beliefs and the accompanying attitude to life and nature that Goethe had unconsciously absorbed as a boy in Frankfurt and never really shed, in spite of great changes in their form and manner of expression. When he tried in old age, in the *Wanderjahre*, to put some of his deepest beliefs into a non-dogmatic form that could be taught to others, the result was the passages about the three kinds of reverence which the Elders in his Educational Province tried to inculcate in their pupils, reverence for what is above us, beneath us, equal to us, and finally self-reverence, or self-respect, as the sum of them all. But attitudes such as these are communicated by personal contact, rather than by any logical demonstration of why they should be adopted by those who have not grown up with them, as teachers in our own age have only too often found. The order of nature, the idea of perfection and completeness that is behind the 'Great Chain of Being', and so on, were also not directly found in nature by the unassisted mind even of a Goethe. Born into another mental climate, he would, one can only suppose, have had quite another conception of the 'Great Mother', and many of the turns of phrase in the *Nature Fragment* strike a modern scientist like Sherrington as unbearably sentimental and false, because they do not fit in with his knowledge and experience, the phrase about Nature's 'friendly game' with all her creatures, for instance, in view of such biological adaptations of means to ends as cancer, or bilharzia, or sheep-rot, of which Sherrington's classical description indicates the great gulf that separates his view of nature from Goethe's.[78]

We may have to suspend judgment about many of Goethe's ideas about botany, then, or reject them, but it is instructive to trace their relationship to his ideas about art and literature, and the 'eternity of the moment', for these are profoundly interesting, and there are close analogies between them all. The habit of mind which reveals itself in these ideas was not a product of the Italian journey. Goethe's botanical ideas, as M. Michéa says, were fixed in their main lines long before he left Weimar.

When Goethe crossed the Brenner, he was already clearly aware of the problem. It was 'fixisme' versus evolutionism, preformation versus epigenesis, mechanical or atomistic explanation of life versus dynamic qualitative transformation producing new forms, not reducible geometrically to preceding forms. And he felt irresistibly attracted towards evolutionism, epigenesis, a vitalist biology. The distinctive influence of the journey itself amounts roughly to this, it showed the poet the same plants in different habitats and gave him, thanks to the exuberant habit of mediterranean vegetation, particularly favourable conditions for observation.[79]

His new *aperçus* were the result of long patient activity including much reading, of works made accessible to Goethe, it is interesting for our purpose to note, especially through one of the tools of culture he owed to Weimar, the library acquired on his advice by the University of Jena from Hofrat Büttner, of which more will be heard later, in the chapter on Weimar institutions. Goethe himself always insisted on the methodical effort which led to his discoveries,[80] for, as M. Michéa says, there is no more creation *ex nihilo* in science than in literature. What is behind it all for him is the profound belief in the unity of nature, the ἕν καὶ πᾶν that he found in Spinoza, as he understood him. The really original and valuable contribution he made, in fact, M. Michéa persuasively argues, is his fruitful pondering over this one idea and application of it to many fields of experience.

We shall come later to the famous discussion between Goethe and Schiller on these matters, which ended with Schiller's declaring that what Goethe had always thought of as an 'Anschauung' was what he would call an 'Idee'. Goethe, predominantly visual in his imagery, seemed to see in his mind's eye as a concrete form the type from which nature, he thought, created a whole series of varying forms, for instance in plants. His Anschauung, as M. Michéa says, is 'une représentation globale des termes positifs d'une série temporelle', a sort of composite image from a cinematographic series of shots.

Cette représentation permet d'embrasser d'un seul regard la totalité de l'être, d'envisager l'état présent d'un objet à la lumière de son devenir. C'est presque en termes bergsoniens qu'il conviendrait d'énoncer le problème. Aux yeux de Goethe, le changement est l'essence des choses. Être, c'est avant tout durer, se développer par une altération continue, et il distingue généralement la *Gegenwart*, le *Dasein*, c'est à dire le fait d'être là, l'être empirique, de l'*Existenz*, du *Wesen*, être substantiel, d'un caractère éminemment intelligible, qui renferme en lui un passé vivant et un futur préformé.[81]

To see the object which is actually before his eyes without thought of its past and future, or to analyse it into a number of parts of which it is merely the sum, does not satisfy either the scientist or the artist in Goethe, for that is to be unaware of the 'geistiges Band' which alone makes an intelligible unit, an 'Existenz', for him of the parts and of this present, past and future. In the *Urfaust* already Goethe had made Faust ridicule the scientists who, as one might say, 'murder to dissect', for his ideas here are very like Wordsworth's, and it is what A. N. Whitehead calls the 'fallacy of misplaced concreteness' that is really the object of his protest[82] (see *Science and the Modern World*, Cambridge, 1929, pp. 72, 103).

> Wer will was lebigs erkennen und beschreiben,
> Muß erst den Geist herauser treiben,
> Da hat er die Theil' in seiner Hand,
> Fehlt leider nur das geistlich Band.
> Encheiresin naturae nennts die Chimie!
> Bohrt sich selbst einen Esel und weis nicht wie.*

The development of Goethe's ideas in the course of the 1780's is made particularly clear by a comparison of two of the essays he wrote on his return from Italy, one on aesthetics, *Einfache Nachahmung der Natur, Manier, Stil*, and one on botany, *Die Metamorphose der Pflanzen*. The subject of the second was so

---

* He who would get to know and describe some living thing must first drive out the spirit in it, then he has the parts in his hand, but alas! without the spiritual bond between them. Chemistry calls this process 'encheiresis naturae' and unwittingly makes a fool of itself.

dear to Goethe's heart that he later wrote a fine poem with the same title, in which he explains to Christiane the mystery of the growth and flowering of plants, infinitely varied in their shape and colour, yet all following the same law, analogous to that which brings lovers together and crowns their love with the fruit of common interests and ways of thinking. In the former essay, taking his examples from painting, he distinguishes three levels of artistic achievement. The first is simple imitation of nature, such as is found in Dutch flower-pieces, where the external appearance of a particular model is reproduced with the greatest possible accuracy, but the result only interests us by its craftsmanship. The second is what he calls by a current term, 'Manier', the simplified representation of a landscape in an individual 'manner', a handwriting or language, so to speak, which is to some extent the personal creation of the artist, arrived at by a certain degree of abstraction, omission of insignificant detail and heightening of effects. A simple modern example, perhaps, would be the highly individual way in which successful *Punch* artists draw faces or figures, each having his own recognisable kind of exaggeration. On the highest level, the artist still, according to this view of art, starts from things found in nature, but what he suggests, in his representation of them, is their essential characteristics (their *Existenz* as opposed to their *Dasein*), perhaps the beechiness of a beech-tree, the liquidity of water, the character of a man, and so on. This demands intuitive understanding of what is typical in particular examples, by mental comparison with others stored in the memory.

Goethe takes as an example a painter who is also a botanist, who as such is interested in the way in which a plant grows. He will not merely show his taste by a good choice of forms and colours, but will try to suggest in his picture the biological function of the different parts of the plant, and in this way achieve *style*. Style is achieved by this particular kind of concentration of significance in the image. M. Michéa reminds us that Lessing had said that the painter, in representing an action, should choose the most evocative phase of it, the one which leads the imagination both forwards and backwards from that point and suggests the whole action. Goethe improves on this with the help of Herder and Spinoza, and wants his artist to suggest, not a particular action, but the slow evolution of living things. His view is an alternative to the normal classicistic notion, e.g. of Winckelmann, of arriving at ideal beauty by collecting beautiful parts from many individuals. It assumes that all living things have a *principle of growth* within that determines their outward form, in which all parts are interdependent and in harmony with each other and the whole, so that no mechanical assemblage of choice features can give the impression of the *organic* form of living creatures, each of which is a unique individual, yet made, or rather grown, in accordance with the laws of its type. The artist, he says, in another essay of the same period ('Naturlehre, Antwort', in *Der deutsche Merkur*, 1789), must begin by paying attention to the differences between individuals. Then, comparing the individuals to each other, by a supreme effort of imagination (like his own in conceiving the *Urpflanze*), he must include the whole group of individuals, whether separate in space or successive in time, in one act of vision and rise from abstraction to abstraction, and finally to the conception of the *type*, seen in its indivisible harmony *sub specie eternitatis*.

The fullness of meaning, of truth to natural law, that Goethe asks for is very like what the Dutch philosopher Hemsterhuis (in *Lettre sur la Sculpture*) regarded as beauty in the arts, that which 'gives us the maximum of ideas in the minimum of time'. Goethe mentions the resemblance himself in the *Kampagne in Frankreich*, in connection with a visit to Fürstin Gallitzin at Münster, and restates his own theory there in the sentences: 'I said that we become aware of beauty when we see some living thing, organised according to natural laws, at the height of its activity and perfection. The sight of it makes us want to copy it, and our own feeling of life is enhanced and our activity stimulated to a maximum',[83] where the vitalist element, the notion of *Einfühlung*, is expressed in a way more persuasive to the modern. For considerered simply as an aesthetic theory along with others, Goethe's notion of 'style' will probably not be found very convincing today, when critical opinion has moved so far away from the 'imitation' theory in all its forms. First there came the Romantic insistence on the creative imagination, unfettered by models, followed, after another long realistic phase, when the aim of many artists came close again to what Goethe had called 'Einfache Nachahmung', by various vigorous reactions, towards symbolism, impressionism, expressionism, and the extreme of abstraction. The particular kind of concentrated significance that Goethe demanded will seem to most artists altogether too scientific, and likely to lead to a neglect, in painting, of the purely painterly qualities, to which Goethe was perhaps not very sensitive, to judge by his apparent blindness to the merits of the French genre painters and so on, so well appreciated by Diderot in his *Salons*, a work that Goethe treated with scorn. The results of his guidance of young artists into the path in which he thought they should go, through the Weimar art competitions and exhibitions he organised, as we shall see later, will strike most unprejudiced visitors to the Weimar collections as disastrous. The interest of Goethe's theory, we suggest, lies rather in the light it throws on his personal habit of vision, on some of his creative writing, though by no means all, even after 1790, and on the nature of his wisdom, the serenity which he frequently achieved in his later years and often succeeded in communicating to others in his more didactic writings and philosophical poetry.

His personal habit of vision after Italy may be illustrated from the following passage (singled out by Staiger in his *Goethe*), from the *Italian Journey*, written on 9 October 1786 in Venice: 'This evening I climbed St Mark's tower; for as I had recently seen the lagoons from above in their glory, at high tide, I wanted to see them now at low tide too, in their humility, and it is necessary to combine these two pictures to have a correct idea of them.' 'The intellectual mastery that Goethe from now on demands and achieves', Staiger comments, 'consists in such a combination of images.'[84] He wishes to see and think at the same time, comparing what is present before him with what he remembers and imagines.

It is the habit of one for whom all value lies now in the real world, which is so much more wonderful than anything he could freely imagine. On the same evening he wrote the often-quoted lines (about small creatures he found on the sea-shore, like sea-snails and crabs): 'What an incomparable, glorious thing anything living is! how well adapted to its conditions, how true, how real! (seiend). How useful my little bit of nature study is to me, and how glad I am to continue it!'

(ii) '*Wilhelm Meister's Apprenticeship*'

Goethe views on 'Bildung' after his return from Italy are of course expressed above all in his great novel, *Wilhelm Meisters Lehrjahre*, the first of a long series of 'Bildungsromane' in German literature, novels, that is, in which the gradual formation of the character and philosophy of life of the hero is the central theme, so that he seems to be conducted by the author through many experiences in varying milieus with this end in view, rather than for the direct entertainment of the reader. No other national literature seems to have developed independently a novel of quite this type, and Max Wundt and others have shown how natural a growth it was in the Germany of Goethe's time. It followed a large number of travel diaries, reflecting the keen interest of the Germans of that century in foreign, though at first not very distant countries, in the concrete details of their political and social life, to begin with, and later in the subjective reactions of the traveller, whether critical or sentimental, as long as they seemed to throw light on the human lot and on human character. For in addition to being increasingly curious to know more about the world outside, readers of that day were becoming fascinated by psychology, an interest fostered by brilliant analysts like Locke and Hume, by the introspective habits of sectarians like the Pietists and by the literary fashion established by Richardson and Rousseau and the large group of novelists and dramatists who followed their lead. No previous century had attached so much importance to education, moreover, and the long Christian tradition which enjoined upon the individual the duty of aiming at perfection was still alive in a number of forms, even in the absence of the confessional. The educated associated it with their study of the classics, through the vogue of Stoicism since the Renaissance.[85] Wilhelm von Humboldt, the supreme artist in self-cultivation in the age of the German Classics, began spontaneously in his twelfth year to try to imitate the Stoics he read about in ancient history, in willing to do things just to prove the strength of the will, and all through the German Enlightenment before him, and even in the Baroque age, one finds the sense of inner freedom to be a leading ideal. Lessing's Nathan the Wise puts it into the words: 'No man need say "I must"' ('Kein Mensch muß müssen'), a phrase approvingly quoted by Schiller, who was attracted to Kant above all by this sentiment. The habit of self-examination of the Calvinist or the Pietist, for whom salvation was all, might become, as with Benjamin Franklin, ticking off the virtues in the thirteen columns ruled in his diary, a way to gain a fortune by acquiring, through good habits, 'the art of virtue'. Wilhelm Meister's friend Werner praises order, frugality and industry in just the same spirit, and it is the middle class in Germany, as the novel makes plain, of which this narrowly prudential view of morality is particularly characteristic.

Goethe's novel began, as we know since the discovery in 1910 of a manuscript copy of its earliest form, as a picaresque type of story, which was to show how a young idealist from the middle class rebelled against the attitudes normal to his station and pursued a more satisfying life as an actor and playwright, believing that through the theatre the public too could be made aware of higher things. Similar ideas about the educative potentialities of the theatre were of course widely held in Germany in the second half of the eighteenth century. They led to the foundation of the so-called 'National Theatre' at Hamburg in 1767, a repertory theatre which aimed at performing plays of literary merit, original German ones if possible, and raising the status of the acting profession. Lessing's *Hamburgische Dramaturgie*, written as day-to-day criticism of its efforts, reminds us of the difficulties encountered, but more successful attempts were made later elsewhere, usually with the support of an enlightened court, until in 1791 Weimar too set up a Court Theatre with similar aims. Goethe, who, on his return from Italy, became, as we shall see, a kind of minister of culture in Weimar, was the obvious choice for the official head of the new theatre, but he undertook the task unwillingly, because he had by now become very sceptical about the ethical influence of the theatre, as well as about the educability of the German public, though still interested in the artistic problems presented by an experimental theatre with high standards, catering for a small élite. His early experiences in the new theatre were not encouraging, so that when he came to revise his theatre novel, from 1794, he completely changed its main theme, while still making use of much of his old material. The hero still moves through various milieus in turn, so that Goethe is able to present different social types in their appropriate setting, using the mental notes that we can still see him making, when we read his letters to Frau von Stein from little Thuringian courts visited in the course of his duties before the Italian journey. A particularly good example is the letter of 3 January 1780 from Homburg, with its classification of types of men and women he has encountered: a prince and heir, a retired minister, a lady-in-waiting, an appanaged prince, a princess waiting to be married off, a rich and beautiful grand lady, another ugly and poor, a court cavalier dependent on his pay—and many others. It was during the years when he was making these observations that Goethe wrote, little by little, *Wilhelm Meister's Mission in the Theatre*, while at the same time he was systematically collecting specimens for his geological, botanical and zoological studies, exploring the natural world on every side in the attempt to understand its laws.

Wilhelm remains in the final version, what he always had been, a passive character, with only a generic resemblance, as an artistically gifted young man of the middle class, to Goethe himself, and the novel becomes a record of his experiments in living, and of the reflections suggested to him by his experiences

and the comments on life of the people he meets. He grows out
of his illusions about the theatre, much as Goethe had grown out
of his about 'playing a rôle in a couple of duchies' as a statesman,
and abandoned other 'false tendencies', such as his ambition to
be a painter. He gradually learns more about his true nature, in
the only way in which Goethe thought a man could 'get to know
himself', not by introspection, but by interaction with his environment. Recent critics have pointed to the 'morphological' ideas
about organic growth that his story seems designed to illustrate.
In studying plants, Goethe looked for 'the law of their inner
nature, by which plants are constituted' and 'the law of external
circumstances, by which plants are modified'. There is a clear
parallel between this conception and that of human destiny as
expressed, for instance, in the poem *Urworte. Orphisch* of 1817,
with its distinction between the 'Dämon', the 'law which
governed your first beginnings', and 'Tyche', the accidents of
circumstance. Goethe's autobiography too was begun with the
intention of illustrating a similar interplay in his own growth,
though in the end much more space was given to the description
of the surrounding world than to the analysis of his own nature.[86]

As a plant turns to the light, so a healthy human being works
out his own salvation, seeking the kind of perfection that is
consonant with 'the law of his inner nature'. It is in this sense
that man is 'good', though as *Faust* in particular reminds us, we
must not interpret goodness in a too narrowly ethical sense. In
Wilhelm Meisters Lehrjahre, Wilhelm's letter to Werner in Book
V (chapter 3) is clearly the key to Goethe's intention, where we
read: 'How does it help me to manufacture good iron' (no doubt
one of the projects he had discussed in the fanciful description of
his activities which he had recently sent to his father) 'if my own
inner nature is full of slag?' We are immediately reminded of
Goethe's own letter to Jacobi in 1782 (quoted above, p. 177).
'What is the use of putting an estate in order', Wilhelm continues, 'if I am at odds with myself? To tell you the truth in one
word: to develop myself, just as I am, that was the wish and aim
I was obscurely aware of from my youth upwards.'

This is of course the passage that more than any other supports the interpretation of the novel as a plea for full development of the personality as the supreme aim in life, a parallel to Suleika's lines

> Volk und Knecht und Überwinder,
> Sie gestehn zu jeder Zeit,
> Höchstes Glück der Erdenkinder
> Sei nur die Persönlichkeit,*

lines which must, however, themselves be read in their context.[87] This is one meaning of 'Bildung', but Goethe seldom distinguishes 'Bildung' as self-cultivation clearly from 'Bildung' as the shaping of an organic whole through the interplay between its 'enteleche', the formative forces within, and its environment, nor this again from the final 'shape' it assumes. In thinking of *Wilhelm Meister* as a 'Bildungsroman' we must keep all these meanings in mind. Wilhelm is constantly discovering that his interpretation of himself is merely a provisional truth, and so it is in this crucial letter. A little earlier (IV, 20) he had himself remarked that fate had so far seemed to lead him to the goal of his wishes without any intervention of his own, so that he had unknowingly pursued his deepest desire. That is also the meaning we are led to see in the novel by the words addressed to Wilhelm at the close: 'You remind me of Saul, the son of Kish, who went forth to seek his father's asses and found a kingdom.' Formal education by others is hardly mentioned, and conscious self-education too is represented as only a part of 'Bildung', though an important one. Both are supplemented by all kinds of experiences, and it turns out finally that Wilhelm has for long been discreetly guided at times by members of the mysterious Society of the Tower, so that the 'fate' which leads him to the goal of his wishes is the result of human foresight and guidance exercised by others, combined with blind chance and his own acts of choice. The express teaching of the Society of the Tower is from the beginning directed against the belief in a guiding fate.

* Nation and slave and conqueror, all admit in every age that the highest happiness of earth's children is personality alone.

'Everyone', Wilhelm hears from its first emissary, the Stranger in Book I (chapter 17), 'has his own happiness (or 'destiny') under his hands, as the artist has a raw material that he wishes to transform into a finished work. But it is the same with this art as with all others. Only a capacity for it is given to us at birth, and the art must be learnt and practised with care.' The second emissary, in Book II (chapter 9), repeats the same lesson, with special reference to the theatre.

The elements in life which are shown as contributing to the 'formation' of Wilhelm are of many kinds. The most important to begin with is art, the art of the theatre which, though it does not in the end prove to be Wilhelm's calling, teaches him much, especially through bringing him into contact with Shakespeare, the literary genius *par excellence* for the world of Goethe's youth. The discovery of Shakespeare seems to stand here for all that great literature and art can bestow on a young receptive mind. In an earlier age, religion, not art, would have been the young man's mentor in the interpretation of life. Here *Hamlet* becomes Wilhelm's bible. Wilhelm conceives the character of Hamlet in a manner that partly reflects his own age, as a brooding genius oppressed by the consciousness of his inability to set the world to rights, and for a time, the one thing that matters for Wilhelm is to produce *Hamlet* worthily, a task that engages him completely and suggests all kinds of problems. In this way, starting from the theatre, Goethe constructs a story which, as Staiger says, seems to answer the question 'whether and in what way it is possible for an individual even in northern Europe at the present day to live in harmony with nature and art',[88] and so conveys to us the fruits of his own experience and reflection.

Even in the first version of the novel, Wilhelm's passion for the theatre brought him into touch with a variety of men and women who were obviously seen by the author in their class affiliations and therefore given characteristic ideas about what is important in life. In the small-town citizen class into which Wilhelm was born, what people put first was security, a good reputation and solid comfort, with individual differences in matters of detail. The actors, on the other hand, he finds to be natural bohemians, living from hand to mouth, disregarding all the conventions to which he is accustomed, but all the more attractive to him for that, because they seem to be following more truly 'the law of their nature' in sacrificing order and comfort for something ideal, their art. They seem to him to possess a spiritual freedom lacking in his own class, cluttered up as its life is with material possessions. Even a baggage like Philine lives for the joy of living as the woman she is, so that she seems to be at the opposite pole to Philistinism when she cries: 'If I love you, what harm does that do you?'—a remark which has reminded some commentators of Spinoza and the intellectual love of God.

His association with actors brings Wilhelm into the company of the patrons they most naturally sought, the nobility, who also prove to have class characteristics that seem more attractive still. Enjoying inherited wealth, which they do not feel the need to conserve as anxiously as his parents had done, they can combine some consideration for order and security with the freedom to follow their bent, but they possess too traditions that may shed on everyday life and social intercourse a kind of grace. It is often an appearance with no substance behind it, like the ornate fireplace, with no chimney attached, in the old palace (III, 3), and their hedonism has little regard for ethical considerations, but when, in honour of the prince, the countess appears (III, 12) in full court dress, Wilhelm cannot take his eyes off her, so natural does she make this rococo creation, like Goethe's Lili (*An Belinden*) who, among all the hideous figures playing cards, had seemed to him nature itself. Wilhelm is so fascinated for a time by the life of the aristocracy that one of his reasons for becoming a professional actor is that on the stage at least he may be seen and admired as a person, as noblemen in real life display themselves. They have a nonchalant grace denied in Germany to a commoner who, off the stage, can earn respect, even if he has brains, only as a means to an end, a useful tool, not a personality in his own right (v, 3). It might seem that the harmonious development he so much desires, and conceives so externally, rating pleasing deportment and address as highly as intellectual maturity and good taste, for all these things are normally denied to his class in society, is for Wilhelm the whole content of 'Bildung'. At best his ideal seems to be the all-round development in the individual of every faculty of man.

But Wilhelm's apprenticeship is not yet over. Gradually he comes to see that it is neither possible nor desirable for everyone to be a universal man, self-contained and total. Instead, we take leave of him in the *Apprenticeship* as a husband and father, or rather as a father and husband, anchored in society and eager to find a definite limited sphere of activity, convinced by his experience and the teaching of the 'Tower' that what he must seek is the harmonious development of those special gifts with which nature has endowed him. No man is a microcosm, and only 'all men together can display all the qualities of humanity' (VIII, 5).

The transition from the old material to the new, from a limited to a comprehensive view of 'Bildung', and from the concrete, realistic style in description and character-drawing to a more abstract and schematic one, is provided by the Sixth Book, the 'Confessions of a beautiful soul', by which we are quite properly reminded of the part played by pietism in the history of what has been called the 'culture of feeling' in Germany,[89] and also in Goethe's own poetic development. The 'Confessions' must have owed much to papers left by the friend of Goethe's mother, Fräulein von Klettenberg, papers apparently known to Goethe but since lost, for the understanding of a world and of types of personality so remote from Goethe's experience, in spite of the passing pietistic phase he went through before his studies at Strassburg. A great deal however is certainly invented, to serve to introduce the new characters whose acquaintance Wilhelm is to make in the later books. The limitations imposed on himself by Goethe in choosing these characters, and the consequent restriction placed on the ideal of personal culture they represent, is well analysed by Staiger.

The nearer Wilhelm Meister comes to his real goal, the more the range of his existence is contracted. No place in public affairs, no mark of distinction, no important office fall to his lot. The army, the government, the church, all general institutions lie outside the area over which the classical laws of culture hold sway. It is only in the circle of the family, with a few friends grouped around it, that the individual still appears as a human being with clear contours. But it must be a moderately well-to-do family. Its strength must not be used up in the fight for existence. Culture of the highest grade, moreover, presupposes a tradition that is not of yesterday. The group chosen must therefore inevitably be an aristocratic one. Within the nobility again certain types must be carefully avoided. The patriotic traditions, for instance, that were lively after the Seven Years War, have no place here. There are neither Prussians nor Saxons, only Germans, in fact not even Germans, but only men, citizens of the world, compelled indeed to live in time and space, but not bound by time and space.[90]

After the earlier books, where the contemporary background is an essential feature, this exclusion of reference to a recognisable present is stylistically rather disturbing.

The fact that the so obviously invented situations and characters of these last books are selected to illustrate certain theoretical possibilities of existence gives a utopian air to the ideals of culture suggested to us by and through them. The characters around Wilhelm and he himself are principally concerned with discovering themselves, defining their attitude to life, rather than applying their ideas of the good life to the improvement of society, though the novel as a whole reflects the endless curiosity of its author about the external world, convinced as he was that a man learns to know himself not merely by looking within, but by responding to the stimuli that come to him from other people, from nature and from the world of culture. From the best that has been thought and known he forms his standards of excellence, and Goethe implies that it is a moral duty to be discriminating, as when he makes Serlo say (v, 1) that the reason why many find pleasure in stupid and tasteless things is that they do not make a habit of setting aside a short time each day for the enjoyment of good music or poetry or painting.

(iii) *The 'Travels'*

To give a full account of Goethe's thought about culture, even down to 1806, one would have to include any number of references in his letters, conversations and other works than *Wilhelm Meisters Lehrjahre* and the *Italian Journey*. Some of these observations, particularly those about art, will be touched upon in chapter 5, but here a few words must be said about the continuation of *Wilhelm Meister* written by Goethe in his old age, in order to indicate what limitations he himself came to see in the older work. Schiller, Goethe's best critic, in his extremely penetrating comments in letters to Goethe as the proofs reached him, missed in particular any suggestion of a religion or a total philosophy of life. This defect is very fully repaired in the *Wanderjahre* in the chapter on the three, or rather four kinds of reverence that are taught to the pupils of the Educational Province. The capacity for reverence is seen as the very essence of religion, and education to reverence as the principal aim in character training, 'the one essential, if a man is to be completely a man', so the essence of 'Humanität'. From the various possible forms of reverence, illustrated from different religions, the ultimate form is developed, self-respect in its profoundest sense, the realisation that man is the supreme product of God and nature. To be able to believe this 'without being dragged down again to the unworthy through conceit and egoism' is the final test of what we might call a religious humanism.[91]

A selfish personality cult is not the outcome of the *Lehrjahre*, as we have seen, but in the *Wanderjahre*, which has as its subtitle 'Die Entsagenden', 'men who renounce', we meet people who even more clearly do not live simply to realise themselves, their inner capacities, but to lead active lives in a changing world, in an age when the French Revolution, the wars and new economic developments have made many breaches in the old 'estates society'. In this not fully integrated novel Goethe seems to try several different ways of presenting this new 'culture' and his hopes and fears concerning it. There is first a hint of the distant, almost legendary past that lives on into the present in simple family life, then a full picture of the good old days that are passing away, when the comfortable home of a cultivated country gentleman displayed the order achieved by generations of rational effort. This is a patriarchal society based on what Shakespeare calls 'degree', where the welfare of the many depends on the inherited wealth of the few, their benevolence and sense of responsibility. But Goethe is not blind to the new conditions that we think of as typical in the nineteenth century, when Europe is overpopulated, and the old craft forms of industry and even the newer domestic industries like that of the weavers in Silesia and similar upland regions are threatened by competition from capitalistic mass-production. Large numbers are faced with the alternative of either emigrating to America, the land of plenty, or accepting the modern techniques, the 'cash nexus' and all the evils of industrialism. There is great danger in abandoning the old traditional ways of life, mere preaching will have no effect and the only hope seems to be that 'equally valid, effective and comforting ways of thinking and feeling will be evoked from men's own breasts' (III, 13). What they will be Goethe cannot say, but certainly the old conception of 'Bildung' must be revised. This is not a time for all-round cultivation but for specialisation. 'Train yourself to be a good violinist and be assured that the conductor will readily assign to you your place in the orchestra.' 'It is best to restrict oneself to one craft. For the most limited intelligence it will always be a craft, for the more gifted an art, and the best, in doing one thing, will do everything, or, to put it less paradoxically, in the one thing, properly done, he will see a symbol of all right doing.' Such are the new maxims produced by Wilhelm's mentor when he is worried about the education of his son, and the full answer in the chapters on the Educational Province elaborates them in detail.

3. FICHTE AND SCHILLER

Schiller is the very type of the idealist in the normal, unphilosophical sense of the word. It is his unceasing concern with ideas of a perfection in life and art that might be attained by men, if they were prepared for heroic effort, that is put first among his characteristics by Goethe in the great poem in his memory, the *Epilog zu Schillers Glocke*, as it is by Wilhelm von Humboldt and all his intimate friends. He was impatient with the second-best and with human weakness, so that he was sometimes harsh with those who lacked his toughness of fibre, like Hölderlin, and a little inhuman and even priggish in his references to those for whom 'cakes and ale' meant more than they did for him. In his heart he probably thought Goethe himself somewhat soft and self-indulgent, for Goethe was not inclined, as he was, to sacrifice everything for rapid productivity by conscious effort. Though Goethe disciplined himself severely, especially in old age, and worked in his intentionally bare and comfortless little study from dawn till dark, it was his prose and his science that benefitted most from his diligence, and his best poetic creations still came to him from mysterious depths of the unconscious mind. He needed, as Schiller did not, to experience life fully through the senses, and enjoyed doing so, but his mind played over it without interruption, linking present, past and future, the near and the distant, the world of books and art and the world of instinctive responses, with results that are evident in the Eckermann *Conversations*, and ultimately in the living fullness of his imaginative work.

(i) *Fichte*

In temperament Schiller was much closer to Fichte than to Goethe, and a book of Fichte's, highly praised by Schiller in *On the Aesthetic Education of Man, in a Series of Letters*, gives us an insight into the ethical idealism that the students of Jena admired so greatly in them both. *On the Mission of the Scholar* is the first set of public lectures given by Fichte in Jena, in the summer of 1794, and published in the autumn, while Schiller was writing the original letters on aesthetics to his patron, the Duke of Augustenburg, which were published in a revised form in his periodical *Die Horen* in 1795. Both books are the work of professors who from obscure origins had risen to fame, without losing entirely the impatience with the ordinary sensual man that had characterised their angry youth. Both distinguish clearly between the elect who are capable of ideas, and the mass of men who, even if nominally enlightened, are interested only in the useful application of ideas to everyday problems. Fichte begins, as we have mentioned, with an abstract thesis, independent of experience, from which he means to deduce his conclusions by purely logical processes, but the unconscious attitudes and temperamental tendencies with which he approaches his subject are clear in every line, as they are in Schiller. It was this non-logical element, made fully evident from time to time in purple patches, that must have given his lectures their undoubted appeal. A contemporary tells us that Fichte used to lecture on the Theory of Knowledge between 6 and 7 o'clock in the morning, and usually appeared booted and spurred, riding-crop in hand, fresh from his morning ride, producing a tonic effect on all his hearers.[92] Another writes:

Fichte's words in his lectures sweep along like a storm-cloud that sheds its fire in separate strokes. He does not move, but he uplifts the soul. Reinhold (his predecessor) wanted to make good men; Fichte wants to make great men. His glance is monitory and his gait defiant. Through his philosophy he aims at directing the spirit of the age; he knows its weak side, and tackles it therefore from the angle of politics.[93]

Our conception of the mission of the scholar, Fichte asserts then, depends on our notion of the true end of man in society, and this is 'to determine himself and not allow himself to be determined by anything else', a statement which follows from his basic axiom that 'man, possessing reason, is his own true end' and does not exist for anything outside himself. The educated man is one who has learned how to control all those tendencies in himself that are incompatible with 'the form of his pure ego', besides acquiring certain skills in reducing things outside himself to conformity with his ideas. The pursuit of perfection is the end of man, and a small élite of scholars or educated men leads in this unceasing advance. Each of his hearers must consider himself therefore a 'priest of truth'. 'You are the salt of the earth,' Fichte assures them (lecture IV), consciously reinterpreting the words of Christ, 'and if the élite among men are defective, where shall moral worth be sought?' It is not, for instance, the function of the state (lecture II) to make its subjects virtuous, for no man may 'make a rational being virtuous or wise or happy against his will', and 'the positive character of society is inter- action through freedom'. Each should be inwardly free and desire to see free men around him, so that the true aim of govern- ment is to make government superfluous. We are strongly reminded of the essay written by Wilhelm von Humboldt about this same time, his *Ideas towards an Attempt to Determine the Limits of Government Activity*, with its key sentence: 'The true aim of man, the one prescribed not by his shifting inclinations but by his eternally unchanging reason, is the highest possible cultivation of his powers to form a harmonious whole. For this cultivation (Bildung), freedom is the first and indispensable con- dition.'

If free scope is assured to the creative impulses of the cultivated minority, Fichte asserts, humanity in general will maintain 'the continual advance of civilisation (Kultur) and the steady develop- ment of all its powers and needs' which is its true end (lecture V). Fichte, we note, like Humboldt and Schiller, is closer to Kant and the Enlightenment than either Goethe or Herder, in his universalistic conception of individual culture. 'The highest law of humanity and of all rational creatures, the law of complete harmony with ourselves, of absolute identity ... demands that in the individual all powers be equally developed, all capacities cultivated to the highest possible perfection.' 'If the powers of all are in essence similar, as they are, being founded simply on pure reason, they should be developed in all in the same way' (lecture III). Expressed in this form, his views sound unduly optimistic, both in his estimate of the future prospects of a liberal society, and in his expectation of all-round development for every- one. Herder and Goethe both seem to us nearer to the psycho- logical truth and to a rational ideal, through their understanding of the historical growth of civilisation, with rise and fall and infinite variety in different places and times, and their appreciation of the uniqueness of each individual, capable of developing as he is only according to his particular endowment and the particular stimulus that an ever-changing world affords. Humboldt's desire for total development is differently motivated. Writing to Schiller (28 September 1795) he says that he can 'hardly resist the desire to see, know, put to the test as much as is ever and anywhere possible. Man seems surely to exist in order to turn everything around him into his own, into the property of his understanding—and life is short.'[94] We have seen that Goethe in his maturity sees the individual as limited in the scope of his abilities and interests, and looks to society as a whole to provide variety. Like the others, however, he has the liberal's confidence that, despite specialisation, social harmony can be achieved without undue interference from governments.

Fichte's lectures are illuminating for our purpose, as an illustration of the widespread acceptance of the ideal of self-cultivation, and an indication of one important channel for the propagation of this ideal. Savigny, visiting Jena in 1799, soon after Fichte's departure, finds no trace of the swashbuckling coarseness for which Jena had formerly been notorious, but this change is a recent one and mainly due, it is implied, to Fichte's good influence on the students' 'Orders' or 'Corps', as they were called later. 'There is much interest in intellectual culture for its own sake. . . . With this audience a man of Fichte's brilliant gifts could perform miracles, and he did, for he ruled the students with a nod.'[95] Fichte followed up this first course with a revised version, *On the Nature of the Scholar*, given in Erlangen in 1805, and he developed some of his ideas on education further in his famous *Addresses to the German Nation*. Practical effect was given to some of his ideas, together with those of Wilhelm von Humboldt, in the shaping of the new University of Berlin. The 1805 lectures emphasise the distinction frequently made by Schiller in his prose writings and the *Xenien* between 'Brotstudium', vocational study, and the free cultivation of the mind. Some of his arguments anticipate those of J. H. Newman in his controversy with the

Edinburgh Reviewers (*Idea of a University*) though his manner
of writing is entirely different, humourless and conveying an
impression of portentous self-importance. The true scholar is
filled, he says, not with the desire to be useful but with love of
his profession and his studies, which he regards as something
sacred and serves as a kind of priest, for how is the divine revealed
to the world directly and visibly except in the lives of god-like
men? The perfect scholar's life is 'the life of the divine idea
within the world, continuing the creation and refashioning the
world completely' (lecture VII). Even as a student therefore he
'avoids all contact with the common and ignoble', with anything
that 'debases the imagination and blunts our perception of the
holy'. It is only the mature man who may be permitted to accept
the common with a smile—the young man should hate it in all
seriousness. 'I am eternal,' he should say to himself, 'and it is
beneath the dignity of the eternal to waste itself on what is
transient' (lecture IV). Fichte's moral idealism is clearly akin to
that praised by Goethe in Schiller:

> Und hinter ihm, in wesenlosem Scheine,
> Lag, was uns alle bändigt, das Gemeine.*

but his egotism mars the expression of it and leads him to advance
the dangerous doctrine, to be repeated in the *Addresses*, that any
power, not ourselves, that takes hold of us, and comes alive in us
instead of ourselves (like his own nationalism in the *Addresses*),
is always divine (lecture VII). 'The Idea', in which and for which
his scholar should live, is an absolute, an undefined abstraction,
very like 'the Spirit' which, for Hegel, becomes manifest in all
history, 'the Word' became flesh, for Hegel's whole philosophy of
history might be regarded as a system elaborated out of the ideal
of culture. Fichte marks an important stage in the process by
which Protestant theology was secularised into German Idealism.

Quite apart from these general considerations, Fichte is interesting too for particular parallels that may be found in the works we

---

* And behind him lay, an unsubstantial shadow, what holds us all down, the
common and mean.

have mentioned to passages in Schiller's *Letters on Aesthetic Education*, written from an avowedly similar point of view and under the impact of the same external event, the French Revolution. There is first the notion already discussed, that the ills of the present are not to be cured by any elaboration of the state apparatus, but rather by an inner change in individual men, brought about by self-cultivation of one kind or another and gradually diffused. Fichte does not rely on an aesthetic but on an intellectual and moral appeal, but he is upheld by the same conviction, based on feeling rather than argument and more indebted to childhood religious teaching, perhaps, than he knew, that the golden age is ahead of us and not, as Rousseau was understood to have maintained, behind. (*On the Nature of the Scholar*, lecture v). Rousseau's contention that culture has contributed towards depraving mankind is rejected, though not contemptuously. He is pitied as a disappointed idealist, acquainted with the civilisation only of the French rococo age, where he 'saw talent and art and knowledge uniting forces in the pitiful endeavour to compel the pleasures possible to jaded nerves to yield up a still more subtle pleasure', or simply 'to find excuses for human depravity'. Like Schiller, and unlike the young Wilhelm Meister, Fichte sees nothing attractive in the elegant amusements of the aristocracy. Yet a retreat to the animal state is impossible. 'Nature is coarse and wild without the touch of man', and though he has involved himself in great temptations through growing refinement, there is still a divine spark within him that makes him seek to be like God, that will not let him rest in mere enjoyment and will bring him through effort to higher things. He should see himself, as an earlier passage had put it (lecture III), as 'a necessary link in the great chain which leads, from the first man's awakening to the full consciousness of his existence, right down to eternity', as the heir of all the ages, thoughts that remind us both of Herder and of the 'Great Chain of Being'. Even in the face of death and destruction, Fichte tells his students, man can say 'I am eternal, and I defy your power. . . . My will, alone with its fixed plan, shall hover, cool and courageous, over the ruins of

8 SCHILLER IN 1804

the universe', a piece of eschatological rhodomontade that must have brought the house down.

(ii) *Schiller*

In the *Letters on Aesthetic Education*, Schiller too has rhetorical patches, but his starting-point is the actual state of the world as he sees it, in the year following the Terror, and his final aim is the betterment of man's lot here below. If freedom had really been made the basis of the new state in France, he says in the original letters,[96] he would have 'abandoned the muses, and devoted his activity to the noblest of all artifacts, the monarchy of reason', a statement which lends colour to the rumour, of which we read, that in 1792 Schiller contemplated going to Paris. While urging now reform from within, he still admits that physical well-being is a preliminary condition for the attainment of mental freedom. 'Man is still very little when he has a warm house and enough to eat, but he must have a warm house and enough to eat if his better nature is to be aroused.'[97] Political freedom, however, is a matter of supreme importance, and if the eyes of the world are on France, it is because it thinks the fate of mankind is being decided there. In reality, a golden opportunity has been lost. 'To solve this political problem in practice, it must be approached by way of the aesthetic problem, because freedom is only to be attained through beauty.[98]

Whatever Schiller's original intentions may have been for the series of letters on aesthetics which he announced to his great benefactor, the Duke of Augustenburg, on 19 February 1793, and began to write six months later, he soon made it clear that he was writing not merely to air his aesthetic philosophy, but, stimulated by contemporary events, to tackle the great problem of the education of mankind to freedom. The French Revolution had failed, it seemed to him, because its human instruments had not been morally equipped for their task, of replacing the power state they had undermined (and which he describes in Letter 3 as the 'Nature state', owing its existence originally to physical force, not to the law of reason), by a state devised by reason to guarantee true freedom. The French aristocracy of the ancien régime, corrupted by culture itself, had been selfish and unprincipled—and the aristocracy of Europe generally, it seems to be implied, is no better. But the mob released by the Revolution had revealed itself as disorderly and brutish,[99] like the natural element of fire, when once out of control—the famous lines in *The Song of the Bell* were probably written with this analogy in mind, and after 1793 Schiller was as convinced of the prime necessity of order in the state as Goethe. If neither class had proved to be truly humane, it had not been for the lack of enlightenment of an intellectual kind in France. Evidently something more was needed, the education of the feelings, in Schiller's view, and it is this that art can supply, and art alone.

A quick glance at history in Letter 6 brings out the contrast between the present state of humanity and that of the ancient world, especially among the Greeks. On the lines of his poem, *The Gods of Greece*, Schiller draws a flattering picture of the harmonious variety, the refinement and solidity of Greek civilisation, seen through the eyes of Winckelmann and Herder as combining all the virtues of supreme 'humanity', and follows it up with an indictment of enlightened Europe, where he seeks this harmony in vain, both in the individual and in society. The specifically human qualities in their totality can only be rediscovered by surveying a mass of individuals, and taking a hint for this quality from one and for that quality from another, like a painter compounding ideal beauty from a number of models. 'Whole classes of men unfold only a part of their gifts, leaving others, as in stunted plants, hardly indicated by the faintest trace.' Advancing civilisation itself was the cause of this fragmentation of personality, for analytic reason had proved beyond dispute the necessity for the division of labour and specialisation of function in society. Schiller does not deny this necessity, but he sees its consequences as few in his century had yet seen them. Intuition and speculation, poetry and the spirit of abstraction have become enemies, and civil society is a huge mechanism made up of lifeless parts. 'State and church, laws and morals were now torn apart;

enjoyment was separated from work, the means from the end, effort from reward. Eternally fettered to a single tiny fraction of the whole, man now cultivates himself only as a fraction. With the monotonous noise continually in his ear of the wheel that he turns round, he never develops the harmony that belongs to his essence, and instead of expressing the humanity of his nature, he merely bears the stamp of his occupation or branch of knowledge.' He is valued therefore (as Wilhelm Meister too was to say in his letter to Werner) not for himself but for his function. This complex new society has to be bureaucratically organised with classified groups, not single men, in view, and individuals regard these laws and regulations with cool indifference as something of little concern to them personally.

'Le déracinement est de loin la plus dangereuse maladie des sociétés humaines, car il se multiplie lui-même',[100] Simone Weil wrote during the last war, at a time when the rootlessness of modern man was clear to all, 150 years after Schiller's essay. It is astonishing that so complete an analysis of a process that has gone on accelerating for all these years, and only now become a common theme of literature, should have been written by a poet in the patriarchal state we have described, where these tendencies were, at any rate in industry, at quite an early stage in their development. But he had read about the great capitals, notably what Mercier said about Paris, no doubt, and used his imagination, as he did when describing Charybdis in *Der Taucher* from what he had seen in a mill-race. He is not, like so many critics of modern civilisation, merely negative. Without specialisation, he sees well, discoveries such as the Calculus, or the *Critique of Pure Reason*, could never have been made, any more than without the telescope astronomers could have observed the satellites of Jupiter. But over-specialisation brings great dangers, which simply must be overcome, for he cannot believe it is nature's intention that in pursuing any single aim, man should neglect his essential self, and remain stunted as a human being.[101]

What Schiller misses then in modern society is precisely what Wilhelm Meister misses in middle-class life. It will be a task for more than one century to bring into being, by the slow improvement of human character, the truly reasonable state which the French failed to achieve through the Revolution. Schiller's remedy is reform from within, not the reform of institutions from without by an all-wise government. It is not the first time that he has expressed awareness of the dangers run by the apostle of reason in politics, because of his single-minded fervour. Years before Robespierre was heard of he had explained, in the *Letters on Don Karlos*, how naturally something of this kind had happened to his hero Posa, an impatient idealist and therefore a potential tyrant. There was perhaps some of Posa's masterfulness in Schiller's own nature. Now, at all events, after the Terror, he is convinced that no modern state can be satisfactorily remodelled until a change of heart has been brought about in the generality of men.

In the ideas he advances about how this may be done, Schiller seems at this distance very much of the Enlightenment, for all his reservations about the efficacity of pure reason, but he is at the same time deeply influenced by the Renaissance of Feeling, the 'Gefühlskultur' that, as we now think, is more truly to be regarded as a movement accompanying Rationalism than as its successor. He is a secularist, but a man of feeling. The thought of ethical advance through a religious revival never enters his head. He wholeheartedly approves of the Enlightenment's severing of traditional religious ties. He paraphrases in Letter 8 Kant's claim, in his essay *What is Enlightenment?* that the movement has marked 'the emergence of man from his self-imposed condition of tutelage'. 'The spirit of free investigation', he exultantly proclaims, 'has scattered the illusory beliefs that so long barred the way to the truth, and has undermined the positions on which fanaticism and deceit erected their thrones.' The motto of his reformers, he says, using the same slogan as Kant in that essay, must be 'Dare to be wise!' Courage will be needed, for it is not easy for the ordinary sensual man, burdened with the struggle for existence, to think for himself, and all too easy to accept, even if without conviction, 'the formulas which the state and the priesthood have in readiness for this purpose'. In the original version of this letter,[102] Schiller speaks his mind much more directly and effectively about the illusions—one thinks of Ibsen's *The Wild Duck*—which prop up for so many, especially among the aristocracy, 'the decaying structure of their happiness'. 'How many there are who justify their whole value in society through their wealth, their ancestors or physical advantages'—a useful corrective to Wilhelm Meister's rose-tinted vision of the same class, and a revelation of the Jacobin strain in Schiller.

The over-privileged, then, and shallow wits who serve them, will go in fear of bold, free thought, and the ordinary mass of the people have not the energy to look up from their labours. The outlook for reform would seem to be dark, but there is still a way in which all can be persuaded to move in the desired direction, namely through their feelings. 'The way to the head must be opened through the heart.' Again a telling passage has been omitted which appeared in the original letters,[103] where the distinction between these two methods of influencing character, through the head and through the heart, is elaborated. There has in many respects been Enlightenment enough and to spare.

The more pressing need of our age seems to me to be the refinement of feeling and the ethical purification of the will. . . .What we lack is not so much knowledge of the truth and of justice, as the effective use of this knowledge to influence the will, not so much light as warmth, not so much philosophical as aesthetic cultivation. This latter I hold to be the most effective instrument for the formation of character, and at the same time one that is independent of political conditions, and therefore available without the help of the state.

Two objections to his views occur to Schiller immediately, and he deals with them in Letters 9 and 10 respectively. If the whole present age is as corrupt as he says, how can the artist be exempt from its influence? Both scholarship (Wissenschaft) and art, Schiller replies, are potentially 'immune from the interference of men'. It is enough for their practitioners to assert their freedom, and this he eloquently urges them to do, relying confidently on the long-term effect of their pursuit of the true and the beautiful.

'The artist' (by which term he means also the poet and all who practise the fine arts) 'is indeed the son of his time, but woe to him if he is also its pupil or, still worse, its darling.' He should 'take the material in which he works (Stoff) from the present, but his form from a nobler age (that of the Ancients) or rather from beyond all time, from the absolute and immutable unity of his being.' Pre-Romantic notions of the inspired 'Vates', the poet as prophet, lie behind this statement, and Schiller seems to neglect the big differences between individual artists and writers, as well as the whole problem of communication, a writer's difficulties with a hostile censorship, for instance. Perhaps Schiller did not fully realise these, in the peculiar conditions prevailing in Germany, with its multiplitity of little states where, as Fichte wrote in his *Addresses*, 'a truth that could not be uttered at one place, could at another ... and so, in spite of much one-sidedness and narrowness, a higher degree of freedom of enquiry and expression was possible than in any other country in earlier times'.

To modern ears, in any case, Schiller's view will sound impossibly idealistic. For him it is enough if the scholar and artist alike 'direct the world towards the good, for the calm rhythm of time will complete your work.... The structure raised by self-delusion and arbitrary action will fall, it must fall, it has already fallen, as soon as you are sure that it is leaning; but it must lean in the inner, not in the outer man.' Once more we hear the pure doctrine of inwardness, of 'Bildung', unconsciously relying on a benevolent Providence. 'Seek ye first the Kingdom of God and His righteousness, and all these things shall be added unto you.' 'Live with your century,' Schiller exhorts his colleagues, preaching art as Fichte was said to 'preach' philosophy, 'but do not be its creature; give your contemporaries what they need, not what earns their praise.... Through the unflinching courage with which you disdain their happiness, you will prove to them that it is not through cowardice that you suffer along with them.' Indirectly, through an appeal to their aesthetic sense, you will move them. 'Drive the arbitrary, the frivolous, the coarse, out of their pleasures, and you will imperceptibly banish these things

from their actions, and finally from their habit of mind.' Show
them your own vision of excellence, and at last 'semblance will
conquer reality, and art nature'. What is impressive about these
words is not their logic, but their emotional appeal, the tone of
voice in which they are spoken, expressive of profound conviction.

The second objection, answered in Letter 10, is that two opposing errors have apparently to be corrected by art, the apathy of
the uncultivated masses, and the debilitated over-refinement of
the few. It is a commonplace that manners may be refined by an
appeal to the sense of beauty, but may they not (as Rousseau had
argued, though his name is not mentioned) be refined out of
existence? Does not history suggest some doubts on this score?
Was not the golden age of art in Greece also the period of political
decline, and are there not parallels to be adduced from the history
of the Romans, the Arabs, and the Renaissance in Italy? 'It is
almost superfluous to draw attention to the example of modern
nations' (including, no doubt, Schiller's own), 'whose refinement
increased *pari passu* with their loss of independence.' Hegel's
striking phrase comes to mind, about the owl of Minerva that
begins its flight only as the shades of night are falling. Is not
political health and vigour preferable to cultural refinement,
artistic excellence? The answer depends, Schiller says, on what
we mean by art, and to know its true meaning we must proceed
in a 'transcendental' way and ask (as Fichte had asked) what is
the true nature of man? Beauty will then be found to be a necessary condition for the existence of true humanity.

There follows now the most abstract section of Schiller's
disquisition, in which he goes beyond Kantian aesthetic notions
and bases his argument, as he admits, on Fichte's *Theory of
Knowledge* (1794), with some reference also to the already mentioned lectures on *The Scholar*. Fichte's theory rises to heights
of subjectivism to which very few in later times have been able
to follow him. It is the kind of view that Goethe has in mind
when he makes his arrogant young Baccalaureus cry, in the
Second Part of *Faust*, as he 'joyously follows his inward light':

Die Welt sie war nicht eh' ich sie erschuf

and

> Wer, außer mir, entband euch aller Schranken
> Philisterhaft einklemmender Gedanken?*

The pure ego 'posits' the world. Schiller's method is, like Fichte's, to work out the consequences that follow by pure logic from an apparently incontrovertible *a priori* statement. Then whatever experience may seem to teach us, about the dubious influence of art on ethics, for instance, may be corrected from insight into 'the necessary conditions of experience', and man's will may be shown to be free in the sense of being completely non-determined, a result that Schiller was always hankering after.

We cannot follow Schiller into the intricate details of his argument, which Fichte (after a quarrel, certainly) did not recognise as philosophy, and modern philosophers, with their antipathy to metaphysics, may be tempted to regard as an elaborate way of throwing dust into the eyes of the reader. Lutz's close analysis shows (it seems to me) conclusively that Schiller had shifted his ground between writing the original letters and the final version, that he uses key-words like 'nature' in a dozen different senses, and that a precise logical argument cannot be conjured out of the work.[104] His philosophy has never been revived systematically by later thinkers (though some of its terms have been used, often with a change of meaning), and the usual accounts of it are, as Lutz says, a loose paraphrase, quoting fine pieces of writing, the strength of which lies, we have suggested, in their art, not their logic, in the direct emotional impact of Schiller's passionate beliefs.

What Schiller starts from as a certainty is the dualism of human nature. Man's two halves, the physical and the mental, are necessary components in a unity which includes them both and alone makes them possible. One can compare the course of his activity in living—so we may perhaps paraphrase Schiller's

---

* The world was not there until I created it.

Who but I freed you from all the bonds of thoughts that hemmed you in like any Philistine?

thought—with the line of a graph, which seems to be attracted simultaneously, but with varying forces, by each of its two co-ordinates. One of them is his pure awareness, his 'ego', the other the material present to his awareness, his changing states of consciousness, the instinctive side of his life, his body, and the external world with which he is in contact through his senses. The first force Schiller calls the 'Formtrieb', the pull (literally 'drive' or 'impulse', because it is thought of as proceeding from within) towards 'form', the mental forming of experience. The second he calls, to begin with, 'the drive of the senses', later the 'Stofftrieb', or 'drive towards matter', the craving for experience through the senses.

This is theory of knowledge on Fichtean lines rather than psychology, and Schiller uses his terms with a tantalising vagueness, but the familiar opposition between body and mind seems to be behind it all. Whereas the tradition coming down from Plato and Christian thought, however, favoured the mind at the expense of the body, Schiller tries to arrive at a notion of totality which will do justice to the activity of both, for mind alone, he says, is an empty capacity without the body's experience of the outer world. Men in general tend to lean decidedly either one way or the other, to be either creatures of sense and appetite, or intellectuals and moralists. This opposition reminds us of the contrast drawn between the Realist and the Idealist in Schiller's later famous essay *On Naïve and Sentimental Poetry*. In Letter 13 Schiller says that cultivation ('Kultur', used here, it seems, in the sense of 'Bildung') should aim at developing both sensibility and reason, in the endeavour to do justice to both body and mind. But in Letter 14 he draws our attention to the capacity we have, through what he calls the 'drive towards play', of suspending or balancing the other two drives. Under its sway men are for the first time truly free, free from the compulsion exercised by natural laws, and equally free from the dictates of reason—in particular, one takes him to mean, Kant's 'practical reason' and the 'categorical imperative'. This play-impulse is, Schiller says, the basis of artistic creation and enjoyment, and it is only when actively or passively engaged in aesthetic activity that man becomes in the fullest sense human—which means, as for Herder, made in God's image, and so semi-divine—because he attains here totality.

Only by being made capable of such 'play' and true 'humanity', we learn at last in Letter 23, can the ordinary sensual man be given the rational insight and the strength of character required by the members of a society, if a satisfactory political order is to be achieved by it. Aesthetic education does not furnish men with these desirable qualities directly, however, for art is not art if it pursues any practical aim, but such education constitutes an intermediate stage, having passed through which a man only needs the appropriate occasion for the exercise of these qualities, and he will find that he possesses them. 'To lead the aesthetic man (the product of aesthetic education) to insight and noble-mindedness, it is only necessary to put him into situations that call for them', as Faust, it has been suggested by Rickert, after union with Helena, is inspired by the sight of the 'wasted power of ungovernable elements', as the tide sweeps in and out on the shore, to attempt the recovery of land from the sea. Schiller himself only comes back to further consideration of the ideal state, the search for which prompted his reflections, in parts of Letters 26 and 27. In the former he writes: 'In men and peoples capable of appreciating art for its own sake, as an honest and independent aesthetic semblance, we shall be able to assume the existence of intelligence (Geist) and taste and every related excellence—ideals there will be seen to rule real life, honour to prevail over wealth, thought over enjoyment, the dream of immortality over absorption in mere existence. There the public voice will be the only thing that is feared, and an olive wreath will be more highly esteemed than a robe of purple.'

Schiller is fully aware that he is using the word 'play' in a special sense which needs explanation, and another difficult term is 'Schein', translated above as 'semblance'. In Letter 15 he admits that it does not seem compatible with the rational concept and the dignity of beauty, which is regarded after all as an instrument of culture, to restrict it to mere play, a word with less exalted associations. 'But what is "mere play", when we know that in no matter what connections, it is play and play alone that makes him complete, and reveals both sides of his nature at once? What you, from your view of the matter, call restriction, I from mine, which I have justified by proofs, call extension. I would claim therefore, reversing common usage, that man's atttitude to the pleasant, the good, the perfect is merely serious, but with beauty he plays.'

Play seems to mean then the free use of its powers by any organic being, including even plants as well as animals, any action not evoked by external compulsion, or by its pursuit of an end. When we *play* at something in this sense, we delight in it for its own sake, as an end in itself and not a means. The notion is very close to that of Kant, when he describes art as a source of disinterested pleasure, or of Burke, quoted by Schiller in his lectures on aesthetics in Jena as saying that beauty arouses satisfaction without the lust for possession.[105] Simone Weil, in our day, has drawn a similar contrast between the aesthetic and the practical attitude in her striking aphorism: 'Beauté, un fruit qu'on regarde sans tendre la main.'[106] For Schiller, to observe how a man 'plays' is the best way of discovering his ideal of beauty, and he points to popular amusements in various countries as a key to the nature of their aesthetic sensibility, to the Olympian games, for instance, in Greece, horse-racing in London and bull-fighting in Spain. If men pursued ideal beauty with a devotion resembling that which they show themselves capable of in such pursuits, but raised to a correspondingly high pitch, they would be like the gods as the Greeks conceived them. 'Man only plays', Schiller claims, 'where he is in the full sense human, and he is only fully human when he is at play' (Letter 15).

Rudolf Lehmann, a philosophical admirer of Schiller's penetration and breadth of view, makes the following general criticism of the *Aesthetic Letters*:

Schiller proceeds by purely speculative arguments, depending on that dangerous extension of the concept of the transcendental, which began in a sense with Kant's doctrine of freedom and was systematically elevated into a principle by Fichte. The abstract definitions and theoretical constructions advanced all lay claim to being necessary conditions of human thought in the matter under discussion. Observed experience plays no part. The validity of the argument, it is thought, is sufficiently vouched for by the high level of abstraction on which it moves, and empirical verification is considered unnecessary. This applies to introspective experience as well as external observation. At the very least, both Schiller and Fichte fail to understand the scope of psychology, and the difference between its sphere and that of the logically transcendental. The relative value of ethical and aesthetic ideals is a question that can be illuminated and possibly decided by logical argument, but the question as to how far the development of the sense of beauty influences the training of the will is one of fact and is only to be solved by the use of psychological methods. Schiller's whole approach rules them out. The concepts from which he starts are so extremely general that psychological accuracy becomes impossible, and where his language suggests that he is aiming at it, it is simply misleading. Neither his 'Stofftrieb' nor his 'Formtrieb' is an impulse in any sense that can be understood psychologically. They are basic tendencies of the human mind, to be understood metaphysically, as constituent elements of man's ideal nature. Schiller avoids, and this is clearly intentional, equating his 'Spieltrieb' with the artistic imagination. It is a striking feature all through that so little light is thrown on the creative imagination of the artist and its laws.[107]

In reply to this criticism it could be argued that if Schiller throws no light on the psychology of the artist, he does make a valuable contribution to what has been called in our day 'literary ontology'. He gets away completely from the 'imitation theory' and helps considerably to clarify the thought of his time about the real nature of a work of art. He calls it a 'semblance' (Schein), something that interests us above all through its pattern, the relationships between its parts, not through the material of which it is made or the references to real-life experience that it may suggest. Following up the idea of Burke, no doubt, already referred to, he says in Letter 25: 'Whereas desire lays hold of its object directly, contemplation holds its object at a distance, and makes of it a true and indestructible possession, just by saving it from the hands of passion', and turning it into 'form'. In the greatest art, the 'stuff' (Stoff) of which it is made (by 'Stoff' Schiller seems sometimes to mean material, the marble of the statue, and sometimes content, derived from experience or from literature) is entirely taken up into the formal relationships. 'The secret of the master in any art consists in this, that he obliterates the stuff through the form.'[108]

In his final letter (27) Schiller suggests a theory about the stages by which men have in the course of time advanced towards purely symbolic constructions, and he links this advance up with the general movement of civilisation, very much as he had done some years earlier in his poem *The Artists*. Art begins, he thinks, with decoration, of objects for use, and of a man's own person. The art of the dance, the imaginative expression of sexual love and the refinement of social relations in general are all seen as part of the process, so that the suggestion in which this letter culminates, that the future may see an 'aesthetic state', 'in which even he who performs a menial function is a free citizen, having equal rights with the noblest, and where rationality (i.e. enlightened despotism), which submits the patient masses to its purposes by force, must solicit their consent', does not appear quite implausible, though at the time of writing, he admits, nothing resembling it exists save in a few highly cultivated circles.

In these rare groups within existing societies, Schiller says, 'conduct is governed not by the unthinking imitation of others' behaviour, but by the fineness of a man's own nature. He moves through the most complex social relationships with confident simplicity and quiet innocence, needing neither to interfere with the freedom of others to maintain his own, nor to sacrifice his dignity in order to appear with grace.' 'Dignity' and 'grace' are antithetical concepts discussed a little earlier at some length in Schiller's famous essay *On Grace and Dignity*, in which he had been concerned with the problem, evidently still a central one for him, of how a man could hope to combine in his person the highest ethical and the highest aesthetic qualities. It is an old problem of the age of 'Humanität', raised by Shaftesbury with his interpretation of the Greek 'kalokagathia' and discussed, as we have seen, by Wieland and Herder.

Shaftesbury had urged that 'the Taste of Beauty, and the Relish of what is decent, just and amiable, perfects the Character of the Gentleman and the Philosopher', and that 'a man of thorough Good-Breeding, whatever else he be, is incapable of doing a rude or brutal Action.... He acts from his Nature.' Wieland, fifty years later, found in Shaftesbury his philosophy of education, emphasising the Greek influence on him. The Greeks, he says, 'expected a noble and well-bred young man to be kalos kai agathos, a Virtuoso, as the most brilliant and subtle of modern writers, Shaftesbury, puts it'. Herder had had certain doubts about this interpretation of 'kalos kai agathos', both terms being applied in Greek, he says, to the ordinary good citizen, and having little to do with 'goodness' in our sense.[109] He shared, however, the general admiration for Shaftesbury. Goethe's *Wilhelm Meisters Lehrjahre* had not appeared of course when Schiller was occupied with his philosophical essays, and the two poets were not yet in close touch with each other, but Wilhelm Meister's unconcealed envy of the nobleman's aesthetic advantage over the commoner, his wish to be admired for himself, as a personality, and not merely for what he can do, is an interesting parallel to Schiller's ideas about the combination of grace and dignity. The middle class in Germany, this whole development seems to indicate, was becoming conscious of its own importance. Some of the intellectuals whom it had produced, at any rate, were not content merely to be useful, as tools for those free to enjoy life, and pursue, like Shaftesbury's Virtuoso, things valuable in themselves. Their new conception of the good life made them wish to count as people.

At all events we find Schiller at this time continually searching for a reconciliation between what he calls 'dignity' and 'grace', in discussions that he maintains on the highest level of abstraction. His argument in *On Grace and Dignity* leaves the unphilosophical reader vaguely uneasy. As so often, Schiller seems to be using very general terms in senses that are constantly shifting. (In the *Letters on Aesthetic Education* similarly Lutz analyses out over a dozen meanings, as has been mentioned, for the one word 'nature'.) An acute philosophical critic has recently found the source of the weakness of Schiller's arguments in his use of metaphorical language, which leads him into confusions of category and vicious circles.[110]

Schiller is not content with showing that some men can possess 'grace' and others 'dignity', or one man display them at different moments. Making a dogma of 'kalokagathia', as Dr Hamburger says, he represents 'grace' and 'dignity' as interdependent and capable of being shown simultaneously. 'It is only grace from which dignity obtains its confirmation, and only dignity from which grace receives its value.'[111] Yet he has said that when displaying dignity, man 'cannot act with his whole nature harmoniously, but only with its rational side',[112] dignity being for him the outward expression of the control of the natural impulses by moral strength. Dignity excludes therefore 'the coincidence of desire and duty, reason and natural impulse', the very state of harmony which in the first half of the treatise was made the condition for the emergence of 'grace'. In this portion Schiller had expressed his disagreement with Kant's extreme rigorism, his insistence on duty as action against the grain, against the natural inclinations. Virtue, Schiller had said, could and should become second nature. 'Man is not intended to perform individual moral actions, but to be a moral being.'[113] Kant seems to him to have legislated not for 'the children of the house' but for 'the serving men', and Schiller puts forward his own conception of a 'beautiful soul', one guided, in effect, by 'moral sense' like Shaftesbury's Virtuoso. This is the perfection of humanity, a state in which 'moral feeling has acquired control of all a man's emotions to such a degree that it can confidently leave the direction of the will to feeling (Affekt).'[114] 'Grace' is the outward expression of the harmonious union of natural impulse and reason, duty and desire.

It is significant, as Dr Hamburger says, that immediately after describing his ideal of perfection, the man in whom 'grace' and 'dignity' are combined, supported if possible by natural beauty and strength, Schiller points for illustration to Greek statues like the Belvedere Apollo so eloquently described by Winckelmann, though in a note he disagrees with some of Winckelmann's terms. For Winckelmann the greatest works always express incorporeal ideas, and especially the nobility of mind which the Greek artist emphasises in his subject. A famous example is the Laocoon interpretation to which Lessing took exception, insisting that it is not because of a noble stoicism that the priest does not in the statue seem to be crying aloud with pain, but because, if he had been shown as doing so, his open mouth would have looked ugly. Schiller finds in such controlled expression what he would call 'dignity', though there is 'grace' in other aspects of the same works.

In reading Winckelmann's rapturous descriptions of the Vatican Apollo and so on we see what Goethe had in mind when he wrote in the *Campaign in France*, describing his discussions with Fürstin Gallitzin in Münster in 1792 about her Greek gems, that 'whenever we do homage to a worthy object, religious feeling enters in', and in his more explicit association of the good with the beautiful in the lines he later wrote in her daughter's album:

Unterschieden ist nicht das Schöne vom Guten; das Schöne
Ist nur das Gute, das sich lieblich verschleiert uns zeigt.*[115]

It seems highly probable, as Dr Hamburger says, that Winckelmann's *History of Greek Art* strongly encouraged the linking of aesthetic and ethical values, and also the extension of the ethical-aesthetic attitude from the contemplation of Greek statues to the interpretation of the Greek models of 'Humanität', the 'kaloi kai agathoi' praised by Shaftesbury. There is some confusion of thought in parts of the *Moralists*, where Shaftesbury identifies beauty and goodness.[116] It persists right down to the age of German Classicism and beyond, and brings about a blurring of

---

* The beautiful is not different from the good. The beautiful *is* the good which shows itself to us pleasingly veiled.

the edges between the good and the beautiful, and also the true, a blurring which it sometimes seems to be precisely the business of 'art' with its idealising 'veil' to produce. In Goethe's couplet above, the good appears in art's veil as the beautiful, and we have seen how in his *Zueignung zu den Gedichten* truth hands to the poet the veil of poetry.

Schiller's theory of culture, though highly speculative when compared with Herder's historical study of 'Humanität' or Goethe's wise analysis of 'Bildung', reflecting his own wide experience of life and art and science, has been found very suggestive by many later thinkers. He is just as deeply convinced as Herder and Goethe of the central importance of the cultivation of mind and heart, both for the individual and for society. His *Aesthetic Letters* expressed a great deal that a small élite among his contemporaries believed, without being very clear about their reasons. The reasons that Schiller supplied for the belief in education through art do not always carry conviction, his work has perhaps supplied more catchwords than genuine arguments to the subsequent handling of the topic, but his tone of conviction and the beauty and persuasiveness of particular passages have had a considerable effect. Most later writers interested in his theme have occupied themselves with the psychological aspect of aesthetic education, which is almost entirely neglected by Schiller, as we have seen, in his eagerness to provide a strict theoretical proof of the harmonising influence of art. In earlier essays he had touched on the psychological aspects of the contrast that he draws in Letter 17 between 'schmelzende Schönheit', which reduces tensions in the beholder, and 'energische Schönheit', which rouses the apathetic to action. One is reminded of the distinction made by Plato in the *Republic* between an 'asthenic' or debilitated type of art, which might weaken his ideal statesmen, and a 'sthenic' or strong type, which arouses enthusiasm. Schiller had distinguished similarly, toward the end of *On Grace and Dignity*, between 'belebende' and 'beruhigende' Grazie, and in *On the Pathetic* between 'die bloß schmelzenden Rührungen' of the German sentimental drama, and genuine tragedy, which stimulates the will to assert itself against the suffering which is man's lot. He approves of the sterner kind of art because of the assurance that it conveys to us of man's potential freedom, his power to assert his will, whether for good or for evil, in spite of opposing circumstance. Even here, however, his interest in the matter is not really psychological, but philosophical. It is the power of the conscious mind over the body that is for Schiller the most striking feature in man. 'Der Mensch ist das Wesen, welches will.'

In his most influential critical essay, *On Naïve and Sentimental Poetry*, Schiller again includes much that is relevant to a theory of culture, though his main object is to distinguish between what seem to him the two outstanding types of writing that have occurred in European literature, the one chiefly among the Ancients (though Goethe shares many of their characteristics), and the other among the Moderns, especially the German and English writers of Schiller's own century. Friedrich Schlegel's distinction between Classical and Romantic is on similar lines and probably owes something to Schiller. In this essay Schiller once more, as in the *Letters on Aesthetic Education* and elsewhere, encourages his readers to look towards the future, thinking of civilisation as a painful advance towards an ideal of life in which the happy harmony of the golden age, if there ever was one, will be regained, as the result of a process of conscious thought and moral effort. In this advance towards a perfection that will never be completely attained, he thinks of poets as the leaders and art, still for him a form of 'Spiel' that fosters inner freedom, as the means they use. The 'natural' harmony that we ascribe to the childhood of mankind, and to favoured ages in the past like that of Greece in its heyday, he sees now in the behaviour of actual children and simple country people, but he finds it too by analogy in landscape. Its distinguishing quality he calls the 'naïve', one possessed only by natural objects or living creatures when they put man-produced 'art' or artifice to shame. Like the beauty analysed in *On Grace and Dignity*, it belongs to these things when they seem to us to 'exist in their own right', to 'produce their effect unaided', phrases which remind us of the 'freedom in (the realm of) appearance' of the earlier essay. 'They are what we once were' ('we' as mankind and as individuals); they are what we must again become. We were nature like them, and our civilisation must lead us, by way of reason and freedom, back to nature.' The ideal will have been reached 'when the will freely accepts the law of necessity', when 'duty' and 'inclination', that is, are no longer in conflict. Then and only then shall we have attained to true humanity, for Schiller, as for Herder, an ideal as well as a natural characteristic.

These familiar ideas are applied on this occasion to the working out of a distinction between two types of poet ('Dichter'), two poles between which all individual poets find their place. At the one extreme are those who, like the Greeks, are 'naïve' in their attitude to nature and art, creating objective works in which their personal feelings and reflections are not directly revealed, 'behind which they are hidden as God is behind the world'. Homer and Shakespeare are the obvious examples. At the other extreme come those who (like Schiller himself) are never unaware of the imperfections both in themselves and the world around them, having within their minds an ideal suggested by reason and imagination. To approach this is their object, so that they may be said to be 'making for nature', for the harmony which they do not possess and believe to lie at an infinite distance. The feelings they express in their work are not evoked by the objects they present, as happens with the 'naïve' poets, who are 'pre-servers of nature', the harmonious nature they see all around them. They result rather from their brooding over the world, from 'reflection'. According to the relative importance in their work of the 'real' and the 'ideal', they can be further divided into satirical, elegiac and idyllic poets. Among recent poets Schiller finds only Goethe predominantly 'naïve', and he has often handled 'sentimental' subjects, like *Werther*. A sentimental writer (in Schiller's special sense, which is perhaps better conveyed by 'reflective') can however be a genuine artist. In his own way he helps mankind in its advance, but only by leading man towards inner freedom, not by merely amusing him or instructing and edifying him.

4. Conclusion

The 'Weimar theories of culture', as we have called them, have taken up many pages even in a bare summary, but they are not so well known now, even in Germany, that it is a waste of time to recall them, and in England they are hardly known at all. The modern historian of civilisation and sociologist will learn little in detail from Herder, the scientist and philosopher little from this side of Goethe, and the student of aesthetics or educational theory little from Schiller, but it would be surprising if the range of these writers' knowledge and the depth of their thought did not still impress the specialist and suggest some fruitful ideas. Some German writers, as Professor Morris Ginsberg has reminded us, find it characteristic of the thought of their countrymen that it is the product of 'the whole man', not of analytic reason only. Hegel speaks of the German 'sense of natural totality' or 'Gemüt' —and it is no accident that this word is untranslatable. Hamann already strongly advocated thinking of this kind, not without effect on the Sturm und Drang age, and a great deal of German lyrical poetry could be described by the words Hegel uses of the 'Gemüt', its 'indeterminate striving for general satisfaction, not directed at any particular aim, but rather concerned with the general condition of the soul'.[117] This sort of fruitful vagueness is at any rate as characteristic of German ways of writing as clarity and purposefulness is of French. Mme de Staël saw social causes behind this national difference, the influence of the salon in France, of the isolation of the intellectual in Germany, and there is certainly some truth in her generalisation. Others about whom we shall speak in the last chapter have seen a connection between German 'inwardness' and the absence of political experience, others again derive it from an innate tendency towards mysticism—perhaps they are reversing cause and effect. At any rate, the habit of musing over things in an unhurried way, keeping the mind's doors open to all kinds of stray visitors from the realm of fact or fancy and giving each a friendly welcome, is apt, one would think, to be a precondition for that free linking up of disparate ideas in which William James saw the chief characteristic of genius. But whatever views we may hold about the quality of these thinkers and their roots in society, it is quite impossible for anyone acquainted with nineteenth-century German culture to close his eyes to their outstanding historical importance. Not only poets and novelists, but philosophers and historians and even scientists drew heavily on this capital for a generation or more, and still left enough to bear useful interest even today.

What is above all important for our present purpose is the light that the writings we have discussed can throw on such notions as 'Bildung' and 'Humanität' as then understood, and we may end this chapter with a piece of evidence to prove that by the time *Wilhelm Meisters Lehrjahre* appeared, interest in these notions was not confined to a few leading writers, but could be counted upon—by booksellers, for instance—among the educated public generally. Turning over the pages of that remarkable review, the *Allgemeine Literatur-Zeitung* published at Jena, we find in the one year 1796 these two titles of books reviewed: *Carolinens Blumenkranz zur Bildung des Geistes* ('Caroline's Garland for the Cultivation of the Mind') and *Ceres, für Bildung des Geschmacks, erster Jahrgang* (the first volume of the periodical 'Ceres, for the Cultivation of Taste'). There is also a review of a book by F. Delbrück, *On Humanität* (Leipzig, 1796). The anonymous critic complains of the vagueness and ambiguity of this fashionable word, and regrets that the author of this new book has done nothing to make things clearer. 'He assumes that our greatest and most famous authors mean by it that development (Ausbildung) of mind and heart which seems to them most desirable, and that we Germans understand by a humane man very much what the Greeks called a "kalokagathos" and the Romans a "vir bonus et prudens".

The qualities of body and mind which on the one hand raise men above animals, and on the other are common to them all, to the extent that they only differ from each other in degree in these respects, constitute the distinguishing characteristics of human nature. We attribute Humanität to a man who develops harmoniously the capacities and powers which constitute the characteristics of human nature, in proportion to the influence that each of them has on our true end.

The author leaves the question open here as to whether Humanität is considered to be the object of a concept arrived at by induction, or of a mere idea.' This is precisely the criticism, it will be remembered, made 140 years later by Meinecke of Herder's use of the same word. Delbrück, says the reviewer, is thinking most of the time about the qualities he finds in Socrates and his finest pupils, but when he tries to consider the concept in itself, an ideal, never completely attainable in reality, is before his mind.[118] This intelligent review conveniently reminds us of the principal conclusion that emerges from our study of the notion of humane culture as it developed between Shaftesbury and the Weimar writers. Man is good—or at least, it is only the good man who is truly human.

CHAPTER V

WEIMAR CULTURAL INSTITUTIONS AND THEIR CREATORS

THE ideas about the good life for the individual and for society which we have been tracing not only found expression in writing, but led immediately to the creation or improvement of cultural institutions in Weimar, through which they exercised a lasting influence on life and thought, not only in Weimar itself, but on wider and wider circles outside Weimar. Goethe's full awareness of the process by which the ideas of a creative minority are enabled to benefit a whole community is clear from the notes of a talk which he planned for a meeting of the 'Friday Society' and which he mentioned to W. von Humboldt in a letter of 3 December 1795. 'This republic of art and science offers a spectacle of much variety and exists, like the German Imperial constitution, not by connection but by contiguity', he says, and he includes among the institutions to be discussed the Art School and art collections, sketching the recent development of drawing and engraving, sculpture, intaglio-cutting, and architecture, then passes on to music and the theatre, and the arts associated with it, to the parks and gardening, and to schools, periodicals and libraries. A further section deals with the sciences, mainly as developed in the institutes of the University of Jena. Finally he got his faithful collaborator C. G. Voigt to describe recent progress in the practical arts and the welfare institutions of Weimar. A close parallel to these notes is to be found in the report made for Marshal Berthier soon after the Battle of Jena, when the existence of the university was threatened.[1]

In the present chapter the outline provided by these two documents is amplified from many sources, so that the gradual evolution of cultural institutions under the stimulus of particular individuals in Weimar may be followed. First the achievements in this field of Wieland and his friends and associates will be described, then those of Herder, and finally those mainly attributable to Goethe and Schiller.

I. WIELAND'S WORK

To begin then with Wieland. In his first years in Weimar, before Goethe's arrival, he had provided the theatre, as we have seen, with the libretto of *Alceste* and one or two other things, and he had aroused interest in these and other Weimar cultural ventures far beyond the boundaries of the small state through his new periodical, *Der deutsche Merkur*. The programme of the paper, as stated in the introduction to the first number, and as revealed in the issues of the first two years, has been described above (pp. 40–8). Its later history down to 1796, when Wieland virtually handed over the editorship to Böttiger, the headmaster of the grammar school, was marked by many changes and vicissitudes. The *Merkur* was never without a certain importance in the formation of opinion, though Wieland never aimed as high as Schiller did with his short-lived *Horen*, but the kind of interest to which it appealed varied considerably from phase to phase. For a third of a century Wieland succeeded in keeping in touch with his readers, the constantly expanding reading-public of the most eventful period in German literary history, which included for the first time not only people of good birth and education, but ordinary tradesmen and shopkeepers with their wives and daughters, the public reached in England first by Defoe and Richardson, and now, half a century later, by their imitators in Germany. It was necessary for him to appeal to 'the medium sort' if his 'factory', as he called it, was to fulfil its primary purpose, of supplementing his modest income in Weimar, but merely to entertain his readers did not satisfy him. He always wanted also to enlighten them and improve their taste.

Except that his general attitude was always liberal and tolerant, almost too tolerant, Wieland followed no consistent policy in his attempts to make his countrymen more reasonable and sensitive.

Until about 1776, as we have seen, he seemed to be fighting a rearguard action for literary conservatism against Storm and Stress hotheads, with their rejection of all the rules, but he knew real genius when he saw it, and had some doubts about Winckelmann's influence on current art. Then until about 1780, with the help of Heinse and others, he tried to prepare the way for a new conception of classical art, while Merck laid about him mercilessly in literary criticism. Sales had meanwhile gone down seriously, never touching again the figure of 2,000 copies which had been attained in the second year, not to speak of the first year, when a printing of 2,500 was far from satisfying the demand. By 1788 the circulation was down to 1,200, and ten years later to 800, though all of Wieland's own best work, *Die Abderiten*, for instance, the first German novel to appear in instalments, between 1774 and 1780, and his finest verse tale, *Oberon* (1780), had made their first appearance in the periodical, together with notable contributions occasionally by Goethe and Herder, and in 1788 by Schiller, who had just arrived in the neighbourhood and seemed to Wieland to have been sent by providence to rescue the *Merkur* when it was nearly, as Schiller said, at death's door. For six years from 1780 Wieland's chief assistant was Bertuch, who had an excellent head for business, as we shall see, and effectively overhauled Wieland's method of production and distribution, in return for a share of one-third of the profits. He found new contributors sharing his own more prosaic interests, in geography, economic matters and popular science, but sales continued to decline. As he became more and more involved in enterprises of his own, a young man called Reinhold, who had been educated by the Jesuits and was at a loose end on the dissolution of the order, was given a chance in 1784 on the business side of the enterprise. Within a year he had married one of Wieland's daughters, and soon after that, in 1786, started the series of eight *Letters on the Philosophy of Kant* which did so much to make Kant known, and earned for Reinhold a post on the newly founded *Allgemeine Literatur-Zeitung* in Jena and soon a chair of philosophy in the university.

From the outbreak of the French Revolution until the Terror, much space was given to political discussion. No German except Gentz, Gooch says,[2] followed the Revolution so attentively as Wieland, and its general effect on the cultivated *bourgeoisie* can best be traced in his writings. He kept his head, and continued to be what he had always been, a cautious liberal. As early as 1777 he had felt that he must protest against the view expressed by a contributor, that 'no pressure must ever be exerted on a people from above, but always from below, through the people itself', and maintain that, in a certain sense, there was such a thing as the divine right of rulers, provided that the ruler was enlightened. Wieland recognised power as a historical fact, and did not consider the masses ripe for it. On the other hand, he clearly saw the need for gradual piecemeal reform in accordance with reason and humane feeling. The liberal ideas of his philosopher Danischmend in the *Golden Mirror* were expounded in a further series of articles in the *Merkur*, and just before the Revolution, Wieland invented another ideal figure, the 'Cosmopolitan', as a mouthpiece for his liberalism. 'The Secret of the Order of Cosmopolitans' (1788) is in some ways a parallel to Lessing's *Ernst und Falk* dialogues on what Lessing held to be the ideal aims behind Freemasonry at its best, the desire of the enlightened few in every country, a sort of invisible church, to rise above the limitations of creed and nation and class. Existing secret societies Wieland rejects, as Lessing had done. What unites his Cosmopolitans is 'sympathy', a capacity for unselfish love and understanding, and their aim is the not very original one of reducing the sum of evil oppressing humanity, and increasing the sum of good in the world. They are internationally minded, but not usually politically active, unlike the 'republican enthusiasts' who make revolutions, for order and moderation are for them the first essentials. Common-sense liberal but not democratic ideas of this kind are behind Wieland's extensive series of articles on the French Revolution. They are well analysed by Gooch, who sums up Wieland's personality as follows: 'Wieland was by temperament and conviction a Trimmer, always praising and usually practising the "golden mean". He hated violence and confusion in religion, politics and literature. He never forsook the Aufklärung for romanticism. He was sealed of the tribe of Erasmus and Goethe, not of Luther and Fichte.'[3]

2. F. J. BERTUCH'S WORK

The name of F. J. Bertuch (1747–1820) was frequently associated with that of Goethe in the early days in Weimar, and for some years they exchanged the friendly 'du' with each other, but we have noted that in the private theatricals Bertuch's activity was confined to the middle-class group, and in other ways too he seems to have been regarded as on the fringe of the court circle of bright young men. He was the son of a Weimar doctor, had lost both parents at an early age and been brought up by his uncle, G. M. L. Schrön, a petty official who also edited the *Weimarische Anzeigen*, the unpretentious local single-sheet Advertiser, appearing twice a week. Naturally enough, his interests turned to the literature and science of the day, rather than to theology, though as a poor boy he first entered the theological faculty, when he went on from the Weimar Gymnasium to the University of Jena. He picked up Spanish from his employer when he was a private tutor, and was getting verses and translations printed two or three years before he came back to Weimar, for reasons of health, at twenty-six, a year after Wieland's arrival. He tried his hand at an operetta with Wolf, as Wieland had with Schweitzer, though not nearly so successfully, and at other minor dramatic pieces, but translations were his stand-by, and he published ten before Goethe arrived, the most important being his *Don Quixote*, which brought in 2,000 talers for him, according to Wieland. In all these ventures he proved himself to be a competent hack-writer and a very astute business man, and his whole career continued on the same lines. He cultivated any acquaintance he could make with literary men, scholars and artists, never losing sight of the possibility of financial gain, and his principal achievement was to convert Weimar culture into marketable articles. He made himself in this way very much disliked by the more distinguished Weimar writers, except Wieland, but it is undeniable that the fame and influence of Weimar in the outside world grew very much more rapidly, because of his activity, and that the little town owed much of its material prosperity and social stability to the many kinds of enterprise that he developed there step by step. His capitalisation of culture foreshadowed in fact much that was to happen in the nineteenth century in Germany as a whole.

Bertuch's success story can only be told in outline here, where our concern is with the give and take between ideas and everyday life. Bertuch acquired a steady if modest source of income (300 talers a year) by becoming private secretary and keeper of the purse to the Duke on his accession in 1775, married the daughter of a college friend next year and soon afterwards acquired with the proceeds of his *Don Quixote* twenty acres of land, formerly the 'Fürstlicher Baumgarten'. In a letter to Merck he speaks of it as surrounded by a wall and containing a pond, a brook, a cottage and vegetable and flower gardens which are his delight throughout the summer.[4] At the end of 1778 he bought an old grinding-mill on this land, which he made into a paper-mill and an oil-mill for the manufacture of paint, then more adjoining plots of land, and from 1780 he began to build a large house, in part of which, from 1782, he ran a factory for artificial flowers, managed by his sister-in-law. This is where Christiane Vulpius was employed when Goethe first met her. Visitors describe the pleasant conditions under which respectable young middle-class girls worked here, who would otherwise have had to go into domestic service.

Bertuch had had the development of arts and crafts and a luxury trade in view when he published a plan for a drawing-school in Weimar in 1774. The Duke and Goethe became interested and it was possible to make a modest beginning in 1776, when the court engaged as drawing-master the young Frankfurt artist G. M. Kraus, known to Bertuch since his first visit to Weimar in 1774, from which Kraus took back the sketches that gave Goethe his first impressions of the place, as he tells us in his autobiography.[5] We have seen above how the school developed, with the help of Goethe and the court. Paints and paper could soon be supplied locally by Bertuch, who in the middle of the 'eighties conceived the idea of publishing, with the help of Kraus, his *Journal des Luxus und der Moden*, to meet a demand hitherto satisfied only from abroad, and incidentally to employ Weimar artists and craftsmen connected with the drawing-school and to advertise their wares. This fashion and luxury journal appeared first in January 1786, and five years later Bertuch obtained the Duke's permission to set up a 'Landesindustrie-comptoir', to act in the first instance as showrooms and advertising agency for Weimar craftsmen, and a clearing house for orders for this kind of goods. The first number of the *Journal* had announced an agency conducted by the editors to facilitate the purchase of luxuries and fashion goods from France, England, Italy and the more distant parts of Germany, and the 'Intelligencer' that accompanied the *Journal* had regularly advertised such wares. Merck in Darmstadt, another man whose head was full of ingenious ideas for making a fortune, though they brought him in the end to disaster, was already running such an agency, for French books and engravings, in 1782.[6]

Before examining more closely this *Journal*, which is a mine of information on social history, we must look at some of Bertuch's earlier periodical publications, one of which is even more influential than the *Journal*. He had given Wieland some help in seeing the *Merkur* through the press and distributing its quarterly issues, which consisted of three monthly numbers in one. From its second year the *Merkur* was printed in Weimar by Bertuch's old acquaintance Hoffmann, the publisher of the *Anzeigen*. Wieland found Bertuch so useful that from 1780, as we have seen, he took him into partnership, to look after the business side of 'the factory', though he also had much to do with the change in the contents of the periodical in the next few years. In the same year 1780, Bertuch started a periodical of his own, which ran for three years very successfully, the *Magazin für spanische und portugiesiche*

Literatur, and in 1782 he wrote a pamphlet, published by the new 'Buchhandlung der Gelehrten' at Dessau, in which he was financially interested, on a subject dear to his heart, *How can a small state best care for its poor and prevent begging?* His answer, foreshadowing his later idea of an 'Industriecomptoir', was in brief 'by the proper organisation of its crafts and industries'.[7]

In 1784 Bertuch planned with the Professor of Poetry and Rhetoric at Jena, C. G. Schütz, a new general review of current literature of all kinds, to rival Nicolai's *Allgemeine deutsche Bibliothek* and the *Göttinger gelehrte Anzeigen*. Wieland was involved in the enterprise too at first, but quarrelled with the others before the first number appeared on 3 January 1785, under the title of *Allgemeine Literatur-Zeitung*. This new review was soon recognised as the most authoritative in Germany and one of the best in Europe, a publication that reflected the greatest credit on Jena for the rest of the century. When Schütz, for reasons that will be discussed later, migrated to Halle in 1803 and published the review from there, Goethe felt it necessary in the interests of Jena to start a rival review, the *Jenaische Allgemeine Literatur-Zeitung*, and to give it all the support in his power. Reading the pages of the *A.L.Z.* in its prime, one acquires a new respect for German learning in that age.

The *A.L.Z.* was not a specifically literary but a general review, very like the *Times Literary Supplement* of today, covering the literature of every branch of learning as well as 'belles lettres'. One sheet, folded to give four quarto pages printed in double columns, in Latin type, with a view to circulation abroad, appeared on every weekday throughout the year. The introductory notice in the first number explained the principles to be followed by the editors. They included strict anonymity, the pros and cons of which were well argued in this preface, and the choice of reviewers from amongst recognised scholars by the editors themselves, with a view to the greatest possible impartiality. Any judgments expressed were to be fully motivated. For foreign books, collaborators would be sought, presumably abroad, who had the books before them. If possible, all books mentioned in the annual catalogue of the Leipzig Fair, and important works not listed there, would be reviewed, with not more than a year's delay. To discourage the practice of piracy, which went on, owing to inadequate copyright laws, well into the nineteenth century, only legitimate editions would be considered for review.

The well-deserved success of the *A.L.Z.* is clear from its constantly growing circulation figures, 600 subscriptions (at 8 talers a year post free) after the first half-year, 2,000 by 1787, 2,400 by 1795. Bertuch made on it an annual profit of 2,400 talers. He was the business manager of the review and an active member of its editorial staff until 1806, the review itself continuing to appear (in Halle) until 1849. Its pronouncements were naturally much disputed but were always taken seriously, owing to the very good choice of collaborators. Space was allotted to the reviews in proportion to the usually, it seems, very shrewdly estimated importance of the book. Few books in the course of a year earned a review extending over a whole number and into a supplement, as happened with Herder's *Ideen*, First Part, reviewed by Kant in the first week of the new journal's existence,[8] but with all books of any importance, space was allowed for a readable summary of the contents as well as for criticism, so that the pages of the *A.L.Z.* are full of historical interest. Works of literary importance form a small minority of those reviewed. They received an amount of space roughly corresponding to the proportion they represented of the total German production, in which 'schöne Künste', a category including art books as well as poetry, drama, novels etc., only made up about 15 per cent, to be compared with about 17 per cent in theology and 8 per cent in history. The theological total remained steady over the next fifteen years or so, but history and 'schöne Künste' went up gradually to 50 per cent or more above the 1785 figures, according to the classified lists regularly published, together with publishers' announcements, personal news about literary men and scholars, university news from Jena and other universities, and so forth, in the 'Intelligenzblatt', a supplement given with the *A.L.Z.*

twice a week. A full index of books reviewed and also of topics treated in the reviews appeared at the end of each annual volume, while at intervals of five years an *Allgemeines Repertorium der Literatur* was taken in hand, that naturally appeared a few years late, and gave a systematic bibliography of the quinquennium, arranged under an elaborate system of headings and subheadings based on the sixteen categories of the Leipzig Fair lists. It included books reviewed not only in the *A.L.Z.* but in a number of other leading journals, German and foreign.[9] The volumes published, mainly the work of the indefatigable J. S. Ersch, cover the period 1785 to 1800.

To indicate the range of topics discussed in the *A.L.Z.*, it may be mentioned that the British books fully reviewed between 1794 and 1799 include at the one extreme the *Philosophical Transactions of the Royal Society of London* and the *Statistical Account of Scotland*, and at the other, Pinkerton's 1790 edition of Barbour's *Bruce*, from which a passage is quoted (in 1794) on the value of freedom. The reviewer finds this work more interesting than 'the Swabian poets in their epics' and thinks that 'it is time that in Scotland too scholars should occupy themselves more frequently and intensively with their older language and literature'. In particular he suggests a combined glossary to this work and two others evidently known to him, *Gavin Douglas* and *Ancient Scottish Poems*.

To return now to the *Modejournal*, as it was generally called, following the title of the periodical in its first year only, we may note that it was even more fully integrated with the activities of the inhabitants of Weimar, town and state, than the *A.L.Z.*, the contributors to which included in its first twenty years almost all the leading literary men and scholars of Weimar and Jena, as well as a large number of distinguished contemporaries outside, all protected by a by no means transparent anonymity. There were 120 of them, Schiller says, in 1787. The *Modejournal* aimed in the same way at an international exchange of ideas, but in matters of what is called in German 'Zivilisation' rather than 'Kultur'. In the 'Intelligenzblatt' or advertising section of the first volume, it is announced that the principal subjects that will be discussed are: fashions, for men and women, including 'accessories' and jewellery, furniture and bric-à-brac, tableware, carriages of all kinds, together with saddlery and liveries, house fittings and decorations, plans for gardens and country villas, and finally matters of general interest, particularly foreign novelties. Each monthly number contained also within its salmon-coloured paper wrapper in addition to the text and advertisements two or more fashion plates or illustrations of objects discussed, some of them hand-coloured.

The advertisements, all confined to the 'Intelligenzblatt', have as much period interest for us now as the text. In the first volume we find, for instance, Viennese fans advertised decorated with subjects such as 'Lotte at Werther's grave' or 'Lotte in a faint, with Albert', as well as with figures from *Figaro*, or children's games. Another Viennese craftsman sells replicas of classical medallions, of Homer, Socrates, Plato, some forty-four subjects in all, from originals in Rome and Florence. Plaster casts by the Weimar sculptor Klauer are available, we are told, in a whole range of classical subjects (in 1786), from a large Medici Venus at 16 talers and a Ganymede at 10 down to small busts of Homer and Cicero at 1 taler, or, at the same price, busts of the following modern celebrities: Voltaire, Raynal, de Villoison (the two latter had both visited Weimar), von Goethe, Wieland, Herder, Jacobi, Bode, Bertuch, Musäus, Oeser, Gellert, Lavater, von Fürstenberg, Hemsterhuis (two more visitors) and Sterne. Another item, in the text this time, which takes us right back to the eighteenth century and reminds us of the physical background to this classicism, is the sentence: 'Every tidy room must contain a spittoon.' The English have one at each side of the fireplace, the Dutch put one on the tea-table, we read, and in an illustration we see a beautiful and practical Chinese spittoon, like a very large egg-cup, with a lead base and a water seal. Among the miscellaneous essays is one concerned with the latest gossip in London about Mrs Fitzherbert, the beautiful young widow whom the Prince of Wales (later George IV) had secretly married in 1785.

By 1790 the contents of the *Modejournal* had undergone a

noticeable change, chiefly because the overburdened Bertuch now turned the editorship over to Böttiger, who was less interested in the crafts and fashion than in travel and the arts, especially that of the theatre. The volume opened auspiciously with Goethe's description of the Carnival in Rome, already published in book form, but too expensive to be well known. French fashion news is still coming in, despite the Revolution, and one of the illustrations is of an officer in the uniform of the Garde Nationale. In May 1788 a correspondent had drawn attention to the antiquity of the art of making terra-cottas in Germany and suggested its revival, and in August of that year the enterprising Lambeth firm of Coade had had a long price-list inserted of their 'lythodipyra', containing about a thousand items, the more ambitious ones ranging from a nine-foot statue of a river-god at 100 guineas through two or three dozen other classical figures to busts of Homer, etc., and a few English kings and queens, two feet high, at two guineas. In November 1789 the ever-adaptable Court Sculptor Klauer had duly announced his first successful attempt to produce in terra-cotta figures, vases, etc., usually carved in stone, and of course more durable than his plaster casts. By May 1790 he had a stock for sale, far less extensive of course as yet than Coade's, but apparently at about half his price. He could offer a vestal virgin or the goddess Hygiaea, six feet high, at 30 talers, where Coade charged 12 guineas for one two feet shorter. Many Weimar gardens and drawing-rooms must soon have been adorned with these fashionable but inexpensive *objets d'art*. One unpretentious work of Klauer's, still to be seen in the sitting-room of the Kirms Krackow House in Weimar, it is particularly appropriate to mention at this point because of its symbolical fitness. It is an earthenware stove, on the blue and white front panel of which Hermes is to be seen, handing over the infant Trade to Winaria, a female figure personifying Weimar, a clear reference to Bertuch's enterprises, to which Klauer owed so much.[10]

Böttiger's theatrical news consisted at first of scraps of information from various theatres at home and abroad, but towards the end of the decade, when the Weimar theatre was at its best, he concentrated his attention on performances here, and annoyed Goethe very much with what he as manager considered to be niggling criticisms. At last in January 1802, after the performance of A. W. Schlegel's *Ion*, which can only have pleased Goethe because of his obsession at that time with the Ancients, Goethe heard beforehand of Böttiger's unfavourable criticism (Karoline Schlegel tells us how closely Böttiger followed the play and how he ridiculed Schlegel's mythology in the interval), and stopped its appearance by a threatening letter, insisting on seeing Böttiger's criticisms in future in advance. In March, the report on the performances of Schiller's *Jungfrau von Orleans* in four German theatres outside Weimar was by 'the management' of the theatre, Goethe himself. But some of Böttiger's work cannot have been entirely displeasing to Goethe, his long account,[11] for instance, in February 1798, of the masked procession on the Duchess's birthday, an allegorical celebration of the Peace of Campo Formio concluded in the preceding autumn. It was devised by Goethe, and described by him more briefly to Schiller in a letter. Here a little irony would, we feel, have been quite in place. The un-inspired occasional poem spoken by Peace is printed in Goethe's works and reminds us, with several others, of the more tiresome side of his position in Weimar,[12] but this kind of work was practice for the genuinely poetical Masquerade in the first act of *Faust*, Part II, and indicates its background in Goethe's experience.

Bertuch's house outside the old Jacobstor, partly built with stone from this disused town-gate, is described in 1787 by Schiller (to Körner, 18 August) as the finest in Weimar, although the massive central portion with its classical architrave and bee-hive was not added till 1800. It is now the Weimar Civic Museum. Schiller particularly admired Bertuch's garden and his ingenuity in letting out most of it in seventy-five allotments, which brought him in 6 per cent on his capital outlay, and yet contriving to make himself a pleasure garden at one end, where his guests could walk for nearly ten minutes following a labyrin-thine path, through a shady wood, past a grotto and the usual features admired in that age. With his salary from the Duke (till 1796) and his profits on the *A.L.Z.* and the *Modejournal* (this latter alone brought in 1,700 talers, which he divided with Schütz), Bertuch must already have had an income of between three and four thousand talers, about twice that of Goethe, apart from their literary earnings, where again he no doubt had the advantage, with his popular translations.

Bertuch still had several ideas up his sleeve. The 'Landesindustriecomptoir' or centre for local industries of which we have spoken, set up in 1791, included a 'geographical institute', where young people trained at the School of Drawing made maps and terrestrial globes. A flourishing publishing business gradually grew up here, for atlases, books and periodicals, at first printed at various presses in the neighbourhood, but from 1800 on the premises. The Centre for Local Industries had become a publishing house, because Bertuch found that his ideas for the development of industry with state support were ahead of the times, though he made propaganda for them in his own *Modejournal* (particularly in articles of August and September 1793), and in 1794 tried to interest the Elector of Saxony in setting up a similar but more ambitious undertaking in Dresden, to serve Electoral Saxony. Papers found in his archives show how he tried to induce the Saxon government to take advantage of the international situation in order to 'throw off the French yoke' and meet the ever-increasing English challenge. A list of fifty different kinds of English exports, mainly luxury goods, apart from textiles, is supplied, with the suggestion that nearly all of these could be produced in Saxony. A document in German, also translated into French for the benefit of the court, sets out Bertuch's arguments and suggestions in detail under more than thirty heads. The emphasis throughout is on increased production for a much wider market by craftsmen who at present make goods to order for local customers. They need encouragement, capital, better training and the advice of well-informed men of taste to rouse them from their lethargy, and all these the Centre could supply, given good premises, e.g. in the Zwinger, and a good director. 'Je crois d'avoir trouvé cet homme', he modestly concludes, and an accompanying letter of recommendation, signed 'v. R.', confirms our conclusion that he meant himself.[13] His self-confidence was unbounded, there are clear signs of patriotic feeling in the documents from which we have quoted, and it is interesting to see how, beginning in Weimar, he gradually extended the area he aimed at fructifying by his enterprise, first to the province of Saxony and after the wars apparently to the German Confederation, though once again his advice fell on deaf ears.

In Weimar itself, however, both in war and peace, Bertuch went from strength to strength, apart from passing difficulties due to the French occupation. In 1811, when he became one of the two aldermen of the town under Chancellor von Müller's new Municipal Decree, based on Stein's in Prussia, he employed 450 men. By this time, in addition to the publications mentioned, he had launched a *Picture Book for Children* in monthly parts (1791) illustrating natural history, partly in colour, with legends in English, French and Italian as well as German with a view to sales abroad, which duly followed, a geographical magazine (*Geographische Ephemeriden*), a gardening magazine, a monthly *Magazine of Trade and Industry*, an expensive illustrated magazine appearing every six weeks 'for the cultivated at home and abroad' under the title *London und Paris* (1798), and a stout monthly for recent and contemporary history, with good war maps, *Die Zeiten* (1805). After the war, two political ventures, the monthly *Nemesis* (1814) and the daily newspaper *Oppositionsblatt* (1817, but suppressed after the Karlsbad Decrees), both democratic in tone, were important new periodical publications. In the way of books, he favoured safe series like the *Blaue Bibliothek aller Nationen* (1790), a collection of fairy-tales, 'Ritterromane' and similar popular fare, or the *Bibliothek der Reisebeschreibungen* (1800), fifty volumes of travels, but he also published local scholarly productions, mainly in science and medicine, his son-in-law, L. von Froriep, who joined the firm in 1801 and carried it on after Bertuch's retirement, being a medical man. Under this heading we may include Goethe's *Beiträge zur Optik* (1791–92). Kanzler von Müller in his funeral oration on Bertuch in 1820 rightly emphasised his share in the stimulation of activities in Weimar and the diffusion of its products: 'His cosmopolitan connections, like a fructifying stream, bore the products of all kinds of research to the most distant lands. He knew how best to foster every promising beginning in the field of learning, and to rouse and stimulate any dormant powers in those around him.' Goethe, however, in conversation with the Chancellor in the following year, called the late lamented 'the greatest of virtuosos in the acquisition of borrowed plumes'.

3. HERDER'S WORK

When Herder came to Weimar about a year after Goethe, to fill the long-vacant post of General Superintendent, that is, head of the Protestant clergy in the state, it was in the hope, as he wrote to Lavater, of 'living for the Lord in living men' and giving up his writing. Like Goethe, he was more attracted by the prospect of exercising a personal influence for good in what seemed a position of unexpected power and influence than in obtaining what fully satisfied Wieland, a pensionable and not too exacting post that would give him more and more leisure for authorship. As things turned out, it was his writing that continued to be the means by which he left his mark on his time and gained lasting fame and influence, while the institutions that he had hoped to remould for years resisted all his efforts and never offered him more than a very limited field.

For six or seven years after his arrival in Weimar nothing but frustration resulted from Herder's more ambitious undertakings, and the influence he exerted on those around him was confined to his purely personal activity, in his preaching, confirmation classes and similar parochial duties, as well as his happy relations with the Duchess Luise as her spiritual adviser. Church and schools as institutions continued almost unaffected by Herder's presence, though he saw many defects in them which he wished to remedy. What he called in a letter to Hamann the 'Sisyphean task' of supervising all the clergy in the state overwhelmed him at first with matters of detail which he took very seriously, even auditing all the parish accounts, and when he did attempt any improvements, he usually found himself at cross-purposes both with the 'geniuses' round the Duke and the 'anti-geniuses' of the Konsistorium. Goethe and the Duke could not understand why he took himself so seriously as a minister of religion, while Herr von Lyncker, the old-fashioned President of the Konsistorium, its orthodox ecclesiastical members and the Minister presiding over the Conseil, Herr von Fritsch, whose opposition to the Duke's innovations has been described above, were not easily convinced that a 'Bellettrist' and friend of Goethe like Herder could be taken seriously by them.

One thing that Herder's opponents soon had to acknowledge was that in the performance of that part of his duties which for a Protestant minister was supremely important, his preaching, he far exceeded their expectations. We have many descriptions of it, some by persons not predisposed to admire, and all agree in putting him very high among the preachers of his time, a master of his art whom no intelligent visitor to Weimar liked to miss, whether in general he liked sermons or not. Schiller, for instance, did not like sermons, as he tells Körner in the letter describing his impressions of Herder.[14] No intelligent man, he said, would defend them, unless he was prejudiced, eccentric or hypocritical. A preacher cannot simply neglect the uneducated, as a writer can. He has to try to satisfy the sophisticated and the unsophisticated in the same congregation, and that is really impossible. All the same, Herder's sermon pleased him better than any other he had heard. It was on the Unjust Steward.

The whole sermon was like a speech that a man makes to himself, very straightforward, popular, natural, more like a sensible conversation than an address. An ethical principle, applied to certain details of ordinary life—lessons that you might equally well expect to hear in a mosque as in a Christian church. The manner of delivery is as simple as the matter, without gestures or exploitation of the voice, the expression on the face serious and sober.

Herder seemed to him to speak as one having authority, conscious of his dignity and entirely at his ease because generally respected. Böttiger, the new headmaster of the Gymnasium appointed in 1791, also hurried to hear Herder preach and wrote down a much fuller description, agreeing with Schiller's in all essentials.[15] New points are that though the preacher had clearly given much care to the logical disposition of his material, he made the transition from point to point so smoothly that an uneducated listener might have more difficulty than he would with the normal sermon, with its numbered sections arranged as in battle order. The master of his art was also to be seen in the striking but impromptu phrasing of a discourse of which the whole content had been carefully thought out beforehand. Herder did not read his sermons, we are told, at least in his maturity, but preached from full notes. He objected to printing them, and if he had to do so, produced a text afterwards which was more bookish in its style than the sermon as actually preached, when he relied on the inspiration of the moment under the stimulus of his surroundings.

For years Herder preached nowhere except in the Town Church that overshadowed his house, but Böttiger heard him first in St Jacob's, in the suburb that already existed outside the wall. This had formerly been the Garrison Church, but in 1787 Herder had suggested that no new incumbent should be appointed, the old one having just moved to another parish, and that services for the court, which had had no chapel of its own since the 1774 fire, should be held at St Jacob's. If these services, for the old congregation and the new, were conducted by the existing court chaplains, of whom he was the chief, the stipend thus saved could be used to supplement those of other clergy and the salaries of school staff. The Duke agreed to this and prevailed over the Konsistorium. By 1791 it had become fashionable for the *beau monde* to attend when Herder was preaching, and Böttiger found quite a crowd out there before nine o'clock in the morning.

The story of the economy effected at St Jacob's illustrates the shifts that had to be resorted to in order to bring about improvements in the schools, the necessity for which had been obvious to Herder from the beginning, though he had been very slow in producing the plan for a training scheme for country schoolmasters for which the Konsistorium had asked him about a year after his arrival. It took him three years, and another three passed before the scheme was approved by the Konsistorium, under pressure from the Duke after Goethe had become interested in August 1783, when Herder and he had at last become firm friends again, as they now remained for some years. With his prickly nature and permanent sense of grievance, Herder was by no means expert in overcoming opposition to his ideas, however reasonable they might be. The scheme he put forward for the improvement of the country schools was exceedingly modest, disappointingly so for his modern admirers, and it reminds us again, as Lehmann says, of the essentially aristocratic basis of Weimar culture. 'There is no trace here of the spirit of Pestalozzi, whose ideas he shared otherwise in such essential points. There is not the faintest glimmer in his mind of the ideal of a good education for all, although he himself was a son of the people.'[16] What Herder asked for and obtained was that he, as General Superintendent, should be given complete control over the selection of boys for training as teachers, from candidates who had been through the lower forms of the Gymnasium and passed a special test. An indefinite number would go on learning, but the six best would be given teaching practice under supervision, as well as further instruction and training from a Candidate in Theology (a theological student not yet appointed to a church), and one or two part-time teachers. They would receive a small payment as teachers in training, but the total annual cost of the scheme would not exceed 200 talers, the amount agreed to by the Estates. Herder knew of course that village schoolteachers were miserably paid, often as little as 25 to 50 talers a year, less than the meanest labourer—the principle, against which he protested, being that you only made a teacher of someone who was not strong enough to follow the plough. He ended his document in 1786 therefore with a characteristic sentence, after pleading for an increase in their pay: 'For what would be the use of all the wisdom of Solomon he had absorbed, if the schoolteacher in years of bad harvest or scarcity ran the risk of dying of hunger with his wife and children?'

Herder did not suggest any extension of the curriculum of the country schools beyond the ordinary teaching of the three R's and the catechism. He knew that few enough of the pupils ever learned even so much, for although a decree had declared school attendance to be compulsory long before this, well in advance of Prussia, it could not be enforced. But Herder himself devised a new and much improved little primer for reading and an edition of the Lutheran catechism with explanations 'for the use of schools and families', in which he expounded in the main a 'reasonable' form of belief, in the spirit of the times, leaving the Virgin Birth and so forth standing out like erratic blocks. He was, however, much concerned about the curriculum of the Gymnasium and applied to its reform ideas that resulted from his own teaching experience and were first adumbrated in his early *Travel Diary*.

In his ideas about secondary education, as Lehmann has shown, Herder went very little beyond J. M. Gesner, the great innovator in classical studies in Germany, who had himself been the senior master at the Weimar Gymnasium for fourteen years, though his influence then had not extended beyond his own classes. His teaching had its full effect only when he went on, in 1730, to the headmastership of the Thomasschule in Leipzig and from there as Professor of Eloquence to Göttingen (1734–60), where Heyne and F. A. Wolf continued his good work. But Herder entered fully into the spirit of Gesner's reform, gave it memorable expression in his annual addresses and greatly improved the Weimar Gymnasium as a place of humane and not merely humanistic education. Like the Weimar Theatre, as we shall see, the Gymnasium, because of the limited funds available, had to perform functions which in larger capitals were divided among two or more such institutions. Only a small minority of its boys went on to the university, and for them it was a grammar school, laying the foundations of their later studies through its teaching of the classics, especially Latin. The others usually left school after reaching the middle forms and for them it served the purpose of a modern school or 'Realschule'. The lower forms, as Herder wrote to the Duke in 1785, 'really constituted the school for the town and state of Weimar in which citizens, shopkeepers, crafts-men, schoolteachers, artists, in fact the most necessary and numerous part of society had to receive its education.' Two earlier attempts had been made, since the old Town School had been turned into a Gymnasium in 1712, and begun to follow the normal grammar-school pattern, in which Latin and religion were the only school subjects that really mattered, to make some allowance for the varying needs of its pupils. Mathematics and modern languages had been introduced into the curriculum, together with German essay-writing and improvements in the teaching of the classics, and even some accomplishments like dancing and fencing, for the benefit of the young aristocrats, not all of whom could be educated at home by tutors, though the majority of them still were at the end of the century. Fritz von Stein, for instance, did not go to the Gymnasium but was prepared for the university largely by Goethe. But the staff was too small and too little specialised for these good intentions to have much effect, and the masters spent most of their time gerund-grinding with unwilling pupils in classes that were far too large.

Herder sensibly proposed, as Gesner had before him, he claimed, that the lower school should be recognised as the 'Realschule' that it was for the majority of boys, and given a curriculum that would prepare them for life, including history and geography, mathematics, taught Socratically, as an exercise in thinking, and a modern language, the time allotted to religious instruction and Latin being correspondingly reduced. The upper school should remain the real grammar school, where Latin and Greek should be taught in Gesner's way, with the emphasis not on grammar but on the content of classical texts selected on the ground of their literary qualities and educative value, in connec-tion with history and, in the sixth form, some philosophy. Greek is not yet given the emphasis it was to receive in Hum-boldt's reform of the Prussian educational system, where the influence of Winckelmann, Heyne, Wolf and the German classical period is evident, a gain that is offset, in Lehmann's view,[17] by Humboldt's mistaken insistence on a classical education as essential not only for all university entrants but for the cultivated and professional classes in general.

Herder's proposals for the reform of the Gymnasium were immediately accepted in principle by the Consistorium and the Duke, and as J. N. Heinze, the scholarly headmaster, and his small staff were most co-operative, they soon began to have some effect on the school, though progress was still hampered by the lack of the money that would have been required to staff and equip the school adequately. For posterity, perhaps the most valuable consequence was the series of School Addresses by Herder, in which he expressed his appreciation of progress made, drew attention to weaknesses, and above all expounded his philosophy of education in passages like the following, which remind the English reader of Newman's *Idea of a University*:

We are men before we become members of a particular profession, and woe betide us if we do not remain men when exercising this calling. The best of our culture and usefulness in our own person comes from what we know as men and have learned as boys, without too anxious thought of what the state wants to make of us. If the knife is once sharpened, all kinds of things can be cut with it, and not every household has a different piece of cutlery to deal with bread and with meat. So it is too with the sharpness and polish of the intelligence. Sharpen and polish it on what and for what you will, so long as it *is* sharpened and polished, and use it afterwards to your heart's content and according to the needs of your station. . . . It is not for his precious studies that a man should educate himself, but for life, for the use and application of his knowledge in all human situations and callings. What I learned as a theologian I try more and more to forget, and my office compels me to do so. Just because of that I am becoming a better tested man and more useful citizen.[18]

In Herder's theory of education there is much of permanent value, like this distinction between the training of the capacities and the accumulation of knowledge, but in many respects he is naturally unable to free himself from the influence of his age.

We have noted the unconscious acceptance of a two-class society that seems to be implied in Herder's much greater interest in secondary than in primary education, though other explanations are possible and Herder had always insisted on the creativity of the 'people' in folk-song and folk art. The coupling of 'Bildung' with 'Besitz' (personal culture with prosperity) that became almost axiomatic, according to Paulsen, in nineteenth-century German thought, would at any rate have been impossible without some such assumption. In other respects too we can discern, profiting of course from the advantages of hindsight, the dim outline of features that later marked the externalisation of the notion of culture in the century that followed. Lehmann points, for example, to the encyclopaedic and theoretical tendencies, relics of the Aufklärung, that still dog Herder as educationist.[19] His conception of the humane cultivation of the individual is wide and deep, he is fully conscious of the connections between the diverse aspects of civilisation, but like Schiller, with his notion of 'totality', he does not seem to question the possibility of all-round development for every pupil, regardless of his inborn aptitudes. In spite of express caveats, his system might well favour the accumulation of dead knowledge that was mistaken for culture long before Nietzsche's protests, and it certainly strikes English observers as over-theoretical. 'Herder's ideal of all-round humanity is in practice reduced to one of universal receptivity. The humane, cultivated man is merely the mirror or the sounding-board of humanity in all its historical manifestations. It is an ideal of culture for scholars, not for men of action, who need clearly defined motives and models.'[20] Goethe in *Wilhelm Meisters Lehrjahre* seems to be much better aware of these dangers, but the German classical writers in general tended to be spectators of life and to regard 'Bildung' as that which makes existence in this imperfect world still tolerable, not as a spur towards efforts for its improvement. It is in this way in particular that 'culture' is affected in this age by the surrounding 'society', by the political, economic and social conditions of the time. 'The humanistic school was full of enthusiasm for the picture of antiquity that emerges from ancient literature and history, without making any move towards transplanting something of the way of life of the Ancients into the modern world. It praised the gymnastic education of the Hellenes and at the same time opposed the introduction of physical training and bodily exercise in general, it glorified the republican freedom of the Greek people and did its utmost to discourage among its pupils the growth of liberal sentiments or political efforts of any kind.'[21]

On the development of the University of Jena Herder did not have any direct influence, though in the Konsistorium he defended the advanced Jena theologians, like Griesbach and Paulus, when they were fiercely attacked in 1794 by the General Superintendant of Eisenach, who alleged that they were undermining the foundations of the family and the state by their ill-considered utterances. There was still one institution in Jena, of course, the *Allgemeine Literatur-Zeitung*, against which Herder was filled with an uncontrollable hatred, which was extended to Bertuch and all associated with the review and at times to the whole university, as the citadel of Kantianism.

It might have been thought that Herder, intent as he was all his life on bridging the gulf between a dogmatic and historical form of Christian belief and his own free religion of feeling, equally indebted, as it seems from the book *Gott*, to Christ and Spinoza, would make use of the opportunity presented to him in Weimar, where he had the support of a singularly open-minded ruler, to devise a form of worship more in keeping than the inherited Lutheran liturgy with the needs and convictions of a 'modern man'. In fact, however, the only modifications of the liturgy that he did introduce were suggested in the first instance by the Eisenach Estates, as the teachers' training scheme had been, and again Herder took three years to make his report to the Konsistorium. It was a very long one, very critical of the existing forms, but the only definite proposals he made for a revision concerned two forms of service, that for baptism, with its exorcism of evil spirits, and that for marriage. For these changes he easily obtained the approval of the Konsistorium, though as so often before he took umbrage at a word used by his colleagues, in his absence, about his suggestion that these changes should be introduced quietly and without comment, to avoid undue attention being paid to them. As usual, the Duke took his side and the changes were made, early in 1788.

4. THE WORK OF GOETHE AND SCHILLER

The culmination of the development of Weimar as a centre of culture came in the glorious decade that may be said to have begun with the publication of the first number of *Die Horen* in January 1795 and ended with Schiller's death, a period regarded, not of course at the time, but certainly very soon afterwards, as the height of the classical age of German literature. How far Goethe himself was from considering the prospects to be favourable in 1795 may be seen from his essay *Literary Sansculottism*, published in the fifth number of *Die Horen*. More precisely than Schiller in his *Letters on the Aesthetic Education of Man*, especially the ninth, which had appeared in the first number of *Die Horen* (see above, p. 276), Goethe describes here the disabilities under which a German writer of his time still labours:

Nowhere in Germany is there a centre of society, life and culture, where writers could come together and develop their talents, each in his own field, with a certain unity of manner and aim. Born at scattered points, educated very differently, left for the most part to their own devices and to the impressions made on them by quite different circumstances, fired by their liking for this or that example in German or foreign literature; forced for lack of guidance into all kinds of experiments and unskilful attempts to test their own powers; only gradually convinced by reflection of what they should do; taught by their own practice what they can do; repeatedly led astray by a large public without taste, ready to swallow the bad with just as much pleasure as the good; then encouraged again by acquaintance with the host of cultivated people scattered over all parts of this large country; stimulated by contemporaries working and doing their best alongside them—it is in this way that German writers finally reach manhood, when they are compelled by concern for their own maintenance and for their family to look about them in the world outside, where they must often, sick at heart, earn by means of works that they despise the income that enables them to produce those things with which their mature mind would now like to occupy itself exclusively. What German writer of merit will not recognise himself in this picture, and which of them will not with quiet sadness admit that he has often enough sighed for an opportunity of submitting the idiosyncrasies of his original genius to the guidance of a general national culture which was unfortunately non-existent? For the cultivation of the upper classes through foreign manners and literature, however much benefit it has brought us, tended to delay a German in his development as a German.[22]

Classical authors and classical writings worthy of the name are not to be expected, Goethe had said a little earlier in the essay, without the support of a national tradition, embodied in a continuous history of great deeds, and maintaining a consistent body of common convictions which the writer too still shares, together with a literary tradition, so that 'it is not difficult for him to cultivate himself, because his nation has reached a high degree of civilisation'. This applies particularly to prose-writers. Mere talent is not enough. 'A weighty piece of writing, like a weighty speech, is always a product of life', i.e. not of the un-assisted imagination. 'Neither author nor man of action makes the circumstances into which he was born and in which he exerts himself. Everyone, even the greatest genius, suffers in some re-spects from his age as in others he benefits from it, and a first-rate national author can only be expected from a nation.' It is absurd therefore for criticasters like Jenisch in Berlin, whose complaint in the *Archiv der Zeit und ihres Geschmacks* of the lack of classical prose writings in German is Goethe's starting-point, to blame individuals. This is 'literary sansculottism'. It is the politically divided nation, German society, that is basically responsible for German culture or the lack of it. Individuals, Wieland for example, the successive editions of whose works reveal him as always improving on his own style, are doing all they can. But, Goethe characteristically concludes, 'we will not wish for the (political and social) upheavals that might pave the way in

Germany for classical works'. Even in 1827 he was still dilating to Eckermann on the advantages enjoyed by countries with a single capital like Paris or London, and lamenting that 'we Germans are of yesterday'.[23] At other times, however, he could now see German unity as a remote possibility.[24]

The early career of Friedrich Schiller illustrates in almost every respect the features regarded by Goethe as typical for the German man of letters, far more completely than his own life, so that it was with the contrast between his own and Goethe's more fortunate lot in mind, we can hardly doubt, that Schiller wrote in 1798 his moving poem *Das Glück*, which begins:

Selig, welchen die Götter, die gnädigen, vor der Geburt schon
Liebten, welchen als Kind Venus im Arme gewiegt,
Welchem Phöbus die Augen, die Lippen Hermes gelöset
Und das Siegel der Macht Zeus auf die Stirne gedrückt!
Ein erhabenes Los, ein göttliches, ist ihm gefallen,
Schon vor des Kampfes Beginn sind ihm die Schläfe bekränzt.
Ihm ist, eh er es lebte, das volle Leben gerechnet,
Eh er die Mühe bestand, hat er die Charis erlangt.
Groß zwar nenn ich den Mann, der sein eigner Bildner und Schöpfer
Durch der Tugend Gewalt selber die Parze bezwingt;
Aber nicht erzwingt er das Glück, und was ihm die Charis
Neidisch geweigert, erringt nimmer der strebende Mut.
Vor Unwürdigem kann dich der Wille, der ernste, bewahren,
Alles Höchste, es kommt frei von den Göttern herab.*

Innate ability, the free gift of the Gods, like beauty, is what Schiller has principally in mind. Nothing can replace this, but nurture, it is implied, makes its contribution too, and the thought

---

* Blessed the man whom before birth the gracious Gods already loved, whom as a child Venus cradled in her arms, whose eyes were opened by Phoebus, and his lips by Hermes, and on whose brow the seal of power was impressed by Zeus! A sublime, a godlike lot has fallen to him, his temples are wreathed even before the battle begins. Life in full measure was dealt out to him before ever he lived it, and before the race was run, the Graces' favour was his.

Great indeed is the man who, his own shaper and maker, compels fate by the force of his virtues. But no force can win him happiness, and what the Graces enviously withheld, his strenuous spirit can never acquire. From what is unworthy, your will, by its serious choice, can preserve you, but all that is highest comes freely down from the Gods.

of time and place and circumstances, stressed in Goethe's essay, is not absent from Schiller's mind in his evocation of Fortuna.

In his birth then Schiller was a provincial, like all German authors, and one with far fewer advantages in the atmosphere of his home and early surroundings than Goethe. His education was perhaps more thorough and systematic in many ways at the boarding-school for the training of officers and officials for the state of Württemberg, the Hohe Karlsschule, which Duke Karl Eugen had just established and for which he forcibly recruited promising boys like the son of Major Schiller, now Superintendent of the Gardens at the Duke's favourite country palace, the 'Solitude' near Stuttgart. Among the formative influences of Schiller's early youth we find on the one hand the uncomplicated Pietistic faith of his parents, and on the other the acquaintance, from below, with the life of a prince's capital, with its gay festivities, its plays and operas, the Ludwigsburg that was Schiller's home from the age of seven until he went to boarding-school at fourteen. The Duke's amours and reckless extravagance had led to twenty years of conflict with his subjects, who had preserved an independent spirit and more vestiges of representative institutions than those of any other German prince, as must have been very frequently heard by the young Schiller before he was forced to give up his ambition of entering the Church, by the route followed by Hegel, Hölderlin and Schelling, through the 'Klosterschulen' and the Tübingen 'Stift'.

The literary examples that fired his imagination at school were serious poets like Klopstock and Haller, then the Storm and Stress writers of the day, notably Goethe, and some English poets and philosophers brought to his notice by his excellent teacher Abel, Shakespeare above all, and moralists like Adam Ferguson, a disciple of Shaftesbury. The text-book for his Edinburgh lectures, the *Institutes of Moral Philosophy*, had just been translated, as we have noted, with comments by Garve. There was also the literature of revolt nearer home, the *Deutsche Chronik* of the journalist Christian Schubart, who was kept a prisoner in a fortress near Ludwigsburg throughout the years when Schiller was elaborating his *Robbers* from the plot of one of Schubart's stories. But the irksome restraint experienced by Schiller and his school-friends at first hand naturally gave rise, by an inevitable reaction, to the dominant mood expressed in all his first writings, and Schiller became, as the phrase goes, the poet of freedom, just at the time when Goethe was undergoing the chastening experience in Weimar which led him, two years after *Die Räuber* appeared in 1781, to deplore, in *Ilmenau*, the praise that had been showered on him when he

> ... unklug Mut und Freiheit sang
> Und Redlichkeit und Freiheit sonder Zwang,
> Stolz auf sich selbst und herzliches Behagen.

Schiller was only twenty when Goethe, now thirty years old, came back with Karl August from their Swiss holiday in December 1779 and attended with him a ceremony at the Karlsschule, now advanced to the status of 'Academy' or university in Stuttgart, at which medals were presented to the best pupils, to Schiller among many others. A year later Schiller completed his studies and became a regimental surgeon in Stuttgart, where the success of his experiments with lyrical and dramatic compositions, and especially the enthusiastic reception of *The Robbers* in Mannheim, convinced him finally of his talent and led him, on his being forbidden to write any more plays, to leave precipitately his native province and security to embark without any resources on a still more hazardous literary career. The year's engagement which he eventually obtained as theatre poet in Mannheim gave him valuable experience and practice. His plays, poems and essays were still experimental and not free from slight concessions to the public taste, the alterations in his *Fiesko*, for instance, or the choice of a domestic drama as his third play, though he made of *Kabale und Liebe* the most original and impressive German domestic drama of them all. Then when the outlook was becoming desperate for him in Mannheim, the generous help and encouragement of cultivated readers of his work, Körner and his friends in Leipzig, gave Schiller new courage and indispensable material support.

Confidence and the determination to aim at the highest are expressed in almost every letter of the Leipzig period. Here is one striking passage from a letter to Körner (3 July 1785):

I do not remember now how we (Schiller and Huber) came to talk about plans for the future. . . . I felt the bold lay-out of my powers, nature's unattained (but perhaps great) intentions with me. *One* half was destroyed by the preposterous method of my education and the adversity of my fate, the *second* and *greater* however by my own doing. I was deeply conscious of that, dear friend, and in the general fiery exuberance of my feelings head and heart have combined in a herculean oath—to make good the past and to start again from the beginning the noble race to the highest goal. My feeling was eloquent and communicated itself electrically to the others. O heavenly beauty of the contact of two souls that meet on the way to divinity!

It is the language of the full-hearted idealist who a little later wrote the *Hymn to Joy*. Exaltation of this order could not last for ever, but it was the inspiration behind the glorification of friendship in Schiller's new play *Don Karlos* and the generous hopes for the future of mankind which Posa in that play is bold enough to express openly to that epitome of tyranny, Phillip II of Spain, unexpectedly winning for the moment his entire confidence with his sincerity. The optimistic secular humanism of the age, as we have found it in Wieland, Herder and Goethe, is a central theme of this play as of *Iphigenie*. The King's confessor, Domingo, sums it up to Alba in his description of Don Karlos, the friend and disciple of Posa:

> Sein Herz entglüht für eine neue Tugend,
> Die, stolz und sicher und sich selbst genug,
> Von keinem Glauben betteln will. — Er *denkt!*
> Sein Kopf entbrennt von einer seltsamen
> Schimäre — er verehrt den Menschen — Herzog,
> Ob er zu unserm König taugt?*

---

* His heart is aflame for a new kind of virtue which, proud and confident and sufficient to itself, will beg no favours from any faith.—He *thinks!* His brain is

In spite of the tragic outcome of the play, a consequence, it seems, of that impatience natural to the rational idealist, which Schiller was to find later (see above, p. 274) in Robespierre, we are left in no doubt about what for Schiller is the goal of human endeavour.

It will be readily understood that the author of *Don Karlos*, on his arrival in Weimar in 1787, found the lively interest in the natural world with which Goethe had infected his friends there rather distasteful (see above, p. 150). He described it as 'an attachment to nature amounting to affectation, a resigned feeling of trust in one's five senses'. What comes out in these words is the difference between what Schiller had inherited from the Enlightenment, with its confidence in abstract ideas and the moral will—a confidence soon to be intensified by his study of Kant—and the interest in individuality and organic development developed by Herder and Goethe out of their Storm and Stress vitalism. In Schiller's style there is even much that still reminds us of seventeenth-century Baroque poetry, whereas Goethe's, in his lyrical poems at least, is as simple and direct as folk-poetry.

In discussing Schiller's theory of culture we have already seen how fully he was conscious of these differences between Goethe and himself at the time when he wrote *On Naïve and Sentimental Poetry*, and how sure he was by then that his own way of writing was not intrinsically inferior to that of his friend and rival, but in his view the characteristically modern type. We have now to indicate, even if very briefly, the stages by which he acquired this new self-confidence and at the same time a more penetrating understanding of Goethe's nature and art than anyone at all had had up till this time, for it is only in this way that we can explain to ourselves how it was possible for two men so diverse in temperament, intellectual habit and poetic sensibility to become, if not really intimate friends, at least literary allies whose wholehearted sympathy with each other's aims, mutual respect and admiration, and reciprocal capacity for creative stimulation has its

in a fever from a strange chimera — he feels respect for man. Duke, is he fit to be our King?

unique memorial in the famous *Correspondence*, in some of the finest writings in German and, not least, in several of the institutions which made Weimar 'classical'.

In 1787, as we have seen, the auspices were not favourable, though if Schiller had not already had some hope at the back of his mind of entering Goethe's circle it is hard to see why he should have made for Weimar at all at that time. In Mannheim he had been strongly attracted by Charlotte von Kalb, an intelligent but neurotic young woman, unhappily married to Major Heinrich von Kalb, one of the Thuringian Kalbs, a brother of the Weimar Treasurer already mentioned. The husband was in the service of the Duke of Zweibrücken, but Charlotte could not bear to live with him there, preferring some pleasant place at a certain distance. From 1784 it was Mannheim, by 1787 Weimar. When Karl August visited Darmstadt in December 1784, Charlotte arranged that Schiller should read the first act of his new play, *Don Karlos* to him, and the Duke showed his pleasure by conferring on Schiller the title of Weimar Councillor. This in itself paved the way for a visit to Weimar, but the immediate occasion in 1787 was apparently an appeal from Charlotte, whom Schiller felt he could now face, though in Mannheim she had represented for him the dangerous temptation reflected in two of his most striking early poems, *Freigeisterei der Leidenschaft* (later toned down into *Der Kampf*) and *Resignation*. She had also initiated him into the court aristocracy's ways of thinking and behaving and its literary taste, acting in some sense as his 'décrotteuse', to apply Chesterfield's term again, to a very different woman from Frau von Stein. Her influence combined with that of Dalberg to turn Schiller's thoughts towards French classical tragedy, verse drama in the grand style, and the result was *Don Karlos*, completed by 1787 and ready for presentation to the Duke, to whom the first act had been dedicated. Charlotte von Kalb was therefore undoubtedly a bridge between Schiller's bourgeois beginnings and his later dependence on Karl August and marriage to a lady of birth, but he never liked courts and courtiers, and the personal factors mentioned would probably have counted for very little if it had not been for Goethe and the high literary reputation of Weimar.

Goethe was still in Italy when Schiller arrived, and the Duke was also away from home. Schiller's letters to Körner show him as extremely detached in his comments on Weimar and its celebrities, the only person he really likes being Frau von Stein. He is struck by the 'Goethe worship' of many people he meets in Weimar, but he quotes Herder too, not a blind admirer, as praising Goethe's complete integrity, the clarity and unlimited range of his thought, which makes him as outstanding as a man of affairs as he is as a poet. Schiller was warmly welcomed by Wieland, who was friendly by nature, admired Schiller's recent work and wanted to secure him for the *Merkur*. All through the following winter Schiller lived quietly in Weimar, working mainly at his *History of the Rebellion of the United Netherlands*, for in writing *Don Karlos*, the theme of which, as he explained it in his letters on the play, was 'the spread of a purer and gentler humanity of feeling', he had come to realise the defects of his education, and with the writing of further historical dramas in view that should interpret the philosophy of history, for the light it could throw on the meaning of life, he had seen the necessity of giving up some years to the systematic study of history and philosophy, hoping to maintain himself meanwhile by essays resulting from his studies. Since the spring of 1785 he had been publishing a periodical of his own, at very irregular intervals, the *Thalia*, which he continued, providing most of the copy himself, until after *Die Horen* had started. The conscious aim at perfection behind all these efforts is clear from his letters, in passages such as this (to Huber, 28 August 1787):

To realise my own value, I have had to witness the impression I make on the mind of several undeniably great men. . . . I have much work ahead of me in order to reach my goal, but I am no longer afraid of it. No path shall be too extraordinary, too strange, that leads me to it. Think for yourself, my dear friend, whether it would not be foolish beyond all understanding if out of cowardly fear of the unusual or irresolute hesitation one were to be cheated of the highest delight of a thinking mind, greatness, distinction, influence on the world, the immortality of one's name. . . . Believe me, an infinitude stands in our power, we have not appreciated the precious possession that is ours. This possession is *time*.

In his ambition to be second to none as a writer, Schiller could not avoid including the study of the Greeks in his course of self-education, for in the age of Gesner and Heyne and Winckelmann their supremacy as artists and as models of 'Humanität' was acknowledged by all the leading German writers, by Wieland, Herder and Goethe in particular. In spite of the quarrel between the Ancients and the Moderns, much the same could be said of almost all the leading writers of Europe, though the features singled out for praise might vary considerably. The practical bias of the teaching at the Karlsschule had not left much time for Greek, but Schiller had had a fair grounding in Latin and had acquired the knowledge of Greek mythology which was then a matter of general education, as is clear from the references in his early poems and plays. *The Letter of a Travelling Dane* of early 1785 shows Schiller's reaction, entirely in the spirit of Winckelmann, on visiting the collection of casts from Greek and Roman sculpture in Mannheim. The first clear sign of a further deepening of his interest in the Greeks is his poem, *Die Götter Griechenlands*, published in the *Deutscher Merkur* for March 1788. This number was open on the table when Goethe visited the Lengefelds on 7 September 1788 and Schiller met him for the first time, though they exchanged only a few words. Goethe had returned from Italy only in June and was slowly getting used to Weimar again, where he felt that no one now understood him. He knew Schiller's early work and was reminded by it of a stage in his own development that was distasteful to him. It is clear from several references in Schiller's letters that he was disappointed at Goethe's taking so little notice of him. He imagines him as a complete egoist, but he cannot help admiring his work, *Iphigenie* in particular, as something of which he himself would never be capable. He admits to Körner (2 February 1789): 'It is a quite extraordinary mixture of hate and love that he has aroused in me, a feeling not unlike what Brutus and Cassius must have had for Caesar; I could kill his spirit and love him again sincerely.'

Goethe meanwhile was quite taken up with his own affairs, but in a memorandum written in a cool official tone he had supported Voigt's suggestion that Schiller, whose first historical work, the book on the Netherlands, had attracted favourable attention a few months before, should be appointed to a vacant chair of history in Jena. Schiller accepted the post, without any enthusiasm, as it was to bring him in only lecture fees and no fixed salary, while it would leave him less free to write. It provided him, however, with a certain status in society and might serve as a stepping-stone. On the strength of this position and his literary earnings he proposed to Charlotte von Lengefeld a few months after taking up residence in Jena in April 1789, and they were married in the following February, after the Duke had granted him a small fixed salary (200 talers), again probably partly due to Goethe's support of Schiller's application. Goethe called on the Schillers in Jena in the autumn, after meeting Körner, who greatly enjoyed his discussions with him and reported them to Schiller. Even after this second meeting, however, Schiller still did not take to him. He showed no enthusiasm for anything, he complained, his way of thinking was too dependent on the senses and 'fingered things' too much for Schiller's liking, but he was undeniably a great man, with a mind that reached out in all directions, always striving for a total view.

For nearly four years after this Goethe and Schiller drew no nearer together. In May 1791, Goethe took over the management of the Court Theatre, and later in that year wanted to put on *Don Karlos*, but it was not given till the end of February 1792, by which time Schiller, who had wanted to revise it, was very seriously ill. Then Goethe was away on his 'Campaign in France' for much of the year, and at the siege of Mainz in 1793, while Schiller, generously supported now by the Duke of Augustenburg, was deep in Kantian philosophy. From August 1793 to May 1794 Schiller was in his native Swabia. It was in the summer of 1794, after Goethe's ready response to Schiller's invitation to collaborate in *Die Horen*, that they met in July after listening to a paper at the Natural History Society in Jena, and continued their conversation about Goethe's notion of the 'Urpflanze' well into the night. Goethe claimed to have discovered the primeval plant by observation, but Schiller insisted that it was not the product of experience, but an idea. They were not in agreement about theories of art either, but they had learnt to respect each other's point of view and to see that they could mean much to each other. The ice was broken at last.

About a month later, after receiving a very friendly letter from Goethe, who said he was looking forward with great pleasure to further exchanges of ideas, Schiller wrote the masterly letter (of 23 August 1794) which set the tone for their further relationship, by explaining how, from very different starting-points and by very different paths, they could, as it seemed to him, arrive at comparable results in their practice as writers. He had derived great benefit from their first conversation. 'The direct view I have had of your mind', he said, 'has lit an unexpected light in me on much that I had not been able till then to think out clearly. I lacked the object, the body, for a number of speculative ideas, and you put me on the right way to it. The imperturbable calm and clarity with which your eye observes things saves you from the danger of being led astray on to side issues, as one is so easily by abstract speculation and by following one's imagination in complete freedom, without any external control.' Two pages follow in which Schiller analyses Goethe's objective manner of thinking and writing and contrasts it with his own, more subjective habit of thought. Goethe seems to him to be attempting what would be impossible for anyone else, 'to take account of the whole of nature in order to obtain light on its individual parts', rising step by step from the simplest forms of life to the most complex, man, 'in order to construct him genetically from the materials of which the whole of nature is built'. If he had been born a Greek, supported by a sound artistic tradition, he would not have needed to go this long way round in order to

9   JUNGFER WENZEL, THE MESSENGER

who walked to and fro between Weimar and Jena, carrying letters,
which included the Goethe–Schiller correspondence, along with
parcels and garden produce.

penetrate to the essential truth of things, but as a German, he has to find a substitute within himself for what reality withholds from him.

The letter goes on to sketch the ideas which Schiller was to develop fully in his essay *On Naïve and Sentimental Poetry*. Poets of Goethe's type, working by intuition, starting from the individual phenomenon but looking for general, eternal features in it, can, Schiller thinks, meet poets of his own type half-way, for these, though they start from general ideas, are intent on finding for them a concrete embodiment. This, as we shall see, is the germ of the classical theory of poetry which Goethe and Schiller worked out between them, which combats the naturalism they found around them and tries to establish new norms for the beauty which, in their view, art must present. Goethe felt sure, on receiving this 'summing up of his existence', as he called it in his prompt and cordial reply, that Schiller's appreciative understanding of him would help him to overcome 'a kind of darkness of mind and hesitation' that he now felt about his own work, and Schiller in his next letter, which was more concerned with himself, expressed the hope that through contact with Goethe he would at last learn how to combine harmoniously the two forces that tended to dominate him by turns, his imagination and his power of abstract reasoning.

(i) *Co-operation in literature and criticism*

Perhaps no product of the German classical age proclaims the ideal aims of its leading writers so clearly as *Die Horen*, and none shows them collaborating so harmoniously in the creation and diffusion of writings that embody the spirit of 'Humanität'. The opening paragraph of Schiller's introduction to the first number speaks for itself:

At a time when the sounds of war close at hand fill our country with dread, when the clash of political opinions and interests renew this war in almost every social gathering, only too often putting the muses and graces to flight, a time when there is no escape in the talk and the writings of the day from this ubiquitous demon of political criticism, it may seem daring, but perhaps also praiseworthy, to invite readers so distracted to join in a conversation of a completely different kind. Present conditions appear indeed to promise little success to a periodical that will maintain a strict silence concerning the favourite subject of the day and pride itself on giving pleasure through quite other topics. But the more men's minds are excited, absorbed and enthralled by the narrow interests of the day, the more urgently necessary does it become to restore them to freedom, and to reunite the politically divided world under the banner of truth and beauty, by arousing a general and higher interest in what is purely human and superior to temporal influences.

He and his collaborators, the editor goes on, will try to rise above the battle and refresh their readers with poetry and prose of high quality that avoids all reference to current events, but by historical contemplation of the past and philosophical anticipation of the future may contribute towards the creation of 'the ideal of a nobler humanity which reason demands, but of which we so easily lose sight in daily life'. By presenting the results of scholarship in an attractive literary form, they wish to break down the barriers that separate the scholar from the writer and to provide both with a wider public, to the advantage of the whole community. The title, 'the Horae', is meant to symbolise this endeavour, for were not these goddesses of order in nature, Eunomia, Dike and Eirene (in Hesiod), 'the daughters of Themis and Zeus, that is, of the law and power; the same law that presides in the material world over the changes of the seasons and maintains harmony in the spiritual world?' The journal will be conducted therefore in the spirit of decency and order, justice and peace—the same spirit, we may note, that inspired great individual works of Goethe and Schiller in this time of crisis, *Hermann und Dorothea*, for example, or *Das Lied von der Glocke*.

Finally Schiller prints the names of twenty-five writers who have promised him their support and announces that contributions will be welcome from any other German authors who will observe the rules on which this 'society' has agreed, one of which, not mentioned here, was that no manuscripts would be accepted that had not been approved, by a majority vote, by a small editorial committee, consisting at first of Schiller and four others, Goethe, Wilhelm von Humboldt, and Schiller's new colleagues in Jena, Fichte, and the historian Woltmann. The best-known of the remaining members of the society were: Archenholtz, K. T. von Dalberg, Engel, Garve, Gentz, Gleim; Herder and 'Kunst'-Meyer in Weimar, Hufeland and Schütz in Jena, with A. W. Schlegel, also there from 1796, Alexander von Humboldt, Jacobi and Matthisson. Of the older poets, J. H. Voss and Boie soon offered contributions. The Weimar amateurs Einsiedel and Knebel came in through Goethe, and two fine poems were sent in by Hölderlin from Frankfurt when he had left Jena. Items were eventually printed by a surprisingly large number of women poets and novelists, Sophie Mereau, then unhappily married to the librarian in Jena and later the wife of Brentano, Karoline von Wolzogen, Schiller's sister-in-law, and four others.

Schiller had been planning such an enterprise as this, as his preface says, for years, but only now obtained the support he needed, from the Tübingen publisher J. F. Cotta, in the first place, whom he won over for it in May 1794, while on holiday in Swabia. Cotta took a considerable risk and kept his own part of the bargain most generously. He had hoped to persuade Schiller to edit a new political newspaper for him, and he did launch a political monthly, *Europäische Annalen*, at the same time as *Die Horen*, advertising it on the last pages of *Die Horen's* first number, but he did not start his important *National-Zeitung* until 1798. Through his enlightened support of Schiller he established good relations with the Weimar writers and became Goethe's publisher. Schiller's circular to prospective contributors[25] and his comments on the enterprise in letters reveal a decidedly realistic aspect of the great idealist. What he evidently expected to accomplish was a unification of the existing reading public in support of a single first-class literary periodical, at the expense of the many existing reviews, each with its own small following, and he offered good terms to those prominent writers who would help him to establish this monopoly.

The *Horen* started off well, with about 1,800 subscribers in the first year, but 300 fell off in the second year, 1796, when the war delayed delivery, and 500 more in the third, when shortage of copy and other difficulties made the last number six months late. It was no wonder that Schiller in the end lost heart and came to take a still lower view of the German public, about which he had long had few illusions. 'Thinking is of course hard work for many of them,' he wrote to Cotta already in 1795 (2 March), 'but we must bring it about that even those who cannot think are ashamed to confess it, and praise us against their will, in order to appear to be what they are not.' A serious tactical mistake was the arrangement made with Schütz of the *Allgemeine Literatur-Zeitung*, one of the original staff of *Die Horen*, to undertake as his contribution to review each monthly number of the new journal in the week in which it appeared, and 'as favourably as was consistent with strict justice'. This was in itself exceptional treatment, and after a few months a young Jena lecturer in philosophy, Forberg, alleged that the *Allgemeine Literatur-Zeitung* was paid for this review. The editor indignantly denied this and threatened to sue Forberg. It came out that payment had been suggested, though only for extra space in the supplementary *Intelligenzblatt*, but the plan had been dropped. Only the one review appeared, in January 1795, and then a year later the first ten numbers of *Die Horen* were fully and favourably discussed in one article, anonymous, of course, but written by A. W. Schlegel.[26] Schiller's rivals made effective use of Forberg's assertion to discredit *Die Horen* and its editor, the tone of whose introductory remarks in the first number had naturally annoyed those whom he somewhat naïvely proposed to put out of business. Outside his charmed circle his enterprise evoked for months a storm of criticism, the writers of which came in for merciless attack from Goethe and Schiller in the *Xenien* in 1796.[27]

Not the least of Schiller's difficulties were due to the failure of his chosen helpers to provide him in sufficient quantity with the work they had promised, and to the relative paucity, as he complained to his patron, the Duke of Augustenburg, of 'good authors and fresh healthy products of genius and philosophical insight', despite Germany's recent advances in the literary field. The middle and lower ranks of her innumerable 'literary men' (some 10,648 in 1795, according to Meusel) were evidently of very little account.[28] Some thought that they had qualified for inclusion in Meusel's list of German learned men by writing a review or two, or a sermon, though he claimed that he drew the line much higher. Schiller was supported regularly at any rate by Goethe, Herder, Wilhelm von Humboldt and, above all, A. W. Schlegel, but Humboldt's essays were heavy and involved. The general level maintained was certainly high, so that *Die Horen* became a model for all later German literary reviews, but after the first year, though there were a few outstanding items, the end of *On Naïve and Sentimental Poetry* and some Schlegel translations from Shakespeare in the second year, Hölderlin's *Der Wanderer* and *Die Eichbäume* in the third, Goethe's main contribution in those years was the endless and, for the general public, unexciting translation of Benvenuto Cellini's memoirs, in eleven instalments, and Schiller, who was busy with *Wallenstein* now, and the poems and ballads for his *Musenalmanach*, gave practically nothing. In the first year, on the other hand, he had provided himself his two best philosophical essays, the *Letters on Aesthetic Education* and the bulk of *On Naïve and Sentimental Poetry*, two of his best philosophical poems, *Das Ideal und das Leben* (Das Reich der Schatten) and *Der Spaziergang* (Elegie) and several others of the highest merit, with other historical and philosophical pieces. Goethe had given, not indeed the *Wilhelm Meister* that Schiller had hoped for, but two verse *Epistles*, the superb but daring (Römische) *Elegien*, and the *Unterhaltungen deutscher Ausgewanderten*, including *Das Märchen*. Herder too had given of his best in recent essays and poems, and most of the remaining original collaborators had been well represented, though some sent in nothing, now or later. *Die Horen* had lived up well moreover to its professed aim of 'ennobling humanity', with Schiller's essays and poems, Fichte's article *On the Arousing and Fostering of the Pure Interest in Truth*, and the essays of Herder and Humboldt. Goethe's *Epistles*, on the other hand, had not been free from ironical implications, and the second had expressed full approval of the concentration of a young woman's interest, for example, on the domestic sphere, as was then normal in Germany:

> Wünscht sie dann endlich zu lesen, so wählt sie gewißlich ein Kochbuch.*

The opening lines of the first *Epistle* had clearly acknowledged Schiller's humanitarian aim:

> Edler Freund, du wünschest das Wohl des Menschengeschlechtes,
> Unserer Deutschen besonders und noch besondrer des nächsten
> Bürgers und fürchtest die Folgen gefährlicher Bücher, wir haben
> Leider oft sie gesehen. Was sollte man oder was könnten
> Biedere Männer vereint, was könnten die Herrscher bewirken?†

But the writer had found himself in a too cheerful mood to take the problem very seriously and had expressed himself as sceptical anyhow about the permanent effects of reading on a man's behaviour:

> Soll ich sagen wie ich es denke? so scheint mir es bildet
> Nur das Leben den Mann und wenig bedeuten die Worte.‡

Goethe's light touch is delightful and much to the taste of his readers, but his attitude to 'Bildung' is really that which is implicit, as we have seen, in the early books of *Wilhelm Meisters Lehrjahre*, where the hero learns from 'life' very much in the manner of *Tom Jones*. A very different view is put forward in the deadly serious contributions of Schiller and Fichte to the first number, on *Aesthetic Education* and *The Pure Interest in Truth*, which must have been felt to belong together, in spite of differences

---

* If after all that she wants to read, she will no doubt choose a cookery-book.

† Noble friend, your desire is the good of the human race, of our Germans in particular, and most of all, of our neighbours and fellow-citizens, and you fear the influence of dangerous books, one we have, alas, often seen. What ought we, or an association of right-minded men to do, what could our rulers do about it?

‡ Shall I say what I think? Then it seems to me that only life educates a man, and that words mean little.

in style, and both went down badly with the public. Fichte shares, and had in fact partly inspired, as we have seen, Schiller's high demands on the aesthetic and intellectual life. For Fichte, books are not written merely to be passively enjoyed. Readers who think so are like 'those oriental voluptuaries who in their baths get special artists to massage their limbs'. To 'have one's mind massaged by artists of another sort' affords a pleasure which is very little 'nobler'. It is a man's *duty* to seek truth and mental consistency, and to act fearlessly in the light of them. Only this makes him a man worthy of the name. The acceptance of the political consequences of thought, hinted at in this passage, came out more clearly in Fichte's second contribution, and was perhaps more important than the stylistic features criticised by Schiller for his rejection of it and consequent quarrel with Fichte.

The difference between Fichte and Schiller was not however absolute on this point. It was rather a difference of opinion about the timing and expediency of action. Schiller, we have seen, by no means accepted society as it was, but the French Revolution had shown, he thought, what disastrous results follow from over-confidence in the power of abstract thought applied to political problems, and of precipitate changes in political and social institutions not prepared for by inner changes both in those who administer the institutions and in society at large. The argument of the fifth of the *Letters on Aesthetic Education* is summed up in the epigram entitled *Der Zeitpunkt* in the *Xenien*:

> Eine große Epoche hat das Jahrhundert geboren
> Aber der große Moment findet ein kleines Geschlecht.*

Schiller's advice to the Germans for the moment is therefore:

> *Deutscher Nationalcharakter*
> Zur Nation euch zu bilden, ihr hoffet es, Deutsche, vergebens;
> Bildet, ihr könnt es, dafür freier zu Menschen euch aus.†

* In our century a great epoch has been born, but the great moment finds a small generation of men.

† German national character.

Germans, you hope in vain to turn yourselves into a nation; Develop your-selves, as you can, all the more freely as men.

He could not tolerate an article by Fichte verging on the political in his expressedly non-political journal, though in founding it he had had to resist those who, like F. H. Jacobi, thought he was unwise in excluding just the subject in which people were most interested. It was in reply to him that Schiller wrote (25 January 1795) that, as he would see from the first number, political subjects could be treated philosophically without any mention of particular states or events (a remark which could refer to Goethe's introductory chapter in the *Conversations of German Émigrés*, with its plea for common politeness in discussing political affairs in ordinary conversation, or to the early letters of his own *Aesthetic Education*), but went on: 'We will continue to be citizens of our time in our physical person, because it cannot be otherwise, but in *mind* it is the privilege and the duty of the philosopher and the poet to belong to no nation and to no people, but to be in the full sense of the word the contemporary of all times.'

These words, with their apparent rejection of any 'commitment' of poet or thinker to the society of his time, might easily be misunderstood as the expression of an ivory-tower romanticism, if comparison with similar passages in other letters, and the intellectual content of Schiller's finest philosophical poems, did not make this interpretation impossible. The central poem, first published as *The Shadow Realm* in the ninth number of *Die Horen*, and finally revised under the title *The Ideal and Life*, expresses superbly Schiller's conception of the relation between the imaginative or intellectual life, not only of creative but also of receptive minds, and the everyday duties of the individuals who house them. The good, the true and the beautiful, embodied by the work of preceding generations in lasting symbols and forming a kind of 'shadow realm' or, as others have put it, an invisible world, of culture, the higher values, independent in some sense of the physical universe, provide those sensitive to them, the cultivated, with a secular form of salvation, open to them not continuously but periodically, at those times when they are free, as they never are for long, from the limitations of men with physical needs, and obligations imposed on them by life in society. Schiller's world of the ideal, or shadow-realm, is clearly akin to Hegel's notion of 'objective' (or, as Nicolai Hartmann prefers to say, 'objectivised') mind, and André Malraux's of the 'musée imaginaire', rather than to Plato's 'world of ideas', although the second title Schiller thought of was 'the realm of forms'. In the context of his thought and of that of his time we must understand it, it seems clear, not as a timeless world of essences, but as a treasure-house of the intuitions of the past, preserved as symbols with a material 'vehicle', paint on canvas, words on paper and the like. Herder's conception of a growing culture and Goethe's of divine revelations to innumerable men of genius similarly presuppose the possibility of the creation, by countless generations of men, of such a superstructure of values, though they seldom explicitly refer to its material embodiment.

Since Schiller's poem, *The Ideal and Life*, expresses perhaps more effectively than any other single work the whole spirit of 'Bildung' and its importance for man in society, it is interesting to note how well, in spite of its difficulties, it was immediately understood, not only by Wilhelm von Humboldt and Goethe, but by the young A. W. Schlegel, who had not yet met Schiller. Having grown up in the same mental climate he was able, in spite of the latent differences between the two men which later led to their estrangement, to seize completely the drift of Schiller's poem and to interpret it in detail in his review of it. In the autumn of 1795 he had offered his services to the *Allgemeine Literatur-Zeitung* and been recommended to Schütz by Schiller, who had great hopes of what he could do also for *Die Horen*. He was asked to review, in rather a hurry, the first ten numbers of *Die Horen*, particularly its poetry and aesthetics, and acquitted himself splendidly, as Goethe and Schiller themselves acknowledged.

This then is how Schlegel understands the general import of a poem that presents, he says, with lyrical warmth and enchanting music the most difficult and abstract of themes.

The sensual nature of man is in conflict with the aspiration towards perfection of his higher self, yet the harmony of both components of his being is necessary to happiness. Is there no means of resolving that conflict? Only one, but he who wishes to attempt it, must first make himself independent of the senses, for it is by them that he is confined to the limitations of animal life. Only what is corporeal in him is compelled to obey the laws of nature; his personality is free. To ennoble it, he must submit himself to beauty at its purest, and this demands an attunement of the mind that removes him completely from the disturbing impressions of the actual and in which, at least while quiet contemplation absorbs him, he forgets the sufferings of life and his own imperfections. Holding life at a distance, he must fill his imagination with ideals of human nature; yet without allowing himself to be lulled into passivity in real life, as if he were already in possession of the unattainable because he can imagine it. No, in action he must seek to approach the ideal by the most strenuous use of his powers, and only feast his eyes on it to throw off the depressing feeling of his inadequacy.[29]

Soon after making his first plans for *Die Horen*, Schiller had begun to think of bringing out also an annual anthology of contemporary verse, like the *Göttinger Musen-Almanach*, which had been in existence since 1769, edited for the last fifteen years by Bürger. On Bürger's death in 1794, Schiller had in fact proposed himself as his successor, but as the publisher had promised the editorship to someone else, he decided on one of his own, having good hopes of making it more attractive than the Göttingen publication, which had gone off badly, or the similar annual collection edited by another of the original Göttingen group, J. H. Voss, which was out of touch with new talent. The first volume, *Musen-Almanach für das Jahr 1796*, came out late in 1795, too late for Schiller's liking, because of the inefficiency of its young publisher, who was therefore abandoned next year in favour of Cotta.[30]

The *Musen-Almanach* did not begin quite so brilliantly as *Die Horen*, but from the first year Goethe and Schiller were the principal contributors and made it into a kind of annual manifesto of Weimar classicism. In the first number their work occupied about four-fifths of the whole, in the second, two-thirds and in the next two about a third. Schiller's policy was at first to reserve his finest poems for *Die Horen*, as well as the longer and more serious poems by others, but even what he had over from the monthly, in the extraordinarily productive year of his return to poetry from philosophy, were poems of high quality, expressing the consistent ethos of his maturity. In *The Ideals*, for instance, he puts the joys of friendship, and of creative work to reduce our debt to the past, above the aims in life which attract the young and inexperienced—love and fortune, fame and certain knowledge, in *The Dance* he sees in the ballroom, where each waltzing couple is freely following a compelling rule, an example of the aesthetic play-impulse and analogies with the motions of the heavenly bodies, and in *Homage to Women* (*Würde der Frauen*) he muses on the differences between the sexes, much as his friend Humboldt had done in prose. Goethe's main contribution was the collection of *Venetian Epigrams*, the expression of disillusion not only with Italy, revisited for a few weeks in 1790, but with the way of the world in general and with apostles of freedom in particular, with 'good' society and with the German public; and of gratitude for what he possesses at home, the love of his Christiane and the favour of his 'Augustus and Maecenas', Karl August. The frontispiece, a head of Apollo, the use of Roman type (whereas *Die Horen* was printed in Gothic), and frequently, though not so often as in subsequent years, of classical metres, were a clear indication of the revival of feeling for the Ancients which became more and more a feature of Weimar taste.

Three thousand copies were printed of this first Almanach, and the terms granted by the publisher, Michaelis, were so good that Schiller soon found it a more lucrative undertaking than *Die Horen*. The editor was paid 300 talers a year for his editorial work and his contributions. Cotta was equally generous, and there was apparently no falling off of the demand in the second year, as was natural, for this was the much-discussed 'Xenien-Almanach'. It was Goethe who, just before Christmas 1795, suggested that Schiller and he should write in collaboration a series of epigrams like the *Xenia* or 'parting gifts' of Martial, about the periodicals that, not quite without reason from their own point of view, as we have seen, had shown so little appreciation of *Die Horen*. Schiller welcomed the idea with enthusiasm, and before January was out they had written two hundred epigrams between them, in the classical form of a distich, a hexameter followed by a pentameter, that had long been a familiar feature in the Almanach edited by Voss, the translator of Homer, and had been used in Goethe's *Venetian Epigrams*. By the end of June they had 676 and thought of bringing out a special volume of perhaps 1,000 epigrams, but then it was decided that Schiller should edit them for the *Almanach*. He gathered the more pungent ones together, some two-thirds of the whole, ending with a series of two dozen distichs, printed later as *Shakespeare's Shade* in the poems, directed against the popular dramatists of the time, and scattered the rest over the volume, mostly in twos and threes, with one big group of 103 *Tabulae votivae*. These and two smaller groups were signed 'G. and S.' but the anonymous *Xenien* proper were also a fruit of intimate collaboration on agreed general lines.

Some thirty periodicals are characterised, mostly unfavourably, and various classes of writers are attacked, in accordance with the intention expressed in *Vorsatz*.

> Den Philister verdrieße, den Schwärmer necke, den Heuchler
> Quäle der fröhliche Vers, der nur das Gute verehrt.*

The 'philistines' are the old-fashioned rationalists with no feeling for contemporary poetry, Nicolai and his friends. The 'enthusiasts' are the 'unco guid' like the Stolbergs, who had objected to Schiller's *Die Götter Griechenlands* and to *Wilhelm Meisters Lehrjahre*, and the hypocrites mostly small fry. Amongst better-known writers, Lessing, Kant and J. H. Voss are treated with respect, F. Schlegel, Reichardt and Georg Forster with disdain, but most of the references are lost on the reader of today unless he is helped by copious notes. It must be admitted that these

---

* Our intention.
Sprightly verses, respecting only merit, may you annoy the philistine, tease the enthusiast and make the hypocrite thoroughly uncomfortable!

most celebrated of epigrams in German seem to us now to be lacking in punch and very seldom amusing, in Emil Staiger's words 'far-fetched and laboured in their wit, feeble in attack', but the excitement they caused, in the year of the Treaty of Campo-Formio, was tremendous. They evoked hosts of epigrams in reply, whole books of them, and they caused widespread and not unjustified resentment of the authority which these two writers had arrogated to themselves.[31] 'The new cultural ideal of a small minority was repudiated and combated by an overwhelming majority of the nation.'[32]

It was the negative *Xenien* that drew the fire of the critics, but if they had looked more closely at the positive epigrams in the earlier part of the volume, they would have found much wisdom in a worthy form, gnomic poetry of a kind familiar to us chiefly from Goethe's later collections. This was indeed a manifesto, in which the deepest convictions of the two poets on a number of serious topics were pregnantly expressed. There was quite early in the volume a group of sixteen distichs by Goethe and eight by Schiller on political and social problems. Goethe's are conservative in a conciliatory tone, like this one:

Der Würdigste

Wer ist das würdigste Glied der Regierung? Ein wackerer Bürger,
Und im despotischen Land ist er der Pfeiler des Staats.*

Schiller's on

Würde des Menschen

Nichts mehr davon, ich bitt euch. Zu essen gebt ihm, zu wohnen,
Habt ihr die Blöße bedeckt, gibt sich die Würde von selbst†

is surprisingly realistic, in its insistence on a certain degree of material welfare as the necessary foundation of 'Humanität', but

* The worthiest.
Who is the worthiest member of the government? A trusty citizen, and in despotic countries he is the pillar of the state.
† Human dignity.
Please, no more talk of that. Give him food and a house to live in; when you have covered his nakedness, dignity will come of itself.

it is what he had said in the *Letters on Aesthetic Education* (see above, p. 271). Yet, as Goethe said to Eckermann, Schiller was more aristocratic than he was, and he certainly did not flatter the crowd:

Majestas populi

Majestät der Menschennatur! dich soll ich beim Haufen
Suchen? bei wenigen nur hast du von jeher gewohnt,
Einzelne wenige zählen, die übrigen alle sind blinde
Nummern, ihr leeres Gewühl hüllet die Treffer bloß ein.*

In the *Tabulae votivae*, which were signed by both poets, what is first insisted on is the need for cultural leadership. Countless millions provide for the survival of the human race, after nature's usual lavish fashion, but true humanity, 'Humanität', is maintained and handed on by the few. (*Die verschiedene Bestimmung.*) A dozen epigrams follow that emphasise this idea of the value of a cultivated personality, like

Unterschied der Stände

Auch in der sittlichen Welt ist ein Adel; gemeine Naturen
Zahlen mit dem, was sie tun, schöne mit dem, was sie sind,†

which sounds like Schiller's version of Wilhelm Meister's letter to Werner (see above, p. 260). A few more deal with pedantry and pretentiousness, inevitable features in a cultivated society. The remaining four-fifths of *Tabulae votivae* are devoted to the 'higher values', truth in religion, science and philosophy, goodness without religious sanctions, beauty, mainly in literature, and the reception of creative work by the critics and the public.

Truth is to be sought in the humanist way, with the help of reason and experience:

---

* Majestas populi.
Majesty of human nature, am I to look for you in the masses? You have always been wont to abide with the few. A few individuals count, the rest are all blanks; their empty throng is but a wrapping for the winners.
† Class differences.
There is a nobility in the moral world too; common natures pay with what they do, fine ones with what they are.

Glaubwürdigkeit

Wem zu glauben ist, redliche Freunde, das kann ich euch sagen,
Glaubt dem Leben, es lehrt besser als Redner und Buch.*

The lesson is hard, however. An error that is our own bosom
child is preferred to truths of other parentage, an insight that
should have made Goethe more cautious than he was in the
distichs that follow, presenting as a truth his undoubted error
about the theory of colours. In philosophy, truth is not to be
found in systems, and in religion, not in creeds:

Mein Glaube

Welche Religion ich bekenne? Keine von allen,
Die du mir nennst! 'Und warum keine'? Aus Religion.†

The aesthetic epigrams seem to express for the most part ideas
familiar from Schiller's essays, but the last group, about problems
of communication, reflect Goethe as well, as in:

Das gewöhnliche Schicksal

Hast du an liebender Brust das Kind der Empfindung gepfleget,
Einen Wechselbalg nur gibt dir der Leser zurück.‡

Even in the group of epigrams headed *Vielen* and *Einer* ('To
many ladies' and 'To one') there are wise reflections, the fruit of
Goethe's experience, in the one case with Charlotte:

Kennst du den herrlichen Gift der unbefriedigten Liebe?
Er versengt und erquickt, zehrt am Mark und erneut's.§

---

* Credibility.
Whom can we believe in? Honest friends, I can tell you. Believe life, it teaches
better than orator or book.
† My creed.
You ask what religion I profess. None of all those you name. And why none?
Out of religion.
‡ The common fate.
When you have nursed the child of feeling at your loving breast, the reader
gives you back a changeling in its place.
§ Do you know the glorious poison of love unsatisfied? It sears you and it
quickens, consumes your marrow and renews it.

and in the other with Christiane:

Kennst du die herrliche Wirkung der endlich befriedigten Liebe?
Körper verbindet sie schön, wenn sie die Geister befreit.*

The *Xenien* were anything but popular, but if Goethe and Schiller had had what we now call publicity in view, which was of course not the case, they could hardly have chosen a more effective way of getting their ideas talked about, if not understood, and thus of arousing interest in the positive achievements, poetry of the very highest order, with which they immediately followed up this broadside against the opposition that had been brought out into the open by *Die Horen*. As we read in the well-informed *Briefe eines ehrlichen Mannes bey einem wiederholten Aufenthalt in Weimar*, an anonymous description of visits to Weimar evidently written by someone in Herder's family or immediate circle, the discussion aroused by the *Xenien* was a perfect gift for German journalists, and people who normally would not buy a book in a whole year had quickly acquired the *Xenien-Almanach*. Within a year of its appearance, Goethe had written *Hermann und Dorothea* and obtained no less than 1,000 talers for it from a Berlin publisher, a measure of the anticipated sale. It came out as a *Taschenbuch für 1798* in the same month, October 1797, as Schiller's third *Musenalmanach*, which contained six new ballads by Schiller and four by Goethe, as well as the second poem in Goethe's second book of elegies, *Der neue Pausias und sein Blumenmädchen*, the even finer first poem, *Alexis und Dora*, having already appeared in the *Xenien-Almanach*. *Wilhelm Meisters Lehrjahre* had come out in 1795–6, after each book had been eagerly read and commented upon admiringly and with discerning criticism by Schiller in his letters. The ballads had led Goethe

* Do you know the glorious effect of love at last satisfied? It unites bodies in fair bonds, and gives minds their freedom.
   Cf. *Römische Elegien*, III:
   Vielfach wirken die Pfeile des Amor: einige ritzen,
      Und vom schleichenden Gift kranket auf Jahre das Herz.
   (Many kinds of wound result from the arrows of love: some are scratches, and the heart is sick for years from the creeping poison.)

back, as he tells Schiller in a letter (22 June 1797), along the 'misty and foggy path' to his *Faust* and he asks Schiller for his advice about it too.

> Fühl' ich mein Herz noch jenem Wahn geneigt?

he asks himself in the *Dedication* to the drama written now, and answers:

> Ihr drängt euch zu! nun gut, so mögt ihr walten,
> Wie ihr aus Dunst und Nebel um mich steigt.*

It is doubtful whether he would have finished Part I in the next few years, however, without Schiller's continual stimulus. At the same time Schiller, in spite of repeated illnesses, was giving his best energies to his *Wallenstein* and, under Goethe's influence, making of the introductory scenes, *Wallenstein's Camp*, an astonishingly concrete picture. So the incomparable partnership went on producing its fruits, not always, of course, at this pace, until Schiller's death, compelling admiring attention first from the discerning few and then, when Schiller's plays won a warm welcome from actors and audiences in Berlin and other leading towns, as well as in Weimar, from a very large number of middle-class and even artisan playgoers. Perhaps Goethe's first reaction to the attacks provoked by the *Xenien* had justified itself after all, when he wrote to Schiller (7 December 1796): 'If I must be honest, the behaviour of the mass of the people is just what I should wish, for it is a not sufficiently recognised and practised policy for anyone who makes some claim to posthumous fame to force his contemporaries to get off their chests everything they have against him. His living presence and activity will always wipe out the impression.'

Meanwhile Prussia, fearing the loss of her Polish gains, had contracted out of the struggle with France in 1795, and it was principally as a result of Prussian neutrality for the next ten years that Weimar escaped the fate of the left bank of the Rhine. Napoleon rose to fame in the campaign in northern Italy and the

---

* You still press on? Well then, have your way, as you rise up around me from mist and fog.

Peace of Campo Formio was signed. Probably in the summer of 1801 Schiller drafted a poem, to which later the title of *German Greatness* was given, and to which we shall return in the last chapter. To the momentous events of these years there is no reference in the correspondence between Goethe and Schiller. The word 'war' does occur in the index to them (in the Cotta edition), but only in the phrases 'war against religion', referring to two letters where both authors express doubts about the Old Testament, and 'war against Reichardt', a literary feud against the well-known composer.

In his appreciation of Goethe's *Hermann und Dorothea*, Emil Staiger shows that this short epic is better composed than the *Iliad* could be expected to be, but goes on to point out how high a price the German poet must pay for his superiority.

He cannot allow himself to move freely between heaven and earth ... and to put into words anything and everything that reveals itself to his eye and that he knows through tradition. He is compelled to withdraw to a modest circle and to be almost too careful in his selection of detail. He is writing a short epic, corresponding in length to three or four cantos of the *Iliad* or *Odyssey*. His world is not the Orbis terrarum but a little German town and a village near by. The number of figures he introduces is limited. He has to refrain from mentioning by name heroes and great personages of German history in the past or present. Even the family names of his citizens would be incompatible with the style in which he is writing. That they are Christian in their way of life may only be unobtrusively indicated, without any reference to dogmatic beliefs. For Homer the true, the real and the poetic are identical. There is nothing in his sphere that art needs to deny itself. For the German poet, on the other hand, the poetic is the beautiful, and the beautiful is an idea. The real must be discreetly arranged into the beautiful. Whatever resists this arrangement is dropped, or retained at most in the form of subordinate marginalia. Goethe may still call this beautiful the true in the deepest sense and urge his time to heed it. What he calls false does not for that reason cease to exist and maintain its irrefutable claims.[33]

Similar examples of the idealisation of the real could be found in plenty in Schiller's poems and dramas at this time, and often disconcert a modern reader. There is, for example, his marvellous evocation of the perfect wife and mother in *The Song of the Bell*:

> Und drinn waltet
> Die züchtige Hausfrau,
> Die Mutter der Kinder,
> Und herrschet weise
> Im häuslichen Kreise,
> Und lehret die Mädchen
> Und wehret den Knaben,
> Und reget ohn Ende
> Die fleißigen Hände,
> Und mehrt den Gewinn
> Mit ordnendem Sinn,
> Und füllet mit Schätzen die duftenden Laden,
> Und dreht um die schnurrende Spindel den Faden,
> Und sammelt im reinlich geglätteten Schrein
> Die schimmernde Wolle, den schneeigten Lein,
> Und füget zum Guten den Glanz und den Schimmer,
> Und ruhet nimmer.*

Karoline and Dorothea Schlegel already were not very like that. Although Karoline was not promiscuous or slovenly in her habits, she was conscious of being thoroughly emancipated as a thinking woman from the older conventions of ladylike behaviour, and so was Dorothea, the daughter, like Karoline, of a very enlightened father and more obviously hampered, as a Jewess, by her background. It is no wonder that when Schiller's *Song of the Bell* was read aloud in this circle, some of them nearly fell off their chairs with laughter.

The last lines of the passage quoted from Emil Staiger, expressed in everyday language, come to this, that the poet, for the purposes of his art, must put the best appearance on things, and this is after all a very old practice among artists, as any

* And within, the good lady of the house holds sway, and as mother rules wisely in the family circle, and teaches the girls, and restrains the boys, and is never without work for her tireless hands, and adds to the produce with orderly planning, and fills with treasures the fragrant presses, and winds the thread round the humming spindle, and collects in the carefully polished chest the gleaming wool, the snow-white linen, and invests goodness with a lustre and gleam, and rests never.

collection of portraits reminds us. It is an endeavour which, on the face of it, seems as worthy of respect as that of the Naturalists, in their inevitable reaction against the epigonoi of German classicism, to make things appear at their worst. What is always difficult to assess is the literal 'truth' of the picture, and the claims made by either party may seem exaggerated to the unsympathetic critic. After the endless disputes on this point, it is not surprising that in our day, and in some degree already among the Romantics, many artists have sought a way out by neglecting the factor of truth altogether, in an art of fantasy or abstraction, though when this happens the theorists immediately try to bring 'truth' in again by the backdoor, by finding it in any revelation of the unconscious mind, and even postulating something like a collective subconscious in which ancestral myths are preserved and repeatedly revived.

It is often with considerations of this sort in mind that the modern reader approaches the German classics, and he may therefore find them impossibly 'serene'. Schiller as we have seen, in his *On Naïve and Sentimental Poetry*, represented the artist as the 'guardian of nature', that is, of the natural, or of 'true humanity'—certainly an 'idea' in Staiger's sense, whereas Goethe thought of him, in *Einfache Nachahmung, Manier, Stil*, for instance, as suggesting in his picture of any individual living creature the slow evolution of living things, the principle of growth as well as the external form determined by it. Applied to society, this way of thinking led Goethe to emphasise in his pictures what Viktor Hehn long ago described as 'natural forms of human life' and illustrated from all periods of Goethe's work, but especially from the one we are discussing. After anticipations in the poem *Der Wanderer* of 1772 and the patriarchal enthusiasms of Werther, comes the determination expressed in Italy to occupy himself with 'lasting relationships' and finally the masterly handling of them, often with Greek plastic art and Homer in view as models, poems like *Alexis und Dora* and *Hermann und Dorothea*, but also parts of *Faust* and of *Wilhelm Meisters Lehrjahre*.[34] Schiller's poems about the typical course of Western civilisation, *Das eleusische Fest* and *Der Spaziergang* (published as *Elegie*) in the tenth number of *Die Horen* in 1795, in their more reflective way, pursue the same aim, well brought out in the concluding lines of this last poem:

> Ewig wechselt der Wille den Zweck und die Regel, in ewig
> Wiederholter Gestalt wälzen die Taten sich um;
> Aber jugendlich immer, in immer veränderter Schöne
> Ehrst du, fromme Natur, züchtig das alte Gesetz.
> Immer dieselbe, bewahrst du in treuen Händen dem Manne,
> Was dir das gaukelnde Kind, was dir der Jüngling vertraut,
> Nährest an gleicher Brust die vielfach wechselnden Alter:
> Unter demselben Blau, über dem nämlichen Grün
> Wandeln die nahen und wandeln vereint die fernen Geschlechter,
> Und die Sonne Homers, siehe! sie lächelt auch uns.*

We have seen from Goethe's essay on *Literary Sansculottism* in *Die Horen* how unfavourable he considered his own times to be for the production of literary masterpieces. In the *Correspondence* he and Schiller are continually exchanging ideas about the theory of literature in their attempt to overcome these difficulties, ideas that are suggested in the first place by the work on which they are engaged at the time. In 1797, for instance, there is a prolonged exchange on epic and drama, when Goethe has just completed his *Hermann und Dorothea* and Schiller is busy with his *Wallenstein*. In these discussions Goethe frequently appeals to the example of the plastic arts. 'The advantages of which I made use in my last poem' (*Hermann und Dorothea*), Goethe writes, for instance, 'were all learnt from plastic art' (8 April 1797). On his holiday in Switzerland with his artist friend Meyer the two made the first draft of an essay on *The Subjects of the Plastic Arts* which was later elaborated by Meyer

---

* Eternally the will varies its aim and its rules, in ever repeated form the cycle of action revolves; but ever youthful, in ever beautiful transformations, pious nature, you honour obediently the old law. Always the same, you maintain, safe in your faithful hands, for the man, what the gambolling child and the youth entrusted to you, all the ages of man in their manifold changes are nourished at the same breast, near and distant generations move as one under the same blue and over the unchanging green, and Homer's sun, O look! still smiles there upon us.

in the first number of the *Propyläen*, and before that led to the joint essay by Goethe and Schiller on *Epic and Dramatic Poetry*, after spoken and written exchanges of ideas, at the end of 1797. In all these discussions they took it for granted that, as Goethe put it, they were compelled 'to forget their century if they wished to work according to their convictions', because of the hopeless 'drivel that passed for principles' with it (25 November 1797). They were confident that they could arrive at principles derived chiefly from Greek literature and art which would be applicable to their own or any age. The result was, however, as Staiger says, that 'Goethean classicism became dogmatic and threatened to transform itself from something produced as if by necessity by personal, biographical conditions into a canonical art, intended to last unchanged and be effective quite independently of the individuality of the poet and his changing moods'.[35]

(ii) *Co-operation in art criticism*

To set out the principles of this Weimar classicism in literature is beyond the scope of this book, but it is instructive to study their application to the plastic arts in the art periodical, the *Propyläen*, which Goethe and the 'Weimar friends of art' now started as a successor to *Die Horen*, and the effect they had in practice, in the work produced by German artists of the time for the competitions organised by Goethe and Meyer. Here the principles of a new classicism were systematically and confidently expounded, but unfortunately to little effect. From his father, Goethe wrote in the well-known little rhyme, he had inherited 'des Lebens ernstes Führen', his seriousness and, we may add, a certain tendency to didacticism, which began to come out in his letters from Italy, but was acceptable there as the fruit of genuine enthusiasm. On his return to Germany, where even his friends seemed to him now to have a confused and undeveloped taste in literature, and still more in the plastic arts, he defended his new insights into Greek and Renaissance art, wrote a few articles for Wieland's *Merkur* on what he had seen at Pompei and so on, as well as the important essay on *Einfache Nachahmung der Natur*,

Manier, Stil discussed above (p. 251), and from 1791 persuaded the Swiss artist J. H. Meyer (1760-1832), whom he had known and admired in Rome, to live in Weimar, for the first eleven years in his own house, that he might have a congenial spirit near at hand. In 1795 Meyer began to teach, with the title of professor, at the 'Freies Zeicheninstitut', as the Weimar art school was now called. An art historian rather than an artist, Meyer seems in general to have lent support to Goethe's prejudices, and when he was entrusted with the expression of their common views, to have had a tendency to warp them into still more dogmatic forms. Then from 1794 Schiller, between whom and Meyer as rival intimates of Goethe there was a certain tension, encouraged him, as we have seen, to aim at raising the level of German taste by working out a consistent theory of art. In poetry, Goethe even now usually wrote first and theorised afterwards, not allowing even Schiller, as we have seen, to read his poems till they were virtually completed. In art, in which he had long practised as a dilettante, 'he set up doctrines of which he had to offer a laborious defence. That he expected them to prevail is one more proof of his dilettantism in this field.'[36]

In spite of his losses on the last year of *Die Horen*, Cotta agreed to publish a new periodical for the 'Weimar friends of art', which meant Goethe, Meyer and Schiller, supported by the classical scholar F. A. Wolf and later by the art historian K. L. Fernow, who came to Jena as professor in 1803, after nine years in Rome. The *Propyläen* began to appear in 1798, with two parts to the volume, and continued like *Die Horen* for three years, the same three years in which the *Athenäum*, the Romantic organ edited by the Schlegels, was also providing intellectual circles with something to take the place of Schiller's periodical.

Goethe's 'Introduction' in the first part makes it clear that he is thinking of a distinctly literary form of painting, produced by cultivated artists for a well-read public. Solemnly he explains the symbolic title. The marble gateway to the Acropolis in Athens suggests for him a 'space between the inner and the outer, between the sanctuary and the commonplace world', a suitable place for the discussions on nature and art between the initiated which are now to be communicated to the public, whose understanding support is indispensable, though it will have much to learn. The whole essay stresses the importance not only of technical training but of all-round cultivation.

As the *Propyläen* articles were unsigned, the second one, on 'Subjects for the artist', written by Meyer, was ascribed to Goethe also. It was the basis for the later formulation of subjects for the prize competitions and for Meyer's criticisms of the prizewinners. In this article Meyer establishes 'rules' for the evaluation of pictures, following classicistic notions of Mengs and Oeser, and Goethe, being uncertain of his own principles in this field, deferred to Meyer's judgment on the works submitted for the competitions, though he probably would not have accepted everything Meyer said about the choice of subjects. What he himself meant by subject was a mental image, the concrete idea for a picture that suggests itself to the artist, and as he had written to Schiller (16 December 1797), in reply to a letter in which Schiller had said how much he longed for a kind of encyclopedia of poetic subjects, 'We know unfortunately from experience that no one can choose subjects for the poet, and that he often makes mistakes in his own choice.' Meyer, on the other hand, meant 'objects' in the external world, and had no compunction about prescribing subjects to artists. His conception of the artistic process is clear from his later article on 'Academies' in the second volume of the *Propyläen*, where such institutions are urged to provide themselves with libraries, containing the works of poets and historians needed by the artist, as well as with collections of casts, pictures and engravings. Although the study of life models is made indispensable, instruction is centred on the copying of pictures.

With the *Propyläen*, as with the *Horen* earlier, copy began to be scarce before very long, and one reason for starting the prize competitions may have been that the editors hoped in this way to make sure of matter for discussion in their pages, while at the same time they provided artists with an incentive for following the advice which had already been offered in the *Propyläen* in Meyer's essay on the choice of subjects for painting and in a series of essays by Goethe, his *Introduction*, the dialogue *On Truth and Probability in Works of Art*, *On Laocoon*, *The Collector and his Family*, and his translation with commentary of Diderot's *Essay on Painting*. The tendency in all is anti-naturalistic, and Goethe, influenced by Schiller, whose voice is recognisable in the words of the philosopher in the *Collector*, goes further than he had ever done in Italy in contrasting art with nature. As in his management of the Weimar Theatre, his aim was a return to conscious art after the marked swing towards naturalism which had been evident since the Sturm und Drang in the German theatre, and also to some extent in painting.

Goethe's general point of view is well conveyed in the following extract from the dialogue *On Truth and Probability in Works of Art*. One of the two speakers asks why a highly conventional work of art like an opera, if everything in it fits together, produces an impression of naturalness, and the answer given is:

Because it is in accordance with your better nature, because it is above but not outside the natural. A perfect work of art is a product of the human mind, and in this sense also a work of nature. But because the scattered objects are brought into a unity and even the most commonplace are taken up into it in their meaning and value, it is above nature. It needs to be appreciated by a mind that has a harmony of its own through its origin and training, and this mind finds something comformable to its nature in whatever is excellent, and perfect in itself. Of this the untrained art-lover has no conception, he treats a work of art like an object that he comes across in the market; but the true connoisseur sees not only the truth of what is imitated, but also the happy results of selection, the subtlety of the composition, the dream beauty of this small world of art; he feels that he must try to rise towards the artist in order to enjoy the work, he feels that he must draw himself together from his distracted life, live with the work of art, look at it repeatedly and acquire in this way a higher mode of existence.

This passage shows that Goethe had the root of the matter in him, however exaggerated some of his dicta may sound. The enemy in art theory is the unsophisticated notion of imitation of nature, representationalism as an end in itself. We have seen how Schiller rose above this in his *Aesthetic Letters*. A later and more explicit attack on it is to be found in the preface to the *Bride of Messina*, a defence of the use of the chorus in tragedy as an anti-naturalistic device. It is not that Goethe and Schiller were afraid of 'frequent sights of what is to be borne'. Schiller's last essay on the theory of tragedy, *Über das Erhabene*, represents tragedy as an 'inoculation (of the spectator) with our inevitable fate', and in Goethe's revision of Lessing in *On Laocoon*, evoked by the archaeologist Hirt's essay in *Die Horen*, he does not object to the contention that the representation of suffering in this statue is not as Lessing had claimed, moderated in the interests of art, but intensified in the highest degree. He maintains, however, that a subject of the utmost horror like this was endowed by Greek artists with what he calls 'Anmut', a pleasing quality (not at all the same as Schiller's 'grace', however) that arises from 'order, intelligibility, symmetry, balance' and appeals immediately to the eye. Seen in its most general outlines from a distance at which the subject could not be recognised, a Greek statue would appear as a pleasing design. In the *Collector* he gives a still more striking example of a Greek sarcophagus in which the dead bodies of the sons and daughters of Niobe are in the carving worked into a pleasing design. 'It is art luxuriating in its power! It does not use flowers and fruit now for ornamentation, but human bodies, the representation of the greatest calamity that can befall a father or a mother, to see their happy family suddenly swept away before their eyes.' In the next letter the same idea is applied to tragedy: 'If we speak about the work of art as if we had been experiencing the actual events in nature that are taken as its subject-matter, even Sophoclean tragedies may be made to appear loathesome and revolting.' The subject, as Schiller had said, must be totally taken up into the form.

In the Diderot essay Goethe brings out more clearly than elsewhere what he means by the 'beauty' which he distinguishes from what pleases the eye (Anmut), and represents as appealing above all to the mind. 'Nature', he says,

organises a living being that leaves us indifferent, the artist a dead one
that is full of meaning; nature a real being, the artist the semblance of
one. To the works of nature the beholder must supply significance,
feeling, thought, effect, emotional influence; in the work of art he
expects to find all that, and it must be there. A perfect imitation of
nature is in no sense possible; the artist is only called upon to represent
the surface of any object. The outside of the vessel, the living whole
that speaks to all our mental powers and senses, arouses our desire,
elevates our mind, makes us happy when we possess it, that is the
artist's concern, to produce the effect of life, strength, perfect growth
and beauty.[37]

In short, the artist's values seem to be objectified, with regard to
a particular aspect of life, in the work of art that it suggests to
him. We see in a portrait, for example, not just what a camera
would have recorded, but the artist's personal reaction to the sitter.

Although Goethe had emancipated himself from the worst
features of the imitation theory, the great stress that he lays on
the importance of the right choice of subject, for poetry, in the
correspondence with Schiller, and for painting and sculpture, in
his *Propyläen* articles concerned with the prize competition,
suggests to us that he still stood under the shadow of that ancient
error. The announcement of the competition, in May 1799,
begins with a reference to Meyer's article in the first number and
offers two prizes, one of twenty and one of ten ducats, for drawings illustrating a by no means original subject from Homer,
Aphrodite bringing Helen back to Paris after his defeat in the
duel with Menelaus. Flaxman's handling of the same subject is
praised as intelligent, but defective in composition and drawing,
and competitors are advised to submit outline drawings with
some shading, adding a little colour if they wish. Entries came
in slowly, only eight artists competing, and their work was
exhibited in the autumn with the usual display of that of the
Weimar School of Drawing. The verdict on their work had been
promised for the first number of the third volume of the *Propyläen*
due to appear in the autumn of 1799, but it came out late and is
dated 1800.

This and the later criticisms of competition work, though

stylistically revised by Goethe, were written by Meyer. The point of view expressed in them is often inconsistent with that put forward in Goethe's own essays and in the successive announcements of competitions, which were written by Goethe. In one instance at least there is a flagrant contradiction, in 1800, when an artist named Wagner was praised by Goethe for not being afraid to copy what was good in a Flaxman engraving, while 'improving' on it, and Meyer deplored the additional figure which constituted this improvement. The chief difference between the two Weimar 'Friends of Art' goes deeper and concerns their interpretation of what was meant by the 'symbolic' treatment which they had invited. For Meyer symbolism was what we should now call allegory, the representation of an abstract idea in concrete form, but Goethe already made the distinction now commonly accepted between allegory, which starts from the abstract, and symbolism, which presents us with a concrete whole completely satisfying in itself, but capable of suggesting 'deeper' ideas, never completely analysable in a point-to-point correspondence between the concrete and the abstract and therefore variously interpreted by different beholders. All great poetry and art had to be for Goethe 'ein unergründliches Symbol', an unfathomable symbol, and in saying this he was drawing attention to a quality foreign to most of the art of the Enlightenment, but highly prized by the Romantics and almost all their successors. Incidentally he was also proving himself to be far less 'naïve' in Schiller's sense and far more reflective than might have been expected from Schiller's famous essay, but at the same time what most foreign critics would probably consider to be typically German.

What Goethe understood by symbolism emerges clearly enough from his own essays in the *Propyläen*, beginning with the preface written by him, and every word shows how highly he now rated the importance for the writer and artist of personal cultivation or 'Bildung'. What is always demanded of the artist, he says in the *Propyläen* introduction, is that he should follow nature, but nature, he now insists, is divided from art by a great gulf which even the genius cannot cross without external aid. To produce a work of art that will rival those of nature in excellence, the artist must penetrate both to the depths of his own mind and to those of the world of phenomena. But 'a man only sees what he knows',[38] so to see the human body as it really is, the artist must know his anatomy, the structure beneath the surface appearance, and in order to vie with nature in creation, it is necessary to have observed how nature goes about her work of construction, to understand the principles of organic growth. More and more as we read on we are reminded of Goethe's own studies in Weimar and Italy. His artist, he says, must know something about stones and their qualities, whether it be for painting, sculpture, architecture or the carving of intaglios. The properties of colour above all must be thoroughly known by the painter, and though the physicist with his spectra will help him little, the Weimar Friends of Art will provide him with a theory, based like electricity on the principle of polarity. Through studies of this kind the artist will discover that he can best express the depths of his own nature by penetrating to the core of the nature that surrounds him, for the two are in essence the same, and art is a continuation of nature. 'When the artist fully grasps any object in nature, it no longer belongs to nature alone. It may even be said that the artist creates it in this very moment, by seizing on that in it which is significant, characteristic, interesting, or rather by endowing it with a higher value than it had yet possessed.'[39] We are reminded of the 'Urpflanze' and of Goethe's delight in discovering, as he thought, a principle, by following which nature's intentions might be understood, predicted and even improved upon, and this he now, through Schiller's influence, agrees to call an 'idea', demanding that his artist should be 'capable of rising to ideas and understanding the close relationship between things that may seem far removed from each other'.[40] The personal reference in all this becomes particularly clear when Goethe, writing here anonymously, goes on to speak of the difficulty experienced by the German artist—and by all his modern and northern colleagues—in his attempt to advance from the formless to form (Gestalt), and to hold on to his intuitions of form, acquired perhaps in Italy, in the face of the German public's indifference and ignorance.

The second point stressed by Goethe in this introduction, after his elaboration of the relation between art and nature, is the importance of the tradition, in the various branches of art and the genres belonging to each, the idea underlying the discussion between Goethe and Schiller about the epic and the dramatic. 'One of the surest signs of decadence in art is the mixing of the genres'[41]—a statement which is particularly striking when we remember Friedrich Schlegel's famous *Athenäum* fragment (in the first volume) which describes Romantic poetry as a 'progressive universal poetry' combining all the genres, as they had been combined, in his view, in Goethe's *Wilhelm Meisters Lehrjahre*, the work praised by him as one of the three main influences on the age, along with the French Revolution and Fichte's *Ideenlehre*.

It follows from this view of art that the artist must be not only highly trained in his techniques but also something of a scholar, and that wide knowledge is equally necessary for the connoisseur and discriminating lover of art. He must correct his inevitable one sidedness. 'A man must as far as possible make his own, in theory and practice, what is opposed to his nature', the light-hearted, irresponsible person aiming at strictness with himself, the stern and serious at a relaxed attitude, 'and each will develop his own nature the better the more he seems to be drawing away from it. Every art demands the whole man, its highest grades all the potentialities of humanity.'[42] The 'native wood-notes wild' of which the Sturm und Drang had been enamoured no longer satisfy, and in the Weimar Theatre Shakespeare himself will be subjected to classicistic revision, but the principle of 'inner form', of creating from inside as nature does, has not disappeared in the new theory. It has been saved by the assumption of the identity of subject and object, the mind and nature, which had become a conviction with Goethe in Italy and for which he found support, like the Romantics, in what Fichte had made out of Kant's theory of perception.

Goethe's programme, as Wolfgang von Oettingen says, 'making inordinate claims on the cultivation and intellectual powers of artists and public alike, demanded that painting of the highest order should present nothing concrete without symbolic intent, and to this end, having mastered what nature and the Ancients could teach, should choose only such subjects as were self-explanatory by a clear appeal to the senses, yet were capable of being purified and ennobled by the strictest feeling for style, the style of Greek vase-painting and reliefs.'[43] The symbolic content could come, as the essays discussed above have shown, from various sources, but the picture must always suggest ideas to the well-stocked mind of the beholder. They might be ideas of what had gone before and what would follow the pregnant moment in a familiar classical episode chosen by the artist, as in the *Laocoon* as Goethe interpreted it, or in many subjects prescribed for the competitions, involving as they did the translation of a succession of events into the representation of a given moment. Or in a landscape painting, to judge by what is said in *On Simple Imitation, Manner, Style*, they might be ideas about the essence of the things represented, resulting from 'close and profound study of the things themselves'.[44]

The work evoked by the competitions, reproduced now extensively in W. Scheidig's monograph[45] and still to be seen, for the most part, in the Weimar Schloss, bears out Wolfgang von Oettingen's severe judgment:

A one-sided, completely unpainterly classicism, a brilliant feat of abstraction, had as little appeal for ordinary practising artists, with sharp senses but little reading to boast of, as for the mass of art-lovers, who knew what they liked and had no desire to change their tastes. More than that, this classicism, if it had spread, would have prevented for a long time the emergence of any fresh and vigorous art, based as it was not on the impulse to translate into paint what is seen by the innocent eye, but on an intellectualised learning very rarely to be found. Goethe was wrong in assuming that every painter of his time would find in Homer, preformed for his use, all paintable motifs to express his own feeling, and he had no conception of the inexhaustible wealth of artistic work, of the highest quality and the greatest variety, that can be produced by the fully developed painting of a flourishing, healthy period.[46]

It was only to be expected that the artists who responded most readily to Goethe's prompting were rather fumbling talents with little of their own to express. Of the more gifted young painters of the time, only K. D. Friedrich of Dresden was awarded a prize for two landscapes he had sent to Goethe in the last year of the competition, without entering for the competition. Goethe was instrumental in arranging for some of his work to be purchased by the Duke. He also took an interest in P. O. Runge, though he knew that Runge did not agree with his ideas. 'We are not Greeks now-a-days,' Runge wrote in February 1802, 'and when we see their masterpieces cannot appreciate them entirely, still less produce such things ourselves. Why should we give ourselves so much trouble merely to turn out indifferent works?' He criticises the subjects proposed for the competitions and those who enter for them. 'These people hunt for subjects', he says, 'as if they had no living power within themselves. Must that kind of guidance come from outside? Have not all genuine artists begun with a feeling and chosen a subject suitable to express it?'[47] Schadow, the Berlin sculptor, of whom Goethe thought highly, also criticised severely the lines on which the competition was being run, especially the undervaluation of craftsmanship which it seemed to him to encourage. His criticism was evoked by a survey of German art centres published in the *Propyläen*, insecurely based on the impressions Goethe had gained from the first two competitions and his correspondence with some of the artists, a correspondence which reveals him as full of human sympathy, but over-eager for confirmation of his own views and therefore amenable to flattery. What he said about Berlin in his survey, to the effect that its artists were too prosaic and naturalistic, could naturally not be accepted by Schadow, who preferred sound technique to the windy allegorising and literary painting favoured by Meyer.[48]

Interest in the annual exhibition soon fell off in Weimar, though at first the takings from the sale of tickets had in each year almost provided the following year's prize-money. In October 1802, an apparently serious notice of the exhibition and appreciation of the prize-winners appeared in the Leipzig *Zeitung für die elegante Welt* which turned out to be a hoax, a parody of Meyer's criticisms, written before the current one had appeared, apparently by Böttiger, that thorn in Goethe's flesh, with Herder's knowledge and approval.[49] Böttiger was evidently getting his own back for the suppression of his *Ion* criticism by Goethe earlier in the year. (See above, p. 305.) The *Propyläen* had ceased to appear after three years, in 1800, Cotta's losses being too heavy to bear. He had sold only about one-third of the copies printed even in the first year. News of the competitions continued to be printed however in the *Intelligenzblatt* of the *Allgemeine Literatur-Zeitung* until Goethe finally lost interest in 1805, after Schiller's death. Schiller had done his duty not only by frequent aesthetic discussions with Goethe but by writing a long letter to the *Propyläen* on one of the exhibitions. The last of Goethe's important writings on art appeared in the same year 1805, as part of a collective volume in honour of Winckelmann. Goethe's preface claims that the Weimar Art Lovers had slowly but surely exerted a considerable influence for good on the German world of art, and in his own sections of the book, particularly in the one headed 'Schönheit', he sums up admirably the doctrine which they had consistently put forward.

(iii) *Co-operation in the theatre*

The Weimar Court Theatre did not begin, like Schiller's *Horen* or Goethe's *Propyläen*, as a missionary effort to 'arouse a general and higher interest in what is purely human', or to educate the public taste. It did come later, however, particularly in the 'classical' decade with which the last few sections have been concerned, to be looked upon and to function as a cultural institution, though never exclusively, because in a small capital with limited resources it had to serve other purposes as well.

When the court began to lose interest in amateur theatricals, and Goethe, for one, was too busy to give them much attention, there still remained a need for entertainment not satisfied by the regular court concerts, balls and assemblies. Late in 1783 Bellomo's company from Dresden was therefore invited to Weimar, to give during a winter season of six months three performances a week, to which the court was admitted without charge, in return for the Duke's subsidy of 300 talers a month. In the summer the troupe could give performances elsewhere, and Bellomo built a theatre at Lauchstädt, a neighbouring spa, for this purpose. The small stock of costumes and scenery which had been built up in Weimar and the court orchestra of about a dozen players were placed at Bellomo's disposal, and in the assembly rooms and theatre built, as we have seen, by Hauptmann, he was able to put on the usual repertoire of operettas, domestic dramas and 'Ritterstücke', under the general supervision of a court official, at first Seckendorff, who had been the keenest of the amateurs. In spite of the subsidy Bellomo was mainly dependent on the general public, who had to pay for their tickets, so that he had to be sparing with experiments. Operettas were popular with all, and in addition to Italian and French works, attractive German ones were now available, by Dittersdorf and others, and from 1782 there came the series of Mozart's operas in the same tradition, beginning with *Il Seraglio*. There was a good supply of domestic dramas and comedies, mostly translated or adapted at first, by actor-authors like Schröder in Hamburg, and then originals by Iffland, another great actor, and the prolific Kotzebue. Schröder had begun in the preceding decade to adapt Shakespeare, in prose translations, to the contemporary taste, and Bellomo followed his lead here too, but only occasionally, and he was equally cautious in staging Lessing and the earlier plays of Goethe and Schiller, with which, except for *The Robbers*, he always ran the risk of losing money. As his actors and actresses were all expected to be able to act, sing and even dance in ballet after a fashion, the level of performance could not be very high, and it was for this reason that in 1790, when Anna Amalia's visit to Italy had made her more fastidious, that she and the Duke took the initiative in setting up a real Court Theatre for which the

Duke, and not a private actor-manager, assumed financial responsibility and was therefore entitled to control through his nominees the theatre's artistic policy.

Goethe was the obvious choice for the official head of the new theatre, but he accepted the post very unwillingly. He had lost his early enthusiasm for the theatre, he was disappointed with the reception of his recent plays as books (*Egmont, Iphigenie* and *Tasso*), and he was preoccupied with scientific studies, particularly with his theory of colour. Moreover, he had no illusions now about the taste of the German public, even in Weimar. In a fragment intended for his autobiography, he wrote in his old age that in the north, the German theatre had not developed naturally, as in the south, but had been 'reformed but not improved' by people with strong moral feelings but no taste. Even the three great actors, Ekhof, Schröder and Iffland, were too conformist and dignified for his liking, too much concerned with 'Humanität' and too little with the appeal that the theatre should make to eye and ear.[50] That he held similar views as early as 1790 is clear from a letter he wrote to J. F. Reichardt (on 28 February), and he expresses essentially the same convictions, fully and with evident personal feeling, in 1805, the year before he married Christiane Vulpius, in the notes to his translation of *Le neveu de Rameau*, where he says: 'The public in general is not capable of judging any kind of artistic talent, for the principles by which it can be done are not innate in us, or handed on by chance, but mastered only by practice and study.' On the other hand, everyone has a standard for moral judgments in his own conscience, and is therefore only too ready to pass ethical judgment on all his neighbours. Goethe strongly deprecates the moral criticism of creative artists in their private lives, which should be left to their families and immediate associates. What is public about them is what they produce by virtue of their special gifts, and this alone should be judged by the world in general.

With this, for him, rather dubious new theatre Goethe therefore went to work, as he says, very 'piano'. When a new company had been recruited, a producer appointed and routine management and finance entrusted to the treasury official, Franz Kirms, who had had to deal for the government with Bellomo's theatre, Goethe could leave the theatre to run itself most of the time. In the first year he wrote an encouraging prologue for the opening performance, of a very ordinary play, Iffland's *Die Jäger* (7 May 1791), drew up standing orders for the troupe, to which he held them strictly, supporting Kirms in all his efforts to keep within his budget, and helped the troupe when he could to build up its repertoire, making much use, like Schröder, of reading-rehearsals, especially for verse plays like Schiller's *Don Karlos*, which the producer first attempted, like most of his colleagues elsewhere, in prose. The general nature of the repertoire remained unaltered, most of the plays being works already staged by Bellomo, and known to the half-dozen members of his company who were retained. Apart from *Don Karlos*, even the novelties were mostly of the same type as before, Mozart's *Il Seraglio* and *Don Giovanni*, two Shakespeare plays in prose, with both of which Goethe lent a hand, then his own *Clavigo*, an old favourite, and a specially written new comedy, *Der Großkophta*, about Cagliostro and the Diamond Necklace. In the second and third year of the theatre Goethe was away for months at a time with the Duke, on the French campaign and at the siege of Mainz, and the company still carried on.

This theatre was in fact three theatres in one, even in its best period, which may be said to have begun when Schiller's *Wallensteins Lager* was given in the improved and newly decorated theatre at the opening of the winter season of 1798. It still had to provide about two-thirds of its running expenses from its takings, so that roughly two performances out of three were of plays and operas—necessarily of the 'Singspiel' type, not calling for a large cast or orchestra—which could be expected to draw good houses. One-third remained for plays of high literary merit which might or might not be effective in the theatre, or even within the comprehension of the average audience. On certain occasions, with *premières* of Schiller plays, for instance, but not normally, these performances too might attract a full house, including the regular patrons from the University of Jena and visitors sometimes from a considerable distance. The Weimar Theatre was a cultural institution because it was able to put on these better plays and operas, even at a loss, and for the rest it was a place of entertainment like the average German theatre of the day, as is clear for instance from the relation between the number of plays by Iffland and Kotzebue performed during the twenty-six years of Goethe's management (some 118) and the corresponding number for works by Goethe and Schiller (37).

Within these limits, however, Goethe, strongly supported by Schiller, carried out the same policy as they did in their periodicals, of offering what they regarded as good or interesting work, without much caring whether the public agreed with them or not. Even with his Shakespeare productions, Schröder in Hamburg had sometimes had to do the same, in his purely commercial theatre in a large town. On one occasion he acted *Henry IV* in the same kind of prose version, boiled down from both parts, that was played in Weimar in 1792, and though it was badly received, he came out in front of the curtain at the close, as was his custom, to announce the programme for the next day, and said: 'In the hope that this master-piece of Shakespeare's, which presents different manners from ours, will be better understood on further acquaintance, it will be repeated tomorrow.' Goethe, of course, made much greater demands on his public than Schröder, but he benefited by the improvement in the dramatic repertoire that had taken place since the days of Schröder's first management, though the supply of good plays was still by no means satisfactory. The outstanding feature about the Weimar Theatre was that it had Schiller behind it, to provide almost every year from 1798 a new play combining stage appeal with literary qualities of the highest order, the nearest approach to a national German drama that has so far been seen. *Wallenstein, Maria Stuart, Die Jungfrau von Orleans, Die Braut von Messina, Wilhelm Tell,* all made their first appearance between 1798 and 1804, as well as translations and adaptations by his hand.

These works of a highly conscious type of art, following on

the long period of self-education that Schiller had imposed on himself after *Don Karlos*, as well as wide reading in the classics of the drama and in dramatic theory, eagerly discussed with Goethe by word of mouth and in the *Correspondence*, were deliberately anti-naturalistic in style, concerned with heroic themes and attempting to interpret the common fate of mankind, as Schiller found it revealed in significant phases of history. Characters of unusual self-awareness and eloquence, language that was dignified and avoided the conversational even in the mouth of the meanest, blank-verse dialogue varied where it was appropriate with lyrical measures, everything removed these plays from the everyday level of experience, but though their atmosphere approached that of opera, the thought and feeling expressed could be understood and shared by all hearers, the philosophical reflections for the intellectuals being balanced by love-scenes and tense situations that gripped all alike.

In his artistic policy in the Weimar Theatre Goethe followed, with renewed zeal when joined by Schiller, the same ideals that are manifest in the periodicals for which the two writers were responsible, the return from 'nature' to 'art', from unbuttoned naturalism, that is, to a creative activity inspired by a particular idea of beauty, derived in the main from classical Greek sculpture and Renaissance painting. Goethe's interest in acting was stimulated by Iffland's performances as a guest of the Weimar Theatre in 1796, and again in the following year. These taught him that even within the realistic convention a good actor should not confine himself to roles in which he remained more or less his normal self, as he was encouraged to do by the traditional system of engaging actors and actresses for a particular 'Fach', such as 'jeune premier' or 'soubrette'. He persuaded or compelled his troupe after this to use their imaginations, and to try to rival Iffland in the range of parts they attempted, transcending their given personality even in commonplace plays. From now on he took a much greater share in the rehearsal of the more important productions. His principal concern was with the spoken word. Through reading-rehearsals and later in actual lectures to young recruits, he taught them to shed the worst dialectal features in their pronunciation, to enunciate clearly and speak to the audience, never up-stage, and above all, to speak verse without mouthing it or destroying its rhythms, for this art had been quite lost through the vogue of realistic prose drama.

He urged them always to think of what would look or sound well, rather than of fidelity to everyday life, in their movements on the stage and in their declamation. To give them practice in speaking verse he translated first the *Mahomet* and then the *Tancrède* of Voltaire into blank verse, and persuaded Schiller to do the same with *Phèdre*, all of which were acted on successive birthdays of the Duchess, always a gala night in the theatre. This fact reminds us again of the court patronage which made this 'theatre of culture' possible and still left its mark on it, for it was the Duke and Duchess and many of their friends who retained their affection for the French classics so familiar to them in their youth, and not Schiller, for instance, or the ordinary educated German who, since Lessing's, day, had been told that in the serious drama, Germany had long left France behind her.[51] A letter from Wilhelm von Humboldt, from Paris, where he had observed with admiration the acting of Talma, the rhythm of his movements, the music of spoken verse, the impression of harmony and grace conveyed by the concerted action of all on the stage, brought home to the 'Weimar Art Lovers' some deficiencies of the German theatre, comparable with those of older German painting, in the emphasis laid on expression at the cost of 'form' in its Italian sense.

In imposing his own new ideal on recalcitrant actors, Goethe often employed extreme measures, marking out the stage in squares for the better direction of their movements and using a baton to control their tempi. The full use of his authority was necessary because Goethe had to rely on training to make up for his troupe's lack of talent, Weimar being unable to compete with Berlin, Hamburg, Vienna and other large towns in the salaries it could pay. He had so much confidence in the efficacy of his methods that he once declared that the best raw material to turn into an actor was a stalwart grenadier. Anything approaching stardom was frowned upon, the strength of the theatre being in the harmonious ensemble effects that Goethe had encouraged from his first prologue on. Some critics found Weimar actors stiff and statuesque, and they did not usually fit in well if they moved elsewhere, but there can be no doubt that the general level of their best productions was high.

The impression of stiffness came in part from the inherent difficulty of the roles that Goethe demanded of his actors, in comedies of Terence played in half-masks, for example, in classical French tragedy or the over-stylised book-dramas of the Schlegels, *Ion* and *Alarcos*, the second of which provoked laughter in the wrong places that Goethe had to quell by a loud appeal to the audience, decorum being required of them too in this 'cheerful temple', as Schiller called it in the *Wallenstein* prologue. Even Goethe's own *Natürliche Tochter* raised even greater problems for the actor than his *Iphigenie*, which he shrank from producing until 1802, when Schiller helped him with it. *Die natürliche Tochter* was the first part of a projected trilogy on the period of the French Revolution, a plan never completed, any more than the epic *Die Achilleis*. The lover of Goethe will find in both the hand of the master, but they are clearly over-influenced by his classicistic theories. Apart from the performances of Schiller's plays and Mozart's operas, where it was possible to strike a happy medium, what was provided by the Weimar Theatre seems to have been either good entertainment in the shape of the ordinary stuff of the theatre of that day, domestic dramas, social comedies and farces or light opera, where without straining itself the troupe made good use of a small stage and by no means lavish equipment, or well-rehearsed and competent performances of plays of mainly literary or even antiquarian interest. Surprisingly few plays of Shakespeare were attempted, and these in verse-translations drastically adapted to classicistic tastes, Schiller's version of *Macbeth*, for instance, or the really extraordinary *Romeo and Juliet* that Goethe made out of A. W. Schlegel's translation in 1812. Strangely enough, not a single

Greek play was attempted, no doubt because Goethe knew too well the limitations of his troupe. His own *Faust I* was never acted while he was manager, though it was published in 1808, nine years before he retired. When the example of other theatres induced Weimar at last to attempt it in 1829, Goethe did not go to see it, though he coached Mephistopheles. He probably felt now that such works, like Shakespeare (*Shakespeare und kein Ende*, 1813), 'are not for the eyes of the body', the words and the inner world they call up being all-important.[52]

It does not seem then that Weimar classicism entirely escaped, in the field of the theatre, the narrowness that made Goethe and Schiller relatively insensitive to the greatness of a Hölderlin, for instance, and led to the production of so much purely academic art in the annual exhibitions. In the theatre, Goethe's unforgivable mistake was his blindness to the greatness of Kleist, at a time, after Schiller's death, when he was giving every support to the Werners and Müllners with their absurd fate-tragedies, again because of a one-sided theory. Emil Staiger's judgment is thus confirmed, that it was a good thing for German literature, when Goethe's classicism was becoming dogmatic, that a new movement was being initiated by the early Romantics, 'whose influence Goethe, to his benefit and ours, could not in the end escape, a movement in which his rigidity was relaxed and his poetic genius again reminded of its most precious possession, its freedom'.[53] His theory had left to poetry too narrow a space for manoeuvre, one that he had already inimitably filled with his *Hermann und Dorothea*.

5. GOETHE AND THE UNIVERSITY OF JENA

The institution through which Goethe exercised the most direct influence on education, and at the same time entered into the closest contacts with living scholars, was the University of Jena, which was under the patronage of four Ernestinian courts, Gotha, Meiningen, Coburg and Weimar. The already mentioned report to Marshal Berthier in 1806 explained that although the town of

Jena formed part of the Duchy of Weimar, these four states were jointly responsible for its university, 'nominating professors and generally exercising supreme control'. After a reform initiated by Weimar in 1766, the total annual subvention was fixed at 7,000 talers, about two-thirds of which sum was contributed by Weimar. Weimar was accordingly much more actively concerned with the affairs of the university than the other three states. Academic self-government had reached a very low ebb in Jena, and Karl August, liberal as he was in many ways, found in the incessant intrigues and quarrels of the professors ample support for his belief in authoritarian methods of government, in this sphere as in others. It was with two or three trusted professors and not with the Senate that Goethe and his right-hand man in so many matters, C. G. Voigt, negotiated in such questions as additional financial aid, the planning of new institutes, new appointments, and even problems of university discipline. Salaries, even those of the full or 'ordinary' professors which came from endowments, were miserably low, particularly in the faculty of arts, ranging from the 459 talers received annually by each of the two senior professors of theology to the 258 talers of the professor of rhetoric.[54] They would all come within what we have called above (p. 67) the 'master-craftsman' income group (200–600 talers). Unless the professors had private means, which was seldom the case, they had to eke out their incomes in various ways. They gave mainly 'private' lectures, for which they received fees, their free 'public' lectures being in the end merely announced and never delivered, they earned what they could by their writing and, if they were medical men or lawyers, by private practice and consultative activities. Frequently they would also let rooms in their houses and their wives might take paying guests at the midday meal. 'Extraordinary' professors, like Schiller, received no fixed salary, unless Karl August gave them a small grant *ex gratia*, as he did to Schiller (of 200 talers) at the beginning of 1790, to enable him to marry.

Goethe was occasionally called upon, as a member of the Conseil, to deal with items of business concerning Jena even before the Italian journey, and he was helped by individual professors there in his scientific studies from the early 'eighties. At that time relief measures for Jena as a town occupied him even more, in particular plans to prevent the flooding of the town when the Saale ran high. Jena was an even quieter little town than Weimar, just spreading beyond its still complete city walls with their seven gates. When Crabb Robinson was there first, in 1802, he found it an ugly place, without good houses or public buildings of any kind. Even Weimar was compared unfavourably by him with his native Bury St Edmunds. Jena had a population of about four thousand, largely dependent on the trade brought by the university. It was its quiet atmosphere that especially delighted Goethe. Here, with pleasant country all round, he could escape from his Weimar social obligations, yet readily find congenial company when he wanted it, men who shared his intellectual interests more fully than almost anyone in Weimar after his return from Italy. From 1794 Schiller and his friends, including for a year or two Wilhelm von Humboldt, were a great attraction for him in Jena, and after Schiller's departure, Frommann the publisher and Knebel, as well as several professors. 'I am always a happy man in Jena', he wrote to Schiller, 'because no place on earth has given me more productive moments.' Here he finished *Wilhelm Meisters Lehrjahre*, wrote *Hermann und Dorothea* and many ballads, and later much of the *Westöstlicher Divan*, the first 'Novellen' in *Wilhelm Meisters Wanderjahre*, and parts of *Dichtung und Wahrheit*.[55] A letter to Schiller (29 July 1800) gives a lively picture of the benefits derived from a single visit to this staple-town of science and scholarship.

Apart from his constant efforts on behalf of certain scientific institutes, and measures to meet various crises in Jena's development, Goethe had little to do with the efflorescence of Jena in the 1790's, which came after a century or so of a vegetative existence. It is not an accident that the university's best days fall within the period between the foundation of the *Allgemeine Literatur-Zeitung* in 1785 and the migration of its chief editor Schütz to Halle in 1803. In those years, Jena perhaps benefited more from

Bertuch's business enterprise than from Karl August's grudging help. The review was able to pay its contributors well, as we have seen, and Schütz naturally relied principally on his colleagues in Jena, who were very glad of this new source of income. A further attraction for scholars in the difficult years of the French Revolution was that Jena, under the divided control of its four patron-states, offered them more freedom of expression than most universities. Karl August was known to be broad-minded in religious matters and well-disposed towards the arts, so Jena acquired a reputation for liberalism, and it naturally shared in the literary glory of the Duchy's capital, especially when it had become the main centre of the new Kantian philosophy. The discerning reviews of the *Metaphysik der Sitten* and the *Kritik der reinen Vernunft* published by Schütz in the first volume of the *Allgemeine Literatur-Zeitung* were what first attracted the attention of Wieland's son-in-law Reinhold to Kant's ideas, and led him to write the 'Letters' in the *Merkur* which did so much to popularise Kant's thought. Reinhold became a professor of philosophy in Jena, and in seven years (1787–94), helped by G. Hufeland, the lawyer, and K. C. E. Schmid, the theologian, he made the university a stronghold of the new philosophy and attracted a great many students. The new universities of Göttingen and Erlangen had drawn so many students away from Jena since about 1750 that numbers had dropped from 1,300 to under 600 in thirty years. By 1790 they were up to 800 again, and in 1793 to 892, the peak for that decade. By 1806 they were down to 200,[56] and Jena's great days were over.

In 1794 Fichte had been appointed as Reinhold's successor, on the suggestion of Hufeland, to which it is surprising to find Weimar assenting, in view of Fichte's decidedly Jacobin reputation. Only a year before this he had published his *Contribution towards the correction of the public's judgment concerning the French Revolution*. He was soon in difficulties with the university's patrons, but he overcame them for a time, and among the young, as we have seen, he had an enthusiastic following. Before he was compelled to leave in the spring of 1799, after the controversy

10   FICHTE ON THE ROSTRUM

about his alleged atheism, he had produced the *Theory of Know-ledge* in which he carried Kant's ideas, as he thought, to their logical conclusion, and provided the new Romantic school with its philosophy. In 1798 Schelling, who had come to Jena as a tutor to two young noblemen two years earlier, was appointed to a chair of philosophy at twenty-three through the influence of Goethe himself, who saw in his 'philosophy of nature' ideas akin to his own. Finally Hegel came to Jena as a 'Privatdozent' in 1801, became an 'extraordinary professor' in 1805 and finished his *Phänomenologie des Geistes* in the dark days of the Battle of Jena (14 October 1806). These thinkers between them esta-blished the new 'absolute idealism'.

As early as 1793, the anonymous author of the *Letters on Jena* (G. F. Rebmann)[57] stated that the university had entirely changed its general character in the last ten years. In the early 'eighties it was still notorious because of the swashbuckling students' 'orders' or clubs. It is from Jena that Zachariä's *Renommist* comes in his well-known satire. He is described as 'a born enemy of freshers and philistines', a coarse fellow who cannot open his mouth without swearing, 'made to be a corporal rather than a son of the muses'. It is duelling that is picked out as the characteristic feature of Jena in the student rhyme:

> Wer von Leipzig kömmt ohne Weib,
> Von Wittenberg mit gesundem Leib,
> Von Jena ungeschlagen,
> Der hat von großem Glück zu sagen.*

But by 1793, though duelling had not disappeared, it was looked upon, according to the *Letters*, as a relic of the past, and many students were too foppish for Rebmann's taste, though he finds them reasonably hard-working. There is ample evidence that the abler students of this last decade of the century were reading Herder, Goethe and Schiller with delight and finding in Kant's *Critiques* and especially in Fichte's lectures and writings

---

* He who escapes from Leipzig unwed, from Wittenberg in good health, from Jena without bruises, can call himself a lucky man.

ideas about the potentialities of the human mind that they might not fully understand but welcomed with enthusiasm. Crabb Robinson, coming to Jena in January 1802, after Fichte's departure, wrote home: 'I never before saw such an assembly of promising youths ... and I found the several students whom I became acquainted with enthusiastic for the new *Idealistical* System.'

Some of the best of Fichte's students, in agreement with his views about the old type of students' 'orders', with their drinking and duelling, started a literary society, usually called the 'League of Free Men', in June 1794, which continued to meet as long as Fichte was in Jena. Its minute-book still survives and gives us a good idea of what 'idealism' meant for these young men, and what is known about their later careers bears out the remark of Steffens in his autobiography, that if Fichte trained few philosophers, many of his pupils became admirable men. 'They meant by freedom action that was freely chosen. It showed itself not by empty complaints about things as they were, but by recognising the given circumstances, and mastering them.'[58] Many of them remained in touch with each other all their lives. 'We love each other as brothers, and honour each other as men,' so ran the fifth article of their constitution, 'and our union does not separate us from anyone whose countenance is human and whose heart is noble.' J. F. Herbart, the philosopher, was one of them, and half a dozen more who became professors. Others were active in public life and in the professions. The story of their society and the brief life-histories of its leading members that Paul Raabe has given us convey impressively a sense of the potentialities for good of Weimar culture.

The political background to the literary and philosophical debates of these young men, who came from all over north Germany and from the Baltic states, was Europe in the first decade after the French Revolution, and this younger generation in Jena hardly differed at all in its reactions to contemporary events from the older men in Weimar and Jena whom they so greatly admired. It is interesting to observe from the minutes the gradual change in their attitudes. In the first three semesters they are carried away by Fichte's ideas in his lectures *Über die Bestimmung des Gelehrten*. The legacy of the Enlightenment is to be seen in their ethical convictions, their very theoretical views about government and their cosmopolitanism, but their confident belief that their human and political ideals are capable of being realised in actual society and the warring nations made conscious of their common humanity belongs specifically, as Paul Raabe says, to the age of German classicism.[59] 'They found their model in classical antiquity, were fired by its greatness and tried to follow its ideals.' Their social evenings devoted to high thinking were no doubt inspired by the *Symposium*, but the Revolution must have had at least some influence on the choice of themes for discussion.

The titles of some of the papers read at these early meetings are revealing. The first recorded was *On the character of ancient and modern greatness*, followed after a business meeting by one on *The rational freedom of man now first dawning in society*. When no new paper was ready, members read aloud for discussion passages from *Nathan the Wise*, Herder's *Humanitätsbriefe* and similar improving works, or from current periodicals. Other titles are: *That patriotism, in the sense in which it has been understood till now, is not only ridiculous but the reverse of a virtue*; *History of the despotism of all ages*; *The duty of the scholar to be active also as a citizen*.

After about a year and a half there is less of a sense of urgency in the proceedings of the Free Men. They are concerned above all with the problem of the harmonious personality, brought home to them by *Wilhelm Meisters Lehrjahre*, which was just coming out. They become more and more of a literary society, read each other papers about *Iphigenie* or *Tasso*, declaim their own or other people's poems, frequently Schiller's. Their maximum membership had been seventeen; before the society fizzled out in the spring of 1799 it was a little group of three or four theological students. The Free Men, as their minute-book shows, had followed the same pattern as Schiller, or Hölderlin, who was for a time on the fringe of the group. From activists, at least in theory, stimulated by the French example, they had developed into onlookers, still convinced of the perfectibility of mankind, but resigned to the indefinite postponement of social and political reform, for

> Aus den Wolken muß es fallen,
> Aus der Götter Schoß, das Glück.*

In the university as a whole political interest had cooled in the course of the 'nineties. In 1792–3, G. Hufeland, the lawyer, had lectured on the French Revolution, to the alarm of many influential personages in the protector-states, who had demanded that his script should be censored, but as Weimar had confidence in him, the affair blew over. Fichte's very popular lectures on *Die Bestimmung des Gelehrten* had raised further apprehension, not through their content but because of the lecturer's Jacobin reputation, and his decision to deliver them on Sunday afternoons (avoiding the hours of church services), ostensibly because of the crowded time-table. His lectures were undoubtedly a kind of lay sermon, on the new gospel of 'Bildung', suggesting what Goethe expressed in the lines:

> Wer Wissenschaft und Kunst besitzt,/Hat auch Religion;
> Wer jene beiden nicht besitzt,/Der habe Religion.†

Few were surprised therefore to find Fichte involved before very long in the 'atheism controversy' which led to his dismissal, not because he was any more unorthodox in his religions than Goethe or Karl August, but because he was an uncompromising radical in the two dangerous fields of politics and religion, and refused to be tactful. He seriously annoyed Voigt, for instance, who with Goethe had taken his side in the matter of the Sunday lectures, by insisting in the following year on republishing, this time with his name on the title-page, his book on the Revolution.

The 'atheism-controversy' began when in the autumn of 1798 an anonymous pamphlet attacked two essays on religion which has appeared earlier in the year in Fichte's *Philosophisches Journal*,

---

* Happiness must fall from the clouds, from the lap of the Gods.

† A man who has scholarship and art has also religion; when a man has not those two, let him take to religion.

one of them by the editor. The government of Electoral Saxony banned the number in its own universities and demanded the punishment of the authors. Goethe and Voigt were again for moderation, but this time the Duke, in his fear of the Revolution, was in favour of drastic action, and Gotha demanded Fichte's dismissal. Fichte, after handing in an official defence of his actions, wrote privately to Voigt in a rather arrogant tone, still further alienating his sympathy, and through him, that of Goethe, so that no influential voice was raised at court for Fichte, and all the protector-states agreed on his dismissal, in April 1799. None of his colleagues left with him, as he had been sure they would, but student numbers showed a marked decline.

The methods adopted by the Weimar authorities when, as not infrequently happened, the students got out of hand, were no less authoritarian than those they used in dealing with the professors. The marked improvement in the intellectual tone of the student population in the 'nineties was not accompanied by the complete disappearance of the traditional disputes and fights with the townsfolk, or 'Philistines', as the Jena students were apparently the first to call them, and unpopular personalities, even among the professors, still sometimes had their windows broken by rowdy gangs. When the professor elected as 'Pro-rector' for a term or two to look after university discipline found that the sanctions at his disposal, confinement of offenders in the university 'carcer' or prison, or the threat of sending them down ('Relegation'), were insufficient, he had to call in the military from Weimar, as happened in 1792, when the Pro-rectors's own home was turned upside down after a student rag. The authorities were particularly nervous just then, of course, scenting revolution in any disorder. Neither Weimar nor the University Senate had given the students any encouragement when a considerable body of them had offered support, in the preceding year, for a plan to suppress duelling, and similar abuses encouraged by the students' 'Orders', by making themselves responsible for dealing with the offenders democratically. But the sixteen hussars and fifty 'Jäger' dispatched to Jena in 1792 were soon withdrawn and the students were promised immunity when it was heard that a migration of five hundred of them to a neighbouring state had been organised, with a view to their settling down at the University of Erfurt. The government needed the taxes they raised from the Jena shopkeepers and householders, who could not pay them if the students departed on whom they depended for a living. Such were the petty considerations Goethe had to face when, as so often, he had to advise the Duke about student disorders. They were serious again in 1795, when Fichte's opposition to the Orders had alarmed many of their adherents, but this time it was possible to deal with the ringleaders severely, because the Reichstag, usually so slow to act, had agreed on a measure intended to discourage universities from exploiting each other's difficulties, in order to attract students, at least when students' Orders, now mistrusted in most states, were behind the trouble.

Though in the next few years, Jena's most flourishing period, there was little trouble with discipline, duelling had by no means ceased when Crabb Robinson was there. In July 1803, he wrote home that nearly a hundred duels has been fought in the last six months. Goethe's worries now were occasioned by the university's steady loss of its leading professors. 'Jena now seems to be on the brink of ruin', Crabb Robinson wrote in September 1803. 'Nearly all the celebrated men who have raised Jena to so great an eminence have suddenly received invitations which they will possibly accept. The Dukes of Saxony to whom the university belongs are poor and cannot bid against the King of Prussia or the Elector of Bavaria.' Perhaps the most serious loss was that of Schütz, not because of his personal eminence but because, encouraged by a Prussian subsidy, very welcome to Bertuch, he took the *Allgemeine Literatur-Zeitung* with him to Halle. It was at about this time that the new Weimar Palace was completed, and Schiller, who had left Jena for Weimar at the end of 1799, was not the only one to contrast the 'new life' in the palace, which had cost so much money and effort, with the decay of Jena.

'I see three months of effort, worry, annoyance and dangers in front of me', Goethe wrote on 1 September 1803 to the Duke, appealing for his co-operation. He played an important part in the negotiations for the new appointments that were necessary, was the prime mover in the setting up of a new *Jenaische Allgemeine Literatur-Zeitung* in rivalry with the old one and made renewed efforts to improve the library and the scientific institutes in Jena.

Goethe had been in close touch with the Jena scientists since J. C. Loder, the anatomist, one of the professors who in 1803 left for Halle, had first helped him with his zoological studies in 1781. He was naturally interested in the specimens, mainly concerning zoology and mineralogy, collected by J. E. I. Walch, bought by Karl August on the professor's death in 1778 and housed in the Jena Schloss, where they were joined in 1783 by the library of Professor Büttner of Göttingen, and various other acquisitions. The keeper of this small scientific museum and library was J. G. Lenz, who lectured on mineralogy in Jena from 1781 and had to wait thirteen years before he was made extraordinary professor, and sixteen more for a normal chair. He had come over to science from theology and philosophy, and Walch too had been a philosopher, keenly interested as an amateur in natural history. It was only in connection with medicine that natural science of any kind was taught in his day. Chemistry was first made independent of medicine through Goethe's influence, because of his need of chemistry in his mineralogical studies. It happened through the appointment of J. F. A. Göttling as extraordinary professor of chemistry, in the philosophical faculty, in 1789, after a period of special training financed by the Duke, who provided a laboratory, also in the Jena Schloss. Botany was similarly divided off in 1792, when A. J. G. K. Batsch was finally made extraordinary professor of botany after five years as a lecturer, helped and encouraged, since his graduation in the medical faculty, by Goethe.

All these pioneers were kept going more by enthusiasm for their subject than by material rewards. Batsch, for instance, had to write works of popularisation like his *Botany for Ladies*, but he was a good systematic botanist, who built up the Botanical Garden, started in the Prince's Garden at Jena in 1794 and supervised not by the university, but by a committee consisting of Goethe and Voigt. It was Batsch who founded in 1793 the Natural History Society (Naturforschende Gesellschaft) which first brought Goethe and Schiller intimately together in 1794. It met once a month in Batsch's house, usually on a Sunday afternoon. Lenz, three years later, founded a Mineralogical Society, and in the critical year 1803 it was given rooms in the Schloss and allowed to prefix 'Ducal' to its title. It will be clear from these few details how much all the new scientific institutions depended on stimulus and support from Weimar, especially from the all-powerful Goethe. In 1803 he was particularly anxious about their fate. Loder had taken most of his collections with him, but now all the scientific museums were brought under the one roof in the Jena Schloss, and Goethe, with Voigt, was given the 'Oberaufsicht', became, that is, the Honorary Director of them all, together with the libraries in Weimar and Jena. The condition under which Büttner had made over his valuable library to the Duke in 1783 had been that he should be given a pension and free accommodation in the Jena Schloss. He lived on until 1801, so it was only then that his library could be freely used, and Goethe was given the task of getting it into order. He spent seven years doing this on occasional visits, with the help of the Weimar librarian, Christiane's brother, C. A. Vulpius, and later he undertook also to unite it with the university library and its various separate collections, organising the re-cataloguing of them all, and establishing them on a proper basis under full-time librarians, responsible, characteristically, not to the university senate, but to the 'Gross-herzogliche Oberaufsicht', i.e., Goethe, who after 1815, when Weimar became a Grand Duchy, was styled 'Minister of State, with the supreme direction of the higher institutions for scholarship and art in Weimar and Jena', a new title for the office he had really held since his return from Italy.

6. GENERAL CULTURE IN WEIMAR

It was natural that at a court where leading figures in literature, scholarship and the arts received so much official encouragement and stood in high social esteem, the general level of taste was high, and conversation at the usual gatherings of those belonging to good society was, at least towards the end of the century, more intellectual and less devoted to idle gossip than had once been the case. There is a hint of Goethe's early memories of Weimar society in the second of the *Roman Elegies*, where the poet rejoices that now in Rome he is safe from the 'fair ladies and the gentlemen of good society' with their inevitable inquiries about uncles and aunts and cousins, followed by 'dreary games of cards'. The first, unpublished version is more explicit about his own experience, when he speaks of being asked 'whether Werther had really existed, and everything was really true, and what town could boast of the unique Lotte?' Schiller's letters from Weimar on his first arrival there draw, as we have seen, quite a favourable picture, and this impression is confirmed by the reports of innumerable visitors. The *Briefe eines ehrlichen Mannes* already mentioned describe the aristocracy in Weimar in the late 'nineties as amongst the most cultivated in Germany, especially those in the immediate circle of the Duchess. They speak of the good talk at her tea-parties in the park in summer and of Anna Amalia's continued interest in literature and the arts at her own quiet gatherings in the Wittumspalais. The ordinary run of people are naturally much as they are anywhere else, but they amuse themselves in a quiet and orderly way at the so-called 'Vauxhall' in the park on Sundays, where there is music, and a great crowd of people promenade up and down, or sit about in the arbours and beside the large circular flower-beds, and at the meetings of the three clubs, one on Mondays for men, with no distinction of rank, others for both sexes on Wednesdays and Fridays, this latter reserved for the nobility. In the winter season there is the theatre, three times a week, Sunday concerts at court and masked balls occasionally at the theatre.

In the early days, as we have seen, Goethe and others had frequently read aloud to some of the court circle, and he had been one of the leaders in devising and producing plays for the amateur theatre, until his official duties and his scientific hobbies had come to take up more and more of his time in the years just before the Italian journey. From 1791, after his second visit to Italy with the Dowager Duchess, he became more and more fond of lecturing to the ladies and gentlemen, especially the ladies, of the court, partly no doubt because of a strong didactic strain in him, inherited from his father, and partly because he thought it was good for them and for Weimar society in general that the results of the labours of the intellectual élite should be shared with them and freely discussed. His high praise for Fontenelle in the *History of the Theory of Colours* shows how much he admired earlier French attempts at the popularisation of scientific knowledge, and these were probably his model.[60] 'Scientists as well as other men of letters and scholars lived in the world and for the world; they had to try to arouse interest in their pursuits too, and did so quickly and easily.'

In July 1791 Goethe organised a kind of small literary and philosophical society in Weimar, a modest version of the Academies in larger capitals, which met to begin with on the first Friday of every month between five and eight o'clock in the evening at the house of the Dowager Duchess. Some of the papers read to it have survived and we have a full report of four meetings by K. A. Böttiger, the newly appointed headmaster of the Gymnasium, who, as a good classical scholar, was at first a welcome contributor to its proceedings, but before long, as we gather from what Goethe said to Chancellor Müller in old age (28 June 1830), 'broke up the society, and disturbed harmonious relations between the leading men in Weimar through his gossip. He tried to use everything he saw and heard merely for his own selfish purposes.'

In his own brief description of the 'Friday Society' (in the *Annalen* for 1796 and in a note commenting on his correspondence with Schiller), dealing with it after its resurrection in 1794, Goethe speaks of it as 'a society of highly cultivated men', each of whom 'talked about a subject of his own choice concerned with his work, his writings and hobbies, and was listened to with generous interest'. At first each took the chair in turn and proceedings were quite informal, even when, as often happened, the Duke and Duchess were present. After each paper, the company stood up and gathered in free discussion round a table where illustrative drawings or specimens had been laid out. The first members were Weimar residents of whom much has been heard already: Goethe, Herder, Wieland, Knebel, Bode the translator, Bertuch, Meyer, Buchholz the chemist, and the high official Voigt, and Goethe mentions also Kraus, Hufeland and the younger Herr von Fritsch, and at their first meetings they agreed on rules for their proceedings. They continued to meet, less regularly after a year or two and then with new enthusiasm from about 1795, usually weekly now and in Goethe's house. If he was not able to be present, Voigt organised the meeting.

At the first meeting to which Böttiger was invited as a guest (4 November 1791) Goethe continued an exposition, begun at an earlier meeting, of his Theory of Colours. These are the talks referred to in the Dedication to the Duchess at the beginning of his *Theory of Colours* (1808), dated 30 January, her birthday. Herder followed with a paper, *True Immortality in Posterity*, published in his *Zerstreute Blätter* in the following year,[61] in which he follows up the thoughts discussed above in connection with the later books of the *Ideas*, about the debt we all owe to the past for our inherited culture, and our highest hope, to transmit these benefits, with anything we can add ourselves, to the future, not in the vain expectation of a lasting name, but in the certainty that only in this way civilisation can advance.

The noblest that we possess is not our own creation. . . . Language . . . inventions . . . maxims and manners have come down to us which not only reveal the law of nature that lies hidden within us, but fire us and give us courage to rise above depression and habit, to shake off prejudices and, through feeling others to be penetrated by the same light of the true, good and beautiful, to be far more closely united with them in friendship and activity than bodies without minds and senses can ever be united. . . . In this way the tree of 'Humanität' rose up above all peoples; innumerable hands helped to tend it, we enjoy its fruits and must assist in its further cultivation.

After this moving little sermon on culture, Voigt produced and explained a document from the time of Frederick Barbarossa, and two of the frequent guests from Jena, Batsch and Lenz, read papers on natural history, illustrated by specimens, eagerly discussed by Herder and the septuagenarian Hofrat Büttner, while the Duke's doctor, Hufeland, pointed out a strange effect produced by light on a framed silhouette. As the meeting had already gone on an hour too long, Bertuch's communication, on Chinese coloured inks, was postponed.

At the second meeting reported by Böttiger, Goethe read a section of K. Ph. Moritz's *Lectures on Style*, Böttiger spoke about 'Tattooing amongst the Ancients', Knebel read an outspoken 'moral rhapsody', Buchholz performed a chemical experiment, Voigt compared some recent Prussian law with Justinian, Bertuch spoke about his inks, and Meyer, Goethe's Swiss friend, showed a picture of 'Castor and Pollux abducting the daughters of Leucippus', in which he had followed Goethe's ideas in his treatment of colour. These few details about a couple of meetings are perhaps enough to convey some idea of the intellectual range of this small circle in Weimar and of the stimulating influence again of the one man, Goethe, in fostering the fruitful interpenetration of ideas and living experience, in other words, of culture and society.

A remarkable example of the results that might follow happens to be recorded. At the third meeting he attended, Böttiger heard the second instalment of a treatise on *Makrobiotik*, or the prolongation of life, by the busy young Weimar doctor, Christoph Hufeland, who had taken over the extensive practice in town and country of his father nine years before this, at the age of twenty-one. The father and his father before him had been personal doctors to the ducal family, but young Hufeland had not succeeded to this honour. His paper, however, made such an impression on the Duke that he decided immediately to make him a professor of medicine at Jena. After eight very successful years in Jena, where Hufeland started the first German medical journal, he was called to Berlin, to take charge of the great Charité hospital, and he became personal doctor to the Prussian royal family, first dean of the medical faculty in the new University of Berlin and one of the foremost doctors in Germany. His autobiography reveals a man of character, whose success was due to hard work and willingness to learn from experience, just the kind of man who would make an impression on a Karl August or a Goethe.[62] His treatise, like his later books and articles, running into hundreds, was written in the two or three hours before breakfast—he rose at five o'clock in summer—and to attend the Friday Society he must have broken his usual routine, which kept him busy with visits between nine in the morning and seven or eight o'clock at night, after which he made up his own prescriptions. He wrote a rhymed version of his *Makrobiotik* on his death-bed, from which we can see how little a modern doctor could have taught him about the rules of hygiene and how strong the ethical foundation of his medical philosophy was. The first three stanzas may be quoted, unpretentious verses, yet astonishingly close in their content to Goethe's practical philosophy, an indication that this, like Kant's ethics, as Korff has suggested, is a distillation of the moral feeling of wide circles:

> Willst leben froh und in die Läng,
> Leb' in der Jugend hart und streng,
> Genieße alles, doch mit Maß,
> Und, was dir schlecht bekommt, das laß.

> Das Heute ist ein eigen Ding,
> Das ganze Leben in einem Ring,
> Die Gegenwart, Vergangenheit,
> Und selbst der Keim der künft'gen Zeit.

> Drum lebe immer nur für heut,
> Arbeit', genieße, was es beut,
> Und sorge für den Morgen nicht,
> Du hast ihn heut schon zugericht.*

* If you want a long and happy life, live hard and sternly in your youth. Enjoy everything in moderation, and avoid what does not agree with you.

'Today' is a strange thing, the whole of life in one ring, the present, the past, and even the germ of the future.

So live always just for today, work and enjoy what it offers, and have no care for the morrow—you have shaped it by your acts today.

Goethe's absences from Weimar on the French campaign and at the siege of Mainz may have had as much to do with the discontinuance of these meetings for a time as Böttiger's intrigues. He may also have found that, after the first year, it was not so easy to persuade his friends to come forward with papers. At any rate, when the meetings were resumed in his house on 27 November 1794, Goethe himself seems to have been much the most active member. The talk 'On the various branches of our activities here' discussed at the beginning of this chapter was intended for this society, though it is not certain that it was read there, and in the note on his Correspondence with Schiller, as in the *Annalen* for 1796, he mentions his reading of a canto of Voss's translation of the *Iliad*, greatly enjoyed by W. von Humboldt. This is the kind of thing that he read later to the 'Wednesday Society' of Weimar ladies that met in his house (*Annalen* for 1807 and 1809), who heard him translate extempore from the *Nibelungenlied*, just published in 1807 by Friedrich von der Hagen. *König Rother, Tristan and Isolde* and various Norse sagas are also mentioned. As late as 1822, the last year covered by the *Annalen*, we read: 'As for social communications, this year was particularly successful in our circle. Two days in the week were fixed for me to lay before our royal personages something of importance, with the necessary explanations. Every meeting furnished some new occasion and the most varied matters were discussed, ancient and modern, artistic and scientific topics always being well received.' Goethe's amazing many-sidedness, his urge to communicate and the cultural receptivity of his circle during a whole generation are brought home to us by these records of social occasions on a high intellectual plane. Even when sights were set lower, as in the 'Mittwochskränzchen' or Wednesday Parties of seven couples that met in Goethe's house in the winter of 1801–2 and came to an end this time through the intrigues of Kotzebue—for both high- and small-mindedness are, alas, equally in evidence in Weimar—some of Goethe's best 'Songs for Social Occasions' were the fortunate result, the *Tischlied* 'Mich ergreift, ich weiß nicht wie, Himmlisches Behagen', and the mischievous *General-*

beichte, a 'General Confession' that shows another side of the
often so solemn Privy Councillor, who here repents sins of
omission like these:

> Ja, wir haben, seis bekannt,
> Wachend oft geträumet,
> Nicht geleert das frische Glas,
> Wenn der Wein geschäumet;
> Manche rasche Schäferstunde,
> Flüchtgen Kuß vom lieben Munde
> Haben wir versäumet.
>
> Still und maulfaul saßen wir,
> Wenn Philister schwätzten,
> Über göttlichen Gesang
> Ihr Geklatsche schätzten,
> Wegen glücklicher Momente,
> Deren man sich rühmen könnte,
> Uns zur Rede setzten.
>
> Willst du Absolution
> Deinen Treuen geben,
> Wollen wir nach deinem Wink
> Unabläßlich streben,
> Uns vom Halben zu entwöhnen
> Und im Ganzen, Guten, Schönen
> Resolut zu leben.*

A letter written by Goethe to Knebel when he was preparing
for publication his correspondence with Schiller (24 December
1824) provides an authoritative final comment on the great days
in Weimar which it has been our aim to recall, and helps to

---

* Yes, we have, let us admit, often dreamed in waking hours, failed to quaff
the refreshing glass of sparkling wine, let slip many a quick tryst and passing kiss
from dear lips.

We have sat silent and tongue-tied while philistines chattered, rated their
tittle-tattle higher than heavenly song, and called us to account for happy hours,
of which we had the right to boast.

If you will give absolution to your faithful worshippers, we will unceasingly
strive, following your bidding, to wean ourselves from all half-measures, and to
live resolutely in the whole, the good, the beautiful.

justify our choice of the death of Schiller as the most suitable point at which to bring this volume to an end.

My correspondence with Schiller [Goethe writes], which is now almost completely assembled, has given me pleasure and instruction; it ends in 1805, and if we remember that the French invasion began in 1806, it is obvious at the first glance that it put an end to an epoch of which we retain today scarcely a memory. That way of cultivating oneself that was a product of the long period of peace in northern Europe, and took ever more intensive forms, was violently interrupted, and all were compelled from youth and childhood upwards to cultivate themselves differently, with the result that in an age of tumult there was no lack of mis-cultivation. All the more unmistakably does this correspondence bear witness to an epoch that is over, will not return, and yet is felt in its effects down to the present day, exerting not only in Germany a powerful living influence. Let us rejoice that we belonged to it and are still the same as we always were, and that our friendship too has proved to be so enduring.

CHAPTER VI

THE LATER HISTORY OF THE
WEIMAR IDEALS

OUR aim has been to describe the many-sided cultural advance achieved in Weimar between Goethe's arrival there in 1775 and the end of the Holy Roman Empire in 1806, the year which Goethe looked upon, as we have just seen, as marking the end of an epoch when the peaceful pursuit of personal culture was the primary concern of his immediate circle of friends. We have tried to trace the history of this attitude towards cultivation in the Weimar circle, to see how the leading writers speak of it in their theoretical discussions about the history and nature of culture, and to ascertain the part played by a few men, for whom personal cultivation was a supreme value, in the shaping of the chief cultural institutions of the state. Avoiding convenient but indefinable abstractions like 'the spirit of the age' or 'classical man', we have tried to explain what happened in Weimar as resulting from acts of choice on the part of a small number of gifted but fallible men, influenced by inherited traditions, foreign example and the particular circumstances of a given time and place. We have seen how one distinguished writer after another followed Wieland to Weimar and stayed on there, for reasons which it is usually possible to discover, though they do not include the conscious desire to bring into existence what has come to be known as Weimar Classicism. Each of them, we have found, with his innate gifts, his inherited and consciously cultivated knowledge, taste and moral attitude, was affected by his new surroundings, but each was at the same time able, through his creative talent, to 'objectify' his own personal reactions to life, both in his successive writings and in his contributions towards creating or reshaping a periodical, a school, a scientific institute or whatever it might be, institutions outlasting the individual and preserving a record of his activity as a mind in fruitful contact with other minds in a settled society, where through their combined efforts a new phase of German civilisation came into being.)

What has happened in the last century and a half, the present-day reader will naturally ask, to make the picture of classical Weimar presented here appear so irrelevant to the understanding of Germany as he knows it, the Germany that our country has faced in two successive wars? The answer would be a very long story, and one of which many features are still obscure, but a brief description will now be attempted, first of the later history of Weimar itself, and then of the gradual dilution and corruption in German society of the ideals of culture which have occupied our attention.

1. WEIMAR AFTER 1806

Goethe himself, as we have seen, after his return from Italy, collected more eagerly than ever, and encouraged the Duke to collect works of art, scientific specimens, books and the material objects of all kinds that constitute the vehicle of culture in any society, thus laying the foundations of the city of museums which Weimar ultimately became. The means available were small, compared with the resources of the great capitals, so that even when Weimar had become a Grand Duchy, after the wars, its external appearance had little to impress its many visitors. The 'Roman House' was built in the park, between 1792 and 1796, as a summer retreat for Karl August, in the classical style now favoured by Goethe, and the same architect, J. A. Arens of Hamburg, planned in its main lines the restoration of the Wilhelmsburg, the completion of which became a matter of urgency when a marriage was arranged between the Electoral Prince of Weimar and Maria Paulovna, the daughter of the Czar. It was fit to be lived in at last in 1808 and a beginning had been made in adorning its interior with murals by German artists, a process continued by Preller and Neher in the 'forties and extended to the Wartburg by Schwind, when it too was restored in mid-century.

What attracted people to Weimar, however, until 1832 was not its buildings or collections, but its peace, its pleasant park and, above all, Goethe, and the highly cultivated society to be found in its hospitable homes. J. J. Mounier, one of the many French refugees who were welcomed there, ran a private school for boys between 1797 and 1802, in premises provided by the Duke at the Belvedere palace, and this school attracted a succession of English boys of good family, offering as it did a substitute for the institutions in Paris now closed to them. Long after Mounier's departure Englishmen of good family, usually fresh from the university, continued to visit Weimar on their Continental tours, and they were still great favourites, during Goethe's last years, at the frequent parties of his wayward but attractive daughter-in-law, Ottilie, who apparently fell in love with several of them in turn and soon after Goethe's death (August had died in October 1830) joined one of them, Charles Sterling, on a long-planned holiday, though she never secured his affections, even after the birth of a child.[1] W. M. Thackeray, in the letter printed by Lewes in his *Life of Goethe* in 1855, says that round about 1830 he was one of 'at least a score of young English lads' who were always welcome at Ottilie's tea-table. 'We passed hours after hours there, and night after night in the pleasantest talk and music. We read over endless novels and poems in French, English and German', some of the shorter items being, no doubt, contributions to Ottilie's private magazine, *Chaos*, a kind of revival, on a much lower level, of the *Tiefurt Journal*. It appeared in printed form, at first weekly and then irregularly, from 28 August 1829 till February 1832. Goethe himself was not present at Ottilie's parties, but Thackeray and most of the young Englishmen had opportunities of meeting him sooner or later, though Weimar was for them 'not Ilm-Athen, but a second spell of university life freed from academic discipline'.[2] Thackeray writes with enthusiasm about the society in Weimar, at court, which was open to English visitors with little formality, and in private houses. After recalling his memories of Goethe himself, he continues: 'Though his sun was setting, the sky around was calm and bright, and that little Weimar illumined by it. In every one of those kind salons the talk was still of Art and letters. The theatre, though possessing no very extraordinary actors, was still conducted with noble intelligence and order. The actors read books, and were men of letters and gentlemen, holding a not unkindly relationship with the *Adel*. At court the conversation was exceedingly friendly, simple and polished' and 'the young ladies, one and all, spoke admirable English'. 'With a five-and-twenty years' experience since those happy days of which I write', Thackeray concludes, 'and an acquaintance with an immense variety of human kind, I think I have never seen a society more simple, charitable, courteous, gentlemanlike than that of the dear little Saxon city, where the good Schiller and the great Goethe lived and lie buried.'

Many other foreign visitors and a host of Germans have left us their impressions of Weimar and Goethe in the later years of his life. One of the most striking accounts is that of Mme de Staël, who naturally spent a month or two there (in 1803–4) while collecting material for the book *De l'Allemagne*, which did so much to create in foreign minds the image of a Germany of poets and thinkers. At the time, Goethe and Schiller considered this formidable literary lady a very great nuisance, and a hint of her own disappointment at not finding in Goethe the kind of person she had imagined as the author of *Werther* still remains in chapter VII of the Second Part of *De l'Allemagne*, when she speaks of the impression of coldness and stiffness that he made on her at first, but she does full justice to the 'esprit prodigieux' that he revealed in conversation on better acquaintance:

C'est un homme dont l'esprit est universel, et impartial parce qu'il est universel; car il n'y a point d'indifférence dans son impartialité: c'est une double existence, une double force, une double lumière qui éclaire à la fois dans toutes choses les deux côtés de la question. Quand il s'agit de penser, rien ne l'arrête, ni son siècle, ni ses habitudes, ni ses relations; il fait tomber à plomb son regard d'aigle sur les objets qu'il observe; s'il avait eu une carrière politique, si son âme s'était developpée par les actions, son caractère serait plus décidé, plus ferme, plus patriote; mais son esprit ne planerait pas si librement sur toutes les manières de voir; les passions ou les intérêts lui traceraient une route positive.

As a corrective to the hero-worship of Goethe's biographers, even Mme de Staël's uninhibited first impressions (in a letter to her father of 25 December 1803) are not without value. 'Goethe', she says, 'me gâte beaucoup l'idéal de Werther. C'est un gros homme, sans physionomie, qui veut être un peu homme du monde, ce qui ne vaut rien à demi.'

Mme de Staël was amazed at the indifference of Wieland, Goethe and Schiller to European politics. They read no newspapers, she said in this same letter, and she thought there was probably nowhere in the world where one would find more abstract and fewer positive ideas than in Weimar. Yet even Weimar could not for ever avoid contact with harsh political realities. After the near-by Battle of Jena in 1806, its fame alone was not enough to protect it, and Karl August only retained his title by joining the Confederation of the Rhine, but at Erfurt in 1808 Napoleon received Goethe and Wieland with great respect. Admiration for Napoleon's genius was widespread in Weimar, and its population does not seem to have been unwilling to pay him the homage that was expected by a conqueror, Goethe himself least of all. The *Weimarisches offizielles Wochenblatt* announced, for instance, on 21 August 1811, that the birthday of His Majesty the Emperor and King had been celebrated in Weimar by band-music from the townhall balcony in the morning, a dinner and reception at court, and illuminations and a civic ball at night. Goethe was meanwhile working away quietly in that small plain study, so different from the splendid rooms where he assembled his treasures of art and received his many guests, at his *Theory of Colours*, at the *Elective Affinities* and *Poetry and Truth*. In his last years, after the liberation to which Weimar had been able to contribute but little, Goethe might well regard himself as the king of letters of his time. Among the tributes that poured in from every side, the seal sent to him on his last birthday by fifteen English admirers, among then Wordsworth, Walter Scott and Carlyle, who had organised the presentation, gave him special pleasure, though perhaps not as much as the message from Byron in 1822, asking permission to dedicate *Sardanapalus* to him. A whole series of artists came in turn to paint his portrait or model Olympian busts of him, the most monumental of all, stylised beyond all resemblance and more than life-size, being the last, by the French sculptor L. J. David. His table-talk was recorded and written up by Eckermann and others of his intimate circle. King Ludwig I of Bavaria honoured him with a personal visit on his seventy-ninth birthday. When he died at the age of eighty-two, having experienced to the full 'the lot of those who live long, of outliving many'—Herder, Wieland, Anna Amalia, Karl August and his own son August—many throughout Europe felt with Carlyle that their greatest had departed. Weimar had won for itself a name of legendary significance.

For the next twenty years or so there was a lull, in the quiet 'Biedermeier' age, but Karl August's grandson, Karl Alexander, a humane and cultivated man, did much in a long reign to revive the old tradition of patronage, most successfully in music, during Liszt's most active years, in the 1840's and 1850's, made socially brilliant by his devoted Karoline von Wittgenstein at the Altenburg. Under Dingelstedt the theatre regained some of its old eminence, and in 1860 an Academy of Art was founded that for a decade or two outshone the older ones in larger German capitals. The persistence of a cultural tradition was as strikingly evident in Weimar as Goethe had found it to be in Stuttgart, and the little state retained too a reputation for liberalism. Weimar became a favourite retreat for retired men of taste and people with some means and children to educate. In 1914 about a tenth of the population were families of this type. With the rapid improvement of communications, the wider and wider diffusion of an interest in literature and the arts and the increase of tourism, the show-pieces of Weimar were one by one adapted to the reception of a stream of visitors, beginning with the Goethe-house in 1885, on the death of the last of the poet's grandsons. In 1896 the

'Goethe and Schiller Archives' were established and handsomely housed, followed in 1897 by the Nietzsche Archives, and as the seat of the Goethe Society and the Shakespeare Society, Weimar became the Mecca of German conference addicts.

It was natural that after the abdication of the Emperor William II, Weimar, symbolising for Germans everything that was opposed to Potsdam, should be chosen as the meeting-place of the Constituent Assembly and that the Republic thus provided with a constitution should be generally known as the Weimar Republic. Developing the arts and crafts to heights of which Bertuch had never dreamt, Gropius assembled at the Bauhaus in Weimar, between 1919 and 1926, one of the most original and influential groups in the history of this century's art and architecture. Politically, however, the promise of the 1920's was not maintained. It was only ten years after Gropius, yielding to hostile criticism, had moved the Bauhaus to Dessau, that the National Socialists set up on the Ettersberg, within sight of Ettersburg palace, frequently mentioned above, the Buchenwald concentration camp. Here 56,000 men and women perished, who are now commemorated in the name of a square near the station in Weimar and by massive monuments on the site of the camp.[3]

2. 'KULTUR' IN NINETEENTH- AND TWENTIETH-CENTURY GERMANY

Turning now to the history of the idea of 'Bildung' and 'Kultur' in nineteenth-century Germany as a whole, we may point first to some of the positive achievements of the Weimar humanists, regarded rather as men with a new conception of culture and civilisation than as creative poets. In their theories of culture, in the first place, the Weimar thinkers were remarkably bold and penetrating for their day in facing up to the consequences of that 'emergence from tutelage' in which Kant had seen the essence of the Enlightenment. They had as yet only vague notions about the beginnings of life on the earth, but they asked the right questions. Without invoking miraculous intervention, they understood clearly enough how civilisation had grown and spread, through the leadership of exceptional men and the accumulation of knowledge and insight made possible through the invention of writing and the development of the fine arts. They aimed boldly at a total understanding of this whole process, seeing no necessary conflict between religion, philosophy and science, which were all 'natural' approaches of man to 'nature'. Above all, they saw man as responsible now for his own future. They lacked the detailed scientific knowledge to rise to a conception like Teilhard de Chardin's of the 'noosphere', but it is perhaps not fanciful to see in ideas like his the modern equivalent of Herder's and Goethe's guesses about biological and cultural history, inspired by the confident belief that the universe, immense and mysterious though it might be, was responsive to rational inquiry, 'erforschlich'. Still nearer to them in spirit is a passage like the following from Lowes Dickinson, a great admirer of Goethe, where a poetic or mythical conception of nature is still combined with evolutionary thought:

Man is in the making; but henceforth he must make himself. To that point Nature has led him, out of the primeval slime. She has given him limbs, she has given him brain, she has given him the rudiments of a soul. Now it is for him to make or mar that splendid torso. Let him look no more to her for aid; for it is her will to create one who has the power to create himself. If he fail, she fails; back goes the metal to the pot; and the great process begins anew. If he succeeds, he succeeds alone. His fate is in his own hands.[4]

Pico della Mirandola, Herder, Goethe, Hegel are direct forerunners of thoughts like these.

It is not only their broad view of nature and history, based on the idea of the supreme importance of civilisation or culture, that became a central feature of nineteenth-century German thought, largely replacing the metaphysical side of the Christian philosophy of life. Equally important was their new answer to the question of the meaning of life for the individual, after the abandonment by the great majority of educated men of the hope of other-worldly fulfilment. Faust speaks for them all when he cries: 'Aus dieser Erde quillen meine Freuden.' The highest values are for them realisable only by individuals in this earthly life, but not by individuals in isolation. To the essentials of the good life belong love and friendship, and the fullest possible participation in the enduring, superindividual activities of civilisation, in thought and imagination. 'Idee und Liebe', thought and love, these make happiness possible, as Goethe says, even in extreme old age. If awareness of a rich inheritance is the foundation of this view of the world, it is dominated as a personal philosophy by the idea of 'Bildung'. For the great poets, naturally, it was the capacity to create that above all else gave meaning to life, but for primarily receptive minds like that of Wilhelm von Humboldt it was the development of the maximum use, for a man's own satisfaction, of the higher faculties. 'A man who can say to himself on his death-bed: "I have understood and transformed into a part of my humanity as much of the world as I could", such a man has fulfilled his aim. . . . He has, in the higher sense of the word, truly lived.'[5]

With Humboldt, as Spranger's admirable analysis shows, this at first sight so high-minded individualism aims at the construction by the self of a personality rounded and perfect like a work of art, and equally justified in its own right. 'Cultivation is brought to bear exclusively on the inward individual, not on a system of universal aims or social goals, not on the attainment of a social ideal or even of a high standard of living. It is precisely the mood which prompted Schiller to ask: 'Can man be meant, for the sake of any external aim, to neglect his inner nature?'[6] A civilised person owes it to himself to aim at this kind of perfection, unlike a 'philistine', who lives for the satisfaction of his material needs. The idealist might easily forget, as we shall see, how many of those around him were compelled by their circumstances to take an illiberal attitude to mere work. A view of life which values so highly the quality of individual thought and feeling presupposes the existence of an élite, exempt from much of the drudgery of life, an aristocracy of talent, if not of birth. We have seen that the Weimar writers, themselves of middle-class origin, adapted themselves without much questioning to the existing structure of the society around them, into which they were absorbed as an aristocracy of intellect. Their duty, they felt, was to do the best work of which they were capable as artists, and in their less creative moments to give their thought rather to clarifying the relationship between the good, the true and the beautiful, and problems of their own art, than to devising ways of enlarging the circle of the cultivated. If they seem to us to have accepted too readily as inevitable the great differences, of which they were well aware, between the privileged classes and the mass of the people, it is because of contingent influences, to which we shall return.

In spite of these limitations, the Weimar writers did arrive at a criterion for civilisation that proved more acceptable to most later thinkers than that of the Christian Middle Ages or of the Enlightenment. Coleridge is in agreement with them, for instance, when he writes in his *Constitution of Church and State*, in a passage quoted by Mr Williams: 'Civilisation is itself but a mixed good, if not far more a corrupting influence, the hectic of disease, not the bloom of health, and a nation so distinguished more fitly to be called a varnished than a polished people, where this civilisation is not grounded in cultivation, in the harmonious development of those qualities and faculties that characterise our humanity.'[7] This is very similar to the criticism of pre-revolutionary France that we have found in Schiller's *Aesthetic Letters*. Coleridge's description of 'cultivation' tallies closely with the German idea of 'Humanität', and his use of the word 'cultivation', the first recorded, according to Mr Williams, where it denotes 'a general condition, a state or habit of the mind', corresponds so exactly with the German use of 'Bildung' that it is hardly possible to doubt that in speaking of 'civilisation' and 'cultivation' he was thinking of 'Kultur' and 'Bildung'.

'Man is never recognised by Bentham', says Mill, 'as a being capable of pursuing spiritual perfection as an end.' That is where Bentham differs from Carlyle and Coleridge, Arnold and Mill, and the other Victorian 'sages' who sought a religious humanism free from superstition (or 'Aberglaube', as Arnold calls it), often with the acknowledged help of Goethe, who, in Morley's words, became 'the founder, guide and oracle of an informal, nameless and unorganised communion of his own'.[8] But the Victorians looked upon 'cultivation', the pursuit by a 'Clerisy' of good states of mind as ends, as a corrective to over-confident industrialism, as Mr Williams has shown. That was not at all the case in Goethe's Germany, where industrialism was in its first beginnings and looked upon by nearly all with hope, as Bertuch's enterprises were in Weimar, little as his money-making attitude might appeal to superior minds. 'Bildung' was something to live for in a world full of injustice and cruelty, to end which seemed for the moment impossible and was nobody's business, though in due time, it was thought, a remedy would be found. Meanwhile there were irrational notions, dogmatic religion, national pride and class prejudice, by which the enlight-ened few would refuse to be bound in their own free minds, aspiring to belong to the 'invisible church' of their like in all countries, as Lessing had said in his *Ernst und Falk*.

If we are looking for parallels in our own country, something closer in several respects to the Weimar view can perhaps be found among the friends of the author of *Eminent Victorians*, strange as that may seem. This at least is the impression conveyed by Lord Keynes in his memoir, *My Early Beliefs*, about the atti-tude to life of what has come to be called 'The Bloomsbury Group', especially of some of its leading members, Keynes him-self, Lytton Strachey, Leonard Woolf, Clive Bell and one or two others, during their early Cambridge days, about ten years before the First World War.[9] Mr Noël Annan, in his study of Leslie Stephen, has pointed to the connection between some of the circle and the intellectual aristocracy descended from members of the 'Clapham Sect', and shown how the 'Bloomsbury attitude' gradually developed out of a purely moral earnestness deeply rooted in religion.[10] One is strongly reminded both of the secularisation of Pietist attitudes which we have found among the German classics, and of the markedly aristocratic nature of their habitual views. These young men came from privileged and well-to-do families, usually connected with banking as well as with sectarian religion and what grew out of it, however much they might take their good fortune for granted. A point not mentioned by Keynes, whose memoir was occasioned by D. H. Lawrence's hard words about a visit to Cambridge in 1914, when a breakfast party with Bertrand Russell and Keynes sent him 'mad with misery and hostility and rage', is that in Cambridge then, Lawrence will probably have been made acutely conscious of his own working-class background. But he was strongly antagonised too, no doubt, by what he will have seen, as Keynes wrote in 1938, as their 'thin rationalism skipping on the crust of the lava, ignoring both the reality and the value of the vulgar passions'.

In the philosophy described by Keynes there is much that recalls the 'inwardness' so characteristic, as we have seen, of the Germans of Goethe's time. It might be a 'thin rationalism' to Lawrence, but it was as strongly opposed as German idealism had been to the Benthamite side of the Enlightenment. It was anti-materialistic and distinctly spiritual in its leanings, a kind of neo-Platonism inspired by G. E. Moore and his *Principia Ethica*. Keynes explains, however, in his fascinating essay that what they 'got from Moore was by no means entirely what he offered' them. They were not interested in ethical theory, general rules and traditional wisdom. They discarded Moore's morals, therefore, while accepting his religion, 'meaning by "religion" one's attitude towards oneself and the ultimate, and by "morals" one's attitude towards the outside world and the intermediate'. And the essence of his religion was for them that

nothing mattered except states of mind, our own and other people's, of course, but chiefly our own. These states of mind were not associated with action or achievement or with consequences. They consisted in timeless, passionate states of contemplation and communion. ... The appropriate subjects of passionate contemplation and communion were a beloved person and beauty and truth, and one's prime objects in life were love, the creation and enjoyment of aesthetic experience and the pursuit of knowledge. Of these love came a long way first.

Keynes saw himself that this religion 'closely followed the English puritan tradition of being chiefly concerned with the salvation of our own souls. The divine resided within a closed circle. There was not a very intimate connection between "being good" and "doing good".' It was not a 'modern "social service" pseudo-religion, but altogether unworldly.' 'Thus we were brought up—with Plato's absorption in the good in itself, with a scholasticism which outdid St Thomas, in calvinistic withdrawal from the pleasures and successes of Vanity Fair, and oppressed with all the sorrows of Werther. It did not prevent us from laughing most of the time.'

The reference to Werther is made here in jest, but a Romantic component, in the introspection and the preoccupation with love of these young men, is the distinctively modern element among the four mentioned. The absorption in the good in itself, the withdrawal from philistine pursuits, and even, in some individuals, the delight in the subtleties of argument, can all be paralleled in the Weimar and Jena we have described, and a closer examination would probably reveal other similarities in these two variants of what we may call a religion of culture, haunted by echoes of sectarian forms of belief. A third variant may be found among the New England writers of Emerson's time, among whom the influence of German transcendentalism is beyond doubt, whereas G. E. Moore's disciples seem to have had only a tenuous connection with the German tradition, chiefly through him. It was 'a very good state of mind indeed' to hear him singing German Lieder at the piano, and in spite of his repudiation of Kant and Hegel, he was a decidedly professional philosopher like them. As described by Keynes, he reminds us in the 'the pure and passionate intensity of his vision' of what is most attractive in the great German thinkers and writers, their singleminded simplicity and self-forgetful absorption in 'das Geistige'. 'The New Testament', Keynes writes, 'is a handbook for politicians compared with the unworldliness of Moore's chapter on "The Ideal".' Taking this as their guide, he and his friends, though there were great differences between them as individuals, and none of them held to the gospel in its purity for long, lived 'in the specious present'. 'We existed in the world of Plato's *Dialogues*; we had not reached the *Republic*, let alone the *Laws*.' As young men at the university in an age of peace and plenty, they quite properly held the world at a distance, as the Weimar writers had done in different circumstances, and like them, they were optimists, who believed in the steady growth of civilisation. Where they chiefly differed perhaps from any German group one can think of was in their sense of humour, their refusal to take themselves too seriously. In Leonard Woolfs's account of the group, an amplification and to some extent a revision of that by Keynes, we are reminded that frankness and humour had always marked the proceedings of the discussion society (The Apostles) in Trinity College that included G. E. Moore and most of the people mentioned above among its members. The Society had been in existence for more than a century and had well-established traditions of its own. Henry Sidgwick had described the Society, long before Moore's time, as filled by 'the spirit of the pursuit of truth with absolute devotion and unreserve by a group of intimate friends, who were perfectly frank with each other, and indulged in any amount of humorous sarcasm and playful banter, and yet each respects the other, and when he discourses tries to learn from him and see what he sees.'[11] We are strongly reminded of what Shaftesbury says in praise of 'a freedom of Raillery, a Liberty in decent Language to question everything', evidently a centuries-old practice among educated Englishmen.

To return to Germany after this excursus, which may help readers to find something in common between the purposes of Goethe's age and one at least nearer to our own, we must first qualify the generalisation that, in Germany, reform of political and social abuses was felt to be nobody's business. We have found individual exceptions to this rule in the history of Weimar itself before the French Revolution, and there were naturally more after an event which aroused hopes and fears in the whole of Europe. But the existing structure of society in this small state was too stable to be much affected by sporadic efforts, or by vague rumblings of discontent. In religious matters certainly the literary men, even Herder, were broad-minded in the extreme, sure as they were of the sympathy of the Duke. The cosmopolitanism of most of the educated class was genuine too, but freedom from class prejudice meant principally the claim of the cultivated, irrespective of their origins, to be treated as gentlemen. Otherwise, as we have said, they formed a consenting part of an 'estate society' in which class privileges were taken seriously and protected by law as well as by custom. This attitude was all of a piece with the prevailing political view, which became more strongly conservative and authoritarian than ever after the outbreak of the French Revolution. In Goethe's Sturm und Drang days in Weimar, when, as he says in the poem *Ilmenau*, he 'unwisely sang of courage and freedom', even the young Duke had been infected by the Rousseauistic notions which were making the ruling class temporarily lose its nerve, and for years Goethe had hoped and striven, in his position of influence, to correct some of the evils he then saw in society, but his efforts had ended in frustration. 'Wenn wir zum Guten dieser Welt gelangen, Dann heißt das Beßre Trug und Wahn', he made his Faust say, the second-best is good enough for us at a certain stage in life. After the Revolution, order, the maintenance of the traditional social hierarchy, seemed to him more important than justice. A kindly, paternal despotism was favoured by the cultivated in Weimar. Even in Goethe's relations with the University of Jena there was no suggestion of democracy, no question of decisions by majority vote after free discussion. There was no enthusiasm for popular education, and cultivation was regarded as reserved without question for the privileged few. The association of 'cultivation' with 'property' (Bildung und Besitz) was not an invention of the nineteenth century, for who in Weimar but the reasonably well-to-do had the leisure for culture or saw any attraction in many-sidedness? Patronage was indeed generously exercised, and many a poor boy was lifted by education or training out of his class, but this was no right that he could claim, but a benefit conferred from above, in the interests of the community, or perhaps chiefly of the ruling class, who needed skilled service.

That society was constituted as it was in the state of Weimar, and in Germany in general, that intellectual and artistic culture was concentrated in a thin layer at the top, inevitably had a profound effect on the literature and art of the time, and on the relation of the creative few to the mass of the people. Goethe and Schiller could never feel that they had the support of a whole nation, and often expressed regret at their comparative isolation, envying countries that possessed capitals 'where the best brains of a great kingdom are to be found in one centre, and stimulate each other in daily intercourse and rivalry', helped by the great libraries and museums and art-collections of a metropolis. Schiller thought seriously of moving to Berlin in his later years. Goethe contrasted the popularity enjoyed by a Béranger or a Burns with the reception of the work of Bürger, Voss, Schiller or himself by the German people. 'What is alive of my own songs?' he asked Eckermann. 'One or another is sometimes sung perhaps by a pretty girl at the piano, but among the people proper there is no echo whatever!... We Germans are of yesterday and a few centuries may have to pass, before enough culture penetrates our people and becomes sufficiently widespread for them to treasure beauty as the Greeks did, for them to show enthusiasm for a song, and for it to be possible to say of them, that it is a long time since they were barbarians.'[12] We have seen what a low opinion Goethe and Schiller had of the German public in the theatre, and in their *Xenien* they included a poem headed 'German Art' which ran:

Gabe von obenher ist ,was wir Schönes in Künsten besitzen,
  Wahrlich von unten herauf bringt es der Grund nicht hervor.
Muß der Künstler nicht selbst den Schößling von außen sich holen,
  Nicht aus Rom und Athen borgen die Sonne, die Luft?*

---

* The things of beauty that we have in the arts are a gift from above, for in truth the ground below does not of itself produce them. Must not the artist himself procure his cuttings from abroad, borrowing from Rome and Athens the sun and air to make them grow?

It is for this reason that Goethe's methods in the Weimar Theatre and the art competitions had to be so dictatorial, and for this reason that ambitious ventures like the *Horen* failed so soon.

Some of the disadvantages under which German writers and artists laboured are at other times ascribed by Goethe to the decentralisation resulting from political separatism, as when he complained to Zelter about the shifts to which he had to resort in Weimar as manager of the theatre, whereas Zelter could do such remarkable things in his concerts in Berlin. But he was grateful too for many good results that came from the multiplicity of cultural centres in Germany and the rivalry between the patrons of the arts. It is clearly for this reason that opera, for instance, and the theatre in general, enjoyed and still enjoy so much more local support than in this country, where arts that can hardly hope to be self-supporting have never been encouraged to anything like the same extent as they were in Germany, in a large number of provincial centres at once, through the patronage of small courts. That for similar reasons the cultivated few in Germany led relatively lonely lives must have encouraged a greater concentration on the things of the mind that can be pursued in solitude. We have seen how Schiller praises, as one of the consolations in life that has not lost its value for him with advancing age, 'Beschäftigung, die nie ermattet', the tireless industry of the German literati, on which Mme de Staël remarked, and which she found quite natural in small towns where 'time fell drop by drop'.

These are some of the contingent elements in the Weimar attitude to culture, features in which the effect of the particular circumstances of the time is now much more evident to us than we can expect it to have been to contemporaries. They are features which we are not likely to find in English thought about culture, even when it has been influenced by German writers. Speaking in a very general way, we find English writers on these topics tending to be liberal and democratic, where the Germans are conservative and authoritarian. The difference is still more marked between the attitude of the English and the German educated man towards political activity, at least until the time of the Weimar Republic, and the revival of democratic ideas after the National-Socialist interlude. A characteristic German pronouncement is that of Thomas Mann in the *Reflections of a Non-political Man* (1917) about the special strength of the Germans which lies in *cultivation* and *obedience*. 'Politics make men coarse, vulgar and stupid. Only the cultivation of the mind makes men free. Institutions are of little account, states of mind of supreme account. Become better yourself and everything will be better.' Later, of course, he saw that 'this dangerous indifference to freedom had fearfully avenged itself, that the absence of political experience in the cultivated Germans and their scorn for freedom had resulted in the enslavement of the citizen to the state and to power-politics', and in exile he made every effort to correct what now seemed to him a fatal tendency in German intellectuals.[12]

It was, however, deeply rooted in German history and is another, and perhaps in its consequences the most regrettable, of the peculiarly German features in the Weimar view of culture. An attitude to politics that had become traditional under authoritarian government, where the individual citizen felt himself to be powerless, had been strengthened by Lutheranism, with its passive acceptance of the will of 'Caesar' in this wicked world, its concentration on personal salvation—a very different point of view, as Troeltsch has pointed out, from that prevailing in Calvinist countries, where the right to rebellion against unjust authority was not easily renounced.[14] The secular substitute for salvation, 'Bildung', now becomes hypostatised in its turn, a quietistic philosophy of life having been meanwhile much encouraged by the vogue of Pietism in the early eighteenth century. Books are written with no real hope that events will be affected by them, as we shall find Fichte admitting, their authors being absorbed in speculation for its own sake, or in the pleasures of the imagination. Even before the Revolution, Schiller had written, in *The Gods of Greece*:

Was unsterblich im Gesang soll leben
Muß im Leben untergehn,*

and when he returned to poetry, after a passing moment of hope
that through the Revolution reason might now be combined with
power, he relapsed into the traditional German attitude and gave
it ever new expression in his philosophical poems. The poem
with which he greeted the coming of the nineteenth century, for
instance, ends with these words:

In des Herzens heilig stille Räume
Mußt du fliehen aus des Lebens Drang:
Freiheit ist nur in dem Reich der Träume,
Und das Schöne blüht nur im Gesang.†
(*Der Antritt des neuen Jahrhunderts*)

The same disregard of the aspect of power comes out also in
Schiller's hopes for the future of Germany. These are most clearly
expressed in the draft of a poem, later called 'German Greatness'
by one of its editors. It was written probably at about the same
time as the last one quoted, in June 1801. A few months earlier
the Peace of Lunéville had confirmed the cession of the left bank
of the Rhine to France. The great powers in Europe, Schiller
begins by saying, are France and Britain, and Germany is at their
mercy. Has the German then any grounds for self-respect?
Schiller assures himself that he has, because Germany would still
continue to exist as a cultural nation even if the Holy Roman
Empire were to be destroyed. He sees that there is a great risk
of this happening as the German princes, backed by Napoleon,
scramble for territory at the expense of other 'estates' of the old
Reich, the ecclesiastical territories, Free Towns and Imperial
Knights. This tumbledown house of the Empire is, however,
inhabited by a vigorous race, strong in the spirit and with no
reason to be ashamed of its *cultural* achievements or its character.
Schiller consoles himself with the thought that 'he who cultivates

* That which is to live for ever in song must perish in life.

† From the hurly-burly of life you must retreat to the sacred calm spaces of
the heart: there is no freedom but in the realm of dreams, and the beautiful
blossoms only in song.

the spirit' is bound in the end to prevail, if there is any meaning in the life of man, if there is a rational purpose working itself out in the world—Schiller's words imply the belief in a secularised form of Providence. He praises the German language for its unrivalled expressiveness, much as Fichte was to do in his *Addresses to the German Nation* in 1807.[8] 'Our language', he says, 'will rule the world', and not only the German language, perhaps, for the German, with his passion for cultivation, 'is chosen by the World Spirit to work, during the conflict of time, at the eternal structure of human culture, to preserve what time brings'. So the final German triumph will be not merely the day of greatness that every nation in its turn enjoys in history, but the culmination of all humanity's efforts, 'the harvest of the whole of time'. We see Schiller here at the stage so well analysed by Friedrich Meinecke in his *Weltbürgertum und Nationalstaat*. Meinecke points to similar utterances of Wilhelm von Humboldt, Novalis and others. Humboldt gave up his civil service post on his marriage, to devote himself entirely to cultivating his mind.[15] The Germans, he was convinced, were destined to be 'the purest mirror of human potentialities' in the modern world, as the Greeks had been of old, to be 'das eigentliche Menschheitsvolk'. The state should interfere as little as possible in the private life of the individual, who needs the maximum of freedom in order to devote himself to his true aim in life, 'the highest and best-proportioned cultivation of his capacities so that they form a whole'. He was therefore better employed following his wide intellectual and aesthetic interests than in attempting, as a civil servant, to cope with the practical problems of government.

All this sounds splendidly idealistic, but history reminds us of the great dangers that result from extreme subjectivity of this kind when it is used to justify action or inaction, in the real world of men. We begin by conditioning ourselves to feel that the things that annoy us, and that we cannot change in the outside world, political and social conditions, for instance, are not really important, that, as Stoicism and Christianity taught long ago, a man has a higher and a lower self, and that it is only the lower self or

the body that hungers for materialistic satisfactions. With training we can progressively kill the desire for them, live in the mind
and be free. It is, as Sir Isaiah Berlin has said, a very grand form
of the doctrine of sour grapes. Kant builds his moral theory on
this idea, that what really matters to us is a certain state of the
true, inner, higher self. Fichte and the Romantics generally
refine on Kant's moral and metaphysical ideas and purge them of
any remaining traces of common sense, which they associate
with the utilitarian Enlightenment. Morality and art and truth
come to be regarded as resulting from a mystical inner vision, to
follow which the creative artist, writer or musician, and those
who love him, must be ready for any sacrifice, for what matters
above all is integrity, that a man should be true to his inner self.
Fichte founds his philosophy on the single principle of the 'Ich-
bewußtsein', the consciousness of self. He made such a bewilder-
ing number of distinctions however between the various kinds of
'ego'—divine, general, absolute, human, individual, finite—
that the ordinary reader frequently misunderstood him. Like
Goethe's Baccalaureus, he might then confuse the absolute ego,
God, who forms the world out of himself and in himself through
creative imagination ('Einbildungskraft'), with the individual
ego, and believe that 'the world did not exist until he created
it'.

In a man like Fichte, the retreat to the inward does not mean
true renunciation. One impression that is left with us quite
clearly by all his writings is that of a strong, even overbearing
personality, and this is how he appears as Hölderlin's Alabanda
in the novel *Hyperion*. He is always mentioned alongside
Freiherr vom Stein as one of the principal inspirations of the
Germans in the movement that led to the War of Liberation. His
influence was exercised above all through his *Addresses to the
German Nation*, one of the most important documents for the
understanding of the further development of the idea of cultivation, contending as it now did with the idea which emerged
during the Romantic period of a political, as opposed to a purely
cultural, nationalism. The *Addresses* are at the same time a

penetrating criticism of some of the weaknesses we have mentioned.

Prussia, selfishly passive since 1795 in its desire to retain a hold over its new Polish acquisitions, had in desperation at last turned on the French and been completely routed at Jena, and Fichte gave his *Addresses* in a Berlin already occupied by the French. As we have seen, he had long had the reputation of a Jacobin, but what mattered most to him now was his nation, of which he had come to think as a 'self' also deserving freedom. He had understood how the inspiration of the democratic idea and vigorous leadership had transformed the French people, and saw no reason why what had happened in France should not happen in Germany too. He had also by this time, from a study of Machiavelli and from personal contacts in Berlin, acquired a new understanding of the indispensability of efficiently organised power for the maintenance of a state.

Appealing from the beginning to 'Germans as such', not to Prussians, Saxons and so on, he impresses upon his audience of Berlin aristocrats and intellectuals that the Germans must rely entirely upon themselves, that the cause of their collapse is weak political leadership, masquerading as liberalism and humanity— one can easily be too tolerant and cultivated for this wicked world, he implies—and he declares that the real enemy is selfishness in the educated class, resulting from a false idea of education. This ardent advocate of freedom maintains now that, before a pupil can be trusted with freedom, he must be conditioned into willing 'the good', so that he cannot possibly will anything else, and can be completely trusted by his teachers. 'You must make him anew, make him in such a way that he cannot will otherwise than you will that he should.' This character-training can best be carried out in boarding-schools, away from contaminating influences.

The pupils must be weaned from old conceptions of an otherworldly religion and educated to a new religious humanism, which seeks satisfaction entirely on this earth. Man must now make himself. The Germans are indicated as the leaders in this movement, because of the purity of their language! Their record in the Reformation and in the achievements of their Free Towns (recently abolished), 'the only republics in modern Europe for centuries', proves what they can do when they are true to themselves. Men must enlarge their conception of the self until it includes first their nation and then the whole of humanity, willingly sacrificing themselves for their nation, finding a vicarious immortality in its independent continuance.

Without political power behind it, the cultural nation—which is all that Herder, it will be remembered, had desired—would never maintain itself in being. Fichte strongly criticises the intellectuals of his day for being so 'uncommitted', as the phrase now goes. He wishes that 'it might become the custom in our nation to think not simply as an amusement and, as it were, as an experiment to see what will result, but as if what we think were expected to be true and really to count in life.' Thought has a great task before it, because 'the battle of arms is over. We begin now, if we will to do so, the new battle of principles, of manners, of character.'

Ten years before Fichte delivered this counterblast to the doctrine of cultivation for cultivation's sake, his *Theory of Knowledge* had been one of the principal inspirations of German Romanticism, along with the French Revolution and Goethe's *Wilhelm Meister*, according to Friedrich Schlegel's already mentioned 'Fragment'. This was in the first or Jena phase of what came to be called the German Romantic movement, usually dated from the first appearance of its periodical, the *Athenäum*, in 1798, immediately after the abandonment by Schiller of *Die Horen*. A. W. Schlegel, the editor of this new and equally highbrow review, which also lasted for just three years, had come to Jena in 1796, as we saw, to review for the *Allgemeine Literatur-Zeitung* and to help Schiller with *Die Horen*. He continued to live there till 1800, with his brilliant, sharp-tongued wife Karoline, and there his younger brother Friedrich joined him at times, with Dorothea Veit, Moses Mendelssohn's daughter, from Berlin. He was there for about a year soon after A.W.'s arrival, and for about two years from 1799. The Jena Romantics and their work might well have been included in our account of cultural activities in the state of Weimar, but their story is so long and complicated that it seemed better to reserve it for later treatment, especially in view of the fact that despite the chronological overlap, the Romantics belong to the next generation, and show so many divergencies from the Weimar Classicism of which they are initially an offshoot that they may well be regarded as opening a new phase in German culture.

Nevertheless, the Romantics stand in very many respects, as was inevitable, on the shoulders of their predecessors, and they take for granted a great deal that had not been easily won. It was not to the same extent a matter of deep conviction with them, but rather a set of ideas with which, as quick-witted intellectuals, they liked to experiment. Their agile minds might soon have found an accommodation between their literary theories and those of Weimar, for to begin with they were enthusiastic admirers of Goethe, some of the first critics in Germany to appreciate his work as it is generally valued now, but they soon became involved in personal differences, especially with Schiller, now a firm ally of Goethe. As the author of the closest study of this conflict says, 'the exaggerations of the Romantic programme were only a consequence of these quarrels'.[16]

Needless to say, the early Romantics accept with enthusiasm the Weimar ideal of personal cultivation, 'Bildung'. An anthology of aphorisms bearing on 'Bildung' could be compiled from their writings, especially from F. Schlegel and Novalis. Even more for them than for Goethe, cultivation is the new form of salvation. F. Schlegel writes therefore: 'The Summum Bonum and the One Thing Needful is culture', or: 'Do not squander your faith and love on the political world, but offer up your inmost being in the divine world of scholarship and art to swell the sacred fiery stream of eternal culture (Bildung).'[17] The early Romantics are nothing if not cultivated. They set a standard in the range of their intellectual and artistic interests which has seldom been reached since. To begin with, they idolised Goethe, wrote excellent appreciations of his mature works as they appeared and spread the gospel of Weimar culture with missionary zeal, particularly in Berlin. Here in 1797 Friedrich Schlegel already found some in Jewish circles who shared his enthusiasm far more readily, for special reasons, than the normal educated German.

In the last thirty years of the eighteenth century the Berlin Jews had been granted a certain measure of emancipation. There were wealthy merchants among them whose wives and daughters had leisure, and both the desire and the requisite intelligence to make up for the defects of their formal education. They took an interest in music, the theatre and literature, and in their cosmopolitan drawing-rooms anyone was welcome who shared their interests. It was here, in 1789, that Wilhelm von Humboldt was first infected with the love of general culture by Henriette Herz and her friends, Dorothea Veit, who left her husband to marry Friedrich Schlegel, and Rahel Levin, who eventually, in 1814, married Varnhagen von Ense. In 1798 Schleiermacher praised these salons to his sister in the highest terms, and they retained their importance down to the French occupation of Berlin. Rahel's attic in the Jägerstrasse in particular was the centre of a Goethe cult. It was a circle, as Brinckmann says, 'into which everyone, royal princes, foreign ambassadors, artists, scholars or business men of every rank, countesses and actresses . . . strove for admission with equal eagerness, and in which each person was worth neither more nor less than he himself was able to validate by his cultivated personality'.[18] The Berlin Jews became for a short time a link between 'a declining and an as yet unstabilised social group, the nobility and actors'—exactly the same groups outside normal middle-class society from whom Wilhelm Meister learned to *be* someone, and not simply to count for what he could do. It was natural that they should welcome an ideal of 'noble humanity' potentially accessible to all men as such, just because of their own lack of an accepted status in society, and the diffusion of Weimar humanism throughout Germany was greatly helped by them.

The homage publicly paid by the Romantics to Goethe does

not extend much beyond the end of the century, for by this time they felt that they had established their own claims to consideration and, having never suffered from excessive modesty, held more strongly than ever that, to use the words of Novalis, 'Goethe would and must be excelled'. They began therefore to extend to Goethe the depreciatory criticism to which Schiller had provoked at least Friedrich Schlegel almost from their first acquaintance. Friedrich had however learnt something from Schiller, for even his notion of the Romantic writer is opposed to that of the Classic at first in very much the same way as Schiller's 'reflective' ('sentimentalisch') type to his 'naïve'. Without embarking on these deep waters, we may here simply note the quite astonishing variety of literatures that came within the purview of one or the other of the Schlegel brothers. They include Greek, in which Friedrich was a really considerable scholar, French, English, Italian, Spanish and later Sanskrit. This was the beginning of the serious comparative study of both literature and language in Germany. It is 'Bildung' with a vengeance, and goes beyond even Goethe's 'inclusiveness' on the purely literary side, though the Schlegels, who shared Goethe's interest in art also, left science at least to others of the fraternity, like Schelling, Ritter and Steffens, with whom it became an *à priori* 'philosophy of nature', where the weakness of Goethe's approach to science was dangerously exaggerated. The effect was to put Germany a good generation behind France and England in the empirical, experimental study of science. We have here a parallel to the neglect of politics, a similar exclusive preoccupation with what the mind can create out of its own resources. But in all matters concerned with 'Humanität' as Herder had conceived it the curiosity of the Romantics was boundless. Among the most fruitful of their discoveries was the neglected German literature of the Middle Ages, together with the folk-tale, the folk-song and all kinds of folklore at home and abroad. With the literature of the Middle Ages they rediscovered their religion.

In Berlin in 1797 Friedrich Schlegel became a close friend of the theologian Schleiermacher, the very type of a cultivated man, but one with an irrepressible religious sense. Within a month of meeting Schleiermacher, Friedrich Schlegel was writing to Novalis: 'I am thinking of founding a new religion. . . . There are subjects left, which neither philosophy nor poetry can deal with. Such a subject, I think, is God, and I have a completely new view of it.' Kant and Fichte had brought philosophy to the threshold of religion, he went on. 'Goethe's *Bildung*, from the other side, strolls in the propylaea of the temple.' Novalis could make a new synthesis of these ideas and between them they would reveal the result to their age in gospels, epistles, apocalypses and so on.[19] It was Schleiermacher who convinced the Romantics that the new culture they were trying to build up would not permeate the whole of life unless it became a religion, and soon he presented to them in his *Addresses on Religion, for the Cultivated among those who Despise It* a view of religion that an educated man could accept, knowing well how few of them in Germany by this time retained any positive beliefs. Then Novalis directed their attention to a model in the past of a religious culture that had penetrated and transformed life, the Christian culture of the Middle Ages in Europe. His picture was as hopelessly idealised as Schiller's of Greece, but it served in the same way to focus the longings of the present. In this unfinished work, *Christendom or Europe*, we find too the quite independent expression of the same conviction that fills Schiller, Humboldt and Fichte, that 'Germany goes its slow but sure way in advance of the other European countries. While they are occupied with war, speculation and the party spirit, the German cultivates himself industriously to be able to participate in a higher epoch of culture, and this advance must in the course of time give him a marked ascendency over the others.' Or as he puts it in an aphorism, using the language of the fairy-tale: 'The German has long been (silly) Jacky. But soon he may well be the Jack of all Jacks. It will be the same with him as it is often said to be with stupid children: he will be alive and have gained sense when his precocious brothers and sisters have long been mouldering in the grave, and he is sole master in the house.'

The rapid changes in the external world of the Napoleonic era could not but leave their mark on the ideas of the Romantics, however faithfully they followed their inward light. Thus their cosmopolitanism, as we saw with Fichte, turned imperceptibly into nationalism, and their freethinking, in the case of several of the leading Romantics, into more or less orthodox Catholicism, not through any clear process of reasoning, but under the influence of events. Both tendencies were reinforced by Burke's *Reflections on the French Revolution*. Herder's historicism, and the disastrous failure, in the view of most Germans of the educated classes, of French attempts to refashion society in accordance with rationalistic theories, fitted in well with Burke's insistence on the value of old institutions, embodying the wisdom of the past. The forces of legitimacy and orthodoxy, defending vested interests of all kinds, sought before long the help of Romantics like Friedrich Schlegel. Later, in Austria under Metternich, Prussia under Frederick William IV and Russia under Nicolas I, advocates of the alliance of throne and altar repeatedly drew on German Romantic ideas.

It was Hegel who finally summed up the German thought of the preceding generation in the most ambitious of the many systems of German philosophy, Absolute Idealism. It held almost undisputed sway during his years as professor in Berlin (1818–31) and for ten or twenty years to follow. Even in its decay it provided a framework for Marx. Where Hegel saw in the concrete events of history nothing but mind, the self-revelation of pure spirit (in his youth he would have said, of God), Marx saw all ideas as the product of concrete events, especially of economic change. Both use the same dialectical method, interpreting history as if it were a continuous logical argument, a method foreshadowed by much that we have found in the leading Weimar writers. Like them too, they are exceedingly well-informed, continually comparing one feature with another in the history of civilisation, finding analogies and asking intelligent questions. Hegel's was a philosophy of history and of the state that seemed to supply an answer to the problems of a politically reactionary age, when a strong undercurrent of liberalism was challenging institutions held to be sacred by the ruling class. It seemed to do justice to the movement of history by representing no stage as final and all as rational in their different ways. Like the Weimar thinkers, Hegel was able to find enough of the ideal in the actual to justify his loyal support of the system of government under which he lived in Prussia, even looking upon the state as the divine on earth, the realisation of the Idea, and therefore a law unto itself.

Largely under Hegel's influence a kind of political mysticism came to be accepted in Germany, to which the liberal-minded Ernst Troeltsch still appeals in 1916 when defending the German idea of freedom against the criticisms of Allied writers. 'Princes and officials regard themselves as the first servants of the state, the citizen feels himself to be a member of the state organism. They are all organs of one sovereign whole, and in dutiful devotion they unceasingly create it. Their freedom consists of duties rather than rights, or at least of rights which are at the same time duties.'[20] The disentangling of the rational and the irrational elements in views like these presents the historian of political thought with a particularly difficult task, but notions like those to which we have pointed in Fichte and the rest, gradually modified by the continued impact of events, the War of Liberation and the establishment of new institutions of the power-state by Stein and Scharnhorst, the unification of Germany under Prussian leadership and the rapid industrialisation of the country, are clearly one important constituent. The history of the century between 1815 and 1914 is reflected in the fact that, for foreigners at least, the German word 'Kultur' had changed into a portent. It had come to be as closely associated with the idea of national power as 'Bildung' was by now with 'Besitz'. In *Unsere Zukunft* (1912) General Bernhardi wrote, for example: 'Thus it is in the general interest of civilisation our *duty* to strive for an extension of our colonial possessions and to unite nationally, even if not politically, the Germans scattered throughout the world, because we regard German Kultur as the most necessary factor in human progress.'[21] Even Meinecke appeals to similar arguments, though in more moderate language, when he asks himself, in August 1914, what Germany is fighting for. 'It is through its achievements for the spirit of humanity that a nation justifies all its selfish strivings, including its struggle for power and its wars. . . . If we are victorious, the victory is not only for us, but for humanity too. We look up to the eternal stars above and confidently entrust our fate to their guidance. "Every nation", Schiller calls to us, "has its day in history, but the day of the German is the harvest of the whole of time."'[22]

The corruption of humane ideals through the pursuit of national power is not, of course, a phenomenon peculiar to Germany, and German critics of British 'hypocrisy' have long been in the habit of pointing to Kipling and English talk about the White Man's burden. 'Why beholdest thou the mote that is in thy brother's eye . . .' is a reminder seldom heeded by cultural propagandists, however, and there will be few of us who do not feel that with Hitler and Goebbels heights of dishonesty were reached that compromised the word 'Kultur' almost past mending.

3. 'BILDUNG' IN THE SAME PERIOD

The gradual degeneration of the idea of national culture was accompanied by a parallel development of the notion of personal cultivation. In a famous monologue, Schiller had made his Wallenstein say that the things of the mind shed a radiance that gives delight but makes no one rich, whereas worldly success comes only through an alliance with the forces of evil.[23] This distinction between the inner and the outer life of man, oversharply drawn for reasons which have been discussed, could not be maintained by the great majority of those who considered themselves educated, in an age of material expansion, and the association of the idea of culture with that of social status, already implicit, though seldom acknowledged, as we have seen, in the essentially aristocratic structure of Weimar society, came to be regarded as normal. To illustrate current opinion in 1893,

Friedrich Paulsen quotes from a newspaper the sentence: 'A man apparently belonging to the educated (cultivated) classes caused a stir through his unusual behaviour in the street.' It is implied here that education or cultivation, for which modern German characteristically uses the same word 'Bildung', can be recognised by external signs, and the normal view at this time is, Paulsen says, that the educated do not work with their hands, that they dress and behave 'properly' and can hold their own in conversation. It is a fairly reliable sign if they use foreign words correctly, and if they know foreign languages there is no doubt at all about their 'Bildung'. To be considered educated or cultivated at the end of the nineteenth century, a man must normally, as a minimum, have attended a secondary school and passed the school-leaving examination, which included two foreign languages. He might have left school in what corresponds roughly to the fifth form ('Untersekunda'), that is, before beginning the more specialised sixth-form work which prepared pupils for the university. In much the same way, an English boy could leave his grammar school in the middle school and still qualify for a 'white collar' occupation.[24]

Among the many factors that would seem to have contributed towards this transformation of the idea of free humane cultivation may be mentioned in particular the reform of the Prussian educational system initiated by Wilhelm von Humboldt and widely imitated in other states, and the constantly increasing use made of examinations for the selection of aspirants to the civil service and the professions, a measure that was unavoidable in an age when patronage and personal recommendation could no longer produce the numbers required. The population was growing rapidly, communications being transformed, trade and industry expanding, and Germany was fast becoming a highly organised, unified nation. Humboldt's philosophy of education was the 'Humanität' for which he had striven throughout his mature life and which he naturally considered the best basis for true education for life, as opposed to vocational training. In the university his influence was certainly beneficent, helping to produce a system that, through the encouragement of learning for its own sake, was to prove for generations a model to all the world of the university as a place of research. But the complete separation of secondary from primary education, and the imposition of a classical education, with a new emphasis on Greek instead of Latin, and on the content instead of the grammatical form of what was read, though an admirable preparation for the best students, did not sufficiently allow either for the different interests, capacities and vocational needs of those boys of average intelligence or lower who were able to secure a higher education, or for the proper use of the vast reservoir of talent that could have been provided by the under-privileged portion of the population, who went to the 'schools for the people' and were not encouraged to think too much for themselves, lest they should lose their traditional respect for their social superiors, and possibly the religious beliefs which were thought to foster it.

What Humboldt failed to realise was that the old pre-revolutionary kind of society, with its more or less fixed stations or 'estates', though it lingered on well into the nineteenth century in Germany, was nevertheless doomed there too. Freiherr vom Stein was busily breaking down barriers between the social classes, especially through his Municipal Reform Edict, and the privileges of the nobility were being much curtailed in the south German states belonging to the Confederation of the Rhine, at the very time when Humboldt was organising a system of secondary education following ideals essentially bound up with the old type of society.[25] The maladjustments that resulted have left their mark on German education until our own time and the ostensible ideal that was being followed, true 'Bildung', was seldom attained because, as Paulsen points out, the educational ideals of any age are always determined by the social élite, and the social élite of Germany at this time was steadily changing its character.[26]

In a somewhat similar way, the triumph of the Reformation in Germany had re-established a clerical ideal at a time when in France and England everything was making for rapid secularisation. After the Thirty Years War, the leading states of the Empire began to imitate France in the rationalisation of government by means of a highly centralised system of administration, which called for many more trained civil servants. A strong impetus was thus given to the utilitarian and socially rewarding aspects of education in the Schools for Noblemen (Ritterakademien) now set up in many places for the dominant social class. The notion of a free cultivation of the mind and heart began, as we have seen, as the private reaction of a few independent spirits like Wieland, Herder, Goethe and Schiller, inspired by Shaftesbury, Rousseau and the Greeks as Winckelmann saw them, a reaction against clericalism and utilitarianism alike. It was a splendid ideal for those who had the ability and the means to follow it, but in the days when railways were being built and the Customs Union was being created, there were few who wished to use the world simply to develop their own personality, to turn it in this sense into their 'property', as Humboldt put it, and many who were eager to learn how to develop the forces of nature and to make their mark among their fellowmen. Schoolmasters filled with the old ideals of 'inwardness' were inevitably in conflict with most of their pupils. Yet culture, or a reputation for culture, still retained its attraction, as a symbol of status at least, with the new élite, of businessmen and administrators of middle-class origin, and the more widely it was sought, the more diluted and external-ised the content of individual culture became, until the cultivated man was only too often replaced by what Nietzsche called the 'philistine of culture'. Much of Nietzsche's satire is of course directed against countrymen of his who are very well informed about all sorts of dead cultures, but do not seem to him to know what culture really means, so that he finds Germany after the Franco-Prussian War utterly undistinguished. Even his positive ideas are largely evoked by this state of things.

It was natural that after an age so rich in genius as that of Goethe and the Romantics, poets and prose-writers alike should for a generation or two find it difficult to achieve an original outlook and style. Even before 1800 Goethe and Schiller saw examples enough around them of young poets who would not, in their view, have produced anything if they had not found a poetic language and a stock of clichés at hand which made it comparatively easy to make up neatly turned verses on conventional subjects. As we have seen, Schiller had to rely for copy on poets, or rather poetesses, of this type in editing the last volume or two of the *Musenalmanach*. Derivative writers, 'forced talents' or 'epigonoi' as they have been called, were common in the rather dull half-century that followed the Napoleonic Wars, when a return to normality was the desire of those in authority, but the general public had still so much to discover in the golden age of German literature, which only now gradually came to be adequately appreciated, that they were ready to welcome much more of the same kind, dramas only too closely modelled on Schiller, novels of 'Bildung' and Romantic fantasies, or nature and love poetry that seemed to come from the heart.

The inward life, the full development by a man of his interests and capacities, of what he is in himself and not of what impresses or is useful to other people, continued to be extolled on the highest level by a Schopenhauer or a Stifter, for example. For Schopenhauer, the contemplative life is the sole means of eluding the blind urge of instinct, the irrational 'will' that leads to action, self-assertion, and thus inevitably to pain and suffering.

The man in whom the intellectual capacities preponderate [we read in a fine passage in the *Aphorismen zur Lebensweisheit*] can take the liveliest interest in life—and in fact cannot dispense with such interests— through the desire to *know*, unhampered by the will. This interest transports him to a region to which pain is in general a stranger, into the atmosphere of the carefree gods. The lives of others are passed in a daze, their every thought absorbed by the petty concerns of their personal welfare, by mean trifles of every kind, so that intolerable boredom assails them as soon as there is a break in their routine, and they are thrown back on themselves, only the wild fire of passion being capable of stirring the stagnant mass. But the man well-endowed with intellectual powers leads a life full of thought, variety and meaning; he is occupied with worthy and fascinating objects whenever he can give himself up to them, and he possesses a source of the purest pleasure in himself. He is stimulated from outside by the works of nature and the human scene, and further by the diverse achievements of the most gifted minds of all times and countries, which only he can really enjoy, because only he can understand and feel them. These choice spirits have therefore really lived for him, it is to him they have really addressed themselves, whereas the others only by chance pick up and half understand a fragment here and there. . . . . A man of this temper leads, in addition to his personal life, a second life, that of the mind, which gradually becomes the real aim of his existence, using the other only as a means. . . . Through continuous growth in insight and knowledge his inner life acquires an integration, an ever increasing intensity, wholeness and perfection, like a work of art in the making. To this the merely practical life, directed towards a man's personal welfare, forms a sad contrast, capable as it is of extension only in length and not in depth.[27]

It is disturbing, on reflection, to find that in this eloquent description of the intellectual life Schopenhauer expressly abandons all hope of a unified attitude to experience. For him, man lives in two worlds, and in this dualism Schopenhauer stands by no means alone among Post-Romantic German writers. Even Stifter in his *Nachsommer*, another work clearly nourished on the Weimar tradition of 'Bildung', does not sustain in us for long the serenity which is his aim. At the Rose House that he conjures up with great art, everything speaks of the humanising of man's environment by the exercise of a carefully formed taste and a sense of order and seemliness. Nature shows herself indeed a loving mother to man, if he takes the necessary measures to preserve her balance—singing-birds encouraged to nest in the garden obligingly keep the roses free from greenfly and the fruit-trees from all pests, while rabbits keep to their allotted territory and prefer the cabbage-stalks thrown to them to the bark of young trees. It is too good to be true. As a work of art, on a theme suggested by experience and elaborated by the poet's imagination into a harmonious and consistent whole, *Der Nachsommer* is delightful, but it is not convincing as an inter-pretation of life, for no vision of the ideal can magically transform stubborn realities.

Are we on the track here, one wonders, of an explanation of the existence of 'the two Germanies', a phrase which, in spite of German criticism, still has a plain meaning for foreign students of German culture between Goethe and Hitler? Is the fatal flaw in the philosophy of Goethe's Germany an over-confidence in the power of 'Geist', of the reason and imagination exercised as independently as possible of empirical knowledge? To say this is not to follow Marx in 'turning Hegel upside down'. It is simply to insist on what Baron von Hügel called 'the innate need of system that renders (the Germans) steady, but also obstinate; virile and brutal; profound and pedantic'. The same need, he continues, 'makes anything that is sufficiently theorised appear to a German as worthy of hearing or even of belief', so that whatever is 'daring, clear, paradoxical attracts *apart from the possibility of testing.*' (My italics). This tendency is contrasted by Baron von Hügel with the attitudes that result from the 'loosely-knit minds and moderate passions' of the British, who seldom reason things out to a logical conclusion.[28] We have seen what extravagant claims were made for the capacities of the free mind by the philosophers of German idealism, Fichte, for instance, and by early Romantic poets, but Schiller and even Goethe, wisest of men, could on occasions treat the deliverances of their own minds as absolute oracles. The great intellectual and artistic achievements of the age led writer after writer to express the hope that German thought would lead the world. But real life continued to present them all with insoluble problems, and nothing is more striking than the fact that so many fine minds in Germany, especially in the Romantic age and after, collapsed under the strain.

Under the influence of bold ideas, not sufficiently tested by experience, the factor of organised power in politics was neglected, as we have seen, by the liberals, the heirs of Weimar, and observation and experiment despised by the exponents of the 'Philosophy of Nature'. Is it not possible, we ask ourselves, that an excessive trust in the magic of thought, and perhaps a certain confusion, common among the German Romantics, between the aesthetic and the practical attitude towards the written word, the acceptance of the 'beautiful' as 'true', may have helped to bring about a cleavage between ideals and action? While the cultivated dreamed and theorised, the children of this world pursued their sectional aims in industry and politics. A remark like the following, by that clear-headed observer of the social scene, Theodor Fontane, certainly suggests that the educated classes suffered in Wilhelminian times from a kind of split personality: 'All pretend to have ideals. They never cease to prattle about the beautiful, the good and the true, and yet they only bow the knee to the golden calf.'

In this the Germans were not of course unique among the nations of Europe. The disillusioned wisdom of Christian thought, at least, according to Dr Reinhold Niebuhr, would see in their conduct something typically human.

In the collective life of man [Dr Niebuhr writes] most evil arises because finite men involved in the flux of time pretend that they are not so involved. They make claims of virtue, of wisdom and of power which are beyond their competence as creatures. These pretensions are the source of evil, whether they are expressed by kings and emperors or by commissars and revolutionary statesmen. But among the lesser culprits of history are the bland fanatics of western civilisation who regard the highly contingent achievements of our culture as the final form and norm of human existence.

In all these forms of fanaticism and pride, men prove that while men's freedom is the source of creativity, the pretension that they are more free of finite conditions than mortals can be generates destructiveness amidst the creativity of freedom.[29]

APPENDICES, REFERENCES
AND BIBLIOGRAPHY

THE STRUCTURE OF WEIMAR SOCIETY IN 1820 ON THE BASIS OF INCOME

(Adapted from H. Eberhardt, *Goethes Umwelt*, Weimar, 1951)

A. *Upper class* (600 to over 3,000 talers per annum)				
	I	II	III	IV
Income in talers per annum	Civil service Local government Police	Court personnel Court theatre Court music	Professional men Clergy Teachers	Merchants. Bank Innkeepers and Shopkeepers
2,000 and over	v. Goethe (3,100) v. Gersdorf (3,000) v. Fritsch (3,000) and three others (6)	Chief Equerry (2,125) (1)	(1)	Bertuch and Froriep (6,000, combined incom Ullmann (3,000) (banker) (3
1,500 to 2,000	Chancellor v. Müller Head of Treasury Treasury official (3)	Marshal of the Court Senior gentlemen-in-waiting Opera singer (male) (1,800) Master of Music (1,800) (5)		
1,000 to 1,500	Senior Treasury, Law and Consistory officials One colonel (16)	High Chamberlain of the Court Equerry 5 actors (10)	Headmaster of grammar school (1)	Elkan (1,200) (banker) Innkeepers; Elefant (1,065) Erbprinz (1,000) (3
900 to 1,000	Senior officials and law officers Mayor Magistrate (11)	Kirms (theatre administration) (1)	Physician and surgeon to the Duke (2)	Shopkeepers (3
800 to 900	August v. Goethe (Treasury official) One captain (2)	Actors (2)	Apothecary Advocates (5)	Shopkeeper (1
700 to 800	Officials Librarian (8)	Theatre manager Actor (2)	Advocates (2)	Shopkeeper (1
600 to 700	Officials Secretaries (8)	Ladies-in-waiting Actor (3)	Clergymen Grammar-school masters (5)	Shopkeepers (5

V	VI	VII	Pensioners	Total
Master-craftsmen	Lower-grade craftsmen, etc.	Unskilled workers		
				(11)
				(8)
				(30)
				(17)
(1)			(1)	(12)
				(13)
			(2)	(23)

B. *Master-craftsmen class* (200 to 600 talers per annum)

	I	II	III	IV
500 to 600	Officials Secretaries (20)	Secretaries Chef Actors Chorus master Leader of orchestra (14)	Deacon Cantor (Court Church) Advocates (6)	Shopkeepers (8)
400 to 500	Secretaries Officials Clerks (17)	Cook Head keeper Veterinary surgeon (10)	Sacristan Teachers Medalmaker (4)	Shop- and innkeepers
300 to 400	Secretaries Clerks (36)	Upper servants (men and women) Actors Musicians (32)	Cantor (Town Church) Language teachers Court barber-surgeon (7)	Shop- and innkeepers (12)
200 to 300	Clerks Lieutenant (52)	Clerks Cooks Silver-cleaners Musicians (49)	Sacristan Barber-surgeons Teachers (12)	Shop and innkeepers

C. *Journeyman class* (under 200 talers per annum)

	I	II	III	IV
100 to 200	Clerks Messengers Sergeant of gendarmerie Actors (52)	Lackeys Ladies' maids Coachmen Actors Members of chorus (133)	Teachers Barber-surgeons (6)	Shop- and Innkeepers Hawkers (13)
under 100	Messengers (41)	Palace man- and maidservants (45)	Private (6)	Innkeepers Hawkers (13)
income not stated	(4)	(7)	(2)	
Totals	(276)	(314)	(59)	(7)

V	VI	VII	Pensioners	
Baker Butcher Tanner Printer (4)			(4)	(56)
Baker Butcher Soapmaker Typefounder Engraver Lithographer (6)			(3)	(47)
6 bakers 2 goldsmiths 2 engravers etc. (21)			(6)	(114)
7 bakers 6 butchers 6 shoemakers 4 tailors etc. (85)			(11)	(213)

V	VI	VII		
32 shoemakers 30 tailors 7 coopers 6 locksmiths etc. (217)	Shop-assistants Chemists' assistants Clerks Compositors Printers Engravers (51)	Men-servants Coachmen (27)	(19)	(518)
Craftsmen (107)	Journeymen (377)	Coachmen Labourers Maid-servants, etc. (840)	(46)	(1,475)
(16)			(149)	(178)
(457)	(428)	(867)	(241)	(2,715)

CULTURE AND RELATED IDEAS FROM CICERO TO HERDER[1]

THE key phrase about the cultivation of the mind, 'cultura animi', which was revived by the Humanists of the Renaissance and eventually gave rise to cultura, Kultur, culture, etc., in the vernaculars, occurs only once in Cicero, in a passage which reads: 'A field, though fertile, cannot be productive without cultivation, nor a mind without teaching. The cultivation of the mind (cultura animi) is the business of philosophy. It removes imperfections, roots and all, and prepares minds for seed sowing. It imparts to them and, as one might say, sows, things which when come to maturity will produce abundant fruit.'[2] What is unique here is the metaphorical use of 'cultura', a word normally used only of the fields, but the notion of the cultivation of the self is common in Cicero and other Roman writers. It is generally expressed by means of the verb 'excolere' with an abstract object like 'the mind' or 'the abilities', and the noun denoting this process of improving by careful attention mind, body, manners, dress, speech and human accomplishments in general is 'cultus'. The past participle of 'colere' is applied with adjectival force to regions or communities, but not to individuals, meaning 'civilised' as opposed to 'barbarous'.

The philosophy that cultivated the mind was that of the Greeks, the Socratic pursuit of wisdom, to which the Romans still ascribed an ethical effect. Hellenistic ideas about 'paideia', which meant not merely the education of children but the never-ending pursuit of wisdom and cultivation by the individual as a primary aim in life, were widespread in the Roman world. According to M. Marrou, it was in this devotion to the things of the mind that the upper classes in the Greek colonies, after the breakdown of the city states, found the link that still bound them together. It is here, if anywhere, that we must look for the beginning of the idea of personal culture, 'Bildung'.

Le véritable héritier de la cité antique [says M. Marrou] ce n'est pas, comme on le dit souvent avec une nuance péjorative, l'individu, mais bien la personne humaine qui, libérée du conditionnement collectif, de l'encastrement totalitaire que lui imposait la vie de la cité, prend maintenant conscience d'elle-même, de ses possibilités, de ses exigences, de ses droits. La norme, la justification suprême de toute existence, communautaire ou individuelle, réside désormais dans l'homme, entendu comme personnalité autonome, justifiée en elle-même, trouvant, peut-être au-delà du Moi, mais à travers le Moi et sans renoncer jamais à son individualité, la réalisation de son être. Plus que jamais, l'homme grec se pense comme le centre et 'la mesure de toutes choses', mais cet humanisme a maintenant pris conscience de son exigence personnaliste: pour l'Hellénistique, l'existence humaine n'a pas d'autre but que d'atteindre à la forme la plus riche et la plus parfaite de personnalité.[3]

For the Greek 'paideia' Cicero uses 'humanitas', man's humanity as opposed to his animality, with some of the force of the Greek 'philanthropia'. It is an attitude arrived at only by men who can exercise imaginative sympathy, and it owes much to training. It was more natural to the Romans in general to think of man in terms of the social group with its inherited institutions, the Mediterranean city-state with its law and order, its arts and crafts, its comforts and luxuries. The word for civilisation viewed in this way is 'civilitas', the way of life of the townsman as opposed to the rustic, who lacks his 'urbanity'.

These words are the forerunners of our modern words for culture and civilisation. In their later development they continued of course to be affected by the historical circumstances in which they were used. In the Middle Ages, for instance, with the development of Christianity and the decay of the Roman towns, 'civilitas' became a narrow legal term, the root of 'city', and 'humanitas' came to mean either mankind considered collectively, or the creaturely as opposed to the spiritual in man, the 'all-too-human'. The idea of self-improvement by conscious effort was still alive, in the Christian virtue of 'moderatio' and the chivalric ideals of 'mâze' and 'zuht', which still echo the Aristotelian ethic of the golden mean, and are shared by the higher estates, the clergy and the military aristocracy, while the great mass of the people, the peasantry and presently the craftsmen and traders of the towns, have their own characteristic attitudes. It is interesting to note that in an Old French history of the crusades, 'urbanitas' is translated by 'cortoisie', for now the city as such no longer provides the best model of refined behaviour, but the king's court. Many features of the courtly ideal, which was rooted in the economic and social conditions of Europe between the Crusades and the Renaissance, lived on into the industrial age, so that Dibelius in his *England*, for instance, finds much in the 'gentleman ideal' which goes back to the notions of chivalry.

With the economic development of the Italian cities and the Revival of Learning many of the expressions already mentioned acquired a new lease of life, often by conscious imitation of the past, though the nature of the new society is reflected in the particular twist given to the old terms. 'Cultus animi' and 'cultura animi' are revived by the learned for self-cultivation, still with an ethical implication. 'Civilitas' can mean individual 'civility', but it is more usually applied to the civilisation of an advanced society, marked by external signs, which the age of discovery, with its new knowledge of backward peoples, prized more than ever. 'Humanitas' became of course from about 1400 the key-word of the Humanists, who combine Christian with Roman ideas. Man is for them made in God's image, and 'humanity' is all that is best in him. The notion of striving for perfection comes from Christian thought, but the emphasis is now laid on what he can do for himself, aided by the Ancients. Pico della Mirandola in 1486 (*Of the Dignity of Man*) makes God say to Adam at the Creation: 'I have made you neither heavenly nor earthly, neither mortal nor immortal, that you may form and train yourself, following what model and ideal you will. You can degenerate into a beast. You can rise to the highest regions of the divine.' The nature of man is a mixture of good and bad, but humility is going out of fashion, especially with the scholars, inspired to a new confidence and pride in man's achievement by their knowledge of antiquity, for them an age of God-like men.

'Civilitas' is still often used in Italy at this time as a synonym of 'humanitas'. It was Erasmus, in the early sixteenth century, who gave to 'humanitas' the fully developed meaning that was to be widely accepted. For him there is no conflict between Christian thought and the 'humanity' derived from the Ancients, in fact he can sometimes hardly keep himself from saying: 'Saint Socrates, pray for us!' In his controversy with Luther he insists on man's freedom of will, his capacity to struggle towards perfection, though he sees him as finally in need of divine grace. With him already, Prometheus is a symbol of human creative power. Yet however much Erasmus praised self-reliant activity, he never lost the humane attitude that is rooted in sympathy with one's fellowmen, and therefore found Luther's violent tone distasteful and harmful to the good cause. Gentleness and understanding he held to be best fostered by the study of the classics, 'literae humaniores', for the promotion of which he was restlessly active in western Europe, believing that such studies benefited also true religion, through the fuller understanding of Christian revelation which they made possible. It is in his spirit that in Cambridge fellows still pledge themselves to serve their college and professors the university 'as a place of education, religion, learning and research'.

In *Of the Advancement of Learning* (1605), Bacon gives to chapter 22, in the second book, the heading 'De cultura animi', and he shows himself conscious of the metaphor employed by speaking of 'husbandry', and by distinguishing between what is in our own power in the 'culture and cure of the mind of man' and what is not, any more than the nature of the soil or the weather are at the farmer's command. Descartes, Hobbes, Spinoza and others can be quoted to the same effect. As early as 1638, in Italy, Bernardo Davanzati uses 'cultura civile' in the sense of civilisation,[4] and Fr D. Bartoli calls personal cultivation simply 'cultura' in 1663, but it is Samuel Pufendorf, the great exponent of natural law, who first seems to have regarded 'cultura animi' as concerned with the training of men for their duties in society.

In the later editions (after 1684) of his most famous work, *De Jure Naturae et Gentium* (first published in 1672), Pufendorf discusses in Book II, chapter 4, the 'duties of a man towards himself in the cultivation of his mind as well as in the care of his body and of his life'. Man shares with the animals the instinct of self-preservation, but both because of his greater endowments, 'which permit a high and productive culture (cultura)', and because of his duty to society, he should take care not merely to preserve himself but to perfect himself as far as possible. A favourite thought of Goethe's is anticipated when Pufendorf claims that 'the more outstanding a person is in himself (sibi ipsi), the more able and worthy a citizen he is considered of the world. Therefore, as man studies to fulfil the laws of that sociableness, for which his Creator intended him, he should properly give his first attention to himself, since he will fulfil his duties towards others more satisfactorily as he exercises himself with greater care for his own perfecting.'[5]

In his discussion of education and the cultivation of the mind Pufendorf constantly quotes earlier writers, and he seems to have followed Bacon's chapter in the *Advancement of Learning* (though he only quotes the *Essays*) in the arrangement of his matter. But his association of the duty of self-improvement with 'that sociableness (socialitas) for which his Creator intended man' provides a link with his central doctrine in the *De Jure* where, as has been generally recognised since Thomasius, he combined the idea of the essentially sociable nature of man put forward by his great predecessor Grotius with the disillusioned doctrine of Hobbes, that man seeks only his own happiness. Appealing to first principles, like the great mathematical thinkers of his century, 'he parts company with the theologians, who founded law on dogma, as well as with the humanists, who founded it on history; though a true son of his time in his erudition, he never wavers in seeking the true sources of his juridical system in the laws of human reason and the nature of things.'[6] His critics regarded his concept of 'socialitas', however, as arbitary and unconvincing. Like many critics of present-day liberal humanism, they did not believe that a man's innate sociability would be enough, without Christian convictions, to induce him to perform his duty towards God and his fellow-men. Pufendorf rejoined, in the preface to later editions of *De Jure*, for instance, that 'the nature of man, in so far as it was made by the Creator a social one, is the norm and foundation of that law which must be followed in any society'. To appeal to Christian revelation or the authority of priests would be to undermine the universality of his teaching, which concerned 'not Christians alone, but all mankind'. The central ideas of the Enlightenment are all here in germ, the exclusively immanent conception of God, the rejection of original sin, the reliance on sound reason rather than on any special revelation.

The controversy evoked by Pufendorf's arguments was naturally fierce and prolonged. His final summing up was called *Eris Scandica* (1686). In *De Jure* he had tried, in the manner of Hobbes, to imagine what the life of man would be like in 'a purely natural state' and had declared that without the help of his fellow-men and his social inheritance, 'separated from all things which have been added by human institution,' he would be little more than an animal himself. The improvement on his 'natural' condition that man achieves through living in society, what he adds thereby to nature, is now called by Pufendorf 'culture', and in thus opposing the two conceptions to each other he is again anticipating one of the favourite themes of eighteenth-century philosophers. 'Culture' means for him in the *Eris Scandica* something which includes both the internal 'cultura animi' praised by so many of his predecessors and also what Pufendorf calls elsewhere 'cultus vitae', the improvement of the external conditions of life through the arts of civilisation, and he uses the word now absolutely, without a following genitive. The crucial passage reads: 'We have considered the natural state of man in a different manner, according as it is opposed to that culture (culturae), which is added to human life through the help, the industry and the inventions of other men, either by their own thought and strength or by a divine intimation.' The state of nature means for him therefore poverty, discomfort, ignorance, defencelessness, the condition that Hobbes had described as resulting from the 'war of every man against every man' that he held to be inevitable in a primitive society where no state, no 'Leviathan' ensures for men peace and protection. There one would find 'no arts, no letters, no society, and which is worst of all, continual fear and danger of violent death; and the life of man solitary, poor, nasty, brutish and short'. Against this view Pufendorf argues that men are forced to be sociable through their desire for happiness as individuals, and so achieve 'culture', at once the product and the mainstay of life in society.

From Pufendorf's time on, the new idea of civilisation or objective culture came to be more and more discussed by leading writers in Europe, but it was a long time before a standard term for civilisation established itself in the principal languages. Meanwhile the older notion of personal cultivation lost none of its interest, as has been indicated above in our study of Wieland and his successors in Germany. There continued to be many variations in terminology, which cannot be followed in detail here. In French 'la culture de l'esprit' was in time contracted to 'la culture', which still normally means personal cultivation, German 'Bildung' but not 'Kultur'. English followed suit, but German developed its own word, apparently by the secularisation of a term that goes back to the language of medieval mystics, and is connected with the idea of man being made in God's image (Bild), and striving to model himself on the image of Christ in his mind. Early in the eighteenth century Arnold and the Pietists speak of 'geistliche Bildung'. When it became necessary to find a translation of Shaftesbury's 'inward form', it was natural enough that 'innere Bildung' should be used, as 'Bildung' was already associated with the inward, and the same word served for the process of 'formation' (in 'formation of a genteel character'). Later uses by Wieland, Herder, Goethe, etc., have been illustrated above.[7]

J. Niedermann suggests that before the notion of 'civilisation' could arise and gain acceptance, three things had to happen. First, it was necessary that the works of man should come to be regarded as possessing high value in themselves, and not merely as reflecting some higher power. From the Renaissance on, and especially from the seventeenth century, when religious beliefs were being secularised one after another, the number of educated men who satisfied this condition was very large.

Secondly, it was necessary that these enduring works should be thought of as forming a whole, which developed according to laws of its own. A step towards this way of thinking about abstract entities was to consider nations as growing in a way that could be compared with living things, as when Bacon in his last essay spoke of them as having a youth, a manhood and an old age. Similarly, instead of writing 'Lives of the artists', scholars attempted histories of art like Winckelmann's of Greek art (1763). The concept of what was later called civilisation is to be found, before Herder, in Bossuet, Voltaire, Vico and Montesquieu, for example, but an agreed word for it had not yet been found, Montesquieu writing of the 'esprit général' of a nation, Voltaire of the 'état de l'Europe' at a certain time, and so on.

Thirdly, it was necessary to arrive at the idea of a social inheritance, that could be handed on, duly augmented, from age to age. With Bossuet, the improvement found was ascribed to the hand of Providence, Voltaire took the secularist view and emphasised the advance of knowledge and the arts from century to century, and there had been theories like Bacon's long before his time, about a regular and even logical progress of mankind. In 1758 came the important work by Goguet, often referred to by Herder, which was really a history of civilisation, though he called it *De l'origine des lois, des arts et des sciences et de leur progrès chez les anciens peuples.*

The first histories of civilisation which called themselves 'Kulturgeschichten' in German came in the 1780's, but Niedermann has found the word 'culture' used in the sense of 'civilisation' in Germany as early as 1765. It is in a ten-page paper by the

French scholar Toussaint, a member of the Royal Academy of Sciences and Letters in Berlin. The title of his essay, as it appears in the *Mémoires* of the Academy in 1767 in French, of course, like everything else, runs: 'Des inductions qu'on peut tirer du langage d'une nation par rapport à sa culture et à ses mœurs.' 'Culture' is here used in the sense of the German 'Kultur', as it was normally used later, and not of the French 'culture', which is what is called 'Bildung' in German, as we have seen. This is quite clear from Toussaint's explanation of what he understands by culture. It includes for him both the useful arts—agriculture and crafts of all kinds—and everything that comes from 'développement de l'esprit', the sciences and literature, in which every nation expresses its own character. In discussing national character the author does not forget to pay a compliment to his patron, Frederick the Great, who is unique in combining in himself 'l'héroisme militaire, les études philosophiques et la culture des sciences, des lettres et des arts'—a phrase in which 'culture' is used in the normal French way.

In 1782 Adelung, the lexicographer, published under the title *Geschichte der Cultur* an enlarged version of an encyclopaedic treatise which he had formerly called *Kurzer Begriff menschlicher Fertigkeiten und Kenntnisse*. Kant used 'Kultur' more or less in its modern sense in 1784, in his *Idee zu einer allgemeinen Geschichte in weltbürgerlicher Absicht*, Mendelssohn in an article of the same year, 'Über die Frage: was heißt aufklären', discusses the distinction that can be made between 'Aufklärung', 'Bildung' and 'Cultur', all of them still bookish expressions, he says, Hegewisch wrote in 1788 his *Allgemeine Übersicht der deutschen Cultur-geschichte*, and several more 'Kulturgeschichten' followed in the next decade. The lexicographers, however, were slow to register the term 'Kultur', the first being Adelung in the second edition of his dictionary in 1793. Campe still regarded the word in 1807 as one that had been 'imposed on the language'.

REFERENCES

INTRODUCTION

1 London, 1958.
2 London, 1949. (Translation of German edition of 1945.)
3 Williams, pp. 59 f.   4 Williams, p. 61.
5 'Die dichterische und philosophische Bewegung in Deutschland 1770–1800', Antrittsvorlesung in Basel, 1867, in *Gesammelte Schriften*, vol. v, pp. 12 ff.
6 'Der deutsche Idealismus', in *Gesammelte Schriften*, vol. IV (Tübingen, 1925).
7 *Geist der Goethezeit*, I, Einleitung (Leipzig, 1923).
8 Williams, p. 62.
9 *Notes towards the Definition of Culture* (London, 1948).
10 'Vorwort des ersten Heftes "Zur Morphologie"', in *Goethes sämtliche Werke* (Jubiläums-Ausgabe), vol. IX, p. 252. For the implications, see E. M. Wilkinson, 'Goethe's Conception of Form', in *Proceedings of the British Academy*, vol. XXXVII (London, 1951).
11 *Das Problem des geistigen Seins*, Berlin, 1933.
12 E. A. Hoebel, 'The Nature of Culture', in *Man, Culture and Society*, ed. H. L. Shapiro (New York, 1956). T. S. Eliot, *Notes*, p. 120.
13 *The Times*, 29 April 1957.   14 *Eris Scandica*, 1686.

CHAPTER I

1 *Werke*, Weimar edition, IV. Abt., vol. XII, pp. 291 ff. (12 Sept. 1797).
2 F. Hartung, *Das Großherzogtum Sachsen-Weimar* (Weimar, 1923), p. 7.
3 Schiller, *Briefe*, ed. Jonas, vol. I, p. 362.
4 *Der goldene Spiegel*, 2. Teil, 1. Kap.
5 *Ibid.* 2. Teil, 8. Kap.   6 *Ibid.* 2. Teil, 15. Kap.
7 *Die Geschichte des Agathon*, 1. Teil, 2. Buch, 3. Kap.
8 German translations of Shaftesbury:
   Advice to an Author (E. von Fenzky), Magdeburg, 1738.
   The Moralists (J. J. Spalding), Berlin, 1745.
   An Enquiry concerning Virtue (J. J. Spalding), Berlin, 1747.
   An Essay on the Freedom of Wit and Humour (F. C. Oetinger), Tübingen, 1753.
   The Characteristics as a whole was first translated by C. A. Wichmann, Leipzig, 1768.
9 *The Eighteenth-Century Background* (London, 1940), p. 44.
10 Quoted in F. Sengle, *Wieland* (Stuttgart, 1949), p. 168.
11 *Characteristicks of Men, Manners, Opinions, Times* (1711), quoted from edition of 1737, vol. II, p. 367.
12 *Ibid.* vol. II, p. 345.   13 *Ibid.* vol. III, p. 287.
14 *Ibid.* vol. I, p. 69.   15 *Ibid.* vol. I, p. 91.
16 *Ibid.* vol. I, p. 109. Cf. vol. III, p. 223.
17 *Ibid.* vol. I, p. 107.   18 *Ibid.* vol. I, pp. 142 ff.
19 *Ibid.* vol. I, p. 207.   20 *Ibid.* vol. I, pp. 157 ff.
21 *Ibid.* vol. I, p. 290.   22 *Ibid.* vol. I, p. 98.

23 *Ibid.* vol. III, p. 162.
24 Eckermann, *Gespräche mit Goethe*, under 12. März, 1828.
25 *Characteristicks*, vol. I, p. 127.   26 *Ibid.* vol. I, p. 129 f.
27 *Ibid.* vol. I, p. 124.
28 *Variété* vol. II, 'Préface aux Lettres Persanes'.
29 *Characteristicks*, vol. III, p. 156.   30 *Ibid.* vol. II, p. 401.
31 *Ibid.* vol. III, p. 138.   32 *Ibid.* vol. I, p. 138.
33 *Ibid.* vol. II, p. 427.
34 *Shaftesburys Einfluß auf C. M. Wieland* (Breslauer Beiträge zur Literaturgeschichte, N.F. 34), Stuttgart, 1913. For Shaftesbury's influence in England, see C. A. Moore, 'Shaftesbury and the ethical poets in England, 1700–1760', in *P.M.L.A.*, vol. XXXI (1916), pp. 264–325. Moore makes Shaftesbury chiefly responsible for the moral tone of English literature since his time.
35 *Werke*, Jubiläumsausgabe, vol. XXXVII, pp. 17 ff.
36 *Werke*, Akademie-Ausgabe, I. Abt., vol. IV, p. 180.
37 *Ibid.*, vol. IV, p. 184.
38 Cf. Hans Weil, *Die Entstehung des deutschen Bildungsprinzips* (Bonn, 1930).
39 W. Andreas, *Karl August von Weimar* (Stuttgart, 1953), p. 154.
40 *Dichtung und Wahrheit*, 15. Buch.
41 Cf. Bruford, *Theatre, Drama and Audience in Goethe's Germany*, chap. V.
42 *Dichtung und Wahrheit*, 15. Buch.

CHAPTER II

1 Viëtor, *Goethe* (Bern, 1949), p. 63.
2 Goethe, *W.A.*, IV. Abt., vol. V, p. 178.
3 Goethe, *W.A.*, vol. LIII, pp. 383 ff.
4 Goethe, *Briefe an Frau von Stein*, 20 Nov. 1782.
5 For topographical description and information on social life the best source is: *Am Weimarischen Hofe unter Amalien und Karl August*, Erinnerungen von Karl Freiherr von Lyncker, herausgegeben von Marie Scheller (Berlin, 1912).
6 F. G. Leonhardi, *Erdbeschreibung der Churfürstlichen- und Herzoglich-Sächsischen Lande*, 2.A. (Leipzig, 1790), vol. II, p. 756.
7 For population statistics see the first chapter of H. Eberhardt, *Goethes Umwelt, Forschungen zur gesellschaftlichen Struktur Thüringens* (Weimar, 1951).
8 For social life and manners, partly based on Lyncker, see C. A. H. Burkhardt, 'Aus Weimars Culturgeschichte', in *Die Grenzboten* (Leipzig), 30. Jahrgang, 1871, and 31. Jahrgang, 1872.
9 Leonhardi, vol. II, p. 756.   10 Eberhardt, chap. II.
11 F. Hartung, *Das Großherzogtum Sachsen unter der Regierung Karl Augusts* (Weimar, 1923), p. 358.
12 *Reise durch Thüringen, den Ober- und Niederrheinischen Kreis nebst Bemerkungen über Staatsverfassung, öffentliche Anstalten, Gewerbe, Kultur und Sitten*, 3. Teil (Dresden und Leipzig, 1796), p. 527. (Quoted by Eberhardt, p. 25.)

13 'A German Court before the War', in *The Listener*, 14 May 1930.

14 *The German Sturm und Drang* (Manchester, 1953), p. 308.

15 *Goethe*, 5. A. (Berlin, 1918), p. 236.

16 *Hufeland, Leibarzt und Erzieher*, Selbstbiographie von Christoph Wilhelm Hufeland, ed. W. von Brunn, 2. A. (Stuttgart, 1937), p. 45.

17 C. A. H. Burkhardt, 'Aus den Weimarar Fourierbüchern, 1775–1784', in *Goethe-Jahrbuch*, vol. VI (1885), p. 149.

18 *Literarische Zustände und Zeitgenossen* (Leipzig, 1838), vol. I, p. 57.

19 See W. Andreas, 'Sturm und Drang im Spiegel der Weimarer Hofkreise', in *Goethe* (1943), pp. 126–49. Also: W. Bode, *Goethe in vertraulichen Briefen seiner Zeitgenossen, 1749–1803* (Berlin, 1918), where the gossip contained in letters of the time is chronologically recorded. The period 1775-86 occupies pp. 103–337.

20 Quoted by Bode, *Der Weimarische Musenhof, 1756–1781* (Berlin, 1919), p. 182.

21 Gisela Sichardt, *Das Weimarer Liebhabertheater unter Goethes Leitung* (Weimar, 1957), which supersedes all earlier accounts.

22 Details in Gisela Sichardt.

23 On Goethe's first years in Weimar, cf. especially: Karl Freiherr von Beaulieu-Marconnay, *Anna Amalia, Karl August und der Minister von Fritsch* (Weimar, 1874). The letter quoted is on pp. 159–63. Also: H. Düntzer, *Goethe und Karl August*, 2.A. (Leipzig, 1888); H. Düntzer, *Goethes Tagebücher der sechs ersten Weimarischen Jahre* (Leipzig, 1889); W. Andreas, *Karl August von Weimar, ein Leben mit Goethe, 1757–1783* (Stuttgart, 1953); W. Bode, *Karl August von Weimar, Jugendjahre* (Berlin, 1913); W. Bode, *Goethes Leben im Garten am Stern* (Berlin, 1919); F. Hartung, 'Das erste Jahrzehnt der Regierung Karl Augusts', in *Jahrbuch der Goethe-Gesellschaft*, vol. II (1915), pp. 59–139; and Hartung's book mentioned above under note 11.

24 Fauchier Magnan, for instance, relies too much on Wieland's enthusiastic first impressions when he writes: 'Goethe surgit donc d'emblée comme le magicien de Weimar, le héros du jour en attendant d'être le héros de son époque.' *Goethe et la Cour de Weimar* (Paris-Geneva, 1954), p. 47.

25 Biedermann, *Goethes Gespräche*, vol. III, p. 97.

26 See Hans Wahl, 'Sebastian Simpel', in *Goethe*, vol. XI (1949), pp. 62–77.

27 Bode, *Karl August von Weimar, Jugendjahre* (Berlin, 1913), pp. 306f.

28 Beaulieu-Marconnay, *Anna Amalia* . . ., p. 212.

29 W. Flach, *Goethes amtliche Schriften* (Weimar, 1950), vol. I, Introduction.

30 *Werke*, J.A., 25, pp. 142f.

31 Well-documented history in Julius Voigt, *Goethe in Ilmenau* (Leipzig, 1912). Further documents in Flach, *op. cit.*, and Eberhardt, *Goethes Umwelt*.

32 'Lebensverhältnisse mit Ober-Berghauptmann von Trebra', in *Goethe-Jahrbuch*, vol. IX (1888), pp. 11–20.

33 'Antiker Form sich nähernd', Nr. 9 ('Erwählter Fels') and 27 ('Felsen sollten nicht Felsen').

34 Bode, *Stunden mit Goethe* (Berlin), vol. VI, n.d. (1910), pp. 215–19.

35 Singer, Holmyard, Hall and Williams, *A History of Technology* (Oxford, 1958), vol. IV, p. 527.

36   Hans Bürgin, *Der Minister Goethe vor der römischen Reise. Seine Tätigkeit in der Wegebau- und Kriegskommission* (Weimar, 1933).
37   *Jahrbuch der Goethe-Gesellschaft*, vol. VI (1919), p. 277.
38   Details in Hans Bürgin, *op. cit.*
39   Flach, *Goethes amtliche Schriften*, vol. I, Nos. 157, 158, 169, 171.
40   Voigt, *Goethe in Ilmenau*, pp. 108–34.

CHAPTER III

1   Bode, *Goethe in vertraulichen Briefen*, pp. 175 f.
2   Gisela Sichardt, *Das Weimarer Liebhabertheater unter Goethes Leitung*, pp. 79 f.
3   Sichardt, pp. 24 f.   4   Sichardt, pp. 16–20.
5   *Am Weimarischen Hofe*, pp. 72 f.
6   See the painting by Kraus, reproduced, e.g., in Bode, *Der Weimarische Musenhof* (Berlin, 1919), opp. p. 314.
7   A. Schöll, in notes to *Goethes Briefe an Frau von Stein* (Frankfurt-am-Main, 1883), vol. I, p. 499.
8   The Kraus drawings have often been reproduced, e.g. in *Goethe und seine Welt*, ed. Hans Wahl and Anton Kippenberg (Leipzig, 1932), pp. 79 f.
9   Printed as the 7th volume of the *Schriften der Goethegesellschaft* (Weimar, 1892), ed. E. von der Hellen, with an introduction by B. Suphan.
10   To Herder, 20 Feb. 1786.
11   Biedermann, *Goethes Gespräche*, under 24 May 1828.
12   'Geschichte meines botanischen Studiums', in *J.A.*, vol. XXXIX, pp. 296 f.
13   Biedermann, *op. cit.*, No. 239.   14   *J.A.*, vol. XXV, pp. 224 ff.
15   'Vorwort zur Farbenlehre', *J.A.*, vol. XL, p. 63.
16   Agnes Arber, 'Goethe's Botany', *Chronica Botanica* (Waltham, Mass., 1946), vol. X, p. 80.
17   Arber, p. 80.   18   Cf. letter to Merck, 27 Oct. 1782.
19   *J.A.*, vol. XXXIX, p. 302.
20   *Forschungen und Fortschritte* (Goethenummer, 1932), p. 17.
21   *Magon-Festgabe* (Berlin, 1958), pp. 175 ff.
22   14 Sept. 1780.   23   10 Aug. 1782.
24   *Wo sich der Weg im Kreise schließt. Goethe und Charlotte von Stein* (Stuttgart, 1957), p. 10.
25   Günther Müller, *Kleine Goethebiographie*, 2. A. (Bonn, 1948), pp. 83 f.
26   *J.A.*, vol. XXXIX, pp. 6 ff.   27   Walter Hof, p. 31.
28   Cf. W. D. Robson-Scott, *German Travellers in England* (Oxford, 1953), pp. 58, 76, and for what follows: Ian Watt, *The Rise of the Novel* (London, 1957), chap. V, 'Love and the Novel'; and Hanna Fischer-Lamberg, 'Charlotte von Stein, ein "Bildungserlebnis" Goethes', in *Deutsche Vierteljahrsschrift für Literaturwissenschaft und Geistesgeschichte*, vol. XV (1937).
29   Fairley, *A Study of Goethe* (Oxford, 1947), p. 114; Trunz in *Goethes Werke* (Hamburger Ausgabe), vol. I, p. 466.
30   See my 'Fürstin Gallitzin und Goethe' in *Arbeitgemeinschaft für Forschung*

des Landes Nordrhein-Westfalen, Geisteswissenschaften, Heft 76 (Köln und Opladen, 1957).

31 Cf. *Faust* II, lines 10247–53.
32 Cf. Herder, *Sämtliche Werke* (Suphan), vol. xv, pp. 73 ff.
33 See, e.g., the notes by Erich Trunz in *Goethes Werke* (Hamburger Ausgabe). vol. II, pp. 592 ff.
34 Werner Simon, 'Stanzendichtung', in *Beiträge zur deutschen und nordischen Literatur,* Festgabe für Leopold Magon (Berlin, 1958), p. 238.
35 Herder, *Ideen,* Book IX, p. 1.

CHAPTER IV

1   R. Haym, *Herder* (Berlin, 1880), vol. I, p. 284.
2   A. Gillies, *Herder* (Oxford, 1945), p. 38.
3   R. T. Clark, *Herder* (Berkeley and Los Angeles, 1955), p. 210.
4   H. Hettner, *Geschichte der deutschen Literatur im achtzehnten Jahrhundert,* 7th ed. (Braunschweig, 1926), Book 3, p. 53.
5   Herder, *Werke,* ed. Suphan, vol. VII, p. 300. ('An Prediger, 15 Provinzial-blätter').
6   Herder, vol. V., p. 484.   7   *Ibid.* p. 487.
8   *Ibid.* p. 495.   9   *Ibid.* p. 498.
10 *Ibid.* p. 510.   11   *Ibid.* p. 516.
12 Goethe, *W.A.,* II Abt., vol. VI, p. 20.
13 Herder, vol. XIII, p. 62.   14   *Ibid.* p. 161.
15 *Ibid.* p. 176   16   *Ibid.* p. 194.
17 Goethe, *W.A.,* II Abt., vol. VI, p. 16.
18 Herder, vol. XIII, p. 283.   19   *Ibid.* p. 318.
20 *Ibid.* p. 336.   21   *Ibid.* p. 338.
22 *Ibid* pp. 344 f.   23   *Ibid.* p. 345.
24 *Ibid.* p. 346.   25   *Ibid.* p. 348.
26 *Ibid.* pp. 351 f.   27   *Ibid.* p. 355.
28 *Ibid.* p. 357.   29   *Ibid.* pp. 358–62.
30 *Ibid.* p. 371.   31   *Ibid.* p. 374.
32 *Ibid.* p. 454.   33   *Ibid.* pp. 380 ff.
34 *Ibid.* p. 383 f.   35   *Ibid.* p. 394.
36 H.-I. Marrou, *Histoire de l'éducation dans l'antiquité* (Paris, 1948), pp. 142 ff.
37 Herder, vol. XIII, p. 395.   38   Herder, vol. XIV, p. 71.
39 *Ibid.* p. 86.   40   *Ibid.* p. 89.
41 *Ibid.* p. 145.   42   *Ibid.* p. 150.
43 *Ibid.* p. 152.   44   *Ibid.* p. 163.
45 *Ibid.* p. 165.   46   *Ibid.* p. 175.
47 *Ibid.* pp. 200 ff.   48   *Ibid.* p. 206.
49 *Ibid.* pp. 204–7.
50 It is interesting to note a hint of this same idea that appears in Shaftesbury's *Moralists,* in the first of the 'Meditations' of Theocles, later translated by Herder, where he says that if we could view 'Nature's seeming waste' aright, namely 'with indifference, remote from the antipathy of sense, we then perhaps should highest raise our admiration: convinced that even the way itself was equal to the end.'

51 Herder, vol. XIV, p. 208.   52 *Ibid.* p. 213.

53 *Ibid.* p. 219.

54 F. Meinecke, *Die Entstehung des Historismus* (München und Berlin, 1936), p. 457.

55 Herder, vol. XIV, p. 243.   56 *Ibid.* p. 251.

57 Erich Franz, *Goethe als religiöser Denker* (Tübingen, 1932), pp. 19f.

58 Goethe, *J.A.*, vol. XXVII, p. 107.   59 *Ibid.* pp. 134f.

60 Herder, vol. XIV, p. 297.   61 Goethe, *J.A.*, vol. XXVII, p. 16.

62 Herder, vol. XVIII, pp. 307f.   63 *Ibid.* p. 314.

64 Herder, vol. XVII, p. 143.   65 *Ibid.* p. 138.

66 *Ibid.* p. 211.   67 *Ibid.* p. 317.

68 Herder, vol. XVIII, p. 161.   69 *Ibid.* p. 207f.

70 *Ibid.* p. 267.   71 Herder, vol. XXVII, p. 197.

72 Herder, vol. XIV, p. 250.

73 P. Valéry, 'Discours en l'honneur de Goethe' (1932), in *Variétés IV* (Paris, 1938).

74 R. Michéa, *Les travaux scientifiques de Goethe* (Paris, 1943), p. 20.

75 Agnes Arber, 'Goethe's Botany', in *Chronica Botanica*, vol. X, (Waltham Mass., 1946), pp. 74–7. Cf. also Sir Charles Sherrington, *Goethe on Man and Science*, 2nd ed. (Cambridge, 1949), p. 30: 'Goethe, though devoted to science, had not at root the scientific temperament. He had not, for instance, along with the urge to discovery the sublime detachment of the scientific thinkers.'

76 *Nouveaux essais sur l'entendement humain*, 1704, quoted by Michéa, *op. cit.*, pp. 44f.

77 A. O. Lovejoy, *The Great Chain of Being* (Cambridge, Mass., 1936).

78 Sherrington, *Goethe on Nature and Science*, pp. 41–3, and *Man on his Nature* (Cambridge, 1940), chapter on 'Conflict with nature'.

79 Michéa, p. 84.

80 Cf. 'Geschichte meines botanischen Studiums', *J.A.*, vol. XXXIX, p. 316.

81 Michéa, p. 87.

82 A. N. Whitehead, *Science and the Modern World* (Cambridge, 1929), pp. 72, 103.

83 Goethe, *J.A.*, vol. XXVIII, p. 185.

84 Staiger, *Goethe* (Zürich und Freiburg, 1956), vol. II, pp. 14f.

85 See W. Wundt, *Goethes Wilhelm Meister und die Entwicklung des modernen Lebensideals*, 2.A. (Berlin und Leipzig, 1932).

86 E. Spranger, 'Goethe und die Metamorphose des Menschen' (1924), in *Goethes Weltanschauung* (Inselverlag, n.p., 1949), pp. 54–87; and A. R. Wachsmuth, 'Goethes naturwissenschaftliches Denken im Spiegel seiner Dichtungen seit 1790', in *Sinn und Form*, vol. XI (1959).

87 See, e.g., E. Trunz's note in *Goethe* (Hamburger Ausgabe), vol. II, p. 570, with its references.

88 Staiger, *Goethe*, vol. II, p. 130.

89 H. Boeschenstein, *Deutsche Gefühlskultur*, I (Bern, 1954).

90 Staiger, *Goethe*, vol. II, pp. 167f.

91 Good interpretation in E. Franz, *Goethe als religiöser Denker* (Tübingen, 1932), and in Spranger, *Goethes Weltanschauung*.

92 H. Schmidt, *Erinnerungen eines Weimarischen Veteranen* (Leipzig, 1856), p. 33.

93 E. Fichte, *J. G. Fichte* (Leipzig, 1863), pp. 52f. (from the diary of F. K. Forberg).

94 For further examples and an account of the growth of Humboldt's ideas, see my article, 'The idea of " Bildung" in W. von Humboldt's letters', in *The Era of Goethe*, essays presented to James Boyd (Oxford, 1959), pp. 17–46.

95 E. Fichte, *op. cit.*, p. 53.

96 *Schillers sämtliche Werke*, ed. Güntter and Witkowski (Leipzig, n.d.), vol. XVIII, p. 126.

97 *Ibid.* p. 133.   98 *Aesthetische Erziehung*, letter 2.

99 *Ibid.*, letter 5.   100 *L'enracinement* (Paris, 1949), p. 48.

101 End of letter 6.

102 *Schillers sämtliche Werke*, vol. XVIII, p. 134.

103 *Ibid.* p. 129.

104 H. Lutz, *Schillers Anschauungen von Kultur und Natur*, Germanische Studien 60 (Berlin, 1928).

105 *Schillers sämtliche Werke*, Säkularausgabe, vol. XII, p. 343. The reference is to *A Philosophical Inquiry into the Origin of our Ideas of the Sublime and the Beautiful* (London, 1756), Part II, section 1, where we read: 'I distinguish love, by which I mean that satisfaction which arises to the mind upon contemplating any thing beautiful, of whatsoever nature it may be, from desire or lust, which is an energy of the mind that hurries us on to the possession of certain objects that do not affect us as they are beautiful, but by means altogether different.'

106 *La Pesanteur et la Grace* (Paris, 1948), p. 17.

107 R. Lehmann, *Die deutschen Klassiker, Herder, Schiller, Goethe, als Erzieher* (Leipzig, 1921), pp. 225f.

108 Letter 22. Cf. for stuff as 'material' the sentence in the aesthetic lectures: 'The nature of the medium, the stuff, must be completely conquered; in a statue, for example, one must not see the marble, or in an actor his own natural character.' Säkularausgabe, vol. XII, p. 351.

109 Herder, *Werke*, vol. II, p. 305 (Fragmente, II).

110 Käte Hamburger, 'Schillers Fragment *Der Menschenfeind* und die Idee der Kalokagathie', in *Deutsche Vierteljahrsschrift für Literaturwissenschaft und Geistesgeschichte*, vol. XXX (1956).

111 *Schillers sämtliche Werke*, ed. Güntter etc., vol. XVII, p. 363.

112 *Ibid.* p. 356.   113 *Ibid.* p. 346.

114 *Ibid.* p. 350.

115 See 'Fürstin Gallitzin und Goethe', p. 24.

116 Käte Hamburger, *loc. cit.*, p. 375.

117 M. Ginsberg, 'German views of the German mind', in *The German Mind and Outlook*, by G. P. Gooch, Morris Ginsberg etc. (London, 1945), pp. 46f.

118 *Allgemeine Literatur-Zeitung*, Jena, 27 July 1796, No. 232.

CHAPTER V

1 Both documents are printed in *Goethes Werke* (Weimar edition), Band 53. The talk is also to be found in the *Goethe-Jahrbuch*, vol. XIV (1893), with notes by E. von der Hellen.

2 G. P. Gooch, *Germany and the French Revolution* (London, 1920), p. 142.
3 Gooch, p. 160. See also Sengle, *Wieland*, pp. 440–53. Wieland's articles are reprinted in the Prussian Academy edition of his works (vol. xv), where they take up about 500 pages.
4 *Goethe-Jahrbuch*, vol. xxxi (1910), p. 11.
5 *Dichtung und Wahrheit*, 20. Buch.
6 Merck to Bertuch, 6 Nov. 1782, printed in *Goethe-Jahrbuch*, vol. xxxi p. 20.
7 A. von Heinemann, *Ein Kaufmann der Goethezeit* (*Bertuch*) (Weimar 1955), and W. Feldmann, *J. J. Bertuch* (Saarbrücken, 1902). Hans Wahl, *Geschichte des teutschen Merkur* (Palaestra cxxvii), Berlin, 1914. Sengle, *Wieland*. Fritz Kröner, *Das Zeitungswesen in Weimar, 1734–1849* (Leipzig, 1920). Friedrich Lütge, *Geschichte des Jenaer Buchhandels, einschließlich der Buchdruckereien* (Jena, 1929).
8 Reprinted with commentary in O. Fambach, *Ein Jahrhundert deutscher Literaturkritik*, vol. iii, pp. 357 ff.
9 See Paul Raabe, 'Zur Bibliographie der Goethezeit', in *Euphorion*, vol. xlviii (1954), pp. 216–19.
10 For Klauer, see Walter Geese, *Gottlieb Martin Klauer, der Bildhauer Goethes* (Leipzig, n.d. (1935)).
11 Reprinted in *Goethes Werke* (Weimar edition), vol. xvi, p. 454.
12 Goethe, *J.A.*, vol. ix, p. 320.
13 Goethe und Schiller Archiv, Weimar, Bertuch-Nachlaß, ii, Nr. 300.
14 12 August 1787.
15 *Literarische Zustände und Zeitgenossen*, vol. i, pp. 104–7.
16 Rudolf Lehmann, *Die deutschen Klassiker als Erzieher* (Leipzig, 1921), p. 111.
17 Lehmann, pp. 117 f.
18 'Vom Zweck der eingeführten Schulverbesserung' (1786), in *Sämmtliche Werke*, ed. Suphan, vol. xxx, p. 123.
19 Lehmann, pp. 126 f.   20 Lehmann, p. 127.
21 Lehmann, p. 128.   22 Goethe, *J.A.*, vol. xxxvi, pp. 141 f.
23 *Gespräche mit Goethe*, under 3 May 1827. See also, e.g., 14 March 1830.
24 *Ibid.*, 23 Oct. 1828.
25 Printed in Paul Raabe's introduction to the photo-mechanical reprint of *Die Horen* (Stuttgart, 1959), and in G. Schulz's fuller study, *Schillers Horen* (Heidelberg, 1960).
26 See Fambach, vol. ii (*Schiller und sein Kreis*) (Berlin, 1957), pp. 104 ff., where contemporary reviews are reprinted, with notes.
27 For the opposition to Weimar, see A. Bettex, *Der Kampf um das klassische Weimar* (Zürich und Leipzig, 1935).
28 J. G. Meusel, *Das gelehrte Deutschland*, 5. Auflage, 12. Band (Lemgo, 1806), p. 1.
29 Reprinted in Fambach, vol. ii, p. 196, from the *A.L.Z.* of 4 Jan. 1796.
30 Wolfgang Seyffert, *Schillers Musenalmanache* (Palaestra lxxx) (Berlin, 1913).
31 See R. Samuel, 'Der kulturelle Hintergrund des Xenienkampfes' in *PEGS, NS*, vol. xii (1937), and the selection of *Anti-Xenien*, written not

merely by nonentities, but by such men as Claudius, Garve and Gleim, reprinted by W. Stammler (*Kleine Texte*, 81) (Bonn, 1911).

32 A. Bettex, *Der Kampf um das klassische Weimar*, p. 231.

33 *Goethe* (Zürich und Freiburg i. Br., 1956), vol. II, pp. 260f.

34 *Gedanken über Goethe* (1887; reprinted Darmstadt, 1921 and later).

35 *Goethe*, vol. II, p. 290.

36 W. von Oettingen, in his introduction to the 'Schriften zur Kunst', *J.A.*, vol. XXXIII.

37 *J.A.*, vol. XXXIII, p. 210.   38 *Ibid.*, p. 109.

39 *Ibid.*, p. 112.   40 *Ibid.*, p. 110.

41 *Ibid.*, p. 116.   42 *Ibid.*, p. 122.

43 *Ibid.*, pp. xiii f.   44 *Ibid.*, p. 56.

45 *Goethes Preisaufgaben für bildende Künstler* (Schriften der Goethegesellschaft 57) (Weimar, 1959).

46 *J.A.*, vol. XXXIII, p. xiv.

47 Quoted by Staiger, *Goethe*, vol. II, pp. 298f.

48 Scheidig, p. 138.

49 Reprinted in Fambach, vol. IV, pp. 651ff. For the full story see *Jahrbuch der Sammlung Kippenberg* (1925).

50 'Deutsches Theater', in *J.A.*, vol. XXXVII.

51 Cf. Schiller's poem 'An Goethe, als er den *Mahomet* von Voltaire auf die Bühne brachte'.

52 For further detail about the Weimar Theatre and a bibliography, see *Theatre, Drama and Audience in Goethe's Germany*.

53 *Goethe*, vol. II, p. 290.

54 *Geschichte der Universität Jena.* Festgabe zum vierhundertjährigen Universitätsjubiläum, ed. Max Steinmetz (Jena, 1958), vol. I, p. 229.

55 See Wolfgang Vulpius, *Goethe in Thüringen* (Rudolstadt, 1955), pp. 183–96.

56 *Geschichte der Universität Jena*, vol. I, p. 309; *Allgemeine Literatur-Zeitung Intelligenzblatt*, 1 Jan. 1794.

57 *Briefe über Jena* (Frankfurt und Leipzig, 1793).

58 *Was ich erlebte*, quoted in Paul Raabe, 'Das Protokollbuch der Gesellschaft der freien Männer in Jena 1794–1799', *Festgabe für Eduard Berend* (Weimar, 1959), p. 337,

59 *Ibid.* p. 342.   60 *J.A.*, vol. XL, pp. 268ff.

61 'Über die menschliche Unsterblichkeit', *Sämmtliche Werke*, ed. Suphan, vol. XVI, pp. 28–50.

62 *Hufeland, Leibarzt und Volkserzieher*, Selbstbiographie neu herausgegeben von Dr W. v. Brunn (Stuttgart, 1937).

CHAPTER VI

1 See Heinz Bluhm, 'The Newberry "Goetheana"', in *PEGS, NS*, vol. XXVIII (1959).

2 Trevor D. Jones, 'English contributors to Ottilie von Goethe's *Chaos*', in *PEGS, NS*, vol. IX (1933).

3 For Weimar since 1800 see e.g.: Paul Kühn, *Weimar*, 4. Auflage bearbeitet von Dr H. Wahl (Leipzig, 1925); R. Wustmann, *Weimar und Deutschland, 1815–1915* (Schriften der Goethegesellschaft 30) (Weimar, 1915).

REFERENCES

4   G. Lowes Dickinson, *A Modern Symposium* (London, 1914), pp. 152ff. The passage is from the final speech, by Vivian.

5   Wilhelm und Karoline von Humboldt in ihren Briefen, herausgegeben von Anna von Sydow (7 Bände, Berlin, 1906–16), vol. II, p. 162.

6   *Wilhelm von Humboldt und die Humanitätsidee* (Berlin, 1909), p. 421.

7   Raymond Williams, *Culture and Society*, p. 61.

8   See W. H. Bruford, 'Goethe and some Victorian Humanists', in *PEGS*, *NS*, vol. XVIII (1949), pp. 34–67.

9   J. M. Keynes, *Two Memoirs* (London, 1949).

10   N. G. Annan, *Leslie Stephen* (London, 1951), p. 124.

11   Leonard Woolf, *Sowing* (London, 1960), pp. 129f.

12   *Gespräche mit Goethe*, under 3 May 1827.

13   *Betrachtungen eines Unpolitischen* (Berlin, 1917). See W. H. Bruford, 'British and German Ideas of Freedom', in *GLL*, *NS*, vol. I (1948), pp. 77–88.

14   Ernst Troeltsch, 'Epochen und Typen der Sozialphilosophie des Christentums', in *Gesammelte Schriften*, vol. IV (Tübingen, 1925).

15   See W. H. Bruford, 'The Idea of "Bildung" in Wilhelm von Humboldt's Letters', in *The Era of Goethe*, essays presented to James Boyd (Oxford, 1959), pp. 17–46.

16   H. H. Borcherdt, *Schiller und die Romantiker* (Stuttgart, 1948), p. 35.

17   *Ideen*, quoted by Erich Franz, *Deutsche Klassik und Reformation* (Halle, 1937), p. 385 (in an excellent chapter on 'Der Bildungsgedanke').

18   In Hannah Arendt, *Rahel Varnhagen* (London, 1957), p. 144. On the role of the Berlin Jews see also: Ludwig Geiger, *Geschichte der Juden in Berlin* (Berlin, 1871); Karl Hillebrand, 'Die Berliner Gesellschaft 1789–1815', in *Unbekannte Essays*, ed. H. Uhde-Bernays (Bern, 1955).

19   Letter of 2 Dec. 1797.

20   'Die deutsche Idee von der Freiheit', in *Deutsche Zukunft* (Berlin, 1916), p. 38.

21   Quoted by Sir Philip Hartog, '"Kultur" as a symbol in peace and war', in *The Sociological Review*, vol. XXX (1938), p. 20.

22   'Um welche Güter kämpfen wir?', in *Die deutsche Erhebung von 1914*, 6.-10. Auflage (Stuttgart und Berlin, 1914), pp. 51f.

23   *Wallensteins Tod*, II, 2, lines 800ff.

24   'Bildung' (1893), in *Gesammelte pädagogische Abhandlungen* (Stuttgart, 1912).

25   See Theodor Litt, *Das Bildungsideal der Klassik und die moderne Arbeitswelt* (Schriftenreihe der Bundeszentrale für Heimatdienst, Heft 15) (Bonn, 1955), p. 59.

26   'Wandlungen des Bildungsideals in ihrem Zusammenhang mit der sozialen Entwicklung' (1899), in *op. cit.*

27   'Von dem, was einer ist', in *Sämmtliche Werke* (Großherzog Wilhelm Ernst Ausgabe) (Leipzig, n.d.), vol. IV, pp. 399ff.

28   Baron Friedrich von Hügel, *The German Soul* (London, 1916), pp. 128ff.

29   Reinhold Niebuhr, *Nations and Empires* (London, 1960), p. 298.

APPENDIX II

1 This appendix is based principally on the full and careful study by J. Niedermann, *Kultur*. *Werden und Wandlungen des Begriffs von Cicero bis Herder* (Biblioteca dell' 'Archivum Romanicum', 28). (Florence, 1941.) This contains a full bibliography of earlier studies, of which there are many, especially by French scholars.

2 *Tusculanarum disputationum lib. II, V (13).*

3 H.-I. Marrou, *Histoire de l'éducation dans l'antiquité* (Paris, 1948), p.142.

4 *Lezione delle monete* (Florence, 1638), p. 108. I am indebted to Professor E. R. Vincent for this information.

5 Translation by C. H. and W. A. Oldfather (from the 1688 edition of *De jure naturae et gentium*) in 'The Classics of International Law', edited by J. B. Scott (Oxford, 1934). I have made one change. The translators write for 'sibi ipsi' 'for his own advantage'.

6 From the introduction by Walter Simon to the work mentioned in the preceding note, p. 11a.

7 F. Rauhut, 'Die Herkunft der Worte und Begriffe Kultur, Civilisation und Bildung', in *Germanisch-romanische Monatsschrift*, N.F. III (1953).
More specialised studies:
Ilse Scharschmidt, *Der Bedeutungswandel der Worte 'bilden' und 'Bildung' in der literarischen Epoche von Gottsched bis Herder* (1931).
Irmgard Taylor, *Kultur, Aufklärung, Bildung und verwandte Begriffe bei Herder* (Giessener Beiträge zur deutschen Philologie, 62) (Giessen, 1938).

SELECT BIBLIOGRAPHY

As specific references are listed above, and the author's general indebtedness to the literature on the German classics is beyond tracing, the systematic bibliography is restricted to two topics, 'The idea of culture' and 'Weimar'. For Goethe and Schiller, there are excellent up-to-date bibliographies, the *Goethe-Bibliographie* edited by Hans Pyritz (Heidelberg, 1955 f.), and the *Schiller-Bibliographie* by Wolfgang Vulpius (Weimar, 1959). For Wieland and Herder, consult F. Sengle's *Wieland* (Stuttgart, 1949), and R. T. Clark's *Herder* (Berkeley and Los Angeles, 1955), respectively, and for other writers, J. Körner's *Bibliographisches Handbuch des deutschen Schrifttums*, 3.A. (Bern, 1949).

Further information on many subjects touched on in this book will be readily found in the *Goethe-Handbuch* edited by Alfred Zastrau, 2nd ed. (Stuttgart, 1955 f.), and in the introductions to Goethe's collected works in the *Jubiläums-Ausgabe*, the *Hamburger Ausgabe* and the *Gedenkausgabe*.

A. THE IDEA OF CULTURE, AND THE HISTORY OF THE IDEA

Arnold, Matthew, *Culture and Anarchy*, London, 1869.
—— *Literature and Dogma*, London, 1873.
Bacon, Francis. *The Advancement of Learning* Book II Chap. 22 1605.
Collingwood, R. G., 'Human Nature and Human History', *Proceedings of the British Academy*, 22, 1936.
Eliot, T. S., *Notes towards the Definition of Culture*, London, 1948.
Jäger, W., *Paideia*, I, Berlin, 1934. (English translation Oxford, 1939.)
Franz, E., *Deutsche Klassik und Reformation*, Halle, 1937.
Hartmann, Nicolai, *Das Problem des geistigen Seins*, Berlin, 1933.
Hoebel, E. O., 'The Nature of Culture', in *Man, Culture and Society*, ed. H. L. Shapiro, New York, 1956.
Litt, Theodor, *Das Bildungsideal der Klassik und die moderne Arbeitswelt*, Bonn, 1955.
Mannheim, Karl, *Ideology and Utopia*, London, 1936.

Marrou, Henri-Irénée, *Histoire de l'éducation dans l'antiquité*, Paris, 1948.

Meister, R., 'Handlungen, Taten, Werke als psychische Objektivationen', in *Erkenntnis und Wirklichkeit*, Innsbrucker Beiträge zur Kulturwissenschaft 5, Innsbruck, 1958.

Moras, J., *Ursprung und Entwicklung des Begriffs der Zivilisation in Frankreich (1756–1830)*, Hamburg, 1930.

Niedermann, J., *Kultur. Werden und Wandlungen des Begriffs von Cicero bis Herder*, Florence, 1941.

Paulsen, F., 'Bildung' (1893); 'Wandlungen des Bildungsideals in ihrem Zusammenhang mit der sozialen Entwicklung' (1899), in *Gesammelte pädagogische Abhandlungen*, Stuttgart, 1912.

von Pufendorf, Samuel, *De jure naturae et gentium*, ed. J. B. Scott, Classics of International Law, Oxford, 1934.

Rüegg, W., *Cicero und der Humanismus*, Zürich, 1946.

Schnabel, F., *Das humanistische Bildungsgut im Wandel von Staat und Gesellschaft*, München, 1956.

Stahl, E. L., *Die religiöse und die humanitätsphilosophische Bildungs idee und die Entstehung des deutschen Bildungsromans im 18. Jahrhundert*, Sprache und Dichtung 56, Bern, 1934.

Troeltsch, E., *Deutsche Bildung*, Berlin, 1919.

—— 'Der deutsche Idealismus', in *Gesammelte Schriften*, IV, Tübingen, 1925.

Weil, H., *Die Entstehung des deutschen Bildungsprinzips*, Bonn, 1930.

Whitehead, A. N., *Science and the Modern World*, Cambridge, 1926.

—— *The Aims of Education*, London, 1929.

—— *Adventures of Ideas*, Cambridge, 1933.

Williams, Raymond, *Culture and Society 1780–1950*, London, 1958.

Wundt, Max, *Goethes Wilhelm Meister und die Entwicklung des modernen Lebensideals*, 2. A., Berlin und Leipzig, 1932.

B. WEIMAR

1. *General, Topographical, Social*

Bode, W., *Damals in Weimar*, Weimar, 1910. (Illustrations.)

—— *Das Leben in Alt-Weimar*, Weimar, 1912. (Illustrations.)

Briefe eines ehrlichen Mannes bei einem wiederholten Aufenthalt in Weimar. Deutschland, 1800. (For authorship see Eduard Berend in *Euphorion*, vol. xx (1913), pp. 160 ff.

Burkhardt, C. A. H., 'Aus Weimars Culturgeschichte', in *Die Grenzboten*, Leipzig, 1871–1872.

Eberhardt, Hans, *Goethes Umwelt. Forschungen zur gesellschaftlichen Struktur Thüringens*, Weimar, 1951.

Feldmann, W., *J. J. Bertuch*, Saarbrücken, 1902.

Gräbner, K., *Die Großherzogliche Haupt- und Residenzstadt Weimar, nach ihrer Geschichte und ihren gegenwärtigen gesammten Verhältnissen dargestellt*, Erfurt, 1830.

von Heinemann, A., *Ein Kaufmann der Goethezeit (Bertuch)*, Weimar, 1955.

Hufeland, Leibarzt und Erzieher. Selbstbiographie von Christoph Wilhelm Hufeland, ed. W. von Brunn, 2. A., Stuttgart, 1937.

Kühn, Paul, *Weimar (Stätten der Kultur*, Band 13), 4. A., bearbeitet von Dr H. Wahl, Leipzig, 1925.

Leonhardi, F. G., *Erdbeschreibung der Churfürstlichen- und Herzoglich-Sächsischen Lande*, 2 Bde., 2. A., Leipzig, 1790.

von Lyncker, Karl, *Am Weimarischen Hofe unter Amalien und Karl August, Erinnerungen*, ed. Marie Scheller, Berlin, 1912.

Scheidig, Walther, *Das Schloß in Weimar*, 3. A., Weimar, 1955.

Schmidt, H., *Erinnerungen eines Weimarer Veteranen*, Leipzig, 1856.

Stahr, Adolf, *Weimar und Jena*, 2 Bde., Oldenburg, 1852.

Vulpius, Wolfgang, *Goethe in Thüringen, Stätten seines Lebens und Wirkens*, Rudolstadt, 1955.

Wahl, H., and Kippenberg, A. (eds.), *Goethe und seine Welt*, Leipzig, 1932. (Illustrations.)

2. The Ruling Family and their Entourage

Andreas, W., *Karl August von Weimar, ein Leben mit Goethe, 1757–1783*, Stuttgart, 1953.

—— 'Sturm und Drang im Spiegel der Weimarer Hofkreise', in *Goethe*, vol. VIII (1943), pp. 126–49.

von Beaulieu-Marconnay, Karl, *Anna Amalia, Karl August und der Minister von Fritsch*, Weimar, 1874.

Bode, W., *Amalie, Herzogin von Weimar*, 3 Bde., Berlin, 1908.

—— *Der Weimarische Musenhof, 1756–1781*, Berlin, 1917.

—— *Karl August von Weimar, Jugendjahre*, Berlin, 1913.

—— *Goethes Leben im Garten am Stern*, Berlin, 1909.

—— *Charlotte von Stein*, Berlin, 1910.

—— *Goethe in vertraulichen Briefen seiner Zeitgenossen, 1749–1803*, Berlin, 1918.

Bode, W., (ed.), *Stunden mit Goethe*, 1904–1915. Bd. 2: Chr. Schrempf, 'Frau von Stein und Goethe', pp. 5–49. Bde. 6–9: Briefe der Frau von Stein an Knebel.

Burkhardt, C. A. H., 'Aus den Weimarer Fourierbüchern, 1775–1784', in *Goethe-Jahrbuch*, vol. VI (1885).

Diezmann, A., *Goethe und die lustige Zeit in Weimar*, 2. A., Weimar, 1901.

Düntzer, H., *Goethe und Karl August*, 2. A., Leipzig, 1888.

—— *Goethes Tagebücher der sechs ersten Weimarischen Jahre*, Leipzig, 1889.

Geiger, L., *Aus Alt-Weimar*, Berlin, 1897.

Hof, W., *Wo sich der Weg im Kreise schließt. Goethe und Frau von Stein*, Stuttgart, 1957.

Vehse, E., *Geschichte der Höfe seit der Reformation*, Bd. 28: *Geschichte der Höfe des Hauses Sachsen*, 1. Teil, Hamburg, 1854.

Wachsmuth, W., *Weimars Musenhof in den Jahren 1772–1807*, Berlin, 1844.

3. The Government of Weimar, and Goethe's Share in It

Bürgin, Hans, *Der Minister Goethe vor der römischen Reise. Seine Tätigkeit in der Wegebau- und Kriegskommission*. Weimar, 1953.

Flach, W. (ed.), *Goethes amtliche Schriften* I, *Goethes Tätigkeit im geheimen Consilium*, Teil I. *Die Schriften der Jahre 1776–1786*. Weimar, 1950.

—— 'Goethe im Februar 1779', in *Beiträge zur deutschen und nordischen Literatur*, *Festgabe für L. Magon*, ed. H. W. Seiffert, Berlin, 1958.

Hartung, Fritz, 'Das erste Jahrzehnt der Regierung Karl Augusts', in *Jahrbuch der Goethe-Gesellschaft*, vol. II (1915), pp. 59–139.

—— 'Neue Mitteilungen aus Goethes amtlicher Tätigkeit', in *Jahrbuch der Goethe-Gesellschaft*, vol. VI (1919), pp. 252–82.

—— *Das Großherzogtum Sachsen unter der Regierung Karl Augusts*, Weimar, 1923.

Voigt, Julius, *Goethe in Ilmenau*, Leipzig, 1912.

4. Art, Music and the Theatre in Weimar

Bruford, W. H., *Theatre, Drama and Audience in Goethe's Germany*, London, 1950 (with bibliography).

von Einem, H., *Goethes Kunstphilosophie*, Hamburg, 1947.

Flemming, W., *Goethes Gestaltung des klassischen Theaters*, Köln, 1949.
Geese, Walter, *Gottlieb Martin Klauer, der Bildhauer Goethes*. Mit 64 Bildtafeln. Leipzig, 1935.
Huschke, W., and W. Vulpius, *Park um Weimar*, Weimar, 1955.
Pischner, H., *Musik und Musikerziehung in der Geschichte Weimars*, Weimar, 1954.
Scheidig W. *Goethes Preisaufgaben* (Schriften der Goethe-Gesellschaft 57), Weimar, 1959.
Sichardt, G., *Das Weimarer Liebhabertheater unter Goethes Leitung*, Weimar, 1957.
Knudsen, H., *Goethes Welt des Theaters*, Berlin, 1949.

5. Goethe's Science

Full German bibliography in *Goethes Werke*, Hamburger Ausgabe, Band VIII, 'Naturwissenschaftliche Schriften', ed. Dorothea Kühn and Rike Wankmüller, Hamburg, 1955.
Arber, Agnes, *Goethe's Botany* (*Chronica Botanica*, vol. x), Waltham, Mass., 1946.
Fairley, Barker, *A Study of Goethe*, Oxford, 1947.
Goethe et l'esprit francais, Actes du Colloque International de Strasbourg, Paris, 1958.
Michéa, R., *Les travaux scientifiques de Goethe*, Paris, 1943.
Sherrington, Sir Charles, *Goethe on Nature and Science*, 2nd ed., Cambridge, 1949.
Wilkinson, Elizabeth M., 'Goethe's Conception of Form', in *Proceedings of the British Academy*, vol. XXXVII, 1951.
—— 'The Poet as Thinker', in *German Studies presented to L. A. Willoughby*, Oxford, 1952.

6. Education. The University of Jena

Briefe über Jena, Frankfurt und Leipzig, 1793.
Bulling, K., *Goethe als Erneuerer und Benutzer der jenaischen Bibliotheken*, Jena, 1932.
Lütge, F., *Geschichte des Jenaer Buchhandels, einschließlich der Buchdruckereien*, Jena, 1929.
Lehmann, R., *Die deutschen Klassiker, Herder, Schiller, Goethe, als Erzieher*, Leipzig, 1921.
Raabe, P., 'Das Protokollbuch der Gesellschaft der Freien Männer in Jena, 1794–1799', in *Festgabe für Eduard Berend*, Weimar, 1959.

Geschichte der Universität Jena, Festgabe zum vierhundertjährigen Universitätsjubiläum, ed. Max Steinmetz, Jena, 1958.

7. The Literary Atmosphere in Weimar

Bettex, A., *Der Kampf um das klassische Weimar*, Zürich und Leipzig, 1935.

Böttiger, K. A., *Literarische Zustände und Zeitgenossen*, ed. K. W. Böttiger, 2 Bde., Leipzig, 1838.

Fambach, O., *Goethe und seine Kritiker*, Düsseldorf, 1953.

—— *Ein Jahrhundert deutscher Literaturkritik*, II–IV, Berlin, 1957–9.

Hennings, A. (ed.), 'Bemerkungen über Weimar', in *Der Genius der Zeit*. Bd. 20 and 21, Altona. 1800.

Das Journal von Tiefurt, mit einer Einleitung von Bernhard Suphan, herausgegeben von E. von der Hellen (Schriften der Goethe-Gesellschaft 7), Weimar, 1892.

Körner, F., *Das Zeitungswesen in Weimar, 1734–1849*. Leipzig, 1920.

Raabe, P., *Die Horen, Einführung und Kommentar*, Stuttgart, 1959.

Schulz, G., *Schillers Horen*, Heidelberg, 1960.

Wahl, H., *Geschichte des teutschen Merkur* (Palaestra CXXVII), Berlin, 1914.

Wustmann, R., *Weimar und Deutschland, 1815–1915* (Schriften der Goethe-Gesellschaft 30), Weimar, 1915.

INDEX

Bruford

Culture and society in
classical Weimar, 1775-1806